War & Peace in Junglemahal

People, State and Maoists

War & Peace in Junglemahal

People, State and Maoists

Edited by

Biswajit Roy

Setu Prakashani

War & Peace in Junglemahal
People, State and Maoists
Edited by: Biswajit Roy

First Indian Edition
May, 2012

1st Reprint November 2019

Cover Designed by
Dilip Ghosh

ISBN No. - 978-93-80677-28-6(Pb)

Published by
Archana Das and Subrata Das
on behalf of Setu Prakashani
12A, Shankar Ghosh Lane, Kolkata-700 006(India)
Phone : +91 33 2219 0704, +91 94330 74548
Delhi Branch Office :
A-43, Mahendru Enclave, Galli No. 3,
G. T. Karnal Road, Post Office-Azadpur, Delhi-1100 33
email : setuprakasnhani@gmail.com

Price
Rupees Six Hundred

Printed by
Graphic Reproduction
8/3, Chintamani Das Lane, Kolkata - 700 009

Typesetting and make-up by
Unique Phototype
49, Guru Prosad Chowdhury Lane, Kolkata - 700 006

In memory of

Samar Sen

Poet, Journalist and Founder-Editor,

Frontier

His legacy is still alive

Contents

Section III

State and Non-state violence and Politics of Peace-making

Section IV

Voices from Junglemahal and Accounts of Activists

Introduction

Sumanta Banerjee

The present collection of essays appears at an important juncture of India's political history. The pursuit of neo-liberal policies by the ruling powers has plunged the nation into the throes of an economic crisis — with farmers forced to commit suicide, villagers ousted from their homes by the predatory industrial houses, rising unemployment among the rural and urban youth, all of which ring alarm bells of an all-round turmoil.

In the political sphere too, the scams involving ministers and senior bureaucrats at the Centre, and the rising trend in corruption and criminal activities among the ruling parties in the states, indicate the collapse of moral values in the polity. Opposed to these regressive and oppressive trends, people are coming out with new forms of collective actions of protest — mass movements against industrial projects that destroy the environment and people's livelihood, agitation against corruption, armed resistance against feudal exploitation and police repression, efforts to build parallel centres of governance with alternative models of development to benefit the poor.

West Bengal's Junglemahal occupies an important position in this trajectory where popular upsurges confront the State. The writers in this collection, from different viewpoints, trace the history of the Junglemahal movement, analyse its achievements and failures, and explore the ways and means of conflict resolutions (between the State and its armed opponents) in such a situation. Some among them hark back to similar efforts of conflict resolution made in Andhra Pradesh some years ago — an important source for driving home lessons and avoiding mistakes. Comparisons are being made between the Indian State and ethnic armed secessionist groups like NSCN(I-M) of

Nagaland and ULFA of Assam, or efforts at dialogue with Islamic nationalist groups in Kashmir.

But unlike NSCN(I-M) and ULFA which are ethnic nationalist movements or the Hurriyat in Kashmir which is a religion-based movement that seeks secession from Indian State and carve out their respective independent nation States, the Maoist movement is a class-based movement that cuts across ethnic, linguistic and regional identities, and operates all across the territory of the present Indian State. The peasants' upsurge in Lalgarh, for instance, is a part of the larger Maoist strategy that stretches from Chhattisgarh through Jharkhand, Odisha (earlier Orissa) and West Bengal down to Andhra Predesh. But again, although subscribing to an all-India strategy, in their tactics the Maoists have remained confined to a narrow terrain — just like the enthno-nationalist and Islamic insurgent groups. The latter have their bases among their respective ethnic (Naga, Kuki, Assamese in the Northeast) or religious (Islamic in Kashmir) loyalties, which are restricted to a few pockets in these areas.

Similarly, the Maoists' strongholds are confined to a narrow stretch in the heartland, which are mainly inhibited by the poor tribal people, whose class interests have been upheld by the CPI(Maoist) through struggles on issues like their demands for economic equity and social justice. Lalgarh is a typical example of the strategy and tactics — highlighting both their socio-economic efforts at benefiting the tribal poor, and at the same time their vulnerability to the military offensive mounted by an intolerant Indian State. Stuck in a pocket in Junglemahal and besieged from all sides by security forces, the Maoist island is facing extinction. With their leader Kishenji killed, and other leaders in jail, the cadres are being forced to surrender by the Mamata Banerjee-led Trinamul Congress government despite her pre-election promise to release Maoist prisoners and enter into a dialogue with them.

The editor of the present collection invited activists and academics — from Bengal as well as other states — to share their views on the overall experience and current ground situation. But can we hear the local people's voice today? In the post-election environment in

Junglemahal, the erstwhile CPI(M)-led *Harmad Bahini* is being replaced by the Trinamul-led *Bhairab Bahini.* The tribal and non-tribal activists of the People's Committee against Police Atrocities are facing same fascist onslaught from Mamata Banerjee's hired goons. Today, TMC-led *Jana Jagaran Mancha* has allegedly forced some of them at gunpoint to join them.

Such nefarious attempts to stifle the voices of the oppressed have to be resisted by civil society and political forces, which are committed to democratic rights. The present collection of essays should urge our intellectuals to raise their voices against the violation of human rights that continue under the TMC-led regime. Beyond the issue of human rights, the essays also touch upon the issue of the Maoist experiments and the challenge that they pose to the Indian State.

In a no-win situation of confrontation, both the Maoists and the Indian ruling powers need to reformulate their strategies and tactics, there is a need for the State to recognise experiments in grassroots democracy — whether Gandhian or Maoist — that empower the downtrodden. The Indian State, which swears by democratic rights, should allow space for such competitive experiments in socio-economic transformations that are being undertaken by the Maoists in their bases in Chhattisgarh, Odisha and Bengal. But the Maoists also will have to conform to the basic obligations to respect democratic rights, within the framework of competitive political experiments.

Editor's Note

We conceived the idea for this book in the wake of the failed peace initiative between the Mamata Banerjee government in Bengal, then newly elected, and the CPI(Maoist) that took place in the backdrop of the civil war-like situation in the forested areas of the western part of the state, traditionally known as Junglemahal (Jungle Mahals in the colonial records and historiography). The socio-political upheaval, after the Singur and Nandigram movement, was triggered by police atrocities on women and children after the Maoists' bid on the life of Mamata Banerjee's predecessor Buddhadeb Bhattacharjee in November 2008. The militant mass movement of tribal and non-tribal people, led by People's Committee against Police Atrocities, gave vent to their pent-up anger against years of police highhandedness which, as humiliating as it was, regularly violated the norms of their community living. It was aimed at the CPI(M)'s one-party rule and misgovernance, too, which perpetuated hunger in this semi-arid region that home to the poorest of Bengal's poor. Named after its epicentre in West Medinipur district, the Lalgarh movement gradually spread to other forested areas, in Bankura and Purulia districts neighbouring Jharkhand and Odisha. The Maoists were the major catalyst for the movement and made political and military capital out of it almost from the beginning.

Since then, the trouble-torn region has gone through a spiral of violence by State and non-State actors — during the Left Front rule and its incumbent successor, the Trinamul Congress-led regime. The bloodshed renewed between TMC and the Centre-state joint forces and the new regime's friends-turned-foes after the May 2011 Assembly polls, which propelled Mamata to power with a massive mandate. It ran parallel to the half-hearted and ill-fated peace process and ended in an apparent victory of the new ruling party following the killing of the CPI(Maoist) politburo member and the party's key leader, Kishenji, in an 'encounter' in November 2011.

The stillborn peace process not only raised questions on the role of the major participants — the state government, the Maoists and government-appointed interlocutors — but also the successive ruling and Opposition parties, civil society and the media. The questions almost echoed the contested claims and blames after the failed peace processes between the Central and state governments and the Maoists since the failed Andhra Pradesh talks in 2004. We felt the need to examine these questions on the problems of peacemaking in the light of the larger issues created by the undeclared civil war raging on in mineral-rich and forested tribal homelands across south-central India with Bengal's Junglemahal being a part of it. This geo-political contiguity makes it necessary for us to broaden the scope of this book to examine Maoist insurgency in the context of the ground realities in the Junglemahals from Chhattisgarh to Bengal. We were also aware that no fruitful discussion would be possible on peace or peace processes without delving into specific contexts of the conflicts. In Bengal's case, it is the Lalgarh movement and the post-poll situation in Junglemahal. Conceptually, this puts the focus from the failed peace initiative to the unresolved issues thrown up by the popular agitation. Similar examinations of other state- and region-specific as well as pan-Indian contexts of conflicts are needed if peace, however elusive, is to be given a chance.

The country has been hearing the impassioned harangues of the hawks in the corporate media and other mainstream public forums, mostly market fundamentalists wedded to global and domestic neo-liberal interests, seeking military solution to the Maoist violence.

But instead of including those, we have focused on the saner voices in civil society, voices that are interested in using democratic means to resolve the conflict and look for sustainable and honourable peace between the warring sides with active participation of the affected people and their representative organisations. Most of the those people have more or less said the structural violence under the current neo-liberal regime in New Delhi and the designs underlying its

FDI-propelled 'development' model are the main sources of the conflicts. They have identified themselves with the increasing trend of people's resistance against the government-corporate combine's plunder of natural resources, large-scale land grabs and gross violations of their constitutional rights not only in tribal hinterlands, but also semi-urban areas. However, debates are going on within civil society, democratic and political forces of different hues, in Bengal as well as the rest of the country, on both the form and the content of people's resistance. We were keen to cover the entire spectrum of this debate in this collection. These include the opinions of people who are generally supportive of or sympathetic to left-wing insurgents and those who have friendly reservations on or harsh criticisms against Maoist strategies and tactics of armed struggle, which include instruments of people's power and killing of political opponents and violations of democratic and human rights.

In this backdrop, we invited contributions from people who were involved in and concerned about the peace processes between the Maoists and various governments since the Andhra talks in 2004 and thus offered hindsight or insight into the failures. We also invited people who were cynical about or critical of such moves from the beginning to present views of the other side. Two articles on the peace initiatives in India's Northeast and the lessons learnt from them have helped widened our perspective. As we evolved our broad theme to make the collection truly representative by inviting and accommodating as many shades of opinions across the spectrum as possible, we realised that the notion of peace itself was deeply problematic and the conditions for sustainable and honourable peace were as conte[illegible] as the causes of the ongoing war. The opinions are largely divided among those that are cynical about and hostile to peace processes in general and the Bengal initiative in particular and thsoe that consider peace in the context of revolutionary strategy and tactics. While the former cite killings of CPI(Maoist) leaders Azad and Kishenji to argue that peace talks are traps laid by the governments to eliminate their armed adversaries or derail the revolutionary resistance, the latter feel such moves will have to be taken despite the setbacks and the risks involved in dealing with deceptive governments. They have common ground with people who consider peace as a much-required socio-political condition for radical democratic experiments and as a respite for the people in the conflict zones.

Some people insist that peace in the form of a ceasefire may be possible only when there is a military stalemate in the war of attrition between the Indian State and its armed challengers. This school advocates peace through war and calls the peace moves ill-timed in the light of paradigms of war and peacemaking both in global and regional contexts. Another school argues that peace would remain a chimera unless and until the warring sides climb down from their maximalist positions and explore a middle ground in tune with today's world, which is witnessing massive protests against neo-liberal regimes and autocracy — from Wall Street to Tahrir Square — and popular experiments in radical democracy and socialism in Latin America. Closer to this position are some others who offer a fresh perspective by linking peace initiatives with broader social movements for justice struggles against governments' neo-liberal policies.

As the debates invariably involve larger ideological and political issues pertaining to Maoist practices, the collection also gives space to the believers and non-believers in 'sandwich theory' that denotes the controversy over distinctions being made between the Maoists and their support base — political parties of all hues and the people whose interests they claim to represent. In the context of Junglemahal, it turned into polemics between people who accused the Maoists of hijacking a broad-based democratic movement in pursuit of their goal to build a guerrilla base and those who defended the Maoists as rightful leaders of a popular upsurge who had earned the trust and respect of the masses by shedding their blood and sweat. In between, there are views which recognise the Maoists' role but highlight the autonomous character and radical democratic potential of the Lalgarh movement in its initial days. The only meaningful peace talks, they say, would be one in which the state government and PCPA come face-to-face after the release of PCPA leaders.

Many of our contributors have blamed the Mamata Banerjee

government for the failure of the peace process, while some of them have also pointed the finger at the Maoists. Others have criticised civil society mediators in Bengal for joining the government-initiated peace process. They accuse them of reposing blind faith in Mamata's pre-poll promises on political settlement in Junglemahal, and thus collaborating in her post-poll doublespeak. Four members of the interlocutors' team, however, have defended their moves, saying the Maoists and the PCPA leadership both had faith in their credentials; they have given their versions of what went wrong with the peace process despite their sincere efforts. They have offered divergent arguments on the role of Mamata government and the Maoists, though. Most of the contributors feel that 'peace' in Bengal's Junglemahal will remain a sham until political prisoners, including the rank and file of the PCPA, are released, police officers accused of atrocities punished, 'encounter' killings probed, Centre-state joint forces withdrawn and Junglemahal's autonomy is ensured.

We have also included experiences and narratives of some activists, both local and Kolkata-based, who had participated in the Lalgarh movement, joined the people's initiative in rural development, witnessed first hand and/or suffered police atrocities. This will help discerning readers to catch glimpses of the movement, particularly in its early stage, that is, before killings and counter-killings became the order of the day. The full tale of the people's revolt against age-old atrocities and its impact on the dynamics of mainstream and subaltern politics and the collective memory of the people of Junglemahal, however, are yet to be told and assessed. That deserves another book.

The articles in this collection are divided into four broad sections despite the thematic overlapping by many contributors. The risk of repetition notwithstanding, we could not avoid it, considering the nature of the debates. The annexure has excerpts from the interviews of CPI(Maoist) leaders, including Kishenji, and those who were involved in various peace processes in India. That apart, the section has some important documents — the Supreme Court order against *Salwa Judum*, the government-run anti-Maoist vigilante campaign, and Planning Commission-sponsored report on bleak ground realities in the Junglemahals across India that explains the expansion of Maoists'/Naxalites' influence. Some reports and documents on the problems and prospects of conflict resolution with left-wing guerrillas in countries like Colombia, Peru, the Philippines and Nepal have been incorporated in a separate section.

Acknowledgments: We thank all our contributors for their support in conducting the debate/discussion on the abovementioned issues on the online edition of *Frontier* weekly. We have made a few reprints of published articles and interviews in view of their continued relevance, courtesy, the *Economic and Political Weekly*, *Forbes India*, *Deccan Herald* and like-minded websites, including *kafila.org* and *radicalnotes.org* and the Balagopal Memorial Trust. This collection would not have seen the light of the day without Soumya Guhathakurta, Sumit Chowdhury and Nilanjan Dutta sharing the burden of networking and editing. This book is as much theirs as mine. We are grateful to Timir Basu, editor of *Frontier,* and his counterpart in *Mainstream*, Sumit Chakravartty, for allowing us to include articles published in their weeklies. We thank Rabin Chakrabarty, who anchors *frontierweekly.com*, for extending a helping hand whenever we were lost in the cyber-jungle. Our thanks also goes out to Sumanta Banerjee, who has been supportive of our effort from the beginning. He helped us to network with contributors outside West Bengal, besides taking the trouble of writing an introductory note to this collection. And thanks to Diptendra Raychaudhuri and Dipankar Chakrabarti for helping get the articles of Swami Agnivesh and Mahasveta Devi, respectively, and Sujato Bhadra for enriching our project by providing some documents on global peace initiatives, not all of which we could use because of space and other problems. Thanks also to Aditi Chowdhury and Pritha Chatterjee who translated three articles for this collection. Finally, thanks to Subrata Das and Srijani Banerjee of Setu Prakashani, and Sandip Mullick and Anirban Ghosh of Unique Phototype for making this publication possible.

Biswajit Roy

Section I

Mamata or Maoists: Who Failed Peace?

Democracy Must Return to Junglemahal

Mahasveta Devi

Bengal's Junglemahal denotes the area roughly covering Bankura, Birbhum, Purulia and the western part of West Medinipur. I have visited many places in this zone for years together. Our *West Bengal Khedia-Shabar Kalyan Samiti* has its office at Rajnoagarh in Purulia. Of course, tribals are there. But non-tribal people also have a substantial presence in Junglemahal. Hindus and Muslims as well as other communities have been living together here for generations.

West Bengal is territorially small in comparison to other states. Inside this state, the laterite land of Junglemahal is pregnant with mineral resources. The sylvan forest of *Sal*, *Mahua* and other trees has been the cradle of communities for centuries. If my memory is not failing me, the erstwhile Left Front government had virtually sold out a substantial area of such land to Jindal group and some other industrial houses. The poor tribals and non-tribals in the area who had toiled hard to cultivate the largely arid land for generations did not know about the wealth stored in the womb of mother earth since time immemorial. Though officially the land was given on a long-term lease to the Jindals, the 'people's government' practically sold out huge tracts of land, originally vested in the government for redistribution among landless or to be used for state-run public projects.

The LF government did not bother either about the region or its people. Instead, it invited the Jindals to exploit the resources of Junglemahal. The colonial legacy of expropriating tribals' land and police-administrative repression on them has continued even during the LF rule. The tribals' alienation from land and agriculture has compelled a good section of their population to migrate from Junglemahal to other areas of West Bengal and other states in search of livelihood as low-paid and exploited wage labourers over the decades. The migration, both seasonal and long-term, has reduced the size of the tribal population in comparison to others in Junglemahal over the decades.

Release Chhatradhar and Other Political Prisoners

I don't know which government will take care of the never-ending exploitation of the people of Junglemahal and when will it deliver.

But the resistance movement led by Chhatradhar Mahato and his fellow travellers in the People's Committee against Police Atrocities has to be judged in the backdrop of pent up anger and frustration since Independence. Regarding Chhatradhar, I want to know how long he will be kept behind bars. I am asking this because the very issue of release of political prisoners has been put on the backburner after the Assembly polls in Bengal. The regime has changed and a new government is in power. When we think what the earlier government failed to do and what we expect from the new one, the issue of release of political prisoners comes to mind naturally.

I am not a political worker, I have tried to share the sufferings of Junglemahal and helped in my humble way as a writer. Once I did not know much about the Naxalite movement in the seventies of the last century. Later, gradually I came to know about it and realised that the concerns for common people was the main inspiration of the movement. I don't know much about Maoist activities in Junglemahal. I have not visited the area in recent times. But I know that the new government in Bengal initiated a peace process with the Maoists. We want to know from the government whether the talks took place. What is its outcome? If it failed, why did it do so?

Kishenji was killed during the peace initiative. Now it is being suspected by many quarters that he was actually gunned down in a 'fake encounter'. We want to know the truth because we too want peace in Junglemahal.

People Despise One-party Rule of All Hues

My humble request to the new chief minister is that it's time to release all those who have been jailed in connection with the Junglemahal agitation. Why is there a need to continue deploying 'joint forces' or other forces in Junglemahal? How does it solve the perennial problems that people of Junglemahal have been facing? We want the return of democracy. The people of the state have invited the new government. People did not like one-party rule in the name of democracy. One should not forget that the CPI(M)-led government had to go because of people's opposition to its politics of hegemony. I will also ask the Maoists to shun the politics of killing. Whether it's the government side or those in the Opposition, we don't want perpetuation of politics of killings but real democracy.

In the meantime, I would like to remind both sides about what interests me more: problems that the residents of Junglemahal face in their daily lives. I have always cared about the issues that affect the common people. I have come to know about the following problems through my interaction with them:

Are there enough roads fit for vehicular movements and otherwise in the area? Roads increase mobility and communication. I know the LF did not do enough during its 34 years of rule.

Is there enough supply of safe drinking water? Is there enough irrigation facilities for those who have cultivable land?

Are there enough primary schools? What are the other moves to spread education? There is a need to take new initiatives based on the new generations of educated locals.

Is there any sustained and effective effort to make girls literate?

Has the new government ensured doctors' presence, at least in some villages? I am referring to it in view of the abysmal condition of state-run the health-care system during the earlier regime.

Afforestation drive is a must in view of the fast depletion of forest in Junglemahal. The unique beauty of the land and its forest as well as environmental balance has to be preserved. I don't know whether the sylvan *Sal* forest near the Jhargram town of my childhood is still there with its serenity and magnificence.

Peace That is More Dangerous Than War

Amit Bhaduri

Crooked are the times.

Crooked because, peace turns out to be more dangerous than war for those who seek peace.

Crooked because, enforcement of law in the name of peace turns out to be more frightening than the lawlessness of war.

Crooked because, lies are given out as facts by those very politicians who pretended until yesterday that they share the anxiety of the people but possess conveniently crooked memories to do exactly the opposite when in power.

Mamata Banerjee's political fortune began to change for the better as the CPI(M) increasingly displayed an almost pathological arrogance towards the people. Its fate was sealed in Nandigram and Singur and, then in Junglemahal. She provided the rallying point in parliamentary politics. But below it lay a deeper issue: the anxiety of the poor of being dispossessed of their land and livelihood, their defencelessness against the brutality of State terror used by the party in power. She pretended to sympathise with the victims.

The Pretender and Her Charmed Circle

Many in the civil society thought they had found a leader who was willing to face the issue of arbitrary State power and ruling party terror in which the CPI(M) had indulged. Many had hoped, even if she cannot provide economic relief to the people, she can at least stop the State machinery from brutally oppressing the people. It has taken hardly six months for her to dash all such hopes, and exhibit tendencies that rely on police force rather than on the people; on empty populism and utter lies to justify State repression. Killing of

Maoist leader Koteswara Rao (Kishenji), with a fantastic story telling of the encounter given out to the media by the chief minister herself foretells the dangerous extent to which she would go to promote herself against the people with the aid of State terror.

In the Junglemahal area of Purulia, Bankura and West Medinipur, Banerjee's party had tremendous electoral success as all but one front-ranking CPI(M) leaders were defeated. These were desperately poor areas of West Bengal and sub-human poverty had been a part of people's life. The CPI(M) had done virtually nothing to alleviate these conditions during its long years of rule. Poverty had made people cynical about ever being able to change their life through electoral politics.

Such cynicism breeds political apathy and despair, possible occasional outbursts but nothing more sustainable. And yet, what Junglemahal witnessed for quite a while before the assembly election was a growing sense of political restlessness and popular resistance. Anyone visiting the area could feel that something was in the air, perhaps a growing sense of identity of the oppressed *Adivasis*.

A sense of solidarity was shaping up against a long history of deprivation, cultural subjugation and most important of all, contempt shown by the State to their life and dignity. Throughout Junglemahal, the combined Central and state police forces and, the CPI(M) supported goons or the *Harmad Bahini* behaved like an occupation army in a foreign land with no accountability. They killed, looted and raped. Local resistance initially with leaders like Chhatradhar Mahato or Lalmohan Tudu simply wanted their dignity to be restored and an apology from the guilty police officers.

The Maoist party provided the backbone of support only from the background, but on all account, they were flowing with the popular mood of anger and outrage not leading it at that stage. However, the people of Junglemahal got back in return more abuse in the form of State terror, more arrests and more torture, rape and killing. Fighting the Maoist influence became the umbrella excuse for all kinds of atrocities committed by the police and the then ruling party.

Mamata Banerjee with the experience of Singur and Nandiram was quick to capitalise politically on the situation by promising (a) unconditional release of all political prisoners and (b) withdrawal of police forces from the area. As soon as she won the election, she started going back on her promises. Political prisoners were not released and she refused to withdraw the Central-state joint forces until an officially initiated peace process had yielded results to her advantage. And then she played the same old gramophone record played earlier by Union home minister P. Chidambaram.

Every time the authorities say they want to initiate a peace process they want their armed adversaries to 'abjure violence'. This peace without categorical guarantee of safety from the government's onslaught is dangerous for underground Maoist leaders who need to initiate first dialogue within the party. In the process they run far greater risk of becoming visible targets for the police who capture and kill them in fake encounters. This happened to at least two Maoist leaders when the peace talk failed in Andhra in 2004, to Azad in 2010, and now it has happened to Kishenji in 2011 with Mamata Banerjee presiding over the killing as the chief minister of West Bengal.

Peace Talk: A Trap to Kill

Clearly the state policy all along has been to liquidate illegally its Maoist opponents in the name of peace talk and, Banerjee has not deviated from this policy. She only made herself more ridiculous by telling absurd stories about how for three days the police surrounded and requested Kishenji to surrender which no villager ever heard. Obviously, she was referring to a silent announcement which only she and her police could hear! Then according to those who saw the dead body, it had unmistakable signs of horrible tortures, burnt marks(under left feet), marks of cutting with a sharp weapon like bayonet (more than 30 marks) and bullet marks.

If the chief minister is to be believed, Kishenji must have been shooting at the policemen while his feet were being burnt, his body and face were being cut up by bayonets and pierced by bullets! The postmortem report like Mamata Banerjee herself was silent about all this. Finally, the official post mortem report done in Medinipur claimed that the bullets were fired from a distance of at least 500 meters. Although it might fit Mamata's fantasy of an encounter, no known rifle used by the Indian CRPF or police is known to have such a long range (between 300 and 450 meters for AK-47 and Insas rifles).

Beyond the land of malicious fantasies and lies, the truth is brutal. Peace talks with the Maoists have become a ploy for trapping and killing them in cold blood. This same pattern has repeated itself over and over again and, the real puzzle is why the Maoists still respond to peace talks. The reason probably is that the Maoists survive mostly on popular support, and, ordinary people everywhere would like to live in peace. It is the pressure of popular demand to which the Maoist leaders yield at great personal risk. Otherwise, it goes without saying there is no trust between the two parties to build the bridge of peace.

For civil societies and concerned citizens vocal in this matter, it is essential to face this fact instead of wallowing in platitudes of the desirability of peace and constitutional rights which the state does not respect, and the Maoists have no reason to respect if the state treat them simply as dangerous outlaws to be killed, not a political party with a diametrically opposite ideology.

There is only one thing we as outsiders can do to call the bluff. Peace talk cannot be initiated in Junglemahal unless an impartial enquiry is held first into the brutalities and killings committed by the police and the CRPF, and all the prisoners released unconditionally to give evidence in particular cases. Only when the guilty are punished the climate for peace would be created without the outrage of the people being exploited politically either by Mamata Banerjee or the Maoists. But this requires a government which depends genuinely on the people and not on the police. Evidently Mamata Banerjee has failed miserably to qualify.

Paribartan: Transgression Masquerading as Transformation

Sumanta Banerjee

The recent events in Lalgarh, and the process of peace talks that ended in failure, have exposed the pathetic role that the stakeholders — Mamata Banerjee government, political parties, civil society groups and intellectuals — played in West Bengal. They have created an environment of stinking hypocrisy and opportunism. Three intriguing cases of turnarounds by prominent intellectuals and groups in West Bengal in the recent months prompt me to express my views.

First, the interlocutors appointed by Mamata Banerjee to negotiate with the Maoists, announced their decision to withdraw midway from the talks because of the continuing violence in Jungalmahal by the security forces. But as soon as Mamata called them over, they made an about turn and accepted her diktat to resume negotiations with the Maoists — despite the fact that Mamata made it clear that she was in no mood to accept any of the demands of the Maoists (e.g., end to the operations of the security forces, release of political prisoners, etc.). True to her norms, the next thing she did was to permit the security forces to kill Kishenji. The team of interlocutors lost its face, and barring one, all of them pulled out from the negotiations (following the Maoists' announcement of discontinuing the talks).

Two, on 21 November 2011, the well-known author and social activist Mahasveta Devi, who was at the forefront of the pro-Mamata campaign against the CPI(M) in the period preceding the assembly election, suddenly made a U-turn and accused her erstwhile heroine of behaving like a 'fascist'. The occasion was a press conference called by the Calcutta-based human rights group, APDR (Association for the

Protection of Democratic Rights), to protest against the TMC government's refusal to permit them to hold a public meeting at a particular spot, demanding the release of political prisoners. Mamata immediately reacted by issuing a stern warning (through a Bengali TV channel) that she did not like such statements. Mahasveta Devi soon knuckled under and retracted in an article in the Bengali daily *Bartaman* on November 24, stating that she did not call Mamata a 'fascist', that she retained her affection for Mamata, and did not want any harm done to the TMC government! Ironically enough, it was on that same day, that Kishenji was killed by the security forces backed by the same Mamata Banerjee on whom Mahasveta Devi was showering her affection.

Three, on November 18, the West Bengal units of the Congress and Youth Congress — which had collaborated with the TMC during the assembly election campaign — in a volte face, organized a rally in south Kolkata to protest against the killing of their cadres by the goons of their ally, the TMC. A few days later, at a public meeting of the Congress party, Union ministers Jairam Ramesh and Pranab Mukherjee, in order to assuage the anti-TMC rebellious mood of their leaders and cadres in West Bengal (represented by Deepa Das Munshi and Adhir Chowdhury), resorted to a damage-control measure by asserting that the Congress was not opting for a voluntary retirement scheme and was determined to retain their identity in Bengali politics!

QUESTIONING THE *BUDDHI* OF THE *BUDDHIJIBIS*

These three cases of somersaults do not indicate any qualitative change in the minds of the Bengali middle class stakeholders in the above mentioned issues that may lead to the emergence of a radical alternative to the present Mamata-led government in West Bengal. They merely reflect their belated realisation of the mistake they made by voting her to power — a mood succinctly expressed in the old Bengali saying: *Chor palaley, buddhi barey* (One becomes become intelligent or careful, only after the thief escapes). And it is precisely on this issue that I am questioning the *buddhi* — intelligence — of Bengali human rights activists, actors and artists, Maoists and

Congress leaders, who went the whole hog in propelling Mamata Banerjee as an alternative to the widely hated CPI(M) regime. To describe their mad rush in her support, one can again use a Bengali term: *kachha khuley chhota* (running heedless of the loincloth, which has slipped away)! The context of the Bengali euphoric idolisation of Mamata Banerjee on the eve of the Assembly elections is well known. During the last three decades, the ruling Left Front wasted the opportunity (that it got in 1977) of bringing about a *Paribartan* (in the human development index terms of health and educational benefits, as well as the political education of the masses). Instead, led by the CPI(M), it installed a regime of patron-client relationship in village panchayats, trade unions, urban localities — where the local party toughs (known as 'wholetimers' who receive monthly wages from the CPI(M), but were totally devoid of any ideological commitment)) doled out benefits to their followers.

It was these apolitical district secretaries and corrupt panchayat heads of the CPI(M) who recruited armed mercenaries (to be known as *harmads*) to suppress any opposition to the dictates that were being issued by their bosses in Alimuddin Street [CPI(M) headquarters in Bengal]. The ruling CPI(M) reached its nemesis in Nandigram, when the villagers resisted its arrogant decision to acquire their land for its ambition of setting up an special economic zone (SEZ) under the neo-liberalist economic model — the same model against which the CPI(M)'s national leaders like Prakash Karat and Sitaram Yechury breathe fire in Delhi. Matching the hypocrisy of the CPI(M) were the duplicity and naiveté of the Bengal Maoists, who in their animosity against the CPI(M) reached the nadir of political degeneration by acting as armed mercenaries of TMC in Lalgarh and other parts to oust CPI(M) cadres and supporters from their village homes, and thus paved the way for the defeat of their candidates in the elections. Contrary to the Maoist party's declared objective of boycotting elections, its leaders and cadres in West Bengal urged their followers to vote for TMC candidates. Their argument was that once voted to power, Mamata Banerjee, in a gesture of gratitude for their electoral support, would release the political prisoners (Maoist activists and their sympathisers) and withdraw the security forces. What was Mamata's reward for them? Their ideologue and military strategist Kishenji (who openly supported Mamata Banerjee during the Nandigram and Lalgarh movements) was eliminated in a swift military action six months after Mamata Banerjee came to power. Was the Maoist strategy of supporting Mamata mere political naiveté or sheer opportunism to seek protection from a leader (otherwise notorious for her congenital anti-communism from her Youth Congress days since the 1970s) just because she opposed the ruling CPI(M)?

Surprisingly, this illusion about Mamata's generosity was shared even by a lot of Left-leaning Bengali intellectuals and human rights activists. In the face of all evidence (of Mamata's past record of lumpen politics, amoral opportunism and administrative inefficiency as a railway minister), they chose to remain blind and contrived instead to create a halo around her, elevating her to the pedestal of the future saviour of West Bengal. Credulity and naiveté among the Bengali intelligentsia almost developed into a new superstitious faith in Mamata's prowess. Let me recount a personal experience in this connection. Sometime at the end of March 2011, I was invited to speak at a small gathering of politically like-minded friends at *Boi-Chitra* (in the Calcutta Coffee House building) on the political situation on the eve of the Assembly elections. In continuation of the spirit of my earlier 'Open Letter to Mahasveta Devi, et. al' (23 August 2010), I pleaded for the development of a Leftist mass movement at the grassroots level on the daily problems of the rural and urban poor, and other deprived and oppressed sections of our society, as a priority over the prevalent leftist obsession with the electoral race alone, which encouraged the people only to depend on one victorious party or another at regular intervals. I warned that Mamata's victory would not make any difference to the plight of the villagers of Nandigram, Singur or Lalgarh, and I humbly suggested that instead of chasing the chimera of *Paribartan* under the chief ministership of Mamata, we should take up the task of *Paribartan* through mass movements from the base — a task that the undivided CPI (although small in size, and with a few elected representatives in the legislatures) carried out in the

1940-60 period. To my surprise, I found among the participants, Sujato Bhadra (a veteran leader of West Bengal's democratic rights movement, whom I respect as a courageous champion of human rights) going all gaga over Mamata Banerjee's credentials, and assuring us that by voting her to power we can ensure the release of all political prisoners and an end to the depredations of the security forces. I was a bit disappointed with Sujato's naïve hopes. I was therefore not surprised when I heard that he had agreed to be a part of the team of interlocutors set up by the Mamata-led government for talks with the Maoists. As expected, the talks did not yield any results, the final blow to them being inflicted by the government itself. But my question to Sujato and his colleagues is: Why did they agree to negotiate on behalf of the government? Even before the killing of Kishenji, could they not read the reality, and anticipate that Mamata (always being an unscrupulous politician) would renege on her earlier promises? Being political beings, could they not read the signs in Mamata's utterances which were tilting towards the Union home minister Chidambaram's line of unleashing the security forces in Junglemahal to finish off the Maoists? The interlocutors may argue that they were pushing the envelope — trying their best to extend the limits of a negotiated settlement. I agree that the doors for negotiations should remain open. But the levers for opening and closing the doors are being operated by the chief minister Mamata Banerjee, who determines the course of action of her appointees — the interlocutors. That she decides is evident from her allowing the joint security forces to kill Kishenji, the main Maoist leader, whom the interlocutors should have met to negotiate. I hope that Sujato Bhadra and his friends realize now that Mamata used them in her electoral campaign, and has now, true to her self, discarded them as toilet paper!

Role of Civil Society: Andhra and Bengal in Contrast

In this connection, it is necessary to recall the difference between the ways of initiation of the process of peace talks between the Maoists and the state in Andhra Pradesh in the 1997-2004 period, and that in West Bengal recently. This method of mediation (between the Maoists and the state) in West Bengal is totally different from the experiment that was carried out in Andhra Pradesh during the 1997-2002 period. Unlike West Bengal, where a group of human rights activists agreed to be appointed by the government as interlocutors, in Andhra Pradesh the Committee of Concerned Citizens emerged as an independent group of persons, consisting of well-respected personalities like retired IAS officer S.R. Sankaran, national president of the PUCL K.G. Kannabiran (both departed), and senior academics, lawyers and journalists. They could arrange talks between representatives of the Maoists and the Andhra Pradesh government, but they failed — primarily due to the intransigence of the police and state administration. Despite their failure, the reports of the Committee of Concerned Citizens remain an important historical record of the prevailing situation in the villages of Andhra Pradesh at that time, the ideology and praxis of the Naxalites, the tensions between them and the human rights groups and, above all, the intransigence of the police administration in coming to a peaceful settlement. But in the context of Kishenji's killing, mediators who are appointed or nominated by the government to negotiate with the Maoists should have second thoughts. Some time ago, Swami Agnivesh was authorized (informally may be) by the Union home ministry to negotiate with the Maoist ideologue Azad. His well-meaning efforts to contact Azad could have been intercepted by the State's predatory intelligence agencies which helped them to follow Azad's movements and whereabouts, and eventually pounce upon him and kill him. So, is the Indian State using the mediators — whether Gandhians or leftists — to locate the Maoist leaders, in their plans to eliminate them? My next query in this connection is directed towards the veteran author Mahasveta Devi, whom I have always respected as a powerful writer and a courageous social activist. I am selecting her in particular because she was at the helm of the group of Bengali intellectuals (including some artists, theatre directors and actors, and film stars) who campaigned in favour of Mamata Banerjee during the last elections. Mahasveta Devi's recent political off-again-on-again relationship with Mamata Banerjee (which I referred to above) intrigues me. To start with, having been an active participant in the communist movement in the 1940s, and a keen observer and canny analyst of the political scenario of West Bengal in the later period (as evident in her fiction), how could she have poured her blessings upon Mamata Banerjee of all persons, at public meetings all through 2010-11 to promote her electoral prospects? How could she have been taken in by the soothing lies of Mamata Banerjee, whose past record as an unscrupulous opportunist lumpen politician had been open for all to remember? What makes her recant her criticism of Mamata, immediately after Mamata frowns upon her in a TV interview? It is up to Mahasveta Devi to reconcile her professed commitment to radical causes with her support to a chief minister who militarily suppresses those fighting for those causes. You cannot hunt with the hounds and run with the hares at the same time.

As for the third party in the game of somersaults, the West Bengal Congress does not deserve any sympathy. It is whimpering today, but should have known better, given the way it had always been treated by Mamata Banerjee in the past. Why did it allow itself to be stampeded by its central leadership into a humiliating electoral alliance with an arrogant TMC?

Compliant and Complicit Bengali Intellectuals

The last decade (2001-11) in West Bengal — which saw tumultuous events — posed challenges to Bengali economists, intellectuals and artists from different fields, as well as social and political activists. Barring a few independent minded people from among them, the majority split into two sections. One chose to remain loyal to the CPI(M)-led government, and the other fell for the lottery tickets offered by Mamata Banerjee. The former willy-nilly became complicit in the atrocities carried out by the state government and the party's armed mercenaries on the common people in Nandigram, Lalgarh and other areas. loyalty among some of them (mainly the older generation) could have been rooted to their misplaced ideological faith in, and emotional attachment to the CPI(M). But as for the rest of this pro-CPI(M) section of the Bengali middle class, their loyalty was motivated by purely apolitical reasons — proximity to the ruling party opening up prospects in their careers in the academia, material benefits in the shape of higher emoluments and perks, among other advantages enabling them to rise up in the ladder of a consumerist life-style. The other section, partly well-meaning in its protest against such atrocities, and partly driven by the same apolitical motive of improving their careers and obtaining favours under a new regime, bought Mamata Banerjee's lottery tickets. As with all such buyers, a few are lucky while the rest are now bemoaning their decision to back a wrong horse. Fast disillusioned by the Mamata government's performance, they are now rubbing their eyes to discover how their hopes were built on clouds of compliance with the mercurial demands of an amoral politician.The sad experience of the last decade should stir up a new generation of intelligentsia in West Bengal, who can break out from the circle of dependence on a bankrupt CPI(M) followed by a populist TMC. They have to come up with a radical left alternative programme that can mobilize the industrial proletariat and the rural poor against the onslaught of the neo-liberal corporatocracy, and also rescue the Bengali middle class society from a state where the moral sense is dead, the social conscience callous, the intellectual capacity dwarfed, enfeebled and confused. It takes a great deal of optimism, however, to envisage the emergence of such an intelligentsia in the near future in West Bengal, which for the next five years will be ruled by a joker selling tickets of a lottery that will never be drawn.

Lalgarh and the Future of the Maoist Movement

This brings me to the next issue that forms the background to the compilation of the articles in the present book — the peasants' movement in Lalgarh that was utilized by the Mamata Banerjee-led Trinamul to bring about the downfall of the widely hated CPI(M)-led LF government in West Bengal. Lalgarh (or, the events surrounding it) is a symptom of both the limited achievements of the Maoist movement and the wider crisis that the movement is facing today — both in terms of the deeper problems of its strategy (of capturing state power through an agrarian revolution) and military tactics (of guerrilla warfare). As for the achievements, as in Chhattisgarh, during their brief hegemony in Lalgarh, the Maoists did indeed carry out socio-economic popular measures — setting up of medical dispensaries, construction of rainwater reservoirs and embankments, provision of drinking water. They could thus institute a parallel administrative mechanism for providing social welfare measures that had been denied to the rural poor by the Indian State for decades. These welfare measures were, however, a part of the Maoist long-term strategy of capturing State power through the tactics of guerrilla warfare. And this is where their tactics are facing a formidable military challenge from the Indian State. The Maoist bases are confined only to a few pockets in a narrow insurgency-friendly terrain — inaccessible hill and forest areas, remote from the seats of power and inhabited by the most deprived and disgruntled poor who are driven to the desperate state of taking up arms to resist the oppression of the Indian State. But they are isolated from the rest of the country, where various popular movements are breaking out (e.g., the anti-POSCO movement in Odisha), the struggles of the industrial proletariat, among others.

In view of these new developments, as well as the recent popular upsurges that are taking innovative forms in other parts of the world, it is necessary for the Indian Maoists to revamp their strategy and tactics to meet the challenges of the 21st century in order to bring about a socialist society.

Kishenji's Death and Some Candid Observations

Sumit Chakravartty

How did Kishenji die? A lot has been written on this subject in several newspapers and periodicals. One need not harp on that issue again. Because one can engage in endless academic discussions and debates on how he died — that is, whether he breathed his last in direct armed confrontation with the police and/or joint forces or whether he was arrested beforehand and thereafter murdered in cold blood — but that would not lead us to anything fruitful or concrete. Those who are direct, indirect or broad supporters of the Maoists will give full-throated backing to the 'killed-in-cold-blood' theory, whereas those who regard Maoists as enemies of the country will say just the opposite, that is, he died in an encounter. Of course, there are among the latter the ideological camp followers of the BJP-RSS as well and, according to them, regardless of 'whether he was killed in an encounter or fake encounter, by killing him the joint forces have done the right thing', and some of them have even given vent to such feelings in newspaper columns. So such a debate will find every participant sticking to her/his position. None will be able to convince or influence the other to change her/his view and accept the former's opinion. It must be admitted in this connection that politicisation of practically every issue has reached such heights in West Bengal that the scope for a really free discussion is exceedingly limited in the state.

But those of us who are neither supporters of Maoism nor subscribe to the state's policy of taking revenge by using the 'tooth-for-a-tooth' dictum have no hesitation in giving primacy to a rational debate based on logic far beyond our respective political views. Here I feel the urge to strike a personal note. Prime Minister Manmohan Singh and Union home minister P. Chidambaram have for quite sometime been issuing statements on behalf of the Centre, characterising the armed Maoist uprising in the Indian heartland as the biggest danger to the country's internal security. But they have not projected in detail the reasons why the Maoist problem has become such a grave danger. So it is not in the least unnatural to think that in their opinion the Maoists have become such a big threat only because of their reliance on arms and can be tackled by military means alone. The reality, however, is different. The architect of the most significant achievement of the 34-year Left Front rule in West Bengal (that is, 'Operation Barga', the wide-scale movement to record the tenancy rights of sharecroppers or bargadars in the state), and now a Rajya Sabha member representing the Trinamul Congress, Debabrata Bandyopadhyay has clearly written: 'From one police station area (Naxalbari) of one district (Darjeeling) in one state (West Bengal) today's Maoist movement has in these 44 years spread to approximately 2,000 police stations areas of 200 districts in 12 states.' Bandyopadhyay headed the expert group formed by the Planning Commission to conduct a detailed study on the rise of left-wing extremism in the *Adivasi* belt of Central India and suggest how best to contain and tackle it; the group released a report in 2008 which remains perhaps the best document to understand the present-day Maoist problem.

In this period, especially in recent times, the Centre and the governments of the states affected by Naxalism-Maoism have adopted the strategy of curbing Maoism with the help of the security forces. At the same time the police budget of the Centre and states has also increased phenomenally. Yet despite all these, leave aside resolving the problem, Maoism has neither been cornered nor contained — rather the Maoists' strength has grown exponentially instead of being reduced. Why? That is because compared to the sixties, seventies and eighties of the last century the decades of the nineties and beyond have witnessed the magnitude of poverty, deprivation and eviction from land of the extremely poor *Adivasis* growing on a massive scale in tune with the neo-liberal measures adopted by the government of India as a direct consequence of its new economic policies. (In concrete terms, since the government, having abandoned its erstwhile activities attuned to the concept of a welfare state, has forcibly taken away the land of the poor and oppressed *Adivasis* and handed over that land to indigenous and foreign corporate institutions in a pro-active manner in conformity with its current course of action, the plight and predicament of the *Adivasis* have taken such a huge scale; and it is these destitute people whom the Maoists have drawn into their fold through political means without resorting to force — of course it would be a travesty of truth to claim that there has not been the slightest use of force, but to insist that they have been forced to become Maoists would also be downright untrue; actually they have by and large spontaneously joined the Maoists precisely because they were debarred from normal life and livelihood. Needless to add, this brings out the failure of the present policies of the government.) And since I gave a detailed exposition of this reality, I was described in a TV channel as a 'closet Maoist'. There was another reason for characterising me thus. I had openly stated that it was impossible to tackle Maoism with the aid of arms alone; the Maoists' theory and violent activities (wherein people-centric political activities are gradually taking a back seat) can be tackled primarily by political means, that is, through political negotiations. This was not to the liking of that channel's anchorperson. Hence, I was branded a Maoist. This did not affect me, however. Because I am fully conscious of my anti-Maoist position (even though that position is unequivocally opposed to the government's strategy of eradicating Maoism solely through military means. I firmly believe that the victims of such a strategy would not be just the hard-boiled Maoists but also ordinary *Adivasis* — what is known as 'collateral damage' — and that is already happening in Chhattisgarh in particular).

Let us now return to the issue of Kishenji's death. As mentioned earlier, no purpose would be served by discussing how he was killed. However, some points need to be raised. If what chief minister Mamata Banerjee has hinted at is true, then she wanted Kishenji to be somehow arrested and not killed. If that was the CM's directive, then why was it not carried out? This question is not at all illogical. It is possible that Kishenji himself did not give that opportunity to the security forces. But still two more questions crop up in this context. The joint forces are learnt to have exchanged fire with two to three persons, including Kishenji. If that was so, then why were 1,000 rounds of fire exchanged as has been reported? A more important query is: such a major operation was conducted in which Kishenji was killed and yet not a single policeman or member of the joint forces suffered serious injury? How is that possible? Mamata has publicly said Kishenji was given three days to surrender, but he did not do so. Consequently, the joint forces were constrained to conduct the operation. The CM can be asked: did she really think a leader like Kishenji would surrender voluntarily? If she thought so, then it does not testify to her political foresight. Mamata has further said: It was in Junglemahal that the Maoists had secretly worked out plans to attack the Kolkata Metro and kill several ministers and leaders, including the CM. It is quite natural for police to furnish such an argument but is it proper for a political leader like Mamata, now in charge of the Bengal administration, to present such a story before the public?

The Statesman had organised a panel discussion in Kolkata in 2010 wherein this writer was one of the participants. Mamata Banerjee had also participated in it. At that discussion one had unequivocally complimented Mamata for having brought the issue of the death of Azad, a top leader of the Maoist party, on the national scene by openly declaring that the manner in which Azad was killed was not proper and that there should be an investigation into his death. When I was explaining at the same meeting why that death cannot be described as 'death due to encounter', Mamata cut me short to say: 'Please refer to the post-mortem report on the death, it is clear from that that Azad was killed due to firing from close range.'

Today, questions are being raised on Kishenji's death as well; it is being said that he was killed in cold blood. Personally, I believe that Azad's death cannot be bracketed with that of Kishenji; even if one accepts the charge that Azad was killed in cold blood, one cannot say the same about Kishenji's death since the logic of 'death due to encounter' is stronger in the latter case. But it is possible that one may be making a mistake by reaching such a conclusion. That is precisely why when several questions remained unanswered (about which I have written earlier) and since human rights activists and intellectuals of varied persuasions have questioned the 'death due to encounter' theory of the authorities, a fullfleged inquiry should be conducted into Kishenji's death as that alone would be able to allay all doubts.

It is necessary to underline some other points connected with Kishenji's death. It is more than transparent from whatever has been published after his death that the Maoists under Kishenji's leadership were isolated from the people of Junglemahal. Because of this isolation from the people, it is becoming increasingly clear that the common people of the area had given information about Kishenji's den to the joint forces. Nonetheless, one basic truth needs to be spelt out here. There is no doubt that the Maoists have built a strong base in Jharkhand and Chhattisgarh, but it must be admitted that such a Maoist base could not be built in West Bengal due to a variety of reasons. However, the Maoists were steadily advancing in that direction. The poor, deprived, destitute *Adivasis* of the area (that is, Junglemahal) were standing by them. That is not because a conspiracy was afoot in West Bengal to throw them out of their land by leasing it out to industrialists as had happened in Jharkhand and Chhattisgarh. That was far from the reality in West Bengal's Junglemahal. That the 34-year Left Front rule did nothing to help Junglemahal develop and ensure basic means of survival and livelihood to its inhabitants while bringing about phenomenal prosperity to local CPI(M) leaders like Anuj Pandey are facts beyond refutation. Side by side the ordinary *Adivasis* of the area had to cope with not just increasing poverty and deprivation but also mounting oppression and repression resorted to by the local police administration and CPI(M) *harmads*. In several places of the region the local people had to experience undeclared curfew at night. And at the fag end of Buddhadeb Bhattacharjee's chief ministership, the CPI(M) *harmads'* wanton atrocities alongside the police had reached such a scale that people could no longer bear such attacks, and thus extended all-out support to the Maoists' violent acts to counter State terror. That was their way of revolting against the prevailing state of affairs. Not to recognise this would amount to blatantly trampling truth and being blind to the actual situation.

But simultaneously what cannot be underestimated is the persisting atmosphere of terror perpetuated by the Maoists under Kishenji's leadership. As a result of the terror, Mamata Banerjee, who had earlier conveyed her desire to hold talks with them, decided to close the door for talks. There came about a radical transformation in the state after the 2011 Assembly elections. Ending the LF's 34 years of continuous and monopolistic hold on West Bengal, the Trinamul-Congress alliance came to power with Mamata as its head. This change of guard has engendered immense expectations and kindled hopes of a new future, and the Maoists should have understood that their movement could not advance in the old style — what is essential is to change the tactics of the struggle a la Lenin in July-November 1917 in Russia. But they did not undertake that task, perhaps out of shortsightedness. Kishenji must take the lion's share of the blame, for he was the initiator of the Maoist movement in Junglemahal.

As a result, what happened was waiting to happen. With killings taking place one after another, Mamata's patience ran out. Some human rights activists and intellectuals sympathetic to the Maoists maintain that as the ruling establishment had launched attacks on the local people claiming them to be Maoists thereby vitiating the environment, the Maoists were compelled to retaliate acts. But what needs to be pointed out is that these were not retaliatory acts, they were unprovoked and had taken place before the joint forces resumed their operations — in fact, the resumption of the operations was the direct consequence of those acts of provocation by the Maoists. Mamata publicly declared that the joint forces' operations (which she had suspended in the hope that that would pave the way for negotiations) would resume soon. But at the same time, she announced a package of measures based on her commitment for the development of Junglemahal. That evoked a positive response from the local people. But there should have been one more announcement: despite the resumption of the joint forces' operations, special care would be taken to ensure that innocent *Adivasis* do not become victims of such operations so as to keep the collateral damage to the minimum. But this specific commitment did not come.

A Major Flaw on Her Part

Yet what cannot be denied is that on account of the people's confidence in Mamata at least at the grassroots, the hopes generated far and wide have had their effect on Junglemahal as well. And her package for the development of Junglemahal has imparted a new dimension to those hopes. In such a situation it was imperative for the Maoists to change their tactics. That did not happen. That is why they have been isolated from the people at large. During the time of the previous dispensation, the CPI(M)'s *harmads* used to join the joint forces whenever the latter conducted operations in the region. It is because of the atrocities committed by the *harmads* that the local people did not cooperate with the joint forces during that period. But now when the operations are being carried out without the *harmads*' participation, the people have been drawn close to the joint forces.

Mao Zedong propounded the 'fish-and-water' theory to build political workers' unbreakable bond with the common people. Political workers can increase their influence over the people by taking advantage of the latter's deprivation, but once the roots of that deprivation are cut, their influence on the people diminishes. This is exactly the way the fish moves about in water. Today winds of change are sweeping Junglemahal. Therefore, the Maoists, who were led and organised by Kishenji, have become isolated from the people as compared to the past. I know, the Maoists and their supporters will speak of the terrorisastion of the people as a result of the joint forcses' operations. Even if that element of terror cannot wished away, it would be deceiving oneself if one fails to recognise the hopes generated among the people there due the winds of change.

It is high time the Maoists engaged in real self-introspection. In this writer's view, they would have to change not just their tactics but their strategy as well. Instead of relying on acts of terror more stress would have to be laid on people-centric politics. It has to be understood that in this country it is not possible to seize power with the help of a peasant uprising as in China if other sections of the people are not mobilised. But that does not mean that the extraordinary resistance they have built up against the government's land acquisition policy in the interest of the indigenous and foreign corporate entities would have to be weakened or terminated. Far from it. But this resistance should be made in essence people-centric — the people's war has to be transformed into a genuine people's resistance to the government-backed corporate land grab wherein large number of people of varied persuasions, from Gandhians and socialists to communists of different hues and even the people following the Congress, can participate. The Maoists may reject my appeal in this regard by harping on the bogey of revisionism, but I know for certain that one day you will be forced to realise your folly on this score. But perhaps by then it may be too late for you to make amends.

In conclusion, I want to add another point. I wish to tell all those who are branding Kishenji as a 'mass killer' that about five thousand people had joined Mallojula Koteswara Rao, alias Kishenji, in his last journey in Peddapalli town in Andhra Pradesh's Karimnagar district. It was not as if all of them accepted the Maoist ideology or support the Maoists' politics. Many came because Kishenji had cut his tooth in politics by participating in the movement centered on the demand for a separate state of Telangana. And it is by now well known that that demand is currently intrinsically linked to the sentiments of all sections of people of Telangana. But most of them who came were drawn to him because they were keen to get a last glimpse of a person who had selflessly dedicated himself to defending and upholding the interests of the toiling multitudes of our land, sacrificing his own petty interests regardless of his politics, howsoever violent and misguided it might have been. Against the backdrop of today's selfish, hypocritical, opportunistic, self-centered, corrupt politicians, would it be too improper and inappropriate and unjustified to ask the public to ponder over what Azad and Kishenji's images signify in India even though they happened to be the leading representatives of an outlawed political outfit?

Mamata, Maoists and 'Peace'-brokers

Dipankar Chakrabarti

Junglemahal, the most backward region of West Bengal, consisting of the largest parts of three districts, West Medinipur, Bankura and Purulia, in the south-west of the state, has been hogging the headlines since the beginning of the last decade. The region since then has become a hotbed of politically motivated armed conflicts. This process was acutely aggravated during the last five years of the Left Front rule. Though there were expectations that peace would be restored in the region with the departure of that regime, the same tradition has been continuing even after the present Trinamul-Congress regime assumed office under the almost absolute leadership of Mamata Banerjee. The present government did initiate some efforts for 'peace' but it ended in a whimper. The failed effort has rather sparked a bitter debate within civil society in general and human rights movement in particular. Let us have a brief look at the ground reality of Junglemahal before we visit the debate.

The Colonial Legacy Continues

But first we must have a look at the socio-economic background of Junglemahal. A large section of the population of the region consists of *Adivasis* or tribals and Scheduled Castes. These downtrodden people have been deprived of any effective development endeavour. In terms of development, this region, termed 'the Western Region' by the government, is like two sides of the same coin: co-existence of rich forests and huge areas of uncultivated land; or of natural beauty and harsh poverty and deprivation. In six decades of the Indian democracy, the tribals have received their share only in terms of alienation, exploitation, discrimination, deprivation and dispossession.

According to the 2004 Human Development Report of West Bengal, these districts ranked 14th among all the districts in the state in terms of human development indicators. It is interesting to note that about four decades earlier, in 1961, their position was nearly the same.

Few years back, the Panchayat & Rural Development Department of the West Bengal government had marked a few thousand villages of the state as 'the most backward' on the basis of the census figures. Most of them are situated in this region. The LF government tried to prove its 'seriousness and sincerity' for the development of the region by opening a separate department for the western region's development, and till recently none other than Sushanta Ghosh [the CPI(M) leader who was arrested for his alleged role in the killings of Trinamul supporters] was its minister-in-charge. Sadly, even after a decade, the region remains an impoverished hinterland.

The question of food security in the region is also very relevant for our discussion. Since the death of five men belonging to the Shabar tribes out of starvation in Amlasole village in West Medinipur in 2004, the name Amlasole has become synonymous with harsh poverty and hunger death. There are innumerable 'Amlasoles' in the region. The features of poverty and backwardness of the region are different from those of other backward regions.Up to 60-70% people depend on cultivation. The number of agricultural daily labourers is much more than marginal and small farmers, wages are low, and cultivation is seasonal and totally dependent on rainfall. Consequently, food security depends on this seasonal cultivation. During the lean period, food consumption level drops by 30 to 40%. More than 50% people remain almost without food for about six months every year.

The half-hearted and incomplete land reform started by the Left Front government has hardly affected the region. In Junglemahal, hardly any patta (cultivation rights) has been issued. The per capita availability of land is high but not usable because of the nature of the land and absence of effective water-conservation measures. A big section of the tribals has to migrate for livelihood to Namal (lowlands in adjoining districts) as migrant labourers every year. Centrally sponsored public distribution and pro-poor projects like NREGA,

Antyoday and *Annapurna Anna Yojana* or the active role of the local panchayats could have partially redressed the problem of food security like in Kerala. But widespread political manipulations have derailed the projects. Thus for sheer survival, the poor have to depend on the 'benevolence' of the money-lenders, or go to other regions for work.

Forests are another age-old source of livelihood for the poor. Thanks to the forest department's nexus with criminals, political leaders, police, timber mafia and administration to loot the forests and the flawed path of development, the centuries-old dependence of tribals on forests is threatened. Tribals who lived for generations in villages nestled in the forests have lost their natural surroundings and a traditional source of livelihood in the wake of rapid deforestation and fake development. Obviously, just food relief cannot solve the basic problems here. Concrete steps like modification of the nature of land, proper use of cultivable land, steps for irrigation and water conservation, as well as ensuring the forest rights of the people are urgent needs. Also required are effective management of the panchayats in people's interests, expansion of the scope for small and cottage industries as well as proper infrastructure for education and health care to uplift the people of the region from the age-old perpetual backwardness.

Shifting Sand of Political Equations

It is a paradox of our parliamentary politics that electoral parties take oath to follow 'peaceful' methods and yet frequently resort to arms whenever their rule and domination are endangered. Junglemahal is a glaring example of this phenomenon. In spite of centuries of poverty and deprivation of the people in this region, no massive people's movement has ever developed here since Independence. Even the land movements organised by the Communists during this period in other parts of the state did not significantly spread to these areas. The Naxalites; first the MCC group, and then the People's War group, and finally after their unity, the CPI(Maoist) tried to organise the people since the 1980s. Their main emphasis was on armed struggle through individual annihilation, and not building people's movement. Initially they were active around Salboni, Lalgarh, Goaltore, Garbeta and Belpahari.

Even as the ruling party, CPI(M) had to take the help of the Maoist armed squads to bring the region under its control from BJP's influence. In the meantime, CPI(M) too managed to develop its own armed squads and naturally it tried to oust the Maoists. The Maoists then tried to maintain their influence with the help of TMC, the new emerging force. The killings in Choto Angaria took place in this backdrop. Five Maoist cadres were brutally murdered in a TMC shelter by the CPI(M) armed goons. CPI(M) thereafter imposed its almost absolute domination in the whole area directly with the help of their armed forces, known locally as *harmads* and indirectly through the obedient police and administration.

The Maoists, no doubt, are dedicated and self-sacrificing, working for the uplift and liberation of the downtrodden people, though many have serious and reasonable differences with their methods. Their strategy was to select the area as a part of their guerrilla zone mainly by armed action so that they could develop the people's army and a liberated area. They were able to influence, through their long association with the local people, a sizable section of the local people, victims of deprivation and neglect, to join them. Though initially they made some efforts to organise the people based on some of their longstanding economic grievances, most of their organisers were arrested. Afterwards, due to the dearth of politically conscious, able organisers and the failure to develop effective mass organisations, their efforts in this respect were not very successful. In contrast, armed actions bore some fruits in threatening or neutralising the local reactionary forces, and consequently their dependence on armed actions became almost absolute. Since then, regular armed clashes between CPI(M) and the Maoists became the main feature of the competitive political violence in the region.

The Maoists mainly operated through their armed squads, consisting largely of the downtrodden people of the region under their influence and increased their campaign of individual annihilation of CPI(M) cadres or sympathisers. CPI(M) too mainly depended on its armed forces, though publicly it vehemently denied their existence. Naturally, it got immense help from the police and administration. Anyone refusing to accept its hegemony used to be termed 'Maoists' and the police obediently arrested them on 'non-bailable' fictitious charges, so that they are forced to spend years behind the bars. It is a tragedy that the main victims of these armed clashes between the warring sides were the poor and belonged to the exploited classes

Since 2006, an almost unprecedented popular upsurge against the government's pro-corporate land-grab policy swept West Bengal, starting with Singur and spreading to Nandigram. Realising that their life and occupation were threatened in the name of 'development', the downtrodden stood up and organized massive protest movements. These grassroots mobilisations were initially not led by any party or individual but grew out of affected people's initiative. The major sections of civil society too stood by them. The CPI(M)-controlled LF government was simply cornered and even forsaken by their erstwhile ardent supporters in the rural areas, as was evident in the Panchayat elections of 2008. Sensing the regime-changing potential of these protest movements and anger of the people, the Mamata Banerjee-led TMC, the main Opposition party in the state, came forward to harvest the fruits. In order to resist the CPI(M)'s armed retaliation in Nandigram, TMC had to take the help of the Maoist armed squads. It led to an understanding between TMC and the Maoists against CPI(M) onslaughts which also spread to an extent to Junglemahal.

Lalgarh Movement

November 2008 onward, a new situation emerged after the Maoists blasted a landmine during the return journey of Buddhadeb Bhattacharjee, then chief minister of West Bengal, from Salboni following the inauguration of the construction of a mega-steel plant promoted by the Jindal group mainly on government land. The police went on a rampage in the adjacent tribal villages, unleashing a reign of terror in 35 villages encompassing the entire tribal belt of Lalgarh. They tortured and arrested innocent people on sundry charges, including waging a war against the State, conspiracy, attempt to murder, use of dangerous weapons and obstruction to justice. In the process, they brutally beat up one woman, Lakshmi, and she had to be hospitalised. During night raids, many women were brutally kicked and beaten with batons and butts of guns. Chitamani Murmu's eye lost her eyesight after being hit by a gun butt. These widespread police brutalities soon became a flashpoint and the tribals had no option but to rise up in revolt.

The long-oppressed people rose up and dared to confront their oppressors. Road blockades were erected spontaneously, and subsequently a People's Committee against Police Atrocities (PCPA) was formed, consisting of people of various anti-CPI(M) political forces including the Maoist cadres and sympathisers. The blockade continued until the first week of December, when the state government had to negotiate with PCPA. For seven months, the government was compelled to withdraw all administrative forces from the area. It was a great victory of the people. Primarily, the people's demands were against State oppression, but subsequently new demands were included against dispossession and marginalisation of tribals from their land, forests and water in the name of development. The movement was spontaneous and spread to other areas, not only in Junglemahal, but also in other parts of the state, reminiscent of the Santhal Mutiny of the 1850s.

The Maoist Blueprint

The Maoists operating in the area had a different plan. They wanted to utilise the uprising to create an area where the absolute rule of their party and their squads would be established. The Maoists had no regard for the tradition and culture of the *Adivasi* samaj. Their political strategy itself was a great divider. Many sympathisers of the Lalgarh movement were aware of the derailment of a genuine and unique mass movement by the Maoists in pursuance of their blueprint. But at the same time, the Maoists had been able to attract the attention of the downtrodden people to their exploitation and deprivation, to the basic economic system responsible for their perpetual backwardness. The people naturally appreciated their support against the ruling party-government nexus, and were ready to accept them as their natural ally had there been no extortion and bloodshed, often for flimsy and dubious `crimes' of the offenders.

After the partial withdrawal of the government forces, the armed squads of the Maoists were the only armed forces in the area. Of course, there were CPI(M) squads in nearby areas. Between 2009 and 2010, more than 300 activists and supporters of CPI(M) were killed, almost all of them being poor *Adivasis*. In some cases, the killings were committed with utmost brutality and the families of the dead were prevented from lifting and cremating the dead bodies. Some were threatened with dire consequences in case of any opposition. The broad democratic nature of the movement was thus ruined. The Maoists virtually pursued the CPI(M) policy to wipe out all other social or political opposition through threats, insults and armed actions, even murders.

Consequently, the Maoists began to lose popular support since the people of Junglemahal did not accept the politics of violence beyond a tolerable limit. This 'hijacking' of the tribal and non-tribal people's resistance movement against police atrocities by the Maoists and its projection as their own creation and under their absolute control, as well as the series of killings they indulged in naturally deprived the movement of the massive support of civil society, though in the initial phase of the Lalgarh movement it had stood by the movement. The State, on its part was just waiting for a convenient moment to step in and label everything to do with Lalgarh as Maoist and arrest its leaders.

The opportunity was provided by the Central government, which banned the Maoists' movement and started the 'Operation Green Hunt' by sending Joint Forces consisting of Central paramilitary forces and the State Armed Police with the concurrence of the CPI(M) controlled state government. The draconian act, UAPA was indiscriminately used flouting the promise of the earlier LF governments (only with two exceptions of using TADA during the 1980s). PCPA was virtually banned, its leader Chatradhar Mahato and a few others were arrested, and ludicrous charges were imposed on them, though none of them found any place in the chargesheets. PCPA activists, being marked by the joint forces as terrorists, were hounded regularly and the forces made their life miserable. Even the ordinary innocent people were persecuted, tortured and arrested on flimsy grounds, and the women were sexually abused by the joint forces, obviously with the active help of CPI(M) cadres and their *harmad* forces.

In the face of this joint operation, the Maoists tried their best to mobilise the people for a mass resistance. When the joint armed forces started their campaign, only the advanced sections and cadres of the Maoists were ready for some resistance with landmines, which were not very effective against the onslaught of the State. The people fled their villages and took shelter elsewhere. Not only the civil rights activists, but also a large section of civil society began to oppose these draconian measures and demanded the release of PCPA leaders and withdrawal joint forces.

Mamata Banerjee: Political Chameleon

With the West Bengal Assembly elections round the corner, a new political equation began to develop in the state. Sailing on the waves of the mass upheavals in Singur and Nandigram and basically usurping the fruits of those movements, TMC led by Mamata Banerjee began to emerge as a prospective alternative force to CPI(M). A clear indication in this respect had been evident after the Panchayat and Parliament elections in 2008-09. It was essential for TMC to win a sizable number of the Assembly seats in Junglemahal to wrest the power from the CPI(M). The ruling Marxists managed to retain their seats in this zone in the Parliamentary polls despite their debacle elsewhere. Consequently, the understanding between TMC and the Maoists against CPI(M) onslaughts that developed in Nandigram, and spread to a certain extent to Junglemahal through the participation of TMC supporters in PCPA activities, was renewed and broadened, so that public anger against the joint forces could be translated into anti-CPI(M) votes.

Kishenji, the top Maoist leader, openly expressed his wish of seeing Mamata as the next chief minister of West Bengal. In spite of some mutual misgivings, both sides came together against CPI(M). Mamata in her election campaigns repeatedly emphasised the necessity to have a dialogue with the Maoists. In her much talked about meeting at Jhargram in August 2010, she made promises to withdraw the joint forces from Junglemahal and to release all political prisoners unconditionally. She also demanded the release of the PCPA leaders, including Chatradhar Mahato, and a judicial enquiry into the alleged fake encounter death of top Maoist leader Azad. The pledge to oppose 'state terror' was included in the TMC election manifesto. In fact, the West Bengal Assembly elections witnessed a revolt against CPI(M)'s autocracy and suppression of democracy as the majority of the people cast their 'negative' votes for TMC and Mamata with the sole objective of ending the CPI(M) rule. The TMC-Congress alliance swept the Assembly polls in May 2011 and Mamata, as expected, became the new chief minister.

But the truth remains that basically Mamata Banerjee was an inheritor of the political ideology of the Congress. The main architects of the Congress autocracy of the 1970's, especially the dark days of Emergency, were her mentors. She followed a domineering method of leadership to control her organisation as well as the political movements of her party. The election fulfilled her long-cherished dream of becoming the chief minister. She was ready to go to any extent to achieve that goal. She skillfully hegemonised the oppositional space in Singur and Nandigram movements and reaped the fruits. She did not even hesitate to utter leftist slogans and take a public stance against suppression of democracy. She skillfully gathered a large number of leading artists, writers and intellectuals, and consequently built a halo around herself.

However, Mamata began to reveal her true self after her remarkable victory in the Assembly polls. She wanted the Maoists to play second fiddle to her party in Junglemahal. The Maoists were obviously not ready to oblige, since that would go against their strategy to make it a part of their guerilla zone. Consequently, their earlier mutual misgivings gave rise to serious contradictions. She refused to honour her pre-election pledges, on the basis of which rested their mutual understanding. Her government rejected the demands for unconditional release of all political prisoners, immediate withdrawal of the joint forces from Junglemahal and public announcement on non-enforcement of the draconian central law, the Unlawful Activities Prevention Act. But peace in Junglemahal was the aspiration of the people, and they expected the Mamata government to take concrete and effective steps to that end. With Mamata's volte-face, the possibility of restoring peace began to fade.

Schism in Civil Society and Role of Mediators

Most of the human rights activists, including many intellectuals and activists who directly or indirectly supported Mamata's call for *Paribartan* (change of regime), now began to oppose her changed stance. Mamata responded to the situation in her inimitable style. She assembled a few pro-changers, who actively took part in the last election campaign in her favour, and who enjoyed the trust of the Maoists and PCPA. She requested them to help her bring peace to Junglemahal. A six-member team of interlocutors was formed on July 7 under her care and guidance. The team's approach was reflected in a joint statement ('a kind of understanding', according to one of the interlocutors), signed by the home secretary on behalf of the state government and the six interlocutors on behalf of a so-called *Nagarik Samaj* (Civil Society). The team included two prominent human rights activists, though they did not represent their respective organisations. (Rather that statement was unanimously opposed and condemned at the south Bengal annual general meeting of the most well-known civil rights organisation in the state).

The statement promised a special package for economic and social development of Junglemahal and protect the rights of forest dwellers, and asked all sides to 'hold fire'. On the question of withdrawal of the joint forces from Junglemahal, it merely parroted the government's stand that they would be withdrawn only after Junglemahal becomes free of arms and peace is restored. It appealed to the Maoists for talks 'to create a democratic atmosphere free from fear and terror', and reflected the government's strategy to entice the Maoist rank and file to surrender arms. It promised not to be 'revengeful against those who surrendered arms' and to offer them 'financial package and social rehabilitation' (though the connection between promises of not being revengeful during surrender and 'impartiality' of the interlocutors was not clear to many). The statement also gave assurance of investigating the 'atrocities and injustice perpetrated during the earlier regime, on the basis of specific complaints'. (No mention was made of investigations regarding atrocities during the current regime!).

No one can deny that an atmosphere conducive to talks must be created before beginning any dialogue. And, in the existing circumstances this could only be created only by keeping the pre-election promises of Mamata Banerjee: release of all political prisoners including Chatradhar Mahato and withdrawal of all cases registered against them, withdrawal of the joint forces from Junglemahal, and immediate stoppage of indiscriminate arrests and illegal detention of the people by the joint forces. It is utter imbecility to assume that without the fulfillment of at least some of these pre-conditions, the essential conducive atmosphere could be created.

Release of Prisoners and Mediators' Faith in Mamata

The two prominent human rights activists among the interlocutors have already lost the confidence of almost all civil rights activists and members of civil society due to their blatant opposition to the emerging movement for the unconditional release of the political prisoners. If we look back at a similar situation in 1977, the very first resolution adopted by the very first cabinet meeting of the first LF government was to release all political prisoners, in keeping with its pre-election promise. Later, due to bureaucratic bungling and interference by the Central government, the process of release was delayed. When the civil rights activists took to the streets demanding the hastening of the process, the then chief minister Jyoti Basu took immediate steps and ultimately all the political prisoners were released. Though the same government later turned into an autocratic regime, this truth cannot be erased. However, the above mentioned two interlocutors tried to do just that and advocated dependence on the Mamata government in lieu of people's movement.

This 'absolute' faith in Mamata Banerjee's benevolence might have endeared them to her, but almost proportionately, civil society widened its distance from them. There was another reason behind this loss of confidence in the interlocutors. Their main spokesperson is also a member of the government constituted review committee for the release of political prisoners, and his experience of that committee's working should have alerted him in time. The government imposed insulting conditions ('muchleka' or undertaking in the real sense of the term) for the release of the political prisoners. Just on that ground, any self-respecting person should have protested and, if necessary, even resigned from the committee, but the members kept mum.

They initially recommended the release of 78 political prisoners, but the government curtailed it down to 52. The later list included two Maoists along with 50 others of KLO etc. Though the chief minister announced the release of 52 of the 78 prisoners before Independence Day in 2011, only some non-Maoist prisoners have been freed so far — not a single Maoist has been released. The names of two Maoist prisoners have been struck off the list, purportedly owing to the pressure of the Central home ministry

Incidentally, in 1977 too, the Central home ministry had opposed the release of the prisoners facing charges of violence, but the LF government refused to pay heed to that objection, since law and order is a state subject. Notwithstanding the stand of the 'fearless' new chief minister of West Bengal, the committee has reportedly recommended the release of some other prisoners and political status for Chhatradhar Mahato and his close comrades. No recommendation has yet been fulfilled. In many cases, public prosecutors in lower courts have opposed the bail petitions of many political prisoners. Had the members of the review committee cared for minimum self-respect, they would have resigned in protest. Alas, this did not happen.

It was also evident from the 7 July statement that Mamata's

administration has forgotten the basic demands raised by her during the LF rule. Naturally, the peace efforts had a very shaky start. After the death of top Maoist leader Kishenji in November in an 'encounter', the interlocutors came to realise the futility of their efforts and they were virtually forced to disassociate themselves from the still-born peace process. But they have neither the moral authority based on widespread respect and public confidence nor the basic honesty of K.G. Kannabiran, the leading mediator in the failed Andhra talks between the Maoists and the Andhra government. Kannabiran publicly confessed after the failure of the Andhra talks: 'We (interlocutors) unwittingly played a treacherous role in believing the bona fide of the government.'

Stillborn Peace Process: Who is to be Blamed?

According to the main spokesperson for the interlocutor team, they had accepted their assignment because of Mamata's sincerity in recognising the political nature of the conflict in Junglemahal and her repeated insistence on opening of dialogue and bringing peace to the region. They also boasted of their own fight against the misdeeds of the LF government, though we shall presently see that they have forgotten how to fight under the new regime. To learn swimming one has to get into water.

The tragedy is that these interlocutors have not even tried to learn how to swim! That is why in all their TV interviews or write-ups after the failure of the peace efforts, they have basically tried to guard and defend the Mamata government, and put all the blame on the bureaucracy, a section of the media and the Maoists. It is their own fault that they were not 'aware' of the machinations of the bureaucracy and the servility of most of the media to the party that is in power.

So far as the Maoists are concerned, they have to bear part of the responsibility because they refused to take into account Mamata's massive mandate, the shifting allegiance of the anti-CPI(M) forces and sympathisers in PCPA and also the post-poll public opinion. They indulged in killings while the dialogue was on, thereby vitiating the process. Their erroneous tactics of mainly depending on armed action and annihilation while neglecting mass movements have cost them a lot. They have lost a sizable section of their sympathisers, thereby harming the cause of liberation of the downtrodden people. The dichotomy in the Maoist position on political freedom as they considered it legitimate for them but refused to extend it to their rivals, including parliamentary parties, also went against them. That the government was to be blamed primarily for the failure was clear to all close watchers of the effort except the interlocutors. We have already noted the government's failure to take confidence-building measures. The government simply ignored the July 2011 charter of PCPA. The charter included the demand for a judicial probe into the fake encounter deaths of its leaders, release of jailed comrades and punishment of police officers who had committed atrocities on tribal women during the earlier regime. It also listed the demands for genuine autonomy for the region, developmental priorities and people's vigilance on the flow of funds, freedom to continue the PCPA-led development activities as well as recovery of vested and tribal land allotted to others like the Jindal group for their steel plant.

Cosmetic Development and *Salwa Judum*

In her first public meetings on July 12 in Junglemahal, Mamata instead tried to entice the people by announcing distribution of subsidised rice among the poor and cycles among school-going girls, and promises on developmental projects like roads, bridges, schools and colleges.

We have taken a brief look into the socio-economic conditions in Junglemahal and noted that concrete steps regarding modification of the nature of the land, proper use of cultivable land, and measures to make water available and ensure forest rights of the people are urgently needed, which were not at all referred to by the CM in her speech. Naturally, real uplift of people from the pit of perpetual backwardness remains a far cry, even if all of her announcements are fulfilled.

Mamata also announced the government's plan to distribute

subsidised food from police stations and BDO offices, the erstwhile centres of exploitation and repression, and consequently hated and feared by the people. She promised a rehabilitation package for those who would surrender. The Maoists and civil society members were most upset with her call to the local youth to 'take up arms for the government and the country'. Finally, a befitting climax was her announcement that 10,000 special police constables would be recruited from Junglemahal, clearly imitating the *Salwa Judum* design of the BJP-led Chhattisgarh government to raise an anti-insurgent armed force also known as special police officers.

The experienced interlocutors did not utter a single word against these autocratic declarations clearly standing in the way of a fruitful dialogue for peace.

One-party Rule: TMC Swapped Role with CPI(M)

One of the interlocutors later confessed (see *frontierweekly.com*): 'Maoists had alleged that the TMC-led *Bhairab Bahini* like *harmads* of the CPI(M) had been terrorising the people.' According to him, 'Some disturbing news indeed came to our knowledge. Under the nose of the new government, the TMC leadership, with the help of the new converts, became super-active to seize (*dakhal* politics) political space in the area totally'. The Maoists requested them to make enquiries. They brought these to the notice of the chief minister, but she denied those allegations and asked them to give 'concrete evidence'.

Let us first see what were the allegations that were raised not only by the Maoists, but also by a large number of people of Junglemahal. The interlocutors themselves said that there was not a single killing by the Maoists for a month since 30 September 2011, the day the interlocutors signed the joint declaration for 'ceasefire'. However, it was alleged that the police and the joint forces were not sitting idle. They were raiding villages, chasing and harassing villagers and preventing them from collecting sal leaves and firewood for their sustenance. Side by side, the new repressive vigilante armed squads formed by the TMC youth, called the *Bhairab Bahini*, began to operate openly in the area just in the style of the CPI(M)'s *Harmad Bahini.*

They were moving with sophisticated weapons with the joint forces in plainclothes and exhorting protection money from the people, branding anyone opposing their demand as 'Maoists' and handing them over to the police.

The administration too played a subservient role by imposing an unwritten ban on the constitutional rights of the people to democratic assembly and freedom of expression. Since the first week of September 2011, the forces arrested nearly 80 people. On October 21, the Lodha Sabar Kalyan Samiti complained before the West Medinipur district magistrate that in the name of search operations, the police and joint forces are torturing innocent people, as a result of which 16 Sabar families in Aulgeria village have been forced to leave their village. This incident perhaps played a role, at least psychologically, behind the 'sudden' outburst of Mahasveta Devi against the government at the press conference of APDR. On October 26, it was alleged that at Patasole village in the Goaltor area, the house of Gopal Pandey was looted by *Bhairab Bahini* members, and when he escaped, his mother, wife and (nine-year-old) daughter were threatened with dire consequences. The police, obviously took no action.

Again, 12 students, belonging to student organisations such as the Jharkhand Student Federation (JSF), *Chatrasamaj* and USDF, who had been campaigning in the villages regarding a convention which they were holding in Kolkata, were picked up by the joint forces from a house where they were staying near Jhargram, brutally beaten up and handed over to the Jhargram police.

Rape Victims and Mamata: Now and Then

On October 15, Mamata Banerjee attended a public meeting at Jhargram where she condemned the Maoists as 'mafia' and '*supari*-killers', for their involvement in the murder of a TMC leader. But just a day earlier, the joint forces and police had raided the house of Sushen Singha in Shushnijobi village under Belpahari police station to arrest him. Not finding him at home, the policemen and the joint forces members allegedly raped his wife Shibani. Unable to bear such indignity, Shibani consumed poison to end her life. She was taken first to Belpahari block health centre and then to Jhargram hospital in an unconscious state. Jhargram SP Gaurav Misra refused to hand over the medical report to the members of the victim's family. Thanks to the efforts of the physicians, Shibani regained consciousness and on her complaints, her family members registered an FIR with the Jhargram SP's office when the Belpahari P.S. refused to do so, on flimsy grounds.

The media carried that news on the day of the CM's meeting at Jhargram. She simply brushed away the charge of rape and called it a concocted story. Ironically, the woman chief minister's remarks were based on police reports. People seem to have not forgotten that during the LF regime, Mamata herself was dragged forcibly by the police from the corridors of power in Writers' Buildings for seeking justice for Chapala Sardar, a rape victim. But the interlocutors 'couldn't' enquire about these allegations, however serious they might be, because they 'did not have that infrastructure'. The cat was out of the bag. If allegations raised by one side of the dispute were not addressed properly or neglected on the plea of lack of infrastructure, can the interlocutors claim to be morally 'impartial' and expect the dialogue to proceed? No, they cannot and that is why the dialogue has failed, and the government's 'peace-efforts' hs ended, at least for the time being.

All Sides Must Introspect

There is no need to indulge in a blame game. Both sides, mainly the government and partly the Maoists, are responsible for the failure. Also, the interlocutors, to quote again the respected civil rights activist Kannabiran, consciously or unconsciously 'played a treacherous role in believing the bona fide of the government'. People aspire for peace, but for that the government must first create an atmosphere conducive to peace efforts. Mamata must not approach the 'Maoist problem' as a law and order issue, but as a human and developmental issue as recommended by the experts' committee formed by the Central government in 2008. Some bouts of relief and doles to the exploited *Adivasis* of Junglemahal cannot uplift their lot; rather it is essential to take concrete steps for solving the basic problems which are at the root of their backwardness. Otherwise, the same Mamata who was so vocal in demanding judicial enquiry into the fake encounter death of Azad will time and again justify the role of her armed forces in the cases of alleged fake encounter deaths of many Kishenjis during her rule

Also, the Maoists must take into cognizance the ground reality. They should ponder over the post-poll desertion of other anti-CPI(M) forces from their side as well as large number of their cadres and sympathisers. They should also ponder over their gradual isolation from civil society and the common people in the wake of their excessive dependence on armed action and autocratic control over mass organisations. Moreover, mediators or 'interlocutors' should be those who are not self-declared 'representatives of civil society', nor celebrities and TV talk show participants, but respected people who are consistent in their approach and enjoy the confidence of the people.

Or else, peace in Junglemahal will remain a cry in the wild.

Maoists Failed to Gauge Post-Poll People's Mood

Debasis Bhattacharya

Will peace return to Junglemahal? This is not a million-dollar but a just a few-thousand-rupee question. The question has arisen because 23 blocks of Purulia, Bankura and West Medinipur became disturbed from the fag end of 2008 and remained so till November 2011. This tribal area had been a hotbed of Maoists activities. Maoists had secretly organised some youth there earlier. During 2003-04, armed Maoists squads were sneaking into Bengal from neighbouring Jharkhand and fleeing back after killing CPI(M) activists. It was known as hit-and-run tactics. This is what Buddhadeb Bhattacharjee, the then chief minister of West Bengal, had told the legislative Assembly and CPI(M) rallies many times. A heinous act was committed on the night of 31 December 2005, when a group of Maoists raided Rabindranath Kar's *kuccha* house at a village in Bandwan block and killed Kar and his wife. This writer visited the house on 9 January 2006 to see the wreckage. Kar was neither a class enemy nor an agent of class enemies. He was an honest and modest person. Yet he was murdered. Why? Kar was a very good organiser. The Maoists killed him to get a foothold in the hilly terrain of the Jharkhand-Bandwan-Jhargram area.

Has any human rights organisation visited the spot to enquire? No. Such organisations visited Gopalpur in Nadia, Karanda in Burdwan, Surul in Birbhum and demanded arrest of the murderers because in all the three cases the victims were Naxalites and murderers were CPI(M) men. Such human rights activists correctly condemned the barbaric atrocities and violations of human rights committed by the police at Lalgarh from the evening of 2 November 2008. But they kept mum about the Maoist attempt to kill Buddhadeb Bhattacharjee and two Union ministers before the police onslaught.

Since then the Maoists under the leadership of Kishenji fought the police in Junglemahal. The following points are to be noted:

1. The Maoists got some foothold and succeeded in recruiting cadres in Junglemahal. Why? It can't be denied that during the tenure of the first and second Left Front government, or even till 1989, developmental activities were experienced in Junglemahal. The rural tribal poor got the taste of development. They could differentiate between post-1977 changes and the conditions which prevailed in the earlier decades during the Congress regime in terms the basic living standard. Politically, CPI(M) became very strong in that area as the party's local leaders were honest and dedicated enough.

2. With the passage of time, the majority of local CPI(M) leaders, better to say, leaders of the committees — from district committees to the local levels — gradually became corrupt, arrogant and non-political. Many of them were elected at various levels of the three-tier Panchayat system. Panchayat Samiti and Gram Panchayat *pradhans* huddled at zonal party committee offices and confabulated how to utilise the funds for local development of MPs, MLAs as well as funds chanelled through the Panchayat department. Funds for numerous Central government-sponsored schemes also flowed in. The CPI(M) leaders spent 60 percent of the funds for development programs and embezzled the rest. The party leaders, panchayat *pradhans* and contractors formed a triangle to swindle the money.

3. By the first half of the 1990s, the CPI(M) leaders built the zonal committee offices with lavish means. By the second half, even the offices of local and branch committees began showing signs of the party's ill-gotten opulence. With the entry of Buddhadeb Bhattacharjee at the helm of affairs at Writers' Buildings, the local leaders started constructing their own palatial buildings in the midst of hundreds of poor households. The poor of Junglemahal saw this vulgar show of wealth and could gauge where the money came from. Dealers of Hero Honda, Bajaj and TVS were happy with the number of motorbikes being sold in Junglemahal during that time. The buyers were mostly the new rural rich with connections with the ruling party.

The people were first disillusioned then angry with the CPI(M) leaders. But out of fear, they could not open their mouth.

4. Yes, the astute Kishenji could feel the pulse of the people as well as the ripening objective situation for his party's offensive. The topography or geographical location of the area and the jungle cover suitable for armed activities drew his attention. His politics emboldened the disgruntled youth to fight CPI(M). The youth who were angry with CPI(M) leaders rallied behind Kishenji. He didn't waste time by offering them political education and instead asked them to swoop down on the CPI(M) local leaders and cadres. Actions immediately followed his instructions. Guerilla squads of four or five youths began killing CPI(M) activists and fled to adjoining Jharkhand by taking the jungle cover, avoiding the highways. About 300 CPI(M) members and sympathisers in addition to ordinary villagers were killed after being dubbed police informers. Some were killed after the verdicts of extra-judicial kangaroo courts.

On 2 November 2008, Buddhadeb Bhattacharjee's convoy was targeted. The incident shook the state and Central administrations. Police action followed. But the forest cover in the region helped the Maoists escape the ensuing security crackdown. Police were at a loss when it came to the forested area. The LF government deployed paramilitary forces from 18 June 2009. More than 5,000 paramilitary personnel were pressed into action, and the joint forces began their operation. The CPI(M) cadres showed the joint forces the way to Maoists' hideouts. Armed CPI(M) cadres were assembled in fortified camps to launch attacks on the Maoists. The presence of camps of armed CPI(M) men became a topic of debate between Bhattacharjee and the Union home minister. As the spiral of violence continued, armed CPI(M) cadres, known as *harmads,* killed nine poor villagers at Netai on 7 January 2011. On the eve of the Assembly polls, CPI(M) lay exposed before the people of the entire country.

Why did Junglemahal become turbulent and violent? Some people were of the opinion that underdevelopment and socio-economic factors were the main reasons. That opinion was wrong. Jalangi and Domkol blocks in Murshidabad district were more underdeveloped than any block in Junglemahal, but the Maoists could not make a dent in that district. Actually, the forest cover in Junglemahal that suited the Maoist concept of an ideal terrain for waging guerilla warfare motivated them to make the region their base.

5. Kishenji deftly gained the support of TMC supporters, subdued under CPI(M) rule, in Junglemahal in 2009-2010. He even issued press statements intending to see Mamata Banerjee as the next chief minister of Bengal. That intelligent statement helped Kishenji win the support of TMC supporters who were needed to provide the fugitive Maoists food and shelter. Kishenji used the media from his hideout with dexterity. The abduction of the officer-in-charge of Sakrail police station and Kishenji's speech under the glare of television cameras before the release of the hostage officer proved this.

6. In the Assembly election, CPI(M) was almost whitewashed from Junglemahal. Anti-CPI(M) voters could exercise their franchise freely for the first time in decades due to foolproof security arrangement of the Election Commission. On 20 May 2011, the new government under the leadership of Mamata Banerjee was formed. The paramilitary forces were kept in the barracks. The *harmads* absconded. Peace was restored in Junglemahal.

7. On 7 July 2011, Mamata Banerjee entrusted six interlocutors, including this writer, to mediate between the government and the Maoists. This writer thinks that Mamata Banerjee had seriously wanted to solve the problem in Junglemahal amicably. But unfortunately, the Maoists began to kill one person after another from the last week of September 2011. Popular leftist leaders like Babu Bose and TMC leader Lalmohan Mahato were killed without reason. The people of Junglemahal and particularly TMC supporters became furious after such murders.

8. The Maoists failed to assess the mood of the people after the change in the political scenario. Even Kishenji failed. The people of Junglemahal were disillusioned with CPI(M) cadres. With the change of government, the CPI(M) cadres either left the villages or became inactive. TMC supporters were found in large numbers in their place. But TMC supporters could do nothing wrong at least within the first

100 days. It was not possible. So the villagers were happy with TMC supporters as well as Mamata, the new chief minister. This change of situation was not taken into consideration by the Maoists. Kishenji also failed to understand that the villagers now wanted peace instead of police raids day and night. So the villagers tried to keep away from the Maoists. The Maoists became isolated.

9. After the political change, police officers managed to get information on absconding Maoists. Fugitive Maoist cadres and sympathisers surreptitiously got in touch with the police to return home. Anarchism and adventurism had to pay a heavy price ultimately. This writer is of the opinion that Kishenji was led into a trap by his close comrades-in-arms, who became police informers. But the anarchist Kishenji was not a coward. This writer, though, differed with Kishenji's political line but respected his life-long dedication and valour. He had been carrying an AK-47 not to surrender but to fight back. Whenever he was challenged by the Cobra forces he used it. The last encounter which ended in his death didn't last long. It was not possible either. In his death, Kishenji has proved that the political line of the Maoists is wrong and not tenable.

10. After the death of Kishenji, the Maoists are on the defensive at Junglemahal. Many Maoists have now become police informers. Some Maoists are surrendering. Sporadic violence may go on here and there. But as the villagers now want peace, they will be able to keep Junglemahal peaceful now.

11. There lies the difference between forested areas of Bastar and Bengal's Junglemhal. The density of forest cover in Bastar is deeper than Junglemahal. The socio-economic factors in Dandakaranya region are worse than that of Junglemahal. Tribals in Jungemhal are poor. Tribals in Jharkhand, Bihar, Odisha are poorer. But tribals of Bastar are poorest in the country. So the political and military line which could be sustained in Dandakaranya would not be replicated for a long time in Junglemhal.

Peace-talk Process in Junglemahal: A Brief Review

Sujato Bhadra

Civil society, various social organisations and human rights organisations continually demanded withdrawal of the joint forces and unconditional release of political prisoners and initiation of a dialogue with the Maoists and other stakeholders. The *Lalgarh Manch*, CAVOW and APDR issued public statements that pending withdrawal of the joint forces, suspension of operations by the joint forces must be carried out as a necessary prerequisite for the opening of dialogue with the Maoists and others. The desire for peace in the rehion was very much in evidence. It is a known fact that the new government in Bengal led by Mamata Banerjee had requested us (six of the concerned citizens — Sujato Bhadra, Debasis Bhattacharya, senior journalist Asokendu Sengupta, Prof Kalyan Rudra, poet Prasun Bhowmick and human rights activist Choton Das) to initiate the talk process with the stakeholders, particularly the armed opposition party (that is, in popular parlance, the Maoists).

On 7 July this year, a kind of understanding was enumerated on seven points. These were agreed upon and signed by the Bengal home secretary and by us. The seven points of understanding are: an economic package relating to health, food and education, investigation into all kinds of complaints in respect of human rights violations at the hands of the joint forces from 2009 to 2011, restraint in the use of arms by the Maoists and also by the joint forces and suspension of their operations, recognition of the forest rights of the people of this tribal region, participation of all people of the area in development and creation of a democratic atmosphere, an end to the situation of threat and fear, and speedy release of political prisoners. The charter also made a general appeal to the members of all armed groups that if anyone would wish to surrender his/her arms, he/she could do so and the government would not take any revengeful action against those who surrender. We had readily agreed to accept the assignment for three reasons: 1) this new government, being sincere to its electoral pledges, has clearly recognised the political nature of the conflict, which is a definite break from the past; 2) repeated insistence on opening of dialogue to end the killings and sufferings of the people of the region and bring peace; and 3) we fought against the misdeeds of the Left Front government to the best of our ability over the years. Hence, it was also our responsibility to bring peace and help the new government build the infrastructure for development of the region.

Our team with utmost earnestness and sincerity formulated a road map towards a peaceful resolution of the conflict. Three stages were identified: 1) the pre-talk phase, where we would have to create a conducive atmosphere and a climate of mutual trust amongst the stakeholders; 2) face-to-face dialogue between the government and the stakeholders; 3) post-dialogue/post-agreement phase. Following the international norms on conflict management, we had categorised the stakeholders into two groups — Track 1: armed opposition party; Track II: all unarmed oppostion organisations operating in the Junglemahal region.

Phase 1

Notwithstanding the prevalent practice of limiting the involvement at the peace talks to only the armed party/parties, we had held detailed talks with Track II (other unarmed democratic oppositional organisations and the jailed leadership of the People's Committee against Police Atrocities and Maoist stakeholders) on 22 July and 6 August 2011; and the talks with Track I (the Maoist party) took place on 28 August and 30 September 2011. We had a series of discussions with the state government on 29 July, 3 and 29 September, and 18 October.

Disadvantage I

To our utter dismay, the Maoists, even after our contact with them had been established and a round of peace talks with them was completed on a positive note on 28 August, took the lives of three activists [of other political parties] in a ruthless manner. This justifiably made the otherwise difficult situation more tough, resulting in enhancement of the administration's prevailing mistrust of them. On September 29, however, thanks to the government's willingness to continue the dialogue process, the peace talks got a chance. It is true that despite the commitment of the new government to release political prisoners that could not be undertaken at a quicker pace. The release of the political prisoners might have accelerated the peace process. However, the Maoists did not include this demand and the withdrawal of joint forces as preconditions for dialogue. We understood that these could have been part of the agenda at the negotiating table.

Major Breakthrough

On our persuasion, the Track I party (the Maoists) declared cessation of arms or 'ceasefire' for one month, albeit on the condition that the government would reciprocate by halting the operations of the joint forces. And there is the indisputable fact that from 30 September to 3 November, no violent incident, no loss of life occurred and no allegation of violence was levelled against the Track I party from any quarter, despite extreme provocation and no formal declaration of ceasefire from the side of the government.We had also successfully persuaded the Maoists to agree to our proposal that in the event of any attempt by any constitutional organisation(s) to arm them or any armed attack on Maoists, they would duly inform the government through us to take legal action against the attackers. Hence, the Track I party not only accepted the authority of the elected government, but also restrained itself from resorting to any counterattack, etc. It is pertinent to note that the Maoists had clarified in writing that though they were politically opposed to the recruitment of 10,000 police personnel from Junglemahal, they had not issued any death penalty warning to any candidate for the post of police constables, etc.

Neither were they harbouring any plan to bodily harm any leader of TMC or the CM, as alleged. Both these positions were communicated to the government. Short-term successes were temporarily achieved.

Furthermore, it may be noted that the Track I party accepted the fact that the movement of the joint forces had been reduced considerably; and Track I and Track II parties also accepted in principle that the total withdrawal of joint forces was not needed for the peace process.

DISADVANTAGE II

The government unfortunately did not appreciate this positive development resulting in failure of the government to seize the historic opportunity (that is, the new situation of de-escalation of violence and considerable reduction of harm to the people since 30 September; this is really a short-term benefit) to cement this breakthrough and enter phase II. Perhaps the government took exception to the condition mentioned above. But the history of the peace-talk process shows that this kind of demand is not at all unique. In fact, the essential prerequisite of dialogue includes restrained use of arms by both parties and suspension of operations. For instance, in Assam, the ULFA, the banned outfit, in July 2011 (four months after its talks with the Prime Minister and Union home minister), had announced unilateral ceasefire which led to the opening of dialogue with the Central and state governments. This declaration was hailed by the government interlocutor, P.C. Halder, ex-IG (Central IB). And prior to the commencement of the peace talks in October in New Delhi, it may be noted, on 3 September 2011, an agreement of 'suspension of operations' was signed between the ULFA and Central and state governments. Instances of former Prime Minister Rajiv Gandhi's peace initiatives and of peace accords in the Northeast, Punjab and Darjeeling are well known and have proved to be sustainable. At the international level we have similar examples. Lack of understanding about the peace-talk process has caused a very difficult situation. Short-term successes seem to be fast disappearing. The long-term benefit of lasting peace appears to be elusive.

Our Note of 24 /10/11 and its Aftermath

On the basis of detailed deliberations with the stakeholders and the government, we had submitted a confidential note to the state government on 24 October and to the Track I party for perusal and for comments, additions, alterations, if any, by the parties within 15 days. To our utter surprise, the confidentiality of the note was leaked and the 'subject matter' became the object of severe criticisms/attacks by a section of the media against the interlocutors. The code of conduct and ethics of peace journalism were not complied with. The government expressed its displeasure (over the phone) over the aforementioned note on two grounds.

Ground 1: whether the interlocutors have a right to give advice to the government. We strongly feel, yes, though in the note we had put forward only some suggestions. By definition, interlocutors/ mediators are not mere messengers. They identify the differences, difficulties and contradictions among stakeholders and try to iron out such areas of dispute through persuasion and create a road map for peaceful resolution of the issue.

Ground 2: whether the government and other stakeholders can be treated as equal. We hold, yes, all stakeholders are to be treated as mutually equal. It is not a relationship between the victor and the vanquished. A cursory glance into the history of the peace talks reveals that it is an essential to treat the armed opposition party as an equal and with respect (which should be mutual) at all stages of the peace-talk process. Issues like legitimacy of the government, superior strength of the regular forces, etc do not come into play. The mighty sovereign Indian State had made peace accords with even 'Bodo militants', and in November with the UPDS of Karbi-Anglong — though both forces are no match for the government of India. Unfortunately, we in our inerface with the leaders of the government of India failed to convince them on these points. Moreover, the government was doubtful of reposing trust in Akash's declaration of cessation of use of arms. We explained this in detail to the government that being the Maoists' state secretary, Akash's political and organisational command over the military section of the party must have prevailed and this was testified in practice. We had pointed out that unlike the ULFA, there is no anti-talk faction in the Maoist organisation.

Our Letter

The positive development did not lead to its logical conclusion; it died half way before it could enter phase II, that is, a face-to face meeting between the Maoists and government representatives did not materialise. Although the assurance of safe passage to the leaders of the party was given, it was decided that some important ministers would represent the government. Separately it was agreed that the government would also talk with the Track II parties and jailed PCPA and Maoist leaders.

From 31 October, the course of developments took a turn for the worse. The Maoist party hurriedly declared its unwillingness to extend the one-month 'truce' any further on the ground that the government did not keep its promise of suspension of operations by the joint forces. The killing of three Trinamul workers allegedly by the Maoists further vitiated the peace-talk process. The government's decision to resume paramilitary operations in full swing resulted in deaths in encounter of two alleged Maoist cadres and one Naga soldier, and the raid and arrests sounded the death knell of the peace talks. This situation of helplessness, on 14 November, we expressed our inability to act as interlocutors and asked for release from our responsibilities. On 19 November, the CM did not accept our request and asked us to try again. We did not refuse her request. But we failed to contact the Maoists. On 23-24 November, the killing of Kishenji brought the peace-talk process to its final end. We, except one of us, resigned on December.

3. It may be noted that we never met Kishenji in the entire period of our interaction with the Maoists. We had no idea about his role as a party leader in this peace-talk process. We had met them [Maoists] last on 30 September. Thereafter we had no direct contact with them and did not have any pre-scheduled date for meeting them. Our mode

of communication with them was never IT devices, as wrongly claimed by some 'investigative' reports.

Challenges Ahead

We are of the following opinion:

1. If the government still desires to continue the dialogue with Track I and Track II parties, then a formal announcement from an appropriate person of the government is necessary with respect to the total suspension of operations by the joint forces.
2. We have reasons to believe that attempts are on to impose the logic of the war economy forcibly on the newly born government. The government has to overcome this pressure.
3. The government has also to tackle effectively the potential spoilers — a part of the media which has been manufacturing public consent for declaring war on its own people, and a section of the police and bureaucrats who stand to gain from the war economy and war mentality. The people of Bengal know that this section of 'trigger-happy' police and bureaucrats was a part of the State terror during the LF regime. They have no experience of peace talks, and they, we are afraid, are not interested in taking lessons from history.
4. As the party in power has more responsibility and accountability, it should therefore show more patience and flexibility; thus the government should discourage any kind of provocative speech or public display that might create hurdles for the peace-talk process.
5. On the issue of human security, it may be noted that normal 'law and order'/'strict justice' approach are not applicable during the period of the peace-talk process. Alternative approaches to security of life and justice (that is, reparations, transitional justice) in the conflict zone are available, and have been widely practised and studies on them have shown positive results.

Aspiration of the Time: Peace

Even in this situation, we are optimistic. That is because all stakeholders, including the government, seem to have finally recognised the value of peace. However, we have miles to go before bringing the stakeholders to the negotiating table. We do hope that using the tools of patience and flexibility with unwavering determination the government and the Maoists can bring peace and development in Junglemahal. This example will surely inspire other states and peace-loving citizens of India to move forward with the slogan of peace.

(Whatever I have stated above constitutes my personal view. For inputs and insights, I am grateful to the other interlocutors. — S.B.)

* The article was first published in the annual issue of *Mainstream* in 2011. It has been reproduced here with minor editing. — Editor

Why the Talks Failed?

Chhoton Das

The controversy over the peace process in Bengal reminded me of a newspaper photograph many years ago. It was a picture of former US secretary of state Henry Kissinger in conversation with vietnam communist leader Le Duc Tho at a meeting during the Vietnam war. They had travelled to Paris for peace talks. According to Mao Zedong, the No 1 enemy of the people of the world was US imperialism, and it was with this enemy that the Vietnam Communist Party was talking peace. The picture conveyed a clear message of the deep commitment of communists to peace. The passage of time has not been able to diminish this desire. The proof of this is the letter of 8 July 2011 from CPI(Maoist) state secretary Akash to the mediators. It was the first letter in the peace dialogue process by the Maoists. We received it on 12 July. I imagine it must have gone through many twists and turns and passed through many hands before reaching us.

Before dwelling on the letter's content, I will say a few things about the genesis of the 7 July meeting with the government. On the night of 6 July, Sujato Bhadra informed me over the phone that the chief minister wanted to talk about Junglemahal. After a moment's silence, I asked who else would be at the meeting. The response was Asokendu Sengupta (who was born and grew up in a village neighbouring Chhatradhar Mahato's), river-expert Kalyan Rudra (member of *Lalgarh Mancha*'s advisory group and an social activist), poet Prasun Bhowmik and Debasis Bhattacharya (founder-member of APDR and its former secretary and veteran journalist). The first three I knew well. In the last Assembly elections, Friends of Democracy issued a call to 'defeat CPI(M)' and we all addressed many meetings together. Consequently, I became quite close to them. How much our joint campaign worked to end 34 years of LF misrule is a matter of research, but I can say with certainty that overnight we were able to greatly increase the number of those in opposition (sans LF supporters). I agreed to Sujato Bhadra's proposal and suggested that it would be good to include a few more friends. We couldn't do it for lack of time, though it would have helped our work.

The First Meeting

The time was fixed for 2 pm on 7 July 2011. We reached Writer's Buildings a little early. The call from the CM's room came before 2 pm. Education minister Bratya Basu was already there, and chief secretary Samar Ghosh, home secretary G.D. Gautam, DGP Naparajita Mukhopadhyay and Kolkata Police special commissioner Shibani Ghosh came in later.

From the experience of meeting officials, presenting deputation or meeting ministers on various issues during the LF's regime, I presumed the meeting would continue for 30-45 minutes at the most. Considering that Mamata Banerjee is the supreme leader of the ruling party, most popular political personality in the state and the 0busiest chief minister, I felt it would be a very short meeting. We would state whatever we had to say, the CM would listen and the government would consider all angles before taking a decision. How long could that take? That's why, a meeting of FOD was also called that evening.

But the meeting dragged on and on. A tug-of-war over preparing a joint declaration on behalf of the government and civil society continued. We endeavoured to make the declaration positive for the people of Junglemahal by including their long-standing, legitimate and democratic demands. If the 7 July proclamation is read with an open mind, one will find that it contained some of the democratic demands that reverberated time and again from rallies on city streets to meetings in towns and villages.

Joint Declaration

Let us take a look at the seven points of the joint declaration, titled 'Special meeting to bring peace and development in Junglemahal'.

Act 2 states: 'In Junglemahal, all incidents of torture, injustice by the previous government will be investigated on the basis of complaint letters.' Did it not reflect the people's demand in Junglemahal and those who had stood by them? Let's have a look at what PCPA had to say: 'A special demand of the people of Junglemahal is exemplary punishment for CPI(M)/*harmad* leaders and police officers guilty of the hellish carnages orchestrated during the previous regime in Chhoto Angaria, Khasmahal, Saatpati, Boiri, Dharampur, Chherabeni, Chunpara, Barikul and Netai among others.' Furthermore, 'We demand judicial enquiry into the killings of Junglemahal's mass leaders Sidho Soren, Lalmohan Tudu, Umakanta Mahato and others in fake encounters during CPI(M) rule and punishment for the guilty police officers.'[1]

The foremost demand adopted in the mass convention called by *Medinipur Suraksha Samiti* in Medinipur on 21 June 2011 was: 'Those party-slave police, under whose patronage these criminals have freely carried on killings, rapes, loot and so on, small or big, must be identified and given harsh punishment.'

The memorandum from *Jharkhand Andolon Samanway Mancha* (JASM) that we were given at the Jhargram meeting of 21 July to forward it to the CM also made similar demands. Present at that meeting on behalf of the JASM were representatives of *Jharkhand Janamukti Morcha*, *Jharkhand Anushilan Party*, PCC-CPI(ML), *Jharkhand Chhatra Federation*, *Jharkhand Kranti Dal* and other individuals. The basic demands of all the organisations and individuals were the same: the culprits must be punished, the government should arrange for exemplary punishment, and all misdeeds of LF rule have to be investigated. Act 2 includes this demand.

Act 5 of the joint statement states: 'In Junglemahal and the whole of West Bengal, all parties have to withdraw arms.' It goes without saying that 'all parties' implied the Maoist party and the government. Why the critics missed this clearly printed line is not clear even now. Later, hard-nosed bureaucrats and a section of the media attacked the substance of this line the most. The charge was that a handful of rebels and a hugely powerful government that had won a massive majority had come together. People who keep track of peace talks know that peace negotiations are not held between the victor and the vanquished; both sides participate on an equal footing.

The country's Prime Minister himself has held meetings with the rebel Naga outfit National Socialist Council of Nagaland (I-M). In recent times, in peace talks with the ULFA, the Centre was represented by secretary-level officials. The ULFA's organisational boundaries are within Assam, but the talks were held with the government of India. Former Prime Minister Rajiv Gandhi signed peace pacts with quite a few minor rebel groups whose influence was limited to just one or a few districts. There are many such examples internationally, too. The Sri Lankan government held meetings with the LTTE, which were mediated by the Norwaegian government. Great Britain has held talks with the century-old Irish Republican Army, which has been accused of killing of Lord Mountbatten and conspiring to kill the former Prime Minister Margaret Thatcher. On 12 January 2012, the Myanmarese government and Karen rebels agreed to cease hostilities, resulting in a temporary halt in the six-decade-long civil war. A group of ministers and senior leaders of Karen National Union signed the peace pact, according to reports.

That every side in a peace talk has equal standing is recognised internationally as well as in this country. For some invisible reason, this notion was assailed in Bengal. The level of this assault multiplied following the leak of our letter of 24 October to the CM.

The Leaked Letter

In that letter, the mediators had requested the government and the Maoists to declare their stands on the five issues that it mentioned to facilitate the next step. Point 3 in the letter said: 'As announced earlier, Maoists will desist from weapons' usage, display or threat. We hope other groups, forums and individuals will abide by this condition.' Point 4 said: 'Joint forces' operations will be halted.' Point 5 stated: 'To maintain peace, police raids on Junglemahal villages will stop.' The letter reached the government office on the afternoon of 24 October.

A few hours later, a popular TV channel displayed the letter with hostile remarks.

Act 4 in the July 7 joint declaration added: 'Government will take lawful measures in the recovery of arms.' Who has arms in Junglemahal? Nobody's talking about the armed opposition party, because 'withdrawal of arms' had been mentioned earlier.

Though its a well-known fact, I repeat that in our country, left and right political parties both use arms in defiance of the law. Till just before the Assembly elections, with the direct backing of the Buddhadeb Bhattacharjee government, CPI(M) led by Sushanta Ghosha, Tapan-Sukur Ali and others had set up more than a hundred armed *harmad* camps in Junglemahal to 'teach' the agitating villagers a lesson. The biggest corroboration of this is the Netai massacre. With the change in the political equation, the villagers, on their own initiative, launched a move to recover the illegal arms from the region. Some were recovered, but those were just the tip of the iceberg. In this context, we'll take a look at PCPA's statement: '... till now only 2-4 percent of the *harmad* forces' cache of arms has been recovered ... almost nothing has been recovered of the ultramodern weapons.' Furthermore, '... on 10 June in the Aguibani area under Jhargram P.S., led by CPI(M) leader Prasanta Das, a more than 100-strong army of *harmads* riding 50 motorbikes launched a horrific assault on the people.'[2] Had the peace dialogue continued, had the above-mentioned point been made strictly operational, it's not difficult to comprehend who'd have been harmed.

These people are shedding tears, assuming the fall of the LF to be the fall of leftism. Along with police and bureaucrats nurtured with care during the 34-year LF reign, these weathercocks, too, were equally active in laying thorns on way to the peace process.

No, the 7 July joint declaration did not carry entirely what we stood for. That 'joint forces would be withdrawn once peace returned' meant that the withdrawal was conditional. Among the demands I have make till now, and still making as a social and human rights activist, the most important is unconditional withdrawal of the joint forces from Junglemahal. In the declaration, however, the government accepted the withdrawal of the joint forces as a final step but not as an immediate task. We had then two options: to walk out of the meeting and thus revoking all the positive steps we had agreed upon, or insisting on implementing the decision to halt the joint forces' operation as our immediate demand, considering the withdrawal to be a strategic demand. We accepted the latter.

Dilemmas over Withdrawal

We started thinking about the controversial issue of the forces' withdrawal by returning to the past. We didn't have to go too far. Just a year or two ago, various democratic organisations as well as eminent civil society figures had said what we later acceded to, that is, a halt to the joint operations pending the withdrawal.

Let me place the views of *Lalgarh Mancha*. The joint forces started operation in Lalgarh on 18 June 2009. A week later the *mancha* issued a press statement whose main point was: stop joint forces' operation in Lalgarh and begin talks.[3] Note that there's no word on withdrawal of joint forces.

On 31 July 2010, another joint statement was issued, saying: 'We're demanding that the operation should stop.' The demand has been published in big size letters. Here, too, there's no demand for withdrawal.[4]

Sometime in June 2009, another leaflet stated: '... So, we are of the opinion that joint operation must stop.'[5] On 12 May 2010, at a press conference at the Kolkata Press Club, APDR general secretary Debaprasad Roy Choudhury issued a statement saying: 'In *Adivasi* and other areas, Operation Green Hunt as well as military, paramilitary and police operations must be stopped and talks started with Maoists and all others.'

The leaflets issued by various organisations voiced the same demand: stop the joint forces' operation. Let the villagers get relief, albeit temporarily, from the torture unleashed by the joint forces. When the situation was ripe for mobilisation, the demand for the withdrawal of forces could be built into a bigger movement. Generally speaking, in a movement there are two demands: immediate and basic. If the immediate demand is attained, the basic demand is strengthened, and the process of achieving it becomes smoother. Tactically, therefore, sometimes the focus is on the immediate demand. No one could deny the ground reality.

The intimate relationship of the poorest of the poor, the forever-deprived people of Junglemahal with the Maoists cannot be denied. The Maoists could not be suppressed even after the deployment of thousands of paramilitary forces along with CPI(M)-led *harmads*, and killing of several Maoists and PCPA leaders in fake encounters and arrest of three CPI(Maoist) state secretaries and hundreds of workers and sympathisers. The CPI(Maoist) state secretary had, in his statement of 30 September 2011, demanded just one condition for the creation of a congenial environment for peace talks. The declaration stated: 'If the state government promises to halt joint operations for one month and abides by its letter and spirit ...' Sujato Bhadra and I had countersigned this declaration by Akash. Even after that, some political personalities and stalwarts of human rights movement have spewed venom against the mediators.

Talks are Possible

Whether we're capable of fulfilling the responsibilities of mediators is linked with the fact whether it's possible to hold peace talks with the Maoists. A view doing the rounds among the left (non-CPI-M and non-LF) and radical left forces is that the CPI(Maoist) is implementing a revolutionary agenda. Land to the tiller, confiscation of foreign funds and capital, declaring freedom for Naga, Mizo and all other nationalities — these are part of their people's democratic revolution. They are pursuing their goal to overthrow the current Indian State and replace it with people's democracy in order to usher in socialism and finally communism. In all this, can there be any compromise or discussion with the government? Whether according to Marxist theory peace talks is possible, Marxist theoreticians will talk or write about it. That's not our forte. In the past, peace discussions have been held and agreements signed in many different situations. In neighbouring Nepal, Maoists participated in talks; Maoists in the Philippines are holding dialogues under Norway's mediation.

Besides, other kinds of rebel organisations and armed opposition parties have held (and are holding) talks at official levels in India and other countries. A ceasefire is on with NSCN(I-M) for a decade and a half — it has been renewed at intervals. For durable peace, NSCN(I-M) is continuing with the ceasefire with the Central government. Recently, ULFA declared a ceasefire and the Centre, acknowledging it, announced a halt in military operations to create an environment conducive to dialogue. All sides have welcomed such moves.

Without going further into such examples elsewhere, let us concentrate on West Bengal. I mentioned Akash's letter of 8 July at the beginning, which says: '... newspapers have written that this committee has been appointed for talks with Maoists. Actually, we want to know what exactly were the issues discussed between Mamata and you, what are the responsibilities she has given you, how much time has she given, what is there in the written agreement and what in unwritten agreement or understanding. Therefore, I'm inviting ...'

I've talked about communists' interest in peace. In this case, all of the state's democratic organisations and individuals have, at different times, demanded talks. All mass organisations in Junglemahal have reiterated that demand. The PCPA has said: 'PCPA has always been ready for discussions with the old as well as the new government.'[6] The open letter also said: 'You can meet with us at any time. We are willing to talk, willing to extend our hand for development.'

Some eminent civil society personalities issued a press statement on 15 June titled, 'Not paramilitary, police action in Lalgarh but issues have to be solved through discussions.' The statementsaid: 'We believe that the state government should discard the path of bloodletting confrontation without delay and find a way to solve the problem through talks with representatives of the agitating people of Junglemahal.'[7]

Lalgarh Mancha issued a statement on 26 June 2009 saying: 'Stop *joint forces' operations* in Lalgarh and *begin talks* (emphasis by author).' In another statement on 14 July 2009, the *Lalgarh Mancha* said: 'To bring back peace, the government has to take the initiative, invite the concerned side/sides for talks, and fulfil this pledge. We appeal to the armed opposition party to set aside arms and respond to the call for talks.'

On 22 June 2009, a procession was organized from Gariahat to Rash Behari Avenue crossing. A leaflet distributed during the procession said: 'No paramilitary, police action in Lalgarh ... problems have to be solved through discussions ... not killings, withdraw arms and take the initiative to find a healthy solution to the problem through peaceful means, through talks.'[8]

A press statement issued by Debaprasad Roychowdhury, APDR general secretary, on 12 May 2010 demanded: 'Military/paramilitary/police operations have to be stopped and talks begun immediately with Maoists and all concerned.'[9] And on 31 July 2010, several civil society stalwarts demanded: '... let this wrong policy end immediately and the course of dialogue be opened.'[10]

In a nutshell, the entire society's demand was that the government start talks for peace. There's no alternative to dialogue in a democracy. The opposite of dialogue is bloodshed, death and loss of life and property or, in other words, social calamity. That's why, rights movements have always demanded peace, and talks to establish peace. After 7 July 2011, the CPI(Maoist) and other mass organisations and Jharkhand parties in Junglemahal, Santosh Rana-led CPI(ML)-PCC and several political groups welcomed the initiative for 'peace talks'. Many organisations and individuals spoke with us directly. On 22 July and 6 August we met with jailed leaders of the CPI(Maoist), PCPA and Ganapratirodh Mancha at Medinipur jail.[11]

Discussions were held in two phases for a few hours in a congenial environment, and views were exchanged freely. In the words of Chhatradhar and the other jailed leaders: Two rounds of meetings were held at which both sides exchanged views displaying respect for each other.[12] We didn't get even an inkling of the critical campaign being carried on outside what they said. This attitude of the prisoners inspired us.

Slander Against Us

All democratic forces in the state agreed on peace talks. A handful among those who had signed a statement titles, 'Dialogue wanted for peace' and marched in processsions, got bogged down in hair-splitting debates on various issues and thus exposed their stand of opposing the peace-talk process. Some among them worked very hard to spoil our relations with the stakeholders and create an environment of mistrust. The chairperson of APDR's West Medinipur district branch informed the organisation's annual general meeting that the mediators told Chhatradhar Mahato in the jail that he would be released only if he gives in writing that he would not get involved in PCPA politics any more and ends his acrimonious relationship with Babu Bose, president of anti-Maoist *Jharkhand Samannay Mancha*. The district APDR president and elderly professor did not say where he got this important information from. It was learnt from a news report[13] that the APDR leadership had adopted a proposal at its meeting criticising 'this conditional proposal for (Mahato's) freedom. It was not clear from the news report whether the respected human rights organisation leaders wanted to know the source of that information. And even though Sujato Bhadra, known as the 'public face of the APDR was among the mediators, no one felt the need to talk to him and find out the truth.

On 10 August, Chhatradhar Mahato and a few of his colleagues sent a protest letter titled, 'Defeat the slander campaign by a section of the corporate media, and written on the letterpad of *Santrash, Durniti O Samrajyabadi Agrasan Birodhi Ganatantrik Mancha* from jail. The letter said: 'No intellectual had asked Chhatradhar Mahato to give an undertaking or cut off ties with PCPA ... the mediators' team held two rounds of meetings with prisoners in Medinipur Jail. Both sides exchanged views, displaying respect for each other.'[14] It was clear from the statement that pro-corporate people had arrived to disrupt the peace-talk process. It's strange that we haven't seen any statement from APDR or the honourable professor after the publication of Ashokendu Sengupta's rejoinder and Chhatradhar Mahato's protest.

The slander continued even after this.

Meeting Maoists

During the peace-talk process, we met the Maoist leadership twice, first on 28 August 2011 and then on 30 September. Akash and the others escorted us to the meeting venue. Akash already knew Sujato Bhadra, and he said this formally before the meeting began. He also said thatb he had participated in meetings and rallies when bhadra was APDR secretary. The discussion was held in an amicable atmosphere and with mutual respect, exactly the opposite of what was being rumoured outside. At the meeting, the Maoists expressed displeasure with the police campaign and asked us to tell the the government to stop it.

Twists and turns, and complexities are part of any peace-talk process, and they were evident during our efforts, too. The situation heated up over the chief minister's promise of recruiting 10,000 special police personnel. It was alleged that the Maoists had put up posters warning people that those applying for such jobs would be punished with death. At the meeting, Akash said that the Maoists were not responsible for the posters and later gave this in writing as well.

While the peace-talk process was on, TMC worker Rabindranath Mishra and JASM leader Babu Bose were killed by Maoists. Babu Bose and his organisation had held a meeeting with us to restore peace in the region, and demanded the release of all political prisoners. But his death dealt a big blow to the peace-talk process. The government's reaction made the situation even more difficult. Charges, counter-charges, blame games became increasingly common, intensifying mistrust on both sides. The result: talks reached the edge of the chasm.

Ceasefire by Maoists, Cold Reaction of Government

It didn't take long, however, for the situation to change because of the goodwill on both sides. At a meeting with representatives of the mediator group on 30 September 2011, Akash announced his party's historic decision to declare unilateral ceasefire. This was the first time since its formation in 2004 that the CPI(Maoist) had declared unilateral ceasefire anywhere in the country. We found the decision to be extremely timely and encouraging. It was a reflection of the wishes of peace-loving people.

But unfortunately, there was no government recognition of this very positive step. The Maoists, of course, kept their promise. They maintaned restraint despite police instigation and unkind comments and threats from government officials at various levels. Between 30 September and 30 October 2011, Junglemahal literally remained violence-free. I don't know whether the government failed to comprehend the importance of the statement by the main stakeholder or whether there was a hidden agenda. A section of the media started a hostile campaign to create suspicion among people about the honesty and sincerity of the Maoists' to peace. The unilateral ceasefire and call for the government's reciprocal's declaration was interpreted as a Maoist game plan to get a respite from the security crackdown in order to regroup. Clearly, the smear campaign was a reflection of the views expressed by police and bureaucrats [a party to all the misdeeds during CPI(M)'s 34-year rule]. The stand of the CPI(M), Congress and the BJP only strengthened this campaign.

It was disappointing that no forceful voice was heard, nobody took to the streets against the campaign of police, bureaucrats and a section of the media. The stand of the the CPI(M), Congress and the BJP is clear; they want to silence all voces of protest. In West Bengal, the CPI(M)-led LF had carried out ruthless repression.

Even though it was late, some citizens became active to take forward the peace-talk process. Their action, however, was limited to issuing statements signed by prominent personalities. In absence of the demand for for peace from all sections of civil society, the poisonous anti-peace campaign continued unabated. It began to drag the situation towards failure.

Since the government did not officially accept the 30 September declaration, doubts surfaced in the minds of the people. The government's statements on this issue used officialese, reflecting the cold bureaucratic attitude towards an essentially political issue, which the government had initially accepted. Ministers and bureaucrats, too, started speaking in the same language. It was forgotten that the government's responsibility was to restore peace and that in the past, governments had taken the initiative for talks in most cases. The onus of taking the peace-talk process towards the desired goal falls primarily on the government, for which steady and restrained behaviour of government representatives is absolutely essential. The same holds true for all other sides.

In the End: Failure

The unilateral ceasefire declared by the Maoists ended on 30 October. A few days later, the Maoists killed a man and his son, both TMC members, suspecting them to be spies to assert their presence in Purulia. The joint forces, waiting in the wings, jumped into the fray and shot five Maoist squad members. A CRPF jawan, too, was killed in the violence. The body language of the government began to reflect a craving for war. Akash's apprehension was reflected in his letter: '... doesn't appear to be sincere about peace talks. So, on this issue, I'm seeking the government's written statement.'[15] Even after this, the Maoists' continued their efforts to attain peace. Akash wrote: ' ... before government representatives sit for talks, it is imperative to create an atmosphere for peace talks. Consider the proposal to set up a monitoring committee.'[16]

The situation was changing rapidly. Mentioning this in our letter of 16 November to the CM, we asked to be freed of the responsibility. Our letter said: 'Given the way contemporary events are progressing, we fear that we are not in a position any more to play a workable and meaningful role.' The letter was also published in the media. Following this, the lexicon of powerspeak began to be shriller from the corridors of Writers' Building. Political goodwill deteriorated and ultimately disappeared. Muscle power, refreshed with additional oxygen, became more active. The road to peace effectively closed. On 23-24 November, the joint forces killed top Maoist leader Kishenji in an 'encounter.' Kishenji's death brought down the curtain on the peace-talk process. At 4 pm on 28 November, Sujato Bhadra sent a fax to the media, which said: 'The prevailing situation in Junglemahal does not allow us to carry forward the peace talk. We have expressed our helplessness and inability to the Honourable chief minister of West Bengal.'

Postscript

This was not the end of everything. Using Kishenji's tragic death as ammunition, a group of people launched a hateful campaign against the mediators. I had never seen these people displaying such deep hope and trust in official reports. Blind hatred impairs people's common sense. That's what's happened here.

We met the Maoist leaders only twice. Our last meeting was on 30 September 2011, almost two months before Kishenji's death. We never met Kishenji. Neither did we have a plan to meet with him nor di the Maoists gave us was any such proposal. Maoist leaders are supposed to use mobile phones. After the arrest of Sushil Roy, the party's central committee issued a circular, telling Maoist activists at every level not to use mobile phones. Nevertheless, the smear campaign against us continued in the media and elsewhere that security forces tracked him down by following our phone calls with the Maoist leaders. *Anandabazar Patrika* published such a report based on conjectures. Though the newspaper publish our team's joint protest letter on 19 December 2011, it did not deter our detractors. Ignoring the statements of friends, and relying totally on the statements of police and bureaucrats, the hate campaign continues, even though the Maoist leadership has not raised any such accusatioin against us.

Translated from Bangla by Aditi Chowdhury.

Notes :

1. *Natun sarkarer prati Junglemahaler janasadharaner dabipatra* — Charter of demands to the new government from the people of Junglemahal, PCPA, 13 June, 2011, p8
2. Ibid, p3
3. On behalf of the *Lalgarh Mancha*, Sujato Bhadra issued the statement, 26 June 2009
4. Among the signatories were Meher Engineer, Sabyasachi Deb, Subhendu

Dasgupta, Premangshu Dasgupta, Swati Ghosh, Gautam Navlakha, Sujato Bhadra, etc.

5. Published by Tapas Chakrabarty (APDR). Among the signatories were Amal Tarafdar (AICCTU), Ganesh Khan (BMC) and Tapas Chakrabarty (APDR).
6. Open letter to civil society stalwarts, Debabrata Bandyopadhyay, Sujato Bhadra and Debasis Bhattacharya, from Gopal Pratihar, Tota Hembrom, Jiten Mahato, Dilip Hansda, Asit Mahato, Santosh Mahato, Joydeb Mahato — published on behalf of PCPA by Dilip Hansda, July 2011
7. Signatories were Bibhas Chakrabarty, Manash Joardar, Amit Bhattacharya, Debabrata Panda, Tarun Naskar (present legislator) Debaprasad Roychowdhury Siddhartha Saha, Sukhendu Bhattacharya, Subhendu Dasgupta and others.
8. Issued by Mahasveta Devi, Bibhas Chakrabarty, Joy Goswami, Kaushik Sen, Tarun Naskar, Aparna Sen, Saoli Mitra, Subhendu Dasgupta, Asokendu Sengupta, Kalyan Rudra, Manas Joardar, Sacchidananda Bandyopadhyay, Prasun Bhowmik, Sujato Bhadra, Amitdyuti Kumar and others.
9. Signed by Manatosh Mukherjee (Secretary DKMC), Amal Tarafdar (AICCTU), Ganesh Khan, Anarul Sheikh, Ratan Majumdar (all BMC), Tapas Chakrabarty, Dipen Das, Nano Ghosh (all APDR), published and distributed by Tapas Chakrabarty (APDR).
10. Dhirendranath Baske, Panchu Ray, Dipanjan Rai Chaudhuri, Sabyasachi Deb, Subhendu Dasgupta, Premangshu Dasgupta, Swati Ghosh, Saswati Ghosh, Gautam Navlakha, Samar Bagchi, Muktesh Ghosh and others.
11. Those who participated in the talks were: CPI(Maoist) state committee's former secretary Sudip Chongdar, state committee member Kalpana Maity (Anu), PCPA leader Chhatradhar Mahato, Sukhshanti Baske, former GPM secretary Raja Sarkhel, Prasun Chatterjee. At the 6 August discussion, others like Asokjiban Ghosh and Chhatradhar Mahato's wife Niyoti Mahato were also prtesent.
12. Letter from Chhatradhar Mahato and others, *Ekdin*, 31 August 2011.
13. *Ekdin*, 9 August 2011.
14. Along with Chhatradhar, the statement was signed by Prasanta Patra, Prasun Chaterjee, Manoj Mahato and Sukhshani Baske, *Ekdin,* 31 August 2011
15. Akash's letter of 26 October 2011.
16. Akash's letter to mediators.

Things Fell Apart: An Interlocutor's Account

Asokendu Sengupta

They made me proud. A few hundred students of Binpur High School. Their school was turned into a police camp. They had been asking the authorities to return their classrooms, their school, so that did not waste their school days.

This is the school where I studied for a year. It was the only high school in the neighbourhood then. Since the school infrastructure and environment were absolutely poor, my father decided to shift me to Jhargram, a town 20 km away. I got a new school, and more importantly I found a picturesque town. But that was a long time ago.

In January 2009, I got an unexpected phone call. 'Can you remember me, sir, I am Babu Bose. I want to meet you.' I replied, 'Why not.' I was in Jhargram then to attend a family get-together. Of course, I knew Babu very closely. He was possibly a student in my first batch in 1975 in Jhargram Raj College and an SFI activist then. Moreover, his elder brother was my classmate in Jhargram Nanibala School. I told him to come to Jhargram. He came, and we discussed many things. Next evening, I wanted to visit his home at Dahijuri, about 5 km from my Jhargram residence. Babu said, 'No sir, it is very risky." Still I went there and met several local people. On my way back, I touched many *sal* leaves and felt they were trembling with suspicion and chill. The time and space had long been transformed. The Lalgarh episode had cast an inauspicious shadow over the everyday life in Junglemahal and Bengal politics.

Lalgarh Episode

Buddhadeb Bhattacharjee, then chief minister of West Bengal, went to Salboni to lay the foundation stone of Jindal group's mega-steel project. That was 2 November 2008. He was accompanied by some other dignitaries, including central government ministers Ram Vilas Paswan and Jitin Prasad. On its way back, one of the vehicles in the convoy triggered a landmine laid by the Maoists. Though the leaders escaped unhurt, six policemen were injured.

A section of the people was against the steel project because forest land and the land inhabited and occupied by the *Adivasis* were practically gifted to the Jindals. But the *Adivasis* did not come to the fore to protest. They have been driven out of their land since the *zamindari* era, their natural claims over land, forest, hills have been scrupulously denied by *dikus* (outsiders) over the centuries. Such exploitation and oppression or deprivation are not new to them. They have raised their voice with or without their traditional arms many a time in the past. But they were defeated by 'civilised' people with gun power and dirty tricks. Since Independence, they have participated in many 'democratic' movements under the leadership of their own clan. The leaders got their share of the cake, Mr Jaipal Singh to Mr Sibu Soren, the common *Adivasis* received nothing. They went back to their tranquil hamlets.

In West Bengal, we have witnessed many major mass movements since Independence. But the participation of the *Adivasis* of Junglemahal in those movements was insignificant. The demand for Jharkhand state or demand for recognition of the Santhali language evoked only lukewarm response from the people of Junglemahal, the strong cultural bondage with the demands notwithstanding. During the Left Front rule, the tragic incident of a starvation death in Amlasole found some space in the media and the incident attracted attention of other political parties and NGOs. But the ripples died down immediately without fury or fire. Why? We need to analyse this in some detail.

Starvation and mal-nourishment are no exception in Junglemahal. The Adivasis do not have any market for their indigenous products. As for minor forest products, they cannot sell them freely. Droughts are almost a regular feature. The government is fully aware of the Adivasis' plight, and the welfare state from time to time declares schemes and projects for their benefit. But the businessmen and the political parties, their leaders and their combinations reap the benefits. People hardly get food or fuel free or at subsised rates. Nor do they get jobs, food, shelters, electricity as promised. It's a long story of deprivation and torture. The *Adivasis* practically accept these humiliations as natural. There are no protests, no demonstrations, no slogans! They do not cry, do not beg, and do not demonstrate.

Jindal's project was just another scheme to grab their land. They might have understood it, but they had long before renounced the path of confrontation. This time also they were ready to move silently out of the frame. Civil society of West Bengal did play a laudable role in the Singur-Nandigram movement, but no protest worth mentioning was registered against the Jindal project. Only a few small political groups, including the CPI(Maoist), and some voluntary groups raised their voices. The CPI(Maoist) was practically a non-entity in Junglemahal at that time. So how the Maoists managed to lay the landmine is still a mystery.

Political Parties in Junglemahal

The role of the political parties in Junglemahal deserves mention. Between 1947 and 1967, the Congress had total political command over the region, with the main opposition party being the CPI. The Socialists did have some pockets of influence. Since 1967, disgruntled Congress members under the leadership of Ajoy Mukherjee and Shushil Dhara put up a strong challenge in Junglemahal. After 1977, the Congress was practically wiped out as a political party. Strangely, within the next decade, the CPI also stood marginalised as a political force. During the United Front regime, even the CPI(M) was a very small party in Junglemahal, operating from only some pockets. In fact, it was the *Parcheesi Raj* system through which the the CPI(M) attracted common people organisationally. School teachers, small traders and petty contractors were brought to the CPI(M)'s fold and they helped widen the party's political base. Since the early 1980s, the party in collusion with the administration and with the help of muscle and money power attacked other political parties aggressively. This was the game plan of the CPI(M) to wrest total political and social control in Bengal, rural Bengal in particular. This policy achieved more or less total success in the Junglemahal region where, till the other day, 'Party' meant the CPI(M). Almost all other parties, including the CPI, were virtually left with only their signboards. They could not put up candidates in most seats to contest the elections at lower levels like panchayats, co-operative societies and school management committees. They were not allowed to organize major political programmes. The CPI(M) almost totally appropriated the political and social space in the region. Only some factions of Jharkhand parties and the 'Naxalites' held some pockets of resistance.

People's Upsurge

In retaliation, police unleashed a brutal attack on the people in the Lalgrah area on the pretext of a combing operation to catch those responsible for the landmine blast. Police atrocities crossed all civil limits. A retired school teacher, respected especially because of his sacrifice and dedication, was tortured and stripped. A woman was beaten up suffering serious injury in her eye. People were subjected to indiscriminate torture, registration of false cases became the orde of the day, and molestation of women became common. Police were accused of perpetrating some other crimes, too.

Immediately after the brutal police operations, people dug up several roads and blocked the entry of police in the area in protest. They demanded justice through a new organisation formed by people cutting across party lines. The name of the organisation is *Pulishi Santras Birodhi Janasadharaner Committee* — People's Committee against Police Atrocities or PCPA. Chhatradhar Mahato was unanimously elected as the PCPA spokesperson. People of neighbouring villages sat together and prepared a charter of demand. Not a single demand in the charter could be described as anti-people or anti-State or communal, though some of them may appear to be funny or queer to urban sensibilities, especially to people who are unaware of the tribal ways of 'dispensing justice'. Initially, the administration paid scant respect to these people's demands. The arrogance and ignorance of the administration made the situation worse, and the movement spread like wild fire in the Junglemahal region. Neither the government nor the CPI-(M) had faced any people's resistance anywhere in the region in the recent past. Hence, both were clueless. The administration desperately tried to divide the people through dubious moves, but failed in its mission.

It may be noted that the original charter did not have any point related to the development of Junglemahal. Oppression and deprivation of centuries were not issues the *Adivasis* wanted to discuss at that moment. Actually, they have virtually adjusted themselves to the economic development plans of the government for tribal regions. Their demands initially circled around the attitude of the administration, which through the Lalgarh operation had attacked the very foundation of their culture. In tribal tradition 'gurus' (teachers) and women occupy a high position. So the torture of teachers and women in public by the police were the last thing they could swallow. The otherwise meek *Adivasis* reacted instanlt to protect their culture.

Subsequently, some political- and development-oriented points were added to the *Adivasis'* chatter of demands to mount pressure on the government and the CPI(M). The struggle against State oppression that was spearheaded by the police and the CPI(M) turned into a bigger struggle, a struggle against dispossession and marginalization — a struggle of the oppressed against the oppressor. The Lalgarh movement was essentially a movement to restore the honour and tradition of *Adivasi* culture. The movement differed from *Adivasi* movements in other parts of the red corridor, because in Junglemahal mining and inflow of corporate capital were not the issues. It was a unique people's movement in free India. It was a movement in which women participated en masse and that too voluntarily.

LF Government Missed the First Bus

The administration, through all-party meetings, tried to defuse the tension. But since all mainstream political parties, except the CPI(M), had lost their significance in the region long before the *Adivasis* identified the CPI(M) as the main partner of the government in the crime, the meetings failed to impress the people. The CPI(M) was in no mood to take this as a lesson and continued its attacks on the *Adivasis*.

To make the government's presence felt in the region, the administration agreed to negotiate with PCPA, albeit after much hesitation. But the mutual mistrust and disrespect left very little space for manoeuvre. The administration's arrogance was a great hindrance. Mr Israel was the only officer in the administration in whom the people had some faith because of his commendable work as Jhargram SDO in the recent. But he was removed from the dialogue process after a few days for reasons best known to the government. This sent a wrong message to the agitators. And it became clear that the government would not punish the errant officers who steered the brutal operations in Lalgarh.

In the meantime, the Parliament election schedule was declared. The Election Commission was responsible for holding the election in West Bengal as per its declared itinerary, and needed the help of the state administration for the job. But in Junglemahal, the very existence of the state government was practically challenged and PCPA gave a call to boycott the election. For smooth and peaceful election, the EC appealed to all concerned to cooperate. Under the EC's supervision all concerned sides participated in the dialogue, the boycott call was withdrawn and a date fixed for next round of talks. Just before the promised date, however, the state government cancelled the talks and deployed joint forces in Junglemahal. Thus it missed the first bus.

Peoples' Movement Hijacked

PCPA was truly a democratically elected peoples' committee. It was an open platform which members of all political parties, except the CPI(M), were allowed to join spontaneously. Chhatradhar Mahato himself was a Trinamul Congress (TMC) member before. Apart from the Maoists, members of other political parties, namely the Congress, Jharkhandis, Naxalites, and many individuals were included in the body. The decisions they had been taking were democratically processed. But the government propaganda machine branded the organisation a frontal organisation of the Maoists and alleged that it had the covert support of TMC. This propaganda created confusion among the people, the TMC leadership became a bit hesitant, and PCPA lost a part of its non-committal support base. But the people's resistance movement got a fresh lease of life after 9 August 2010.

On that day a meeting was held at the Lalgarh Ramkrishna School ground in which people's participation was overwhelming. The meeting was addressed by Mamata Banerjee, who criticised the Centre and the state government both for perpetuating terror in Junglemahal. She condemned the murder of Maoist leader Azad, too, who had agreed to participate in peace talks. That meeting was also addressed by Medha Patkar, Swami Agnivesh, Mahasveta Devi and some other leaders and intellectuals. All the speakers criticised the state government for promulgating Section 144 in the Lalgarh area for more than a year and supported the basic demands of the people of Junglemahal. People's participation in the meeting was overwhelming.

But the Centre-state joint forces branded PCPA activists terrorists, hounded them and made their life miserable. It became very difficult for them to maintain contact with their own people. It was at this crucial juncture that armed Maoists capitalized on the situation. The Maoists provided the *Adivasis* armed security and food. But it was no free lunch, for the Maoists demanded their pound of flesh from PCPA and captured the platform. They gagged the voice of most of the people who were connected with some other party or had different political leanings. The Maoists killed the activists of some other parties and threatened others with dire consequences in case of opposition. Hence, the democratic nature of the movement was ruined.

The Maoists pursued the same tactics practised by the CPI(M) earlier to eradicate all other social or political opposition. The CPI(M) had the overt support of the administration. The Maoists had no such support, and in many parts of Junglemahal they lost popular support because the people of Junglemahal did not accept the politics of violence, at least beyond a tolerable limit. The Maoists had no idea of the tradition and culture of *Adivasi* society. And their political strategy itself was a great divider.

It is true that through their political activities, the Maoists had been able to attract the attention of a wider spectrum of society to the magnitude of deprivation and hunger in Junglemahal. The people of Junglemahal can never forget the unwavering support of the Maoists in their fight against the CPI(M)-government nexus. In fact, the people were ready to accept the Maoists as their natural allies had there been no extortion and no kangaroo court. The *Adivasis* were indeed made aware of their rights by the Maoists, and economic and development questions were discussed in right earnest. But the *Adivasis* did not want to forego their culture and social order — things that did not find a proper place on the radicals' agenda.

This does not mean that the people of Junglemahal wanted flush out the Maoists. The Netai mass killing by the *Harmad Bahini* of the CPI(M) once again proved that the CPI(M) wanted to perpetuate its rule through its armed cadres and by terrorising helpless people. On the other hand, the brutal acts, partisan attitude and corrupt practices of the joint forces angered people further. Rejecting both these forces, the people of this area had no option but to fall back upon PCPA. Amid all these goings-on the over-enthusiastic Maoists had hegemonised PCPA.

The Assembly Election

The people of the region considered the 15th West Bengal Assembly elections a chance to express their free will. The Maoists and the Maoists-controlled PCPA had to a large extent been isolated from the people. Several of their activists were brutally murdered by the joint forces. Many CPI(M) activists, too, were killed. The people of Junglemahal were no longer ready to accept the bloodshed, police operations, CPI(M) armed camps and Maoists' kangaroo courts. But nobody cared for them. Meanwhile, Mamata Banerjee had become the symbol of struggle for natural justice. Her election promises, apart from her speech at Lalgarh on 9 August 2010 inspired the people of Junglemahal to vote for TMC candidates. The Maoists were a divided lot — a section supported Mamata, while another backed Chhatradhar Mahato and still anothwer understandably kept itself away from the election.

During the election, it became clear that CPI(Maoist) was no more a monolithic organisation. Signs of discord were perceptible. Chatradhar Mahato, the popular representative of the people till about a year ago, lost the election by a huge margin. Interestingly, a small section of Kolkata-based radicals, who fought against CPI(M) misdeeds elsewhere, supported the Chhatradhar Mahato's candidacy, but was frustrated by his defeat.

The day Mamata was sworn in as chief minister, some individuals and groups demanded unconditional withdrawal of the joint forces from Junglemahal and unconditional release of political prisoners. They claimed that since these were part of Mamata's election promises, she must honour them. It may be noted that the TMC election manifesto does not support their claim. Her promise was that police would not implicate innocent people in false cases, false cases against individuals would be withdrawn and police would not be used to oppress the people. After only about a month in office and restored peace in the Darjeeling hills through negotiations, Mamata turned her attention to Junglemahal. In that one month, a review committee had been formed under the chairmanship of Justice Malay Mukherjee to study the cases of political detainees.

Peace Initiative: Mamata Government and Mediators

On 7 July 2011, Mamata requested a group of concerned citizens to take the initiative to restore peace in Junglemahal. She appointed six individuals, including this author, to act as interlocutors. This infuriated a section of intellectuals, some of whom were self-proclaimed champions of the Junglemahal movement. They questioned the credentials of the six people. Some even launched personal attacks against the interlocutors. I know some of them were sceptics, whil others had serious doubts about our capability. Interestingly, a section of the media was also unhappy with the composition of the interlocutors' team. This heterogeneous combination of detractors remained busy slinging mud on the interlocutors' team.

On 7 July 2011, we discussed different aspects of the problem in the CM's chamber, where the chief secretary, home secretary, DGP and other officials were also present. Education minister Bratya Basu, too, was present at the meeting. It was decided that the interlocutors would try to bring all the stakeholders to the negotiation table in order to bring peace and to create a congenial atmosphere that might help start development work in the region. A joint declaration signed by the six interlocutors (or Team Six) and the home secretary was made public by the CM herself at a press conference.

We need to discuss one important question here: Why the peace move was considered so important? The main stakeholders were indeed the Maoists and PCPA. But PCPA had practically lost its relevance in Junglemahal after the Maoists took control of the platform. And the Maoists had lost spontaneous popular support in the region. Maoists or no Maoists, some facts remain unaltered. The people of the region have been deprived of their rightful claims over their land and forest for years. They have witnessed the terror of the State forces, some have lost their relatives in encounters, false cases have been registered against many, and they have been denied their human rights — right to live with dignity. The Maoists, their mistakes and misadventures notwithstanding, firmly stood by the oppressed at their hour of crisis for a couple of years to bring to the world's notice the negligence perpetuated by the State in Junglemahal.

Furthermore, it is an established fact that peace is a prerequisite for development work everywhere. So, it is the duty of every pro-people government to take positive steps to bring peace. Mamata's government was eager to build its pro-people image. At the same time, it was aware that the Maoists were capable of spreading violence and stall development work. Hence, it was a compulsion on the part of new government to buy peace.

Positive Maoist Response

The Maoists responded positively to the peace initiative because they read the pulse of the people. People wanted peace and development, and the Maoists dare not go against their wishes. The development of the backward region is an important point even on the Maoists' agenda. So the Maoists welcomed the peace move.

We met several groups of Jharkhandis and Naxalites and some individuals at Jhargram, who submitted a joint memorandum. The meeting was attended by, among others, Babu Bose who was later killed by the Maoists. The same day we met a group of prisoners, including Chhatradhar Mahato, Sudip Chongdar, Prasun Chattopadhyay and Raja Sarkhel, in Medinipur Central Jail. All of them welcomed the peace move. Through us, they urged the government to release the political prisoners immediately. None of them demanded total withdrawal of the joint forces immediately. Some people who attended the Jhargram meeting even said that the presence of joint forces created a sense of security among the people. Some of course argued that the joint forces' operations must stop first.

We received dozens of complaints against the police and paramilitary forces. At the next meeting in Medinipur Central Jail, apart from leaders who were present at the first meeting, Niyati Mahato (wife of Chhatradhar), Anu Maity and Asokejiban Ghosh were also present. On both occasions, Chhatradhar talked with me separately for a while. I cannot disclose the reasons for the separate meetings here. I can only say that they were personal and the request came from Chhatrdhar's end.

Some civil rights activists and intellectuals had said that the Maoists might not take us seriously and might not agree to surrender their arms. Such fears were baseless. In our joint declaration, no stakeholders, including the police, asked anyone to surrender arms. Rather they were asked only to stop the use of arms during the peace process. Responding to our call and rubbishing all speculations, Akash, secretary of CPI(Maoist) West Bengal state committee, invited us to discuss the peace agenda.

Two of us, risking our lives, met him at a Maoist hideout. At this meeting and through an interview published on a website, the

CPI(Maoist) made it clear that it wanted peace and development. The Maoists, in fact, admitted that the presence of the joint forces had reduced crime and violence in the region, and after the new government came to power, all sorts of operations by the joint forces had considerably been reduced. The same interlocutors met Akash and his companion again to prepare the ground for peace talks.

We met the stakeholders atn hideouts, in jails, behind closed doors. We talked across the table. We received positive and warm response from all the stakeholders and the people. Everybody, leaders and the people, farmers and office workers, whom we met by appointment or by chance, told us in unequivocal terms to bring peace at any cost. At any cost! But, what is that cost?

Peace at Any Cost

Peace is not a commodity that can be purchased in an open market. It is a lifestyle to be achieved through practice. It is simultaneously a political, social and psychological process. The yearning for peace fortunately exists in Indian culture. Teachings of the *Upanishads* and the *Gita*, the writings of Rabindranath Tagore, the movements of Gandhiji and several others have underlined the importance of peace in society. We do have some idea of peace, but its cost we have not pondered over seriously. With the advent of open market economy, we have succumbed to the wishes of world markets; we have surrendered our idea of society, idea of values and idea of peace. Somerset Maugham wrote that peace is nowhere to be found except in your mind. This was never the guiding principle of developed nations.

Now, modern States under the influence of market forces consider comfort as peace. We have allowed our government policies to use us to be pawns of a corporatised world economy with the hope of bringing more comforts to the life of individuals. The worldwide cry for war against terror is a double-edged ploy created by the market players. The problems of the state of West Bengal have been further accentuated by the pretensions of left politics.

The LF big brother, the CPI(M), in order to silence all dissenting voices had been using strong-arm tactics. From Marichjhapi to Nandigram, the administration faithfully implemented the strong-arm policy of the government, from Bijan Setu to Netai, the 'Party' meticulously implemented its policy of elimination of the opposition. The 'Party' in course of time has become a pot full of poison with a lid of honey (*Bishakumbha Payomukham*). It has spoilt the culture of peace-loving Bengali people and instead cultivated a politics of *dakhal* (absolute domination) through money and muscle. Peace was brought in the LF regime through bloodshed or through persecution. The 'Party' resisted even saner people from pursuing peace through dialogue.

We held several rounds of talks in Writers' Buildings with the new chief minister in the presence of top state government officials. Apart from the top functionaries of the state administration, some senior ministers like Partha Chatterjee, Purnendu Bose and Malay Ghatak were present at one meeting or the other. Leaders like Pradip Banerjee and Kalyan Banerjee, too, participated in the discussions. We discussed many things at those meetings, and the meetings lasted for hours. We had reason to believe that the CM was serious in promoting the peace talks. It was decided once that Partha Chatterjee might represent the government at the meeting with the stakeholders to discuss peace, and the stakeholders would be given 'safe passage'. It was also decided that Chatterjee and other senior ministers might visit jails to talk with the detained leaders. All the stakeholders accepted these proposals and welcomed the spirit. Still peace talks met with several obstacles.

Obstacles: Mutual Misgivings and Clashes

The Maoists alleged that the TMC-led *Bhairab Bahini*, like the *Harmad Bahini* of the CPI(M), had been terrorising the people. Some disturbing news came to our knowledge. We brought these to the notice of the CM. She denied them and asked us to give concrete evidence. The Maoists requested us to make enquiries. But, we couldn't. We did not have the infrastructure to do so. Moreover, in our opinion it was not the duty of the interlocutors to run after miscreants of any party. It was our strong belief that mistrust and miscommunication gave birth to many misgivings. We engaged ourselves in building mutual trust among stakeholders.

However, it will not be out of place to say that acts of a section of police embarrassed our position as interlocutors and as members of civil society. In some cases, when the peace move was on, police denied some organisations their right to demonstrate, harassed social workers with fabricated allegations. Interestingly, a section of the TMC leadership was not satisfied with our role. It tried to open a parallel channel by instituting a separate committee of interlocutors. But to its utter dismay neither Mamata nor the major stakeholders approved of this move.

A large section of the CPI(M) members and sympathisers lined up to join TMC after the Assembly elections. Under the nose of the new government, the TMC leadership, with the help of the new converts, became super-active in seizing (*dakhal* politics) political space in the area totally, factionalism made the problem more complicated. Other political organisations alleged that this was a repeat show of the same tragic drama based on the doctrine practised in the past by the CPI(M).

Bureaucrats to be Blamed

To our utter dismay we found the attitude of the state bureaucrats was very much against the peace move. The lukewarm response from the bureaucrats, we learnt, made the works of the review committee for prisoners (undertrials, etc.) tough. Recommendations of the committee, we observed, had been coming very slowly and that too did not percolate in time. Consequently, bail petitions of many prisoners were opposed by public prosecutors in lower courts. It is true that the LF government had amended the relevant rules in such a manner that awarding the status of political prisoner to a person had become cumbersome. But, I must say, that the rule was not the only hurdle.

The bureaucrats practically refused to understand the importance of awarding the status of political prisoners to a jailed activist. At times, bureaucrats, too, spread rumours. Once we were told that the Maoists had put up posters opposing the recruitment for the police department and threatened people with dire consequences, like death. Such posters would send a wrong message to the people regarding governance, senior bureaucrats claimed. Though the Maoists opposed the recruitment proposal, they disowned the posters. The government decided to recruit some eligible persons from Junglemahal in the police department, which was heavily criticised and opposed by rights activists that compared the move with *Salwa Judum* of Chhattisgarh. Their arguments were not tenable, but the state government did not make any serious effort to dispel the apprehensions.

One day, through one of my friends, Dr Binayak Sen enquired about the status of the peace move. I invited him to my flat and we had a long discussion. He appreciated our efforts, the CM's seriousness about the peace move apparently convinced him. But Dr Sen expressed concern over the police recruitment. I tried to dispel his fears, but possibly failed. We agreed to further discuss the issues related to Junglemahal and the peace move in future, but unfortunately could not.

From my personal experience as a member of Team Six, I must say that inefficiency of our bureaucrats and failure of the intelligence department are very serious deficiencies. Distinguished political personality Babu Bose was brutally murdered in a marketplace. We condemned it in no uncertain terms. But the incident once again vindicated the weaknesses of the administration. Babu had a chequered political career. He opposed the CPI(M) and the Maoists voth in his area for a long time. Everybody knew that he was on the Maoists' hit list. One of his close aides was murdered by Maoists. He participated with us in the first meeting held in Jhargram to discuss the peace process. Police did not understand the importance of protecting his life. Not even a guard was posted to protect him. Police got the news of his murder after a considerable time and failed to arrest the culprits.

MAOIST KILLINGS AND CEASEFIRE

The murder of Babu and two other important TMC workers by the Maoists had almost jeopardised the peace process. We criticised such acts of barbarism and warned the Maoists of the consequences. The government was ready to take stern measures, including full-scale operations. We somehow managed to defuse the tension. Our appeal was heeded by all concerned. The Maoists offered to hold back arms for one month, promising total restraint. They asked the government to declare officially that there would be no joint forces' operations. It was known to and acknowledged by them that except for some routine exercises there were no operations, major or minor. Also, on many occasions, Mamata openly declared that her government had practically stalled the operations. Asking for official declaration was unnecessary and that was a sign of mistrust.

It was our understanding that apart from the political parties, people's participation should be ensured to restore peace. People trust Mamata, respect her, and love her. People welcomed the development schemes declared by Mamata. But as chief minister, she has to implement her schemes through the government machinery. People who were tortured and humiliated by this machinery till only a few months ago had reason to despise the government offices and officials. Police camps in schools and health centres were still there in many places despite people's objection. In many places, the Maoists obstructed the functioning of BDO offices and panchayats. To remove all such obstacles and to build mutual trust we, on several occasions, requested the government to form a monitoring committee to look into the progress of peace and development works. The government did not agree. Instead of monitoring the committee, a very senior officer suggested in the CM's chamber that interlocutors might be asked to campaign in Junglemahal in favour of various government schemes. Fortunately, a senior minister immediately rejected the foolish proposal. I mention it here only to explain the mindset of the bureaucrats. They do not know the history of peace talks, do not care to learn the culture of the people. Ignorance and arrogance have prevented them from learning from history and culture.

Anyway, the Maoists kept their promise. No untoward incident took place between 30 September 2011 and 3 November 2011. During this period, we hoped that the government would open a dialogue with the Maoists and they would be invited to the negotiation table. But that did not happen and some foul and unpalatable remarks made the situation more complex. The administration read the offer of the Maoists as a retreat of a depleted force and planned to crush them militarily. Suddenly, the police attacked Maoists' hideouts. The Maoists retaliated and caused the deaths of innocent people. The peace process was halted again. Still we were hopeful that good sense would prevail. We appealed to both sides. But a press statement of the Maoists questioned the seriousness of the government and effectiveness of the interlocutors. We requested the CM that we might be relieved under the changed situation.

Mamata, Media and Civil Society

But the CM insisted that the peace process should continue. Rather she prevailed upon us to continue. As the party supremo she could not tolerate the senseless killings of her party comrades, as a humanist she lamented the killings. And as chief minister, she, with all sincerity, was earnestly pursuing peace. But sections of the media, government machinery and civil society refused to give her necessary support. They had been continuously spreading rumours and placing hasty demands and making uncharitable, irresponsible comments.

Team Six also felt tremendous pressure from those groups. Since assuming the responsibility, we decided not to open our mouth to the media nor to write on the subject. But we were continuously pricked by many. Let me give one example. A Bengali daily painted me as *muchlekar feriwala* (peddler of surrender bonds). It reported that I told Chhatradhar Mahato in Medinipur Jail that if he agreed to sign a bond declaring his wishes to join TMC then he would be released immediately. It was true that Chhatradhar and I sat at a separate table in a corner, not once but twice, discussed several issues confidentially. But I did not ask him to sign any bond. The crafty reporter did not care to check his 'Breaking News' from me or from Chhatradhar.

Based on the news, the APDR condemned the 'bond move' in strong terms. The organisation did not care to contact me either. Both Chhatradhar and I had to write to the editor. Both the protest letters were published, but no apology was tendered. Several other concocted stories appeared elsewhere; even a leading Bengali newspaper gleefully joined the race. It went to the extent of holding us responsible for the 24 November 2011 incident: the killing of Kishenji.

After that incident we felt that our mission had failed and we had no reason to continue as interlocutors. One of us differed. The rest of us sent our resignation letter to the CM and we left the job with a heavy heart.

Conclusion: Not All Quiet on the Western Front

Kishenji *Khatam* (Kishenji Eliminated) was the headline of the highest selling Bengali daily the next day. It clearly vindicated the attitude of the media house controlled by the exponents of free market. The bureaucrats appeared to be happy. They were possibly convinced that the coveted peace had been achieved through State-owned arms. They do not know that bullets can never bring peace. The fight between State forces and their armed adversaries may continue. But, the lesson of history is loud and clear — neither side can liquidate the other militarily. Ignorance is bliss for the warring camps indeed. Only hapless people have to pay. The Union home minister, the torch-bearer of the war against terror in India who is also the champion of globalised market strategy, has reasons to be elated. It may be noted that at least four important Maoists could not be released by the state government, despite the recommendations of the review committee because of the objections raised by the Union home ministry.

As far as I understand, the chief minister was deeply shocked by the turn of events. She sincerely wanted peace and I hope she will carry on her agenda for peace with renewed energy and strategy. People certainly demand that give peace a chance. Unfortunately, the main demands — restoration of the honour of the culture of the *Adivasi* samaj — are lost in the political hullabaloo. Now, the onus, I presume, rests on civil society to draw a transparent road map for peace.

On Maoist Struggle in Junglemahal

Ashim Chatterjee

That the governments, both central and provincial, consider the brutal killing of Com. Koteswara Rao, alias Kishenji, a major success in the operation to crush the popular struggle in Junglemahal, is apparent from the unabashed glee exhibited by government spokespersons in their reaction to the incident. In fact, both the Central home minister as well as the chief minister of West Bengal expressed their satisfaction over the successful operation and boasted of delivering a mortal blow to the struggle in Junglemahal launched by CPI(Maoist), popularly known as Maoists. Naturally the fate of the struggle in Junglemahal in the post-Kishenji period has come up on the agenda of concerned quarters and is doing the rounds in the media. It has become a matter of public enquiry. That Kishenji had been an important leader of the Maoists and his loss will be felt deeply in Junglemahal, can not be denied. But, as pointed out by Plekhanov, the role of an individual, however important, can never be a decisive factor in determining the fate of any course of history. Only the prevailing objective condition has a determining role. So long the objective condition demands, the struggle will remain relevant as it will go on representing the hopes and aspirations of the people.

It is a pity that awareness regarding the actual condition of Junglemahal is very poor in the rest of the country. Even our urban intellectual friends whose sympathy lies with the people of Junglemahal and who often are vocal about the poverty and underdevelopment in the troubled zone do not understand the depth and dimension of the misery of the people there. The real cause of the rebellion of the people can never be understood without a proper understanding of the poverty of the people and its root cause, their exploitation and oppression, their deprivation and fear of losing their self-identity based on their culture and lifestyle because of continuous onslaught from outside. Actually, Junglemahal is the victim of the tyranny of the rich as well as of nature. Blessing of nature in the form of fertility of land is almost absent here. The land is mostly composed of laterite soil. As one moves from the fertile land of south Bengal to the western region of the state, the land becomes increasingly barren, hard and stony with low water-absorption capacity. It makes multiple crop production impossible. So, mono-crop production is the rule without any option of intensive cultivation round the year. Naturally, the wage-level here is very low. Irrigation system is almost non-existent. Crores of rupees have been spent on the much talked about Kangshabati river reservoir project. Though its command area is quite large, the area under effective irrigation is small.

The people of Junglemahal have traditionally depended on the wealth of the forest for survival. But the forest laws after Independence have deprived them of their traditional forest rights. The situation has improved marginally after adoption of Joint the Forest Management Bill. But the plunder of forest wealth by forest contractors persists through the unholy nexus of forest officials and contractors. Joblessness is rampant in Junglemahal. Almost all government jobs, including teaching posts, are filled up by outsiders. Local people do not get any opportunity here. Though 'Kurmali' is the local language, the medium of instruction in schools is Bengali, which the local students are not comfortable with. Teachers, mostly outsiders, do not understand Kurmali. So, there is little communication between the teachers and the students. The social scenario is equally disturbing. High caste residents, though small in number, are vastly influential. Of the local population of Junglemahal, consisting of Jhargram subdivision of West Medinipur, a part of Bankura and a part of Purulia, 20% are Scheduled Tribes, 22% Scheduled Castes and almost 50%. Other Backward Class people, including Mahatos. Yet Junglemahal suffers from acute high caste domination.The resentment of the people against this injustice done to them over the years is, no doubt, just. CPI(Maoist) took up these issues and worked diligently to earn the confidence of the people. It successfully mobilised the people, organised them to take the path of revolt against the existing unjust system. It cannot be denied that the people of Junglemahal supported the the Maoists wholeheartedly at that time and Maoists developed a strong mass base there.

Mistakes of Maoists

In this backdrop, the present day development of the political scenario in Junglemahal is astonishing. That the Maoists are facing severe setback is no secret. The Maoists have lost their mass base and are actually on the run. The loss of Keshenji is a clear pointer to this disaster. One may wonder over the real reason for this debacle. Already leaders of the ruling parties have claimed credit for it. Others think that this disaster denotes the success of the operations of the joint forces deployed in Junglemahal. All these are over-simplification. The real reason for this disaster lies with the Maoists. The Maoists themselves are responsible for it. Deviations inherent in the political line pursued by the Maoists are the real reason. The correctness or incorrectness of the political line decides the fate of any struggle. What are the deviations? Long ago many, including myself, pointed out these deviations. Firstly, over-dependence on modern weapons. Arms, no doubt, are necessary, but over-dependence on arms leads to non-reliance on the people. Long ago Mao pointed out that the revolutionary war is the war of the masses. A revolutionary war can only survive by unleashing the initiative, activity and creativity of the masses. Secondly, over-dependence on the forest terrain. The question of terrain is, no doubt, important, but its role is never determining. Thirdly, establishment of party hegemony by force over mass organisations. One can cite the case of People's Committee against Police Atrocities or PCPA as an instance. PCPA initially was a vibrant organisation consisting of different groups and parties opposed to police atrocities in which Maoists were the only armed group. The Maoists later drove out all other parties. As a result, PCPA became a rubber stamp organisation of the Maoists, and in the process PCPA lost the effectiveness in mobilising the people. Experience shows that whenever revolutionary war degenerates into a war of party supremacy instead of war of the masses, it becomes suicidal for the war as well as for the party. Fourthly, in the name of fighting revisionism, the Maoists carried out annihilation of lower-rank CPI(M) cadres and supporters, mostly poor tribal peasants. The fight against revisionism is a political struggle and not a military war. The culture of seeking a military solution for any contradiction among people is self-defeating and suicidal. Fifthly, there was weakness in their approach to the class question. Maoists often ignored the class question, as it became evident from the class analysis of the victims of their execution. Most of them were poor people who had been branded, rightly or wrongly, as police informers or agents and executed according to the verdict of the kangaroo courts where the Maoists played the role of prosecutor, judge and executioner.

But it is more evident in their selection of areas, which they would turn into their bases. In the late sixties and seventies, when we started organising peasants for armed struggle, we chose Gopiballavpur, Debra and Baharagora in West Medinipur as our struggle zone because of the sharp feudal contradictions in those area. We consciously did not choose the hilly or forest areas of Belpahari or Lalgarh. One should not forget that armed struggle for communists is the product of the development of class struggle. It is evident that the forest or hilly terrain was more important to the Maoists as strategic areas than the question of class contradiction. Thus the struggle that started with great promise degenerated into a series of startling military adventures of roving guerrilla bands. Many people wonder what the relationship of this struggle is with the Naxalite movement of the sixties. The present Maoist struggle is both a continuation as well as vulgarisation of the past movement. It denotes not only a deviation from Naxalbari, but also departure from it.

I think time has come for the Maoists to reconsider their position on two questions seriously. Firstly, we will deal with the question of strategic boycott of elections. One cannot but note the fact that the Maoists, while mouthing the slogan of boycott, tried to use the Assembly elections in Andhra by extending support to Y.S.

Rajasekhara Reddy in 2004 and recently in West Bengal to TMC. As a result their position on election has become opportunistic. Secondly and more importantly, comes the question of establishment of red political power through the formation of base areas in Chinese style. The applicability of this theory in Indian condition needs reconsideration. Dealing this issue, Comrade Mao in his article 'Can Red Power Exist in China' had laid down certain conditions, most of which are absent in Junglemahal. But more important is Mao's emphasis on the existence of historical circumstances in China that created the opportunities for the establishment of red base areas. According to Mao, red political power existed in China because of the war among the ruling classes. Elsewhere, Comrade Mao pointed out that whenever the wars among warlords would intensify, the base areas could be extended and viceversa. In contrast, in the Indian situation, there are contradictions and splits among the ruling classes, but there is no war among them. Therefore, the historical circumstances that lead to the establishment of base areas are absent here. Of course, establishing base areas in hilly regions or forest areas is possible. It should be established and taken advantage of. But it cannot be the mainstream strategic goal. Commenting on the Chinese Revolution, Comrade Stalin had said, 'In China, armed revolution is fighting against armed counter revolution. This is one of the peculiarities and one of the advantages of the Chinese Revolution." Such a situation does not exist in India.

Mamata and the Stillborn Peace Initiative

Now, that TMC led by Mamata Banerjee is in power in West Bengal, a few words regarding the peace initiative taken by the State government for settling the Maoist issue is necessary. Earlier, when she was not in power, Mamata had demanded withdrawal of the joint forces from Junglemahal, a judicial probe of Com. Azad's murder, political solution to the Maoist problem and release of political prisoners while addressing the Lalgarh rally along with Swami Agnivesh and Medha Patkar. But after coming to power, she made a volte-face. She asked for more paramilitary forces, maintained silence on 'encounter deaths' and, instead of unconditional release of political prisoners, announced a 'case-to-case review' of all cases pending against political prisoners through a review committee formed by her government. This is not at all surprising. As everyone knows, TMC is a party without any definite ideology or programme. It always takes adhoc positions on every issue. Expecting consistency from a party without any ideological programmatic commitment is ridiculous. Those who forget it become jokers in the eyes of the people. It is a pity that our friends from the civil society movement, who took responsibility of the peace initiative on behalf of the government, ended up being puppets of the government. It is now evident that the peace initiative was premature and cosmetic. For buying peace, Mamata declared attractive packages for Junglemahal. But packages are not on the agenda of the Maoists — they are after political power. It is no hidden agenda — they have declared it openly. They cannot be blamed for it. After all, the question of political power is the central question of every political party. There are two ways of achieving it. One is the transfer of power through elections, the path taken by Mamata, while the other is seizure of political power through armed struggle, the path taken by the Maoists.

And the two will never meet. As it stands even a temporary meeting is not possible. Earlier, when both were fighting CPI(M), the Maoists were natural allies of Mamata; they stood side by side. After TMC came to power, the earlier alliance became irrelevant; they stood face to face. For the success of the peace initiative, Mamata demanded total arms surrender from the Maoists, which was not acceptable to them. As for the Maoists, they demanded a safe sanctuary in West Bengal as well as unconditional release of their fellow activists. This is not acceptable to Mamata. So, the strife will go on making it clearer every day that a military solution to the problem is neither desirable nor possible. If these points as well as the deviations mentioned earlier are taken care of and rectified, the Maoist struggle still has great potential. Otherwise, a single spark cannot make a prairie fire. A spark will remain a mere spark, splendid but impotent.

Mamata or Maoists: None Cared for Democracy

Santosh Rana

The Indian State represents the class interests of the imperialists, domestic bourgeoisie, particularly the big bourgeoisie, landlords and other exploiting classes. Neo-liberal economic policies followed since the nineties have made the lives of millions of toilers miserable. The situation is graver in the central Indian plateau inhabited by *Adivasis*. The CPI(Maoist) has been trying to build an insurrectionary movement in this region and has achieved some success. Its plan is to convert this area into a base area and continue its protracted armed struggle against the State. In this perspective, there is no common ground between the Indian State and the Maoists for dialogue. Even then, the State may be forced into a dialogue only if there is a countrywide movement in support of the Maoists. There are movements of the working class, the peasantry and other toiling masses against the neo-liberal offensive of the State. But these movements are still in a defensive mode, trying to extract some concessions through parliamentary and other forms of struggle. In the runup to the Chinese revolution, a situation arose after 1935 when Japan invaded China and the Chinese people demanded the end of hostilities between the Communists and the Kuomintang and formation of a national front against Japan. After the Xian incident in 1936, when a section of the Kuomintang army revolted and arrested Chiang-Kai-Shek, the Kuomintang agreed to a ceasefire and the national united front was formed. In Sri Lanka, there were periods of ceasefire between the Sri Lankan government and the LTTE. This was possible because the LTTE represented a national cause and there was scope of dialogue between the government and the LTTE regarding the nature of autonomy or self-determination for the Tamils. A ceasefire between the Indian State and the Naga insurgents has been continuing for a long time. This has been possible because the Nagas have fundamentally agreed to a solution within the Indian Union and the differences that exist are on the question of areas to be included in Nagaland. The Naga struggle is also a national struggle. In contrast, the Maoists have not raised any partial or intermediate demand.

Lalgarh Movement: Looking Back

In November 2008, there was a genuine people's uprising in Lalgarh and adjoining areas. People came out on the streets agitating against police atrocities and demanding withdrawal of police camps. Many social and political forces, including the Maoists, *Bharat Jakat Majhi Marwa* (a social organisation of Santhals), various Jharkhandi parties and two Left parties [CPI(ML)-ND & CPI(ML)-PCC] participated in it. In the 2008 Panchayat election, Lalgarh Block (Biṇpur-1) was won by a combination of two Jharkhandi parties. Since the 1980s, this zone, which is part of the Jharkhand cultural region, has supported the Jharkhand movement. After formation of Jharkhand state with only part of Bihar in it, there was disappointment in the adjoining areas in West Bengal but the demand for autonomy did not die down. For the 2008 uprising, the police barbarity was the immediate cause while the aspiration for autonomy and self-rule was the underlying current. At one point during the movement, there was a dialogue between the People's Committee against Police Atrocities (PCPA) and the state administration. At that point, it was possible to press for dialogue over the demand of autonomy for Junglemahal. Such forms of autonomy could have been negotiated which in turn would have helped build organs of people's power at the village level (like the Soviets in pre-October 1917 Russia). We know that the Bolsheviks were not the leading majority of the Soviets. But the slogan of the Russian revolution was: 'all power to the Soviets'. We had put forward our proposals to the PCPA, but it was rejected under instruction of the Maoist leadership.

The Maoists had a different understanding of the movement. They tried to convert the area into a 'guerrilla zone' where no other political party would be allowed to function. Over and above, the Maoists started attacking democratic institutions and political forces. This destroyed people's unity in Junglemahal. At this point, the Trinamul Congress encouraged and helped the Maoists to launch attack on others. The Maoists had a difference with the *Majhi Marwas* regarding the course of the movement. The Maoists decided to resolve this difference by murdering *Majhi Marwa* leaders. Sudhir Mandi, a *Majhi Marwa* leader and chairman of Belpahari Panchayat Samiti from 2003 to 2008 was killed. This silenced the *Majhi Marwas* and they withdrew from the movement. Later, the Maoists killed many leaders and supporters of the Jharkhand movement, the latest being the murder of Babu Bose, a popular leader of *Jharkhand Andolan Samanway Manch*. After the parliamentary elections, the Maoists attacked our [CPI(ML)-PCC's] mass organisations in Lodhasuli area and closed down our office. Two veteran peasant leaders Rajani Pal and Hariram Pal were severely beaten up and driven away from their village Gohira. Upansu Mahato, the leader of a movement against pollution by sponge iron factories was driven away from his village. We had a trying time but we decided to avoid a confrontation and withdrew from the area. During this period, we approached many supporters of the Lalgarh movement in Kolkata and Delhi and organisations like APDR and *Bandi Mukti Committee* and requested them to intervene but nobody cared. During 2009 and 2010, more than 300 activists and supporters of CPI(M) have been killed, almost all of them being poor *Adivasis*. In some cases, the killings were committed with utmost brutality and the families of the dead were prevented from lifting and cremating the the victims' bodies.

When the joint forces were sent after the Parliament election, the situation worsened. The joint forces resorted to large-scale torture and arrest of villagers, including rape. It further worsened after the CPI(M) set up armed camps with the help of, joint forces. They captured many villages in Medinipur (Sadar), Salboni, Garbeta, Goaltore and parts of Lalgarh. People were forced at gun point to give free service in the armed camps. The *Sangrami Bam Samanway*, a forum of like-minded political groups, organised a march from Goaltore to

Sarenga demanding closure of armed camps after which CPI(ML)-ND cadres were brutally attacked by CPI(M) armed cadres from the camps.The Maoist squads could not operate in these areas and they moved to new areas in Jhargram, Nayagram, Sankrail and parts of Gopiballavpur-II, where the CPI(M) organisation had collapsed and the Maoists got full support of the Trinamul Congress. Actually, the PCPA committees which were formed in these areas were joint platforms of Maoists and TMC. This situation continued till the Assembly election of 2011. In the Assembly election, sections of the Maoists supported Chhatradhar Mahato, who contested as an independent candidate in Jhargram constituency (Lalgarh constitutes a major part of it), and in all other seats in Junglemahal they supported the Congress-TMC combine. In Gopiballavpur, Nayagram, Salboni and Medinipur seats, they used their fire-power in support of TMC.

After the Assembly election, there was a radical change in the situation. The CPI(M) units were totally demoralised, some of them left the area and others, particularly the corrupt elements joined TMC. Earlier, TMC had a very weak presence in Junglemahal. It could not win any even of the 23 *panchayat samitis* in the *panchayat* election in 2008. After the Assembly election, it thought that a golden opportunity had come to capture the area. Mamata Banerjee rushed to Junglemahal with offers of some rice at a cheap rate and some jobs in police and home guard. Before the Assembly election, Subhendu Adhikary (TMC MP) was holding public meetings and processions demanding withdrawal of the joint forces and release of political prisoners. After the election, it forgot about it and demanded that the Maoists surrender their arms and work under the TMC umbrella. The Maoists refused to succumb to the TMC pressure. Rather they tried to fill the vacuum created by the withdrawal of CPI(M) from Junglemahal. But they failed to judge the mood of the people. The upsurge of 2008 had died down. Moreover, their line of indiscriminate killing and extortion had alienated them from the people. In some areas, there was spontaneous resistance to their activities or the people told them politely to leave the area for some time. Some people even refused to pay the levies imposed on them. The Maoists thought that a few more killings would create a favourable space for them. They killed Lalmohan Mahato, a popular figure in Jhargram rural area and Babu Bose, who had a valiant record of struggle against CPI(M) atrocities during the LF rule. These murders further alienated them from the people. Many Maoist squad members and PCPA leaders were young unemployed youths with no political and ideological training. Some of them had actually thought that the overthrow of CPI(M) is the ultimate goal. Many of them started to surrender. The Maoists should have taken note of the Assembly election results when Chhatradhar Mahato lost his deposit in Lalgarh.

Drama of Talks

The drama of the talks between the Mamata Banerjee government and the Maoists was staged to hoodwink the people who had supported TMC with the expectation that it would restore democracy. Mamata's sole aim was to win seats in Junglemahal and capture power. Now that that target has been achieved, TMC has changed tune about its commitment to release political prisoners and withdrawal of the Centre-state joint forces. If the new government had any sincerity it would have released Chhatradhar Mahato and other PCPA leaders and started talks with them. On the other hand, the Maoists should have started dialogue with other democratic and left forces to build a powerful movement based on the demand for the release of political prisoners. They did the opposite. Babu Bose, a leader of JASM, was killed by them. I hold that neither the Mamata government nor the Maoists was sincere about the talks and peace. Both sides were trying to establish their exclusive control over the area.

So the talks between state government and Maoists ended in a tragedy: the murder of Kishenji. The interlocutors chosen by the state government were sincere in their efforts but that was not enough to bridge the unbridgeable gulf. Kishenji's killing is the unmistakable pointer to this fact. The state government and the central paramilitary forces are claiming that there was an encounter and according to the chief minister's statement, the 'Maoist guerrillas had fired 1,000 rounds on the security forces.' How was it possible that not a single person from the security forces was killed or injured? It is highly probable that Kishenji was captured and killed. It may be that some others, too, were killed. Junglemahal had witnessed the killing of Lalmohan Tudu and Sidhu Soren in fake encounters during the LF regime. A demand for judicial enquiry has been raised from many quarters this time too. Mamata Banerjee, who as opposition leader had demanded inquiry into the 'ecounter' killing of Maoist leader Azad should have ordered a judicial enquiry into his fellow CPI(Maoist) politburo member Kishenji. What will happen to the Maoist movement in Junglemahal after the death of Kishenji, people are asking. There is no doubt that it is a big blow to the movement. But the fact is that Kishenji's death is a consequence of severe weakening of the movement. The police had got specific information about his movements and it is highly probable that insiders leaked information. But whether the movement will be able to overcome its weaknesses depends on many factors.

The real issues before the people of Junglemahal are autonomy (under the Sixth Schedule of the Constitution to start with), individual and community forest rights (Community Forest Management instead of Joint Forest Management), scheduling of Kudmi Mahatos (who constitute more than 25% of the population of Junglemahal) as Scheduled Tribes, admission of *Adivasi* students in medical and engineering colleges, jobs, health-care facilities, irrigation, etc. Mamata Banerjee has not yet addressed any of these issues.

The JASM has been consistently raising these issues but many of its activists were killed or had to leave the area in face of both State and and Maoist terror. The only area which has withstood both terrors to some extent are Gopiballavpur-I and parts of Gopiballavpur-II blocks, where the people had gone through the historic peasant uprising of 1969-70. The people are trying to build a genuine mass movement on right to forest produces and land, 100 days' work, autonomy and other issues. The issues are also getting response in other blocks of Junglemahal. If the Maoists reappraise their activities and unite with other Left and democratic forces, the TMC offensive can be resisted and a genuine mass-movement on people's issues can be built.

Much Ado About Nothing

Dipanjan Rai Chaudhuri

The idea of talks between CPI(Maoist) and the government brings to mind the hoary verse: *Ajaa yuddhe, Rishi sraaddhe, Pravaate meghadambaru, Daampatya kalahe Naiba naiba ch.* Start with a bang and end in a whimper.

The Maoist party has chosen the path of armed struggle to overthrow the Indian State and build a people's democratic state in is place. The insurgencies familiar to the post-1947 rulers of India were centred on independence, that is, secession to form a state outside the Indian union. Such are the aspirations of the Kashmiri or the Naga people, while the Maoist party aims to overthrow and replace the Indian Union itself. It is for this reason that the head of the present Union government has called the Maoist insurgency as the greatest danger for the Indian State. Obviously, there can be no talks on the strategic plane between sides holding such mutually exclusive views.

One cynical opinion regards talks to be aimed at rest and consolidation on the part of the Maoist party, and surveillance to locate, arrest and assassinate rebel leaders, on the part of the government. While it is true that there is no long-term strategic meeting point of the two sides, and, in the short term, outwitting each other's surveillance, technically and otherwise, is bound to be attempted, it would be wrong to think that there is nothing more that can arise from talks.

Of course, the Maoists will not surrender their arms. Their point of view would be that they might as well wind up their party. On the other hand, the Indian Union is bound to resist militarily any armed action by Maoist forces. It would be daydreaming if one expects the Indian Union to give up the policing of whole regions to armed

Maoist forces or to allow *janatana sarkar* or rebels-run parallel local government. Neither the Indian Union nor the states have the wisdom of allowing direct political space to sections of the people who want this. In Bengal this is the origin of the disaffection of the hill peoples, the Kamtapuri and greater Cooch Behar movements.

Ceasefire Plus: Beginning of Democracy

So, as far as arms and armed action are concerned, the most that can be expected from the talks is reciprocal sheathing of arms, a ceasefire. Now, if the ceasefire can include an agreement on 'no murders, no arrests', withdrawal of the paramilitary forces, release of political prisoners and the right of all political forces, including the Maoists and their critics, to free political campaigning, this would be a step towards democratisation of the political process in the Junglemahal. Such a beginning would have been a popular one at this juncture. It is strange that even so little a give-and-take proved to be beyond negotiation, and this is the basis of the rumour of anti-talks lobbies being active on both sides.

Roughly half the members of the present Lok Sabha have criminal charges against them, and in the case of one-third of the members the charges are serious ones like murder and rape. Such 'political' elements dominate the countryside, forming part of the bad gentry. Their partners are the police and government officials. Such three-wheelers represent the Indian Union before the poor, looting their entitlements without shame and suppressing their protests in the name of resisting extremism. Sixty-five years of such experiences have resulted in a substantial loss of legitimacy of the State in the eyes of the poor across regions. Hegemony is no longer possible in these pockets and the State can only preserve its dominance by naked violence as in Kalinganagar, Jagatsinghapur, Noida, Pune, Singur, Nandigram and Lalgarh. The importance of the Maoists resides precisely in the fact that they are the only force to have come to the defence of the people everywhere, albeit with a programme of counter-violence which appeals to the people more and more as the State ratchets up violence against the people.

However, these forces are weak in most areas and the Indian Union can think of physically annihilating them. The Union defence minister has created a paramilitary campaign, Operation Green Hunt, for this purpose. The Union is not too anxious to sit at the table with the Maoists just now. If the people can withstand Operation Green Hunt, and the pockets of Maoist influence expand, then only the Union will really become interested in talks.

Political Space for People of Junglemahal

Even then, there can be a positive outcome to such talks only if the Union sheds its narrow view that the problem in areas like Junglemahal is primarily one of Maoist insurgency and recognises the fact that a large section of the people is rejecting the legitimacy of the present body polity and wants more political space directly for itself. If the Union talks to the people and accepts the principle of allowing political space to people to administer themselves, this would mean a transition of the Union into a really federal structure. People are sovereign and if they want more direct political space, if they want a transition to a maximally federal State, they are quite within their rights to do so. The Maoists would not like this compromise, because, after all, the Indian ruling classes will retain ultimate power over the State. But the self-governing enclaves will have more political power than the states do today, and land reform and democracy will expand in scope. In any case, it would be an interim step arising from the balance of forces. On the other hand, the ruling classes, and especially the big conglomerates would never like so federal a structure and their possible exclusion from such areas especially if, as is likely, the land was found to cover valuable minerals.

All sides would be dissatisfied, but this is the hallmark of a good compromise. But why would either side agree at all to a compromise it does not like? This can happen only in a situation of stalemate, a balance of power where neither side sees a quick victory on the horizon. And it would be temporary. The ruling classes will never give up their power over the State, and revolutionaries will never rest till they can do just this.

Advantage Indian Union

At present, the Union is sure of victory and would blow away consideration of such drastic diminution of its powers as poppycock. The governments in Delhi and Kolkata are upbeat after torturing Koteswara Rao to death. The Union dismisses completely the decisive factor against it — galloping distrust and alienation, leading to increasingly widespread and determined opposition by the people. The Maoists, too, are sure of expanding their spheres of influence and would regard any agreement, however temporary, with the Indian State as liquidation of the revolution. But they are yet to demonstrate that what they practise on the ground is tuned to Indian reality and radically different from the old formula of individual killing. Why have darlings of the people like Koteswara Rao to hide and die in forests?

Leaving aside the future and subjective evaluations thereof by the two sides, the present is not objectively a stalemate. It is an advantage situation for the Indian Union. So, talks are unlikely today, and even if they occur, nothing more than a temporary ceasefire seems possible.

Peace Must Have People on Its Side

Ranabir Samaddar

With the Lalgarh movement taking a critical turn a few years back, an undeclared civil war started in West Bengal. Many thought that the decade of the sixties was coming back and we were about to witness the return of 1967-68. But that is not the case. That was a revolt, this is a war. I do not have the scope here to explain the distinction between the two. This is also not the occasion to ruminate on philosophy and the philosophical issues involved in this distinction. But let us be aware, a war is on. Society will have to pay a heavy price — both in humanitarian and human rights terms.

The upsurge of the *Adivasis*, the indigenous people, in vast swathes of Junglemahal, including Binpur, Salboni, Jhargram and other areas now in the news was one part of this war. Doubts about the legitimacy of rule and the capacity of rulers to rule became widespread. Its credibility was at an all-time low. Along with this there were two more factors, unnoticed for long and now demanding attention.

The first point: Even after the debacle in the form of the Partition of 1947, West Bengal had begun its life in a new way — not looking back but deciding to go forward grappling with issues of the time. West Bengal regained its singular nature. By singular I mean building up a collective but a singular existence or identity. Much of it was possible due to the left movement and spread of Leftist politics in North Bengal, central Bengal, Gangetic Bengal and Junglemahal in the south-western part of the state; also the representational system and a common administration tied all these parts in one common political-cultural whole. However, this project of building up a collective Bengal was in ruins in the later years of the Left Front rule owing to its Kolkata-centric rule, upper-caste dominated party politics, corruption, neglect of agriculture, mad rush to invite monopoly capital and neglect of the need for balanced development.

The second point was even more ominous. A large section of the upper echelons of police and bureaucracy administering this state had no connection whatsoever with the people of the land. Some of the names of these top officials and administrators are now familiar to us in the context of the police suppression in Junglemahal. These big officials were the mandarins of an all-India rule. Their job was to maintain the all-India rule in this state. Hence, they took it as their job to brief the rulers in the state in a specific way. Thus even a simple event of lodging a complaint became a matter of security/insecurity, any strong protest became sedition, and in general popular activism appeared in governmental gaze as a programme of creating terror.

The only recourse for these police and administrative officials was — send armed police, un-uniformed armed party cadres, paramilitary forces and all other government personnel to terrorise, threaten, coax, browbeat, beat, arrest, kill, damage or destroy peasants' houses and drive away the protesting people in order to pacify and sanitise the area. The rulers became intoxicated at the new prospect of using strong methods — but in the process they lost all sense of justice.

Clashes between rulers and the angry people seemed inevitable from the way events unfolded. Different groups of people started facing repressing measures. We had already seen a variety of these measures in Nandigram. There was a further cause for alarm in the initial phase of the civil war as there was no clear demarcation line between the two combatant sides. Throughout the state, in various parts various groups of people were up in arms with their respective demands, claims, backgrounds, and stories of deprivation and exploitation; clashes and skirmishes were evident everywhere. It was almost inevitable that this would develop into an all-round bloody conflict, and high police and administrative officials would be able to persuade the political leaders that only strong-arm methods would bring society under submission.

It is not enough to say that dialogue should return to politics. In ordinary course, meetings take place between say a district magistrate and a leader of an agitating group of people. DMs and ADMs used to call local leaders for discussion; they still do it today. But clashes do not stop because of that. Just as ceasefire, which means 'cessation of hostilities' is part of war, there has to be ceasefire in this social war also. If the rulers want to avert the impending disaster, they will have to talk at all levels of society, they will have to say to those who are being ruled that they had committed grave errors, and that they would now have to place dialogue at the centre of their governing policy. There is no shame in admitting mistakes and going for corrective measures.

Setback for Peace Politics

Now of course after three years of war and with Maoist leader Kishenji's death, the curtain has come down over peace-making efforts in Junglemahal and in the entire country — at least in the near future. The mediators' group has resigned in the aftermath of his death. The human rights groups have accused the government and the joint forces of summary killing. The government denies the charge of staged killing. It says in an innocent style, as if nothing has happened, that the rebels can still surrender and come for peace talks. As of now, peace politics has received a tremendous setback.

What is the political cost of the killing of Kishenji and the subsequent developments? One may ask: Cost to whom? I am not speaking here of the government or those who rule, for they may have gained. The nice covers have fallen. Rulers are talking of loss and gain through killing. I am not talking of the rebels either who must have suffered heavy damage due to the death of one of their leaders. The rebels may think that their path is not of peace, and/or they should think of retaliation.

I am speaking here of the entire society — conflict-torn, trouble-torn, and death-torn.

Junglemahal, which hitherto was in the back of beyond, beyond the pale of developed India, removed from the gaze of the administration, has experienced in recent years restiveness to an unparalleled degree. Women of lower classes, youth of poor peasant families joined politics, and then the militants' ranks. No amount of developmental promise can galvanise a society in the way in which the people of Junglemahal mobilised and activated their own society. Peace would have allowed women and youth of poor peasant families to join popular peasant politics, become politically articulate, and thereby become the pride of any democracy. It is the entire society that will now bear the cost of this extinction of the possibility of peace in Junglemahal.

Bhadraloks (upper caste educated Bengali middle class) would not have been able to do what peasants had done in organising villages and hamlets in resisting arbitrariness, highhandedness and coercion. The villagers were not prepared to wait for misery and ignoble deaths any longer. By the logic of the situation, in order to defend the killing — encounter or no encounter — the state government has to now go to any length to prove that the Maoists are bloodsuckers. The mass media, particularly the television channels, are now busy hosting warmongers in talk sessions, discussions and chat shows. These are the kangaroo courts of the channels. Leaders and cadres of various political persuasions will be compelled to take sides thus resorting to extreme views — in short to defend killings. This happened in Kashmir. It helps no side. It only results in an increasing orientation of the polity towards fascist psychology. We may say polity's 'fascistization'. As a result politics takes a back seat.

Maoist Mistakes and Mamata's Impatience

It will not give any sane person pleasure to say that the Maoists have been paid back in their own coin, though the Maoists now seem to be partially distanced from the local population because of the killings they indulged in. If they believe in the efficacy of the death penalty, as the case seems to be, that is a backward belief, because the death penalty awarded by the Maoist courts only mimics the State. It will not end the trend of surrender and the joining of State ranks by surrendered militants. Likewise the death penalty as a rule is not an answer to informers. More often than not these backfire.

The people's courts of the Maoists that give out verdicts of death penalty are based on the same institutional principle of punishment and revenge that they seek to oppose. It will be a long time before they realise that people's struggles to be victorious have to be based on alternative principles. They must win the battle for hegemony while they fight the battle for political power.

Apart from resuming killing when the new regime began, which was wrong, the Maoists also underestimated the overall political milieu of a new party in power. Gun was not the answer. Apart from holding patience and caution, building a mass movement for peace was the answer and still the call of the day.

Such a call for peace will mean building public opinion in favour of the withdrawal of the joint forces, end of summary killings, arrests and harassment of villagers by policemen and party toughs, and demand for peace, bread, water and dignity. The Maoists may have shown an inclination for peace talks. But expecting the government to come down was unrealistic while not building up a peace movement and popularising concrete demands was a gross error. Peace politics is more dangerous and risky than war politics.

In the time of war, lines are fairly clearly drawn. The line of peace is crooked. The party of peace must maintain alertness, have people on its side, and know how to concretise demands, fight for small causes, and help the middle space to survive. The middle space is the peace constituency. Yet the middle space is only middle, it cannot become the principal agent of peace. Possibly one lesson from Kishenji's death is that peacemakers cannot steer the course towards peace, unless the rebels by themselves have found out the way towards peace while maintaining guard.

The urge for combat will be great. All the more reason, therefore, for the intelligibility of peace politics to be studied deeply. Not without reason Yasser Arafat used to say, 'Peace of the brave.' The same is true for the government. If it had wanted peace, the way was not to open coffers for more recruitments for police jobs, let loose the joint forces, keep peasant leaders behind bars, and talk hot and cold. Yet West Bengal chief minister Mamata Banerjee in her high strung, highly publicised meeting at Jhargram (on 15 October 2011) threatened the Maoists to lay down arms, stop their activities and come to the talks' table in seven days, or else, she declared, she would order counter-insurgency operations. Her impatience was evident. From impatience comes error in judgement.

This impatience is of a leader wanting to appear as a no-nonsense person ready to be tough with proverbial Bengal radicalism. It is at the same time matched by her tolerance of crimes that happened before she came to power, courting those who had oppressed the people at ground level for so long and welcoming them to her party, and allowing her strongmen to do the same things that their predecessors had done to tribal peasants of Junglemahal for the past decades. The impatience will possibly prove costly.

Three Obstacles

Three things in this situation strike an observer: The poverty of ideas towards unlocking closed situations, hence impatience and playing to the gallery, and third, the role of the Union government and the security lobby. Let me explain these three one by one.

The first concerns the poverty of ideas. The West Bengal chief minister could have thought of autonomy for the Junglemahal region to ensure common property resources, local ownership of forest and other natural resources, and the right of the local population's groups to determine their priorities of life, namely whether they want drinking water, education, public health provisions, proper implementation of the rural employment guarantee scheme, or jobs in a counter-insurgency militia to be raised by the government to repress their own people.

The second is the phenomenon of impatience. The point to be noted here is that governance through dialogue requires patience. Timely response does not mean haste and breaking trust. The trust Mamata had won from various quarters was won through months and years of hard work. It can be destroyed in a day. When a ruler thinks that she/he does not need trust and her own sense and judgement is enough, and that she/he can use intemperate language in abusing the adversary, we must take it then that serious errors in judgement will duly follow. She has only to look back at the way the previous rulers failed. Her predecessors had thought that what they would decide was enough. Dialogue was redundant.

But more importantly, why the impatience, why this sudden decline in the dialogue trend, and the poverty of imagination towards innovative solutions? Why do rulers in India not learn from the disaster called Kashmir where time and again opportunity had emerged, the adversary had declared ceasefire, possibilities of dialogue had opened up, yet nothing was done and the stalemate continues? This is where the third feature of the situation comes to notice, namely the rapid securitisation of the scenario. With the advice of the Union home ministry, Mamata went back on her pre-poll promises, did not release the political prisoners, did not meet the victims of police repression, did not compensate them and did not take any measure for rehabilitation.

And third, the advice of the Union home ministry has rarely contributed to peace anywhere, because everywhere it has substituted politics with considerations of security. Its advice does no good to state governments which have to face the heat of conflicts, and survive the fire of protests and rebellions. The options of the West Bengal chief minister to negotiate the sharp bends of popular politics are getting limited by the day. The Union government's tight monetary policy, inflationary steps encouraging price rise, random privatisation and destruction of small businesses and peasant farming leave no chance for her to protect her people, whatsoever she may desire. Likewise she has to depend on the financial largesse of the Centre for day-to-day survival of her government. On top of these, she has to depend on the coercive machinery of the Centre to quell militant protest. She has to thus abide by the torrent of advice coming from the Centre. Populism will mean increasingly less in this situation.

Lessons for the Governments and Rebels

If the Maoists, as Mamata says, cannot keep on killing people and call for peace talks at the same time, she has to understand that if the joint forces keep on operating, the government too cannot expect the

Maoists to come for peace talks. For peace and reconciliation, the government must walk the extra mile. Or will the inevitable errors in judgement begin so early, inevitably, because Mamata is not seeing anything beyond populism and one-upmanship? There was an alternative way for her — the alternative was in finding policies for economic regeneration and building an accommodative polity. It is up to her which way she will go.

Yet, if not equally, the armed radicals of West Bengal are also responsible. They took the wrong lesson from the failure of peace talks in Andhra Pradesh and their casualties. The path of peace and the striving for hegemony is long and tortuous. If the Maoists claim to be the vanguard of politics, they cannot allow the gun to command their destiny.

Peace as a Weapon of War against People

Partho Sarathi Ray

The collapse of the so-called 'peace talks' process in the Junglemahal of West Bengal as a result of the brutal killing of Mallojula Koteswara Rao or Kishenji, senior politburo member of the CPI(Maoist), by security forces in what is evidently a false encounter, is highly instructive, as it deepens our understanding of the nature of such attempts at making 'peace', and also raises disturbing questions about the entire proposition of peacemaking in the context of the peoples' struggles that have been or are going on in India over the last decades. It is also to be understood that although the murder of Kishenji was the culmination of the process that has been going on for the last ten months since the formation of the Trinamul Congress (TMC)-led government in West Bengal, it is in reality a byproduct of a much more dangerous process that has led to the stamping out of the democratic surge that Junglemahal had witnessed over the last four years. This understanding about the nature of these so called 'peace talks' is important for the revolutionary forces and peoples' movements that are actively struggling against the Indian State and interests that the latter serves, and also for members of the so-called civil society who stand in solidarity with such struggles.

Every one knows about the immediate context of this particular 'peace process': the newly elected TMC-led government in Bengal appointed a committee of interlocutors, who, styling themselves as representatives of civil society, signed an agreement with the government to take an initiative to 'peacefully solve the problems of Junglemahal' (quotation from the text of the agreement signed by the home secretary on behalf of the Bengal government and the interlocutors 'on behalf of civil society', published in *Jago Bangla*, the

TMC mouthpiece, dated 14th-15th July, 2011). Following this the interlocutors initiated a process of discussions with representatives of the state committee of the CPI(Maoist). After a couple of round of such discussions, in an increasingly vitiated atmosphere created by continuing atrocities and a clampdown on all democratic activities in Junglemahal by state security forces and TMC-organised vigilante forces and retaliatory strikes by the CPI(Maoist) armed squads against the leaders of the TMC-led vigilante forces, the peace talks completely collapsed at the end of November 2011 by the killing of Kishenji.

Neo-liberal Plunder and *Adivasi* Resistance

Amidst all these happenings, which kept public attention riveted on the statements and counterstatements emanating nearly everyday from the contending parties during that period, what was lost from attention were the 'problems of Junglemahal'. Were the problems of Junglemahal just one of violence and counter-violence, which could be solved by laying down of arms by the cadres of the CPI(Maoist) and other non-state actors? Was it just a problem of underdevelopment, which could be solved by the 'development packages' declared by the chief minister Mamata Banerjee? Or is there something deeper in it, something that lies embedded in the particular history of Junglemahal, and also ties it to the general context of the struggles of the exploited and oppressed masses of India?

To understand this context, we need to take a relook at the recent history of the Junglemahal, the history of the struggles of the *Adivasi-moolvasi* people of the region which culminated in the historical Lalgarh uprising in 2008. As is again well known, the *Adivasis* of our country have historically borne the brunt of exploitation and oppression by all dominant forces, be it the British who first brought the forests under a system of governance and opened the way for the dispossession of the *Adivasis*, or the settlers from the plains, the *dikus* (outsiders), who started a cycle of exploitation which continues unabated till today. Independence did not bring a substantial change in the situation; rather the *Adivasis* paid a disproportionate price also for the great developmental projects of modernising India, projects that provided the minerals, water and electricity for a developing urban, industrial society in the country. Liberalisation and globalisation in the beginning of 1990's added another dimension to the problem by opening up the vast mineral resources in the *Adivasi* areas, hitherto mostly accessible only to the public sector companies, for predatory exploitation by various national and multinational corporations. For these corporations, increasingly backed by globalised, financialised capital, this was the last frontier in India. And as their depredations increased in the *Adivasi* areas, so did the resistance of the *Adivasi* masses. People all over the world, when pushed to the wall by capitalism, have fought back, and the *Adivasis* of the eastern and central parts of India, with a long history of resistance and rebellion, have never ben found lacking.

This period also witnessed another phenomenon which ran parallel, and counter, to the process of globalisation: that of the development of an armed struggle based among the peasantry, with the stated aim of an agrarian revolution and with the strategy of 'protracted peoples war'. This struggle, waged by the CPI(ML) Peoples' War in Andhra Pradesh and CPI(ML) Party Unity and the MCC in parts of Bihar and Jharkhand, spread to the *Adivasi* areas, and found a fertile ground there to develop and flourish. The objective conditions in these areas, the extreme poverty and marginalisation of the people, the government-small contractor-big company-political party nexus which kept the cycle of exploitation and oppression running and the inaccessibility and inhospitability of the terrain provided ideal conditions for the Naxalite parties to gain widespread influence and popular support. Not only that, a fact that is easily overlooked, the *Adivasis*, with their little stake in the Indian political and economic systems, with little dependence on privately-owned agricultural land and with strong notions of collective/community ownership, proved to be a potent revolutionary force. Hence, when the CPI(ML)-PW, which had just merged with the other two Naxalite parties to form the CPI(Maoist), was crushed by the government in Andhra Pradesh in the course of another such 'peace talks', the party found a ready refuge among the *Adivasi* population of Dandakarnya in Chattisgarh, where a liberated zone was established and subsequently gave rise to the *janatana sarkars*, the unique experiment in people's governments of the *Adivasis* in the region.

Junglemahal: Different Trajectory but Same Aspirations

The Junglemahal region in Bengal also did not remain untouched by these churnings, although it took a different trajectory because of the differences in geography and socio-economics of the region. Junglemahal was not the direct target of corporations in search of mineral wealth, but that did not lessen the misery of the people there. Here people were the victims of a nexus of forest officials, *tendu* leaf and timber merchants, contractors and corrupt functionaries of political parties which kept the people mired in poverty, exploitation and indignity. People owned little land, and in the absence of irrigation facilities, return from agriculture was meager. This led to mass out-migration of the work force for agricultural work in other parts of the state or to other states, especially during the cropping and harvesting season. The income from this was not sufficient to maintain the families throughout the year, and in the lean season there was widespread hunger and even starvation deaths.

Therefore, people were dependent on supplemental income from forest produce, but also they were greatly exploited by the nexus between forest guards and forest produce mafia. Prices for forest produce like *tendu* leaves, *sal* leaves and *babui* grass was abysmally low. Even access to the forest produce was at the whims and fancies of the forest guards, and I have heard horror stories of how getting beaten up or being sexually harassed was a daily reality in the lives of *Adivasi* men and women trying to extract firewood or *sal* leaves from the forest. Absence of developmental measures such as schools, health centres, roads, electricity and irrigation facilities was the norm. The panchayats, be they led by the CPI(M) or the Congress or various Jharkhand Party factions, were equally corrupt and a large section of political party leaders fattened themselves on money for government schemes and on contracts for government work.

In this scenario, towards the end of the 1990's, appeared the

Maoists. They organised the people on the issues of development, demanding water, electricity and health facilities, and also demanding remunerative prices for forest produce and the end of harassment at the hands of forest guards and the police. The modes of the struggle were overground and constitutional, with deputations to BDOs and marches to government offices. But the government, instead of paying heed to these genuine demands, responded with brutal oppression. The West Bengal police descended in full force on the quiet hamlets of Junglemahal, letting loose a reign of terror in the form of beatings, torture, molestations of women and thousands of false cases. These times are well documented in the series of reports titled, 'Inside Midnapore' by the veteran journalist and human rights activist Nilanjan Dutta, which appeared in The Times of India in 2002. The Maoists resisted this state terror, and organised the people to resist it. Therefore, it is not surprising to hear a villager say in one of the reports of Dutta: 'If one has to do *janayuddha* (people's war) for a health centre, one might as well do it.' The people also achieved some significant victories, as the Maoists could enforce a substantial increase in the price of minor forest produce such as tendu leaves. I have heard local officials in the region privately admit that this was one of the major contributors for bettering the lot of *Adivasis* in the entire forested region of east-central India. The Maoists gained widespread popular support and developed a strong base in the region, with many of the leading cadres such as Sasadhar and Suchitra Mahato arising from the local communities. It is therefore only the abysmally ignorant who say that the Maoists were a non-entity in the region in 2008-09 when the Lalgarh uprising broke out.

The Reign of State Terror

This pattern of State terror continued through the decade of the 2000's with very little noise made about it by the civil society or by opposition parties in West Bengal. Schools came to be permanently occupied by the police, and people were faced with daily indignities of beatings, harassment and raids. False cases became a curse on the livelihoods of people who were daily wage earners, and who could ill afford to waste days to attend courts or report to police stations. The police atrocities began during the night of 5-6 November 2008 in the wake of the land mine blast targeting the convoy of Buddhadeb Bhattacharjee who was returning from inaugurating the proposed Jindal steel plant and SEZ in Salboni. This was the final straw that broke the camel's back, and the people rose up in anger.

It is worthwhile to note that the people had already been primed by the brave resistance of the people of Nandigram against land acquisition, and the initial modes of resistance such as digging up the roads and blocking entry of the police, were borrowed from the Nandigram experience. However, Lalgarh went far beyond, and came to challenge the entire foundation of the state by challenging the State's right to administer a people whose humanity the State was not ready to recognise. This was articulated in a very cogent, but also in a very earthy manner by the demand that the superintendent of police responsible for the atrocities should publicly hold his ears and ask for forgiveness. In response to the democratic aspirations of the people, the Peoples' Committee against Police Atrocities (PCPA) was formed. The remarkable events that followed this upsurge have been well documented, and constitute a glorious part of the annals of peoples' movements in India. But the beats of the *dhamsa-madal* was sullied by the sound of gunfire. From day one of the uprising, the people, especially those who took leading roles in the PCPA, was under attack by the vested interests in Junglemahal, at that time mainly represented by the ruling CPI(M). The state, and the ruling political powers, represented by the CPI(M), would not countenance such a direct challenge to the authority of the state and to the established order of things. Many of the local leaders of the CPI(M), whose corruption in the panchayats was well known, had fled in the wake of the uprising. Together with them were forces and individuals who had been discredited and sidelined by the mass uprising, such as the traditional social leadership of the Santhals, the *Majhi Madwa*, and various Jharkhandi factions which controlled many panchayats in the area. The armed CPI(M) cadre, together with some of the latter elements, were actively backed by the State, to mount attacks on the rallies and the peoples' marches. Those of us, viewing the entire uprising, through the romanticised vision of an idealised exercise of democracy in an ideal context of peace and non-violence, were in for a disappointment. The mass violence broke out in June 2009, in Dharampur, in consequence of a vicious attack by CPI(M) cadre on a rally led by women. People rose up and destroyed the palatial house of Anuj Pandey, the local CPI(M) overlord, and killed his armed henchmen who had terrorized the area. In this mass upsurge, the Maoists, who had been the organisational backbone of the movement because of their longstanding presence and organisational work in the area, came to the fore. And then the Left Front government of West Bengal, in collusion with the Congress-led UPA government in the Centre sent in the joint state and central security forces to 'reoccupy', Junglemahal. They were joined by the armed mercenaries of the CPI(M), the *Harmad Bahini*, organised by the CPI(M) leaders who returned in the wake of the joint forces. Junglemahal conveniently went under the ambit of Operation Green Hunt which had already been going on for some time in the adjoining forested regions of central India. A period of darkness descended over Junglemahal, which has increasingly deepened despite the change in government in West Bengal.

At this juncture, it is worthwhile to note the context under which the 're-occupation' of Junglemahal by the state forces took place. The Prime Minister had repeatedly stressed that the Maoists were the 'greatest threat to internal security' in India, and had also emphasised that the struggle being waged by the Maoists in the forested, mineral-rich tracts of central India was the most serious deterrent to investment by corporations in the region. As a response, Operation Green Hunt, had been unofficially launched across four states, Chattisgarh, Jharkhand, Maharashtra and Odisha since the end of 2008. The Junglemahal of West Bengal is contiguous to the forested regions of Jharkhand, and constitutes a crucial part of the so called 'red corridor', the zone under Maoist influence from ranging from north Bihar to the Andhra-Karnataka border. How could the State allow such a crucial region to be 'destabilised' by a de facto liberated zone? Therefore, it was inevitable that the Lalgarh movement had to be crushed. Some people argue that the Lalgarh movement was not on the basis of the struggle for protecting *jal, jangal, zameen*, from the corporations, which is the basis of the resistance struggles in the rest of the forested regions. However, what needs to be realised is that although there were no direct proposals by corporations to invest in the Junglemahal of West Bengal, except Jindal's infamous project at Salboni, the state clearly feared that the influence of Lalgarh would directly affect the adjoining regions of Jharkhand and Odisha which were, and are, lucrative prizes for corporations. Therefore it was imperative for the state to stamp out the peoples' resistance in Junglemahal, and this also brings us to the crux of the matter that whether peace is at all possible, or meaningful under these circumstances.

Mamata Government Continues Same Policies

Therefore, when Mamata Banerjee came to power, overthrowing the 34-year stranglehold of the CPI(M), things did not change. Mamata Banerjee and her party had based their election campaign in Junglemahal on the promise that the joint forces would be withdrawn and the numerous people imprisoned under UAPA and other cases would be released if they came to power. In absence of a strong campaign by the Maoists and the PCPA against what was doublespeak of Mamata considering her previous record, the people of the region voted for the TMC. However, as was to be expected, these promises were not to be kept. Operations by the joint forces were stopped for a total of fifteen days, from 15th May till 1st June, 2011, till they resumed, although at a subdued scale and in a much more insidious manner. However, the atrocities continued, and reports of beatings, of villages being besieged and houses being ransacked, and of indiscriminate arrests started to come in again. There was a complete clampdown on democratic activities such as meetings and rallies by peoples' organisations such as the *Nari Ijjat Bachao Committee.* Three hundred arrests, including those of the remaining leaders of the PCPA have taken place over the last eight months. At the same time, the network of patronization-intimidation, which the CPI(M) had so skillfully honed, was re-established. The TMC organised a local vigilante force, in many places led by ex-members of PCPA, by the name of *Jana Jagaran Manch* which has come to be locally called as the *Bhairab Bahini*. The *bahini* let loose a reign of intimidation, forcing people to join up and act as informers. It acted in close coordination with the joint forces, and created a *Salwa Judum*-type situation where the vigilante force on one hand became the eyes and ears of the State forces and on the other expanded and established the territorial control of the TMC in various areas. Complementing this mechansm of intimidation were the mechanisms of patronisation, and the government and the TMC skillfully used the developmental schemes declared by Mamata Banerjee to gain control over the people. To be eligible for any of the schemes — rice at Rs 2 per kg, free cycles for girl students, police jobs — one is required to be loyal to TMC. And this loyalty had to be expressed in the form of participation in the *Jana Jagaran Manch* and opposition to the Maoists or PCPA.

Peace Talks: A Subtle Strategy to Put Out the Flame

While these were the State's overt strategies on the ground in Junglemahal, it continued the 'peace talks' as a much more insidious strategy to root out the resistance in Junglemahal. The basis of the peace process was the appointment of the interlocutors to open the channels of dialogue with the Maoists. The interlocutors signed the abovementioned agreement with the state government, which conveniently failed to mention any of the original demands of the PCPA, on the basis of which talks were being held between the PCPA and the state government at the time when the joint forces were sent in. It promised to provide all sorts of socioeconomic, democratic and cultural sops, but significantly failed to address the question of the dignity of the *Adivasi* people.

The problem was that the original demands of the Lalgarh movement questioned the entire basis of the state government, and therefore had to be kept out of the pale of any 'peace process'. Instead, the agreement contained egregious points such as 'the joint forces would be withdrawn from Junglemahal *after and if* the region (emphasis by author) has been free of weapons and peace has returned.' This was a complete negation of the position of all civil society and democratic organizations, both in the Junglemahal and the rest of Bengal, on the basis of which movements had continued against the erstwhile LF government for the previous two years. The demand for the withdrawal of the hated joint forces was always unconditional, and was never contingent on the return of 'peace' in the Junglemahal. Secondly, the agreement did not clarify what was meant by peace; did it signify a return to the status quo ante, marked by the atrocities and the human rights violations of the previous decade? And definitely making the Junglemahal 'arms-free' did not include the arms in the hands of the most heavily armed agency in the region, the security forces. Equally egregious was another point in the agreement (point 4). It stated that 'those who want to surrender with arms would be given social rehabilitation and a special financial package by the government'.

It is unbelievable that an agreement between a group of people who were taking on the role of interlocutors on behalf of civil society included surrender conditions for members of the organisation with which they were going to interlocute. Would the interlocutors be dangling this carrot in front of the leadership of the organisation when they were going to talk with them? This was a clear violation of any interlocution process because it constituted an attempt by the State to break the ranks of the organisation by enticing its members with offers of financial packages and rehabilitation. Therefore, the thrust of the so-called 'peace process' was very clear from the text of this agreement itself. And the subsequent events have made it further clear. The question that it raises is that whether a 'peace process' is at all possible in a situation where it is a war to the finish for both the contending parties. For the State, it is very clear that the survival of the neo-liberal trajectory that it has adopted is contingent upon the destruction of people's resistance all over the country.

It is immaterial whether the resistance is armed or unarmed, 'peace' for the state means the peace of the graveyard, an open field for the operations of capital. That is why the state has besieged three villages over the last six years in Jagatsinhpur district of coastal Odisha, where the villagers are resisting the proposed steel plant of POSCO. That is why people resisting the depredations of capital, and the semi-feudal power relations through which capital works in many parts of the country, from people opposing big dams in Assam to people resisting local moneylenders and liquor dealers in Narayanpatna in Odisha, are all at the receiving end of the State's repressive measures. On the other hand, it is also a question of survival for the people who are resisting the State and for the resistance movements being led by the CPI(Maoist) or other organisations, as the neo-liberal policies of the State are targeting the basic resources on which their lives and livelihoods are dependent.

These conditions are by definition non-negotiable, as the success of the capitalist project is contingent on the destruction of the resistances against it, and the survival of the people is contingent on being able to push back the offensive of the State as has been seen in other parts of the world such as in Latin America. This struggle is fundamentally different in nature from the secessionist struggles, where the status of the territory under contention is negotiable and there are various alternatives available between complete subjugation and complete independence. The war going on in Junglemahal and other parts of the *Adivasi*-populated regions of India, is based on the question of the survival of a people and their control over the resources needed for survival. There will be stalemates in this war but there will be no peace. Under these circumstances, the state will use peace as a weapon of war, just as it uses 'development' as a weapon of war.

The 'return' of peace to Junglemahal is meaningless, unless it signifies a just peace, a peace based on the dignity and prosperity of the masses. Without that the 'return' of peace is a mirage, a mirage that will disappear as soon as the illusions of normality are destroyed by the brutal reality of life in Junglemahal today.

Phantom of Peace

Nilanjan Dutta

Peace is not an absence of war; it is a virtue, a state of mind, a disposition for benevolence, confidence, justice. — Spinoza

Politics is war without bloodshed while war is politics with bloodshed. — Mao

There is much in common between war and politics. War is all about politics and all wars are political. Politics is essentially war — for the domination of nations, resources, or for that matter, minds. Only bloodshed makes the difference — whether we will call it war or simply politics. And that is a thin line — so accustomed have we become to see bloodshed, who cares for it any longer? Peace, on the other hand, is something fundamentally different. It does not depend on whether blood is being shed or not, or whether, in other words, two conflicting sides are at war. For the two sides to reach a state of peace, they must reach a state not simply of equilibrium of force or might, but precisely of equality, of mutuality, and, as Spinoza says, of justice. Until this state is reached, there can be truce but not peace, because underneath the apparent tranquillity there remain inequality, injustice, and violence. More so, if the tranquillity itself is brought about by violence. And let us remember, it is not easy to bring about tranquillity in a war scenario through violence on a routine, mundane scale. If there is tranquillity without peace, be sure that it was preceded by tremendous violence. If history has not recorded it, memory and consciousness certainly did. Some day, they might speak — rather cry out hoarsely — to make us understand that what we had thought to be peace was an illusion.

Unfortunately, we cannot hear the murmur of 'non-peace' until they become as loud as mine-blasts. We always wake up the day after. Then, we wonder how chapattis travel from barrack to barrack and *sal* twigs are passed on from village to village faster than the speed of e-mails. We do the same thing every time it happens. Because we see the leaders of our political 'mainstream' doing the same thing every time. Searching for scapegoats. Playing blame games. Contemplating more violence. And in the intermissions, talking 'peace'. ('tis the time's plague when madmen lead the blind — remember?)

Where the Buck Stops

Two days before the death of 76 CRPF jawans in a Maoist attack in Chhattisgarh's Dantewada on 6 April 2010, Union home minister P. Chidambaram visited Lalgarh, then the hotbed of insurgency in West Bengal, and remarked that the 'buck' should stop at the chief minister's table. Thus, he made the Left Front government primarily responsible for controlling (or not controlling) the rebellion. After the Dantewada incident, Chidambaram admitted that something had gone 'very wrong'. He said, 'I have been asked directly or indirectly where the buck stops after the attack. The buck stops at my desk.' What was it that had gone 'very wrong'? Let us hear from an observation of the Supreme Court of India: 'People do not take up arms, in an organized fashion, against the might of the State, or against fellow human beings without rhyme or reason. Guided by an instinct for survival, and according to Thomas Hobbes, a fear of lawlessness that is encoded in our collective conscience, we seek an order. However, when that order comes with the price of dehumanization, of manifest injustices of all forms perpetrated against the weak, the poor and the deprived, people revolt.' (Order dated July 5, 2011 by Justices B. Sudershan Reddy and Surinder Singh Nijjar on Writ Petition (Civil) No. 250 of 2007, Nandini Sundar & Ors. Versus State of Chhattisgarh.) But the home minister had other things in mind. The Naxalite (or Maoist) problem, according to him, had blown up to such proportions because it did not receive adequate attention during the last 10 years or so. This time, the 'menace' must be fought 'to the last drop of our blood'. If public memory is short, politicians' is shorter. The Naxalite issue is not 10 years old. Forty years ago, in 1970, the then Prime Minister, belonging to the same party as Chidambaram's, had expressed her resolve in Parliament to 'fight to finish' the Naxalites. And on 10 May 1973, the late CPI parliamentarian Bhupesh Gupta, raising a question on the killing of his nephew in Calcutta, said, 'Even though dubbed as terrorist, he had no fear under British rule of being shot down in the street by the police in an action described as an encounter.' The then Union minister of state for home, K.C. Pant, replied, 'But now that the house is ours, we have to do something even if it is our nephews and nieces who try to destroy it from within'.

After the irreplaceable loss of 76 lives in the 'battle of Sukhma', we found the same debate going round and round again. 'Call in the air force, bomb them to splinters,' some 'responsible' persons started demanding. Thankfully, some others, including the chief of air staff, expressed doubts whether this could be the way to deal with the rebels who are 'our own people' after all. When home-grown militant Maoism announced its birth in the fields of Naxalbari in North Bengal in 1967, analysts identified the root cause as underdevelopment. The initial revolt was crushed within five years. Or so it was thought. Four decades later, when it is again tearing through the spine of the country, the buck stops at the same place: lack of development (this development, by the way, has nothing to do with the spurious 'development' dream global capitalism is showing us every day — it is the accessibility of all to the conditions of fulfillment of civilised human needs).

What was being done about the 'root cause' in the intervening time? Those at the helm of affairs have no answer to this riddle, and so have started talking in riddles themselves. Those among the people of Lalgarh who were fortunate to meet the Union home minister during his visit had this experience. When they poured out their problems before him — the lack of health care, drinking water, irrigation, ration, and what not — he gave them the proverbial chicken and egg option: 'Drive out the Naxals from your area and don't provide any moral or material support to them ... If they are ousted from your areas, I can pressurise the government to initiate development works then.' Did the buck lie with the people now? Which came first — lack of development or rise of insurgency? And what should have been done first — removal of underdevelopment or driving out the Maoists? But this is how our great 'strategists' work. After a heavy exchange of fire at Lakshmanpur near Lalgarh on 25 March 2010 in which the joint forces even used mortars, the police were sure that a number of Maoists had been injured at least. And they must have been receiving treatment from village quacks, since there were no hospitals or nursing homes within commutable distance. So now the forces stepped up 'vigilance' on quacks, virtually cutting off the only healthcare providers in these remote villages from the needy people. The health centres set up by the People's Committee against Police Atrocities (PCPA) were raided and shut down. A few makeshift medical camps organised by the forces were expected to fill the void.

Such 'strategies' to separate the Maoists from the people only increased the distance of the administration from the masses. Contrary to the theory currently popular among some sections of the media, academics and 'civil society' activists, the Maoists did not fall from the sky and impose themselves over the poor 'innocent' people of Junglemahal. Nor is there is any justification in thinking that the people have been forced to suffer 'sandwiched' between the State forces and the Maoists. That would be denying the people their active role in course of history of Junglemahal. Even if we keep aside the turbulent Seventies for the time being, various Naxalite groups that later merged to form the Communist Party of India (Maoist) have been working in the region for a long time, at least since the mid-1990s. On different occasions, they have organised people to demand their basic rights like drinking water, healthcare, irrigation facilities and decent wages for the forest dwellers who pick kendu leaves for making bidis. Alongside, they have spread the message of armed revolution, which seems to have had a good number of takers among the local poor (there is no reason to believe that all the Sorens, Tudus, Baskes and Mahatos that we hear about had been herded like sheep to join the armed 'gangs'). And if the Maoists were able to draw sustenance from the latter, it must have been possible because of a mutual dependence and commonality of interest at some points. One such point is that the people are often reminded rudely by the course of events that the 'democratic' means of protests and demands have always met a dead end. Ten years ago, in the winter of 2002, an old man in Banspahari village told me candidly, 'If one had to do *janajuddha* for a health centre, one might as well do it.' (He punned on the word *janajuddha*, which means people's war. He could have meant waging a war by the people, or joining the CPI(ML)-People's War, one of the Naxalite groups organising armed struggle in the area at that time.) Let us recall that Maoist influence in Chhattisgarh grew manifold after the murder of Shankar Guha Neogy, one of the strongest proponents of non-violent people's movement in India since Independence. The same is true of Lalgarh. The PCPA was a vastly popular platform of the local tribals and poor that could not have gone underground because of its sheer strength of numbers. The government dragged its feet on its demands for months, and stopped all negotiations abruptly. Though not yet banned, it was virtually pushed underground as it was branded as a Maoist front and its leaders began to be hounded and killed. As a reaction, the tribals announced the formation of their own 'Sido-Kanhu People's Militia'. And the official strategists immediately equated it with the People's Liberation Guerrilla Army (PLGA) of the Maoists.

Riddles and Real Issues

There are riddles galore in the story. Was it just bad timing that on a day (22 February 2010) when Maoists responded to Chidambaram's 72-hour ceasefire offer with a 72-day proposal if the government too halted its operation, a contingent of joint forces marched to the house of Lalmohan Tudu, president of the PCPA in Lalgarh, and killed him along with two associates? At least in Lalgarh, there was a difference between the present wave of Maoist insurgency that is sweeping a large stretch of India from south to north and the nature of the unrest in this region. It is a part of the forested laterite terrain popularly called Junglemahal, covering parts of West Medinipur, Bankura and

Purulia districts of West Bengal that extends up to the Dalma hills of neighbouring Jharkhand, where the Maoists have a strong base. As much as 39.86% of the population in the Binpur I block of West Medinipur district, of which the Lalgarh police station area is a part, lives below the poverty line. The land is mostly mono-crop, and there are little irrigation facilities. As a result, a large number of people from the area travel to distant places as migrant labour, contributing to the agricultural or 'developmental' activities in other parts of the country at low cost. There are few sources of safe drinking water and fewer health centres to care for those suffering from disease and malnutrition, pregnant women, nursing mothers and children. A building in Lalgarh meant to be a government health centre was turned into a police camp after being kept unused for about a year.

True, underdevelopment is all too apparent among the local population, mostly tribal and Dalit and it has brewed discontent. But that was not the issue when the recent upheaval took place in Lalgarh that eventually catapulted the Maoists to centrestage. What was at stake was the dignity of the local people. Even as the state failed to deliver any of its civic responsibilities towards these poor citizens, it had made them its whipping boys (and girls). They had gotten used to raids, beatings and arrests whenever some 'Naxalite incident' took place anywhere in the district. Like what happened on 2 November 2008. On that day, West Bengal chief minister Buddhadeb Bhattacharjee and Union steel and mines minister Ram Vilas Paswan narrowly escaped a landmine blast while returning after inaugurating a special economic zone being set up by the Jindal group at Salboni for building a steel plant. Though the spot was about 50 km away, the police swooped down on Lalgarh. Three teenage students — Aben Murmu, Gautam Patra and Buddhadeb Patra — were picked up by the police as they were returning from a village festival at night, tortured and charged with waging war against the state. Lakshmimani, the wife of Dipak Pratihar, a resident of Kantapahari village who was one of the 10 people arrested, was badly thrashed. Altogether 35 villages were raided. In Chhotopelia, seven women faced police violence on the night of 6 November. Chhitamani Murmu lost an eye and Panmani

Hansda suffered fractures. All were battered with rifle butts, sticks and boots.

This time, Lalgarh turned around. The next day, it was a very different scene. Thousands of women and men armed with bows, arrows and axes blocked all main roads and declared that the blockade would continue until the police officers responsible for the assaults came and apologised to the people. The State did not take any conciliatory measures and the people's mood hardened. The reins of the movement passed on soon from the hands of the traditional tribal organisation *Bharat Jakat Majhi Marwa Juan Gaonta* to a unique people's committee — the *Pulishi Santras Birodhi Janasadharaner Committee* or PCPA. There was no control by any established political party and all decisions were being debated and adopted by an assembly of thousands. Five women and five men were elected from each village to form the committee. A 13-point People's Charter was drawn up, which included the withdrawal of all 'false cases' registered against the local people since 1998 and compensation for victims of police atrocities, apart from the initial demand for an apology.

Blockades began to come up throughout Junglemahal and even in far-flung tribal populated districts, raising apprehensions of a 'Second Santhal Rebellion' in the media as well as the administration. After a month-long battle of nerves, the schoolboys were released. Medical treatment was arranged for the assaulted women, though Chhitamani did not get her vision back. And one by one, the police camps in Lalgarh were shut down. The PCPA reciprocated by relaxing the blockade, though the 'police boycott' continued as the demands for apology, case withdrawal and compensation were yet to be met. A round of negotiations started before the parliamentary elections on 30 April 2009. The PCPA let Lalgarh vote peacefully and even its leader Chhatradhar Mahato exercised his franchise in style, flaunting his electoral identity card. The negotiations continued for a couple of months after the polls, but no progress was made. For a long time since the blockade started, the Maoists, even if they were present, remained in the background. The PCPA, apart from carrying on the movement, initiated several community services such as setting up health centres, planning small irrigation facilities and building village roads through voluntary labour. The role of the Maoists in all these activities rather resembled that of well-meaning NGOs. Though several 'development'-related demands were later added to the PCPA agenda, those were never really made bargaining points. Meanwhile, there were several negative developments. The ruling CPI(M), too eager to regain lost grounds, began amassing armed cadres along the borders of the blockaded region. There was talk of a 'Nandigram-style' action. Skirmishes became frequent along the 'borders', leading to the exodus of hundreds of people. And inside the rebel territory, those who still belonged to the CPI(M) were forced to sever relations with the party on pain of 'punishment'. Soon, 'spies' began to be exterminated one by one. In course of this chain of events, the Maoists began to emerge from the wings.

Making of the Enemy

Maybe, the state thought it easier to deal with a known enemy, a structured political party like the Communist Party of India (Maoist), with which it was already waging war in neighbouring provinces, rather than an enigmatic 'people's committee." The Centre was already planning an all-out offensive and the West Bengal government, though still run by the LF had a communion of interest with it in this case. So, the negotiations with the PCPA were abandoned after 12 June 2009. The Maoist party was banned. Chhatradhar Mahato was arrested by police officers posing as journalists working for foreign media. He and several other PCPA activists were put behind bars under the Unlawful Activities (Prevention) Act. Thus the 'people's committee' was to be buried with the Maoists — perhaps that's what some strategists thought. Operation Green Hunt ruled the day — and the nights. Not only for the people of Junglemahal, but also for all 'Maoist sympathisers' in other districts including Kolkata. Until Shilda happened. In a daylight operation on 15 February 2010, the guerrillas, reportedly led by a woman, obliterated an entire camp of the Eastern Frontier Rifles in this small town close to Lalgarh, killing 24 jawans and losing five of their own. And notwithstanding the cries and agitations of the relatives of these foot-soldiers of the State, the home minister on 19 February offered the 72-hour truce. The language of violence had been spoken — and understood. The killing of Lalmohan Tudu completed the circle. The Centre-state joint forces were bang on target. This middle-aged man had come home for his daughter's ensuing secondary examination. They shot him and his neighbours Suchitra Murmu and Yuvaraj Murmu, claiming they were planning to attack another paramilitary camp. The following day, Chidambaram announced his fax number in which the Maoists could send in their offer. And Maoist leader Kishenji in turn gave out a phone number through the media, where the home ministry could call for negotiations. It was now a battle of nerves between 011-23093155 and 9734695789. This is how people are reduced to numbers, perhaps.

But No One Dialed. And Nothing Was Discussed

Again, after midnight on 25 July, a large contingent of the joint forces moved into the Metala forest in the Goaltore police station of West Midnapore district. They spotted three synthetic tents in a clearing amid the trees, two black and one orange. The informants had told them that the big catch was in the orange one. So, they closed in on that from all sides. According to police, a fierce encounter followed which lasted for about five hours. Ashish Tiwari, a jawan of the Combat Battalion for Resolute Action (Cobra), was killed. After the gunfire stopped, six bodies — including that of a young woman — were found in the camp. Five of them could not be identified immediately. But there was no confusion about one. He was none other than Sido Soren, the 23-year old general secretary of the PCPA, whose real name was Bhuta Baske. 'Soren was a hardcore Maoist,' the superintendent of police said. But was he always a guerrilla hiding in the jungles? On 12 June 2009, only 13 months before he died, he was sitting at the Midnapore circuit house and talking coolly with many of the top guns of the administration and the police. It was the last negotiation meeting that the state had with the PCPA. A number of decisions were taken at the meeting, such as the release of several minors and 'sympathetic consideration' of the cases of the others held in the wake of the Lalgarh agitation, to pave the way for peace. It never took place. Before that, the joint forces' operation was launched. With the killing of Sido, the entire founding leadership of the people's committee had been either eliminated or imprisoned. At one point, even the Maoists had kept an avenue open. Gour Chakraborty, a senior leader who was doing political work openly, was appointed the official spokesperson of the Maoists in West Bengal. He was arrested under the UAPA as he came out of a TV studio in Kolkata after a talk show. It was a unique experiment of the CPI(Maoist) in West Bengal that failed. Soon, Chakraborty's function was taken over by the ethereal voice of Kishenji over telephone lines of the media. And then, Kishenji, too, was eliminated in an 'encounter'.

The Day After

Meanwhile, there was a great 'change' in the political scenario of West Bengal. The LF regime fell after 34 years in the wake of a massive electoral victory of the Opposition Trinamul Congress. Mamata Banerjee became chief minister replacing Buddhadeb Bhattacharjee. Before the election, she and her party had promised in numerous speeches and publicity materials that justice would be done to the people of Junglemahal. Political prisoners would be released. The joint forces would be withdrawn. Nothing happened. There was not even any mention of resuming the unfinished talks with the PCPA. Instead, she just appointed a team of 'civil society representatives' to talk with the Maoists, now totally underground. After a couple of rounds of 'preparatory' parleys, the talks failed to take off and the 'interlocutors' gave up.

Perhaps, the strategists and advisers of the new regime now think that peace talks are no longer necessary. For, the signs of 'peace' that they were looking for are already there in Junglemahal. People turned out to vote in large numbers, indicating the return of their faith in parliamentary democracy. The villages that were once bastions of the PCPA are now Trinamul Congress strongholds. The remnants of the Maoist squads are on the run. And thus, our policymakers remain buried in self-satisfaction. At best what they can aim at is a transition from politics with bloodshed to a war without bloodshed, not peace with justice. Until they wake up to the shock of a 'third rebellion'. Till then, justice will continue to elude Junglemahal. Till then, Junglemahal will remain in a state of war — with or without bloodshed. Unless the realisation dawns that peace without justice is *maya.*

'If You Want Peace, You Must Go to War'

Rana Bose

Analytical pieces have appeared in various magazines about the peace process that was initiated last year in West Bengal's Junglemahal by Mamata Banerjee, the chief minister of West Bengal. These efforts soon bit the dust and had to be virtually aborted. The intent of this piece is to ask a series of questions (and perhaps provide some answers) related to the past practices in the international arena of initiating peace negotiations between warring parties and/or a rebel force and the State and relate them to the recent experience in West Bengal.

The Path of Peace Negotiations

There are certain fundamental precepts and definitions that need to be visited when one discusses the mechanics and success of peace negotiations.

The process followed towards one defined objective may be unsuitable when deployed against another. First of all, there is peace treaty — an agreement between two or more hostile parties, usually countries or governments — which formally ends a state of war between the parties. Or, an armistice, which is an agreement to stop hostilities between nations without a peace treaty. Or, a surrender, in which an army agrees to give up arms, decommission and be integrated into society or into a regular army. Or, a ceasefire, in which the parties may agree to temporarily or permanently stop fighting, as negotiations are initiated. Some folks may argue about these definitions and add or subtract some clauses here and there but in the broad scope of things, there is not too much else that one needs to enunciate.

The Proportion of the Strife

In approaching such a negotiation, certain important measurement indices need to be considered to have an objective evaluation of the proportion of the strife. Otherwise, one would play into the hands of one of the parties, instead of preventing violence. In any negotiation for cessation of hostilities, it must be understood that both parties are equal and not beholden in any way to the other. There have been cases in history where peace talks were initiated in order to suppress a group of 300 guerrillas, but 8,000 peasants were killed and military coup d'états staged with US support to enable the political manoeuvrings of the ruling elite and their foreign backers (in this case the right-wing military dictators and the United Fruit Company in Guatemala in the 1960s or ongoing attempts to encircle the FARC in Colombia while drawing its leadership into negotiations and killing off their leaders one by one).

In other cases, over 40 battalions of armed forces of the State, including helicopter squadrons have been held at bay by small bands of mobile guerrilla units belonging to two different insurgencies, as in the Philippines (Moro National Liberation Movement/Islamic National Liberation Movement and the Maoist New Peoples' Army) for nearly 40 years. In each case the extent of the violence, structural or physical, the actual balance of forces of the two contending armies, the areas under their respective controls, the list of demands from both sides or one side, as the case may be, the stages of the negotiation and as well as the authority, independence and credibility of the intermediaries who have been engaged in carrying out the mediation, must all be quantified.

In other words what weight (not moral authority or credibility but physical presence and mass following) do the rebels carry, what weight the interlocutors carry and what weight does the government carry? Also, if the State launches military operations using paramilitary special forces, helicopters, drones and snipers to militarily defeat the rebels and if the revolutionary or rebel group declares itself to be engaged in 'people's war' against the State using its mobile guerrilla units, its regular army units and all means of guerrilla war, landmines and rocket launchers, are the two forces effectively at war then, even if they have not declared war formally? While one side uses the rhetoric of 'war on terror', the other side may state that it is involved in a 'war of resistance'. One does not have to declare oneself to be formally at war in order to carry out hostilities over an effective area. If the theatre of conflict is widespread, it is natural that a cessation of hostilities is tantamount to calling for a ceasefire.

Therefore, to reinforce the categories raised earlier, the following questions need to be asked:

Are we looking at a temporary cessation of hostilities, as in a ceasefire prior to negotiation on demands?

Are we asking for a surrender of one of the forces, like when there are two feuding forces — as has been the case in the past in South America and in Africa or even in the Northeast provinces of India?

Are we asking for demobilisation of one of the forces and their possible integration into a new or existing force? Perhaps, as in the debates raging on in Nepal and even in relation to the Karen rebels in Myanmar or in India's North East.

Are we asking for a semi-permanent peace treaty with areas remaining under the physical control of the two parties concerned, until a democratic unification is possible?

Is the State using the peace treaty as a ploy to have areas not under its control vacated, so that its 'development' activities could be pursued? Is it a precursor to forced displacement of the resident population?

Had a stage been reached where the two contending military forces had arrived at the conclusion that no one could obliterate the other?

There are other possibilities as well, which are admixtures of the above situations. However, the first task is to define the objective.

The Route to Negotiations

When it comes to taking the route of negotiations, both parties must follow certain ground rules and definitions about the objective conditions for negotiations. Peace negotiations cannot be started on an ad hoc basis or on the basis of individual directives.

1) The State (government) must constitute a peace council or a negotiating committee within its ruling junta or cabinet. The rebels must constitute the same within their organisation. Without such an organised thought process within both sides, one is often subjected to the flamboyant directives of individual leaders. 'I am for talks. Go talk peace. That is my directive'. Such a stand is short-sighted, nearly egotist and Machiavellian. Governments often do not have elected leaders who have studied the history of peace negotiations worldwide and the careful steps that must be followed to ensure their success. Similarly, rebel leaders must seek a detailed mandate from their highest-level organisation. Otherwise, there is a tendency towards bravado without socio-economic purpose. So both the parties must have a peace council that the leaders are subject to and intermediaries can rely on and which has possibly carried out a strategic exercise, even to the extent of being a simulation exercise of all possibilities as the negotiations unfold. Was this in place during the recent peace initiatives in Bengal?

2) The term interlocutor means not just a messenger in the middle between two bosses, but an independent leader(s) who has the authority from civil society as well to negotiate firmly with both sides. It is the pressure of the civil society that must result in 'talks', not the directives of the current sate government. Had the situation reached such an untenable point that the large masses of civil society were demanding immediate peace negotiations in Junglemahal? Or was the state government in a rush to demonstrate how it could carry out its version of 'development' in a hurry, which the previous regime had miserably failed to accomplish? There was a time when civil society in Bengal was demanding peace talks. However, it eventually seemed to have lost its momentum and instead seemed to have become a tactic of the newly elected government to deflect the demands of the civil rights movement to meet its own election promises (withdraw its forces and release political prisoners).

3) Interlocutors or intermediaries must have well-known national credentials and neutral stature. Typically they could be former judges, well-known citizens whose scientific, artistic, academic, administrative

or social organising skills have earned them nationwide (if not international) respect, which has not been marred by any kind of partisan political engagement in the past. Also, they should not have received any favours from the existing state government. Such interlocutors do not necessarily have to be of human rights and civil liberties background, and preferably not of a law-and-order disposition. From Amartya Sen and Jean Dreze to P. Sainath, Medha Patkar, Anand Patwardhan, Arundhuti Roy, Aruna Roy, B.D. Sharma, Prashant Bhusan and a whole host of others have been essentially pointing out the structural violence that is inherent to the socio-economic development that has been followed in the country for 64 years.

The government's own expert committee has declared that the onslaught in the tribal areas and the signing of countless memorandums of understanding (MOUs) are tantamount to the 'biggest land grab since Columbus.'. The Naxalite agenda is not a mysterious bombshell or meteor that hit the country from outer space. It has been in the national mind space for 40 years and more so since Manmohan Singh declared in 2005 that they were the 'biggest internal security threat to the country'. Therefore, it is natural that one would expect a peace negotiation with the Naxalites to have a national stature.

4) There is the need for a code of secrecy to be observed throughout the process of negotiations. Leaks to the press, by one or the other party, are a sure guarantee that trust cannot be built and the negotiations are bound to fail. Neither police nor the media in India should have any inkling about the process. Both these set-ups in India tend to repeat officialspeak, almost like a disease. The negotiations must be initiated in absolute secrecy and while the negotiations are on, neither of the two parties nor the interlocutors should make hostile or conflicting statements. It has always been found that during negotiations, one side leaks information to either its policing forces or to sections of the media to thwart an unfavourable trend or to carry out an 'elimination'. This has been made clear recently.

5) Since the rebel forces are typically 'underground', it is essential

that after the initial outer perimeter is set up, through link-persons, the actual venue for a face-to-face discussion in the first stage itself be fixed at a place under the command and control of the rebels and they must call the shots in terms of surveillance, security and passageway. They must decide where, when and how many people they are prepared to meet. At this stage we are not talking about a high-level meeting in a plush office setting around a table. As negotiations proceed successfully, the rebels are often disposed to appointing an 'open' representative to represent them at a meeting with the state.

6) As the discussions advance and several levels of preliminary tasks and negotiations are completed by both sides, it may be necessary that meetings are held under the auspices of a neutral and foreign observer, perhaps even in a neutral country. These tasks could include socio-economic policy implementations under joint command, key prisoner release and a decision not to pass any adverse commentary on each other.

7)It is also essential that the United Nations is duly informed of these proceedings by this stage. The human rights situation is pathetic in India, especially in Bengal. A Maoist prisoner was found dead in his cell recently and as per the Asian Human Rights Centre, there has been an average of four deaths a day in India in police or judicial custody (http ://www.achrweb.org/). It is natural that such a peace process should be watched closely by international organisations.

Accompanying all these target objectives, there could be supplementary demands seeking socio-economic justice, joint monitoring of human rights violations, political prisoner release, withdrawal of paramilitary and vigilante forces and reparations.

The Questions to be Asked

Did the all members of intermediaries' team handpicked by Mamata Banerjee have the national credibility that the task required? Sincere and selfless as they were, these interlocutors were essentially unknown outside Bengal, except for Sujato Bhadra. Typically, it became a 'provincial'-minded approach, almost a localised diktat, with no national characteristic — whereas the Maoist belt around Junglemahal comprises Bengal, Jharkhand, Odisha and Chhattisgarh, without taking into account the non-contingent states of Bihar, Maharashtra and Andhra Pradesh. The interlocution was dead before it got off the starting block, because it had no national presence. Were the recent attempts at peace negotiations in Bengal and, for that matter, the previous attempts at negotiations in Andhra — where the negotiators acquired legendary status (Sri Sankaran, K.G. Kannabiran) for their extraordinary zeal and earnestness to bring about peace — and even the poorly conceived attempt by Swami Agnivesh, all of which resulted in the killings of Naxalite leaders, justified by the objective conditions on the ground? Were certain absolutely essential steps taken prior to commencing these negotiations? The answer is 'No'. In Bengal, there was no theoretical basis, nor did any objective condition exist, for any negotiation or a face-to-face other than a unilateral and temporary declaration of ceasefire by one side (the Maoists). Given that violence and strife was becoming unbearable for the common masses of Junglemahal, the government should have reciprocated (the Maoists' gesture) with a complete withdrawal of the joint forces and various vigilante forces (which it did not, but pretended to do). Only then detailed negotiations could have been contemplated. The only aspect that was on the cards was a ceasefire and a reciprocating withdrawal.

The Stalemate Condition

As per the Philippine National Democratic Front case, the basis for negotiations from the point of view of a popular resistance war is that a stalemate condition must be reached. A resistance army typically engages in tactical offensives and opens countless guerrilla fronts. Eventually a stalemate is reached. This is what happened in Algeria during the FLN's national liberation struggles against the French colonisers, in Dien Bien Phu again with the French, and later on in Vietnam with the Americans and, to a certain extent, in Guatemala, Colombia, Nepal and the Philippines.

Even the Taliban, whose social development policies are starkly regressive but primary agenda remain one of ridding their country of foreign occupiers, pursue an effective strategy that eventually enables secret negotiations (as Hilary Clinton has admitted), have been able to open a 'foreign office' in Qatar. Civil society and international opinion overwhelmingly demand 'peace talks' and a cessation of hostilities. Not all peace negotiations have been successful and many have resulted in horrendous backstabbing and the killing of the peace negotiators themselves. Far from reaching any such stage, the conditions in Bengal were marked by inadequate political development and political organisation of the region, repeated internecine revenge killings, 'area domination' exercises by vigilante groups and the absence of any professional revolutionary resistance army that could hold sway against the joint forces and thereby also earn the respect of the rural *Adivasi* population. It is noteworthy that some of the key organisations and leaders of various mass fronts that were set up have gone on to flip sides. This of course is a separate discussion, but the key here is to understand that the objective political conditions did not exist for a stalemate to be reached. The new government of Bengal also did not try to provide any openers by lifting the ban on the Maoists and their various mass organisations or remove the charges under the Unlawful Activities (Prevention) Act against some key leaders. In other words there were absolutely no substantial peace offerings from the state government to begin with.

Peace Talks in Ireland, the Philippines and Guatemala

In Ireland, a peace process had been initiated in the 1980s (through a well-known intermediary Father Alec Reid), even though the British government kept denying it right into the 1990s. Eventually, it led to discussions between the Sinn Fein (the political overground arm of the Irish nationalist movement) and the Social Democratic Labour Party of John Hume. Through a steady, detailed process by 1993 there was a joint declaration of peace, followed by several temporary ceasefire declarations by the Provisional IRA after 1994. There was international involvement and awareness throughout the negotiations. Ceasefire and decommissioning was not the priority item on the agenda in the beginning. No serious politician in his/her right mind asked for 'surrender, or else ... ' like some local neighbourhood tough talker would. During this entire process, there were many breakdowns, but the process eventually co-opted Senator George Mitchell of the US who developed the Mitchell Principles, based on which Gerry Adams, the leader of Sinn Fein, eventually convinced the IRA to decommission by 2005. The IRA has not disbanded, but has chosen to use 'exclusively peaceful means' to further its struggle. Furthermore, the negotiations led to the repeal of the British Ireland Act of 1920.

In India, however, the British sedition Act of the 1890s is still in force. (Nobody in India seems to be terribly bothered about this Act, even though several hundred *Adivasis*, who have no voice, have been jailed based on the Act, never mind the very eloquent Dr Binayak Sen). 'The Belfast Agreement included a devolved, inclusive government, prisoner release, troop reductions, targets for paramilitary decommissioning, provisions for polls on Irish reunification, and civil rights measures and 'parity of esteem' for the two communities in Northern Ireland.' (Wikipedia). The Sinn Fein today is the second largest political party in Ireland, commanding enormous respect among the electorate.

In the Philippines, as per a recent report on the website of *countercurrents.org*, the Philippine New People's Army (NPA), 'has a definitive 5-year program in place to reach a stage of 'strategic stalemate' by enhancing its armed forces to platoon and company strength, augment its organs of political power (at the urban and rural municipality level through mass organisations) and concentrate on implementing the 5-hectare land ceiling limit in areas under its control'. In the meantime, internationally monitored peace negotiations continue in The Hague. NPA continues to hold on to its arms and areas of control. There is no undue rush to secure local 'developmental' advantages in the name of the peace process. There is no demand for NPA to demilitarise or disband for development to take place.

The fundamentals need to be worked out first. Whose life is affected? Whose livelihood has been spurned for centuries, whose education, health and sanitation have been ignored? Who has been denied access to grow his/her own food? Whose land has remained un-tilled and un-harvested? These are the fundamental questions that both sides and the intermediaries should have reviewed before entering the peace process. And not who has how many SLRs, motorbikes and detonators, and who has killed how many of the other. Since 1974, the Filipinos have instituted a National Democratic Front (NDF) comprising 17 organisations, and their political pressures have allowed the initiation of 'peace negotiations' in The Hague that could take place only after several initial joint declarations with the government had been achieved. Even there, the Arroyo and Aquino governments engaged in subterfuge on several instances.

According to the same website: 'The 4 points of discussion in the current negotiations of NDF with the Philippine government are: 1. Mutual respect for human rights (there is agreement on that); 2. Agreement on socio-economic reforms, viz. land reforms, nationalizations, etc. (these are in the second stage of negotiations); 3. Political and constitutional reforms; and 4. End of hostilities. He (Fidel Agcaoili, chairperson of the Netherlands-based NDF monitoring committee, the negotiating arm of NDF), asserted that The Hague declaration which initiated the discussions, clearly also stated that there would be no pre-conditions on each other, no demands for ceasefire and no imposition of each other's constitution on the other.'

The detailed negotiations on point 1 allowed for joint monitoring of violations of human rights and other detailed steps. This is a step-by-step process based on objective conditions that the Filipinos have implemented in their negotiating process. Not all of it has been successful.

In Guatemala, it took almost 30 years of negotiations between the rebel guerrillas, the involvement of the UN, assisted by the governments of Norway and Spain (Oslo accord), the involvement of Catholic bishops, at least 15 different peace accords with detailed procedures, joint civil liberties monitoring programmes (while the US was busy assisting in one coup after the other, which resulted in the killing of some 8,000 peasants between 1966 and 1968 and a massive carnage in the countryside till the mid-1980s) and eventually a series of high-level negotiations which led to a pluralist parliamentary system. Four rebel guerrilla groups united to have a common front in negotiations, which eventually led to restoration of some form of democracy by 1985. The process was achieved through a careful step-by-step approach to the peace process. Not all is well in Guatemala now. In a small country of only 13 million people, over 200,000 lives were lost, but the peace process was very structured, even though it was repeatedly sabotaged.

Vietnam, Laos and Cambodia

The Battle of Dien Bien Phu marked the end of French involvement in Indochina. Vo Nguyen Giap's Viet Minh forces handed the French a stunning military defeat (through extraordinary political and military campaigns), and on 7 May 1954, the French Union garrison surrendered. At the Geneva Peace Conference, the French negotiated a ceasefire agreement with the Viet Minh, and Independence was granted to Cambodia, Laos and Vietnam. That was of course a different type of peace accord, with the colonial masters beating a hasty retreat. Soon after, there was the Evian Accord in Algeria and once again France had to pack up and leave after Ben Bella and the legendary FLN brought the war to their doorstep. (The Americans are shy to sign any peace accords, except one attempt in Vietnam — the Paris Accord — which failed in 1973 with Richard Nixon sabotaging the accord through Henry Kissinger and resuming the bombing of North Vietnam, although Kissinger got the Nobel Peace Prize with North Vietnam's Le Duc Tho for it).

An argument could be made in this case that a foreign colonising force was being fought against in Vietnam, which is of little relevance to Junglemahal. Unfortunately, in this new world order, the same colonising wars are being fought invariably through proxy. Irrespective, US Army's elite divisions with some of their most advanced tank regiments were involved in Joint Counter Insurgency Exercises just a few miles from New Delhi last year. Similar exercises have been conducted with other nations as well. Today, a war can be upgraded in no time with 'foreign engagement' deep in the interior of the country and it would be made to look quite natural and normal.

Conclusion

So, the question is what were the interlocutors in Bengal thinking when they agreed to take up this task, under the conditions that prevailed in Bengal with Mamata Banerjee at the helm? What was the theoretical understanding of the objective conditions for 'peace negotiations' that led them to accept this responsibility? Without a historical understanding of the immensity and national/international scope of the peace process on the part of the interlocutors, without an objective analysis of the contending forces and the absence of a groundswell of political opinion in the wake of a strategic stalemate, a peace process could be a dubious affair. With rebels negotiating for some breathing space and the government trying to pull off little 'coups' (some prize surrenders, some 'encounters' some announcements for jobs and building bridges), the overall strategy for 'peace' was ill-conceived from the beginning. It was disadvantageous for the citizens who seek peace and the rebels who have a cause. The State will of course always talk peace and make war.

(The title for this essay was the result of a discussion the author had with a person who has experience in peace negotiations in the international arena. It can be construed in two ways. First and the preferable one perhaps is that when you want peace, you must go about it like when you plan a war, with precision, with stealth and a careful analysis of the objective situation and a detailed appraisal of the strengths and weaknesses of the contending forces. The other interpretation is that if you want peace, you must actually wage war to a point of advantage where a stalemate is reached and peace negotiations are inevitable. That is a military tactic and was not the topic of discussion for this essay.)

Politics of Area Domination and Peace

Partha Sarathi

As Mamata Banerjee realised her long-cherished dream to capture power in West Bengal, establishing peace in the trouble-torn state, particularly in Junglemahal of Bengal, was high on the agenda of the new government. But the question haunting our mind was how the new regime would try to establish peace: through the might of the State or through peace negotiation with the Maoists? The second option eluded sections of civil society as the Maoists and Trinamul Congress (TMC) entered a tacit understanding before the state Assembly elections in May 2011 to defeat their common enemy, the CPI(M) and the Left Front government.

But their bonhomie was short-lived as, after a few failed efforts to bring the two sides (the Maoists and the state government) to the peace-talk table, events took a sudden turn when the Centre-state joint armed forces surprised one and all by killing to Maoist leader Kishenji in an 'encounter'. It seemed the new rulers of Bengal were simply not ready to miss the opportunity to eliminate the top Maoist leader while pretending to continue the peace process by appointing interlocutors. With the withdrawal of the mediators from the process apparently feeling betrayed by Kishenji's killing, the chances of restoring peace through negotiations became bleak. But was this turn of events unexpected at all?

It was apparent from the very beginning of the so-called peace-initiative that both sides were responding to the process in order to create public opinion in their favour and ultimately gain the upper hand in the ensuing battle that seemed inevitable judging by their different ideological stand-points. On the one hand, the Maoists would in no way be ready to bid farewell to arms and join the so-called mainstream politics as advocated by the parliamentary parties. They are committed to capturing power through armed struggle. They regard the Indian State as the principal enemy which they aim to overthrow through a 'protracted people's war'. They were ready to negotiate peace in the changed political situation after the last Assembly elections principally to show their sincerity to the peace process and gain some time to expand their organisational network in the state.

On the other hand, the State would in no way allow an armed insurgent group to expand its base to newer areas under the garb of peace initiative. TMC gained much ground in Junglemahal during the election campaign, albeit with the help of the Maoists, and wanted to consolidate its gains in the post-election period at the cost of the Maoists. Anyone familiar with the fast-changing ground reality in Junglemahal will wonder how Bengal's new rulers and the Maoists could come to terms even for a short-lived peace when both sides are bent on ground-domination, which had become the common practice of all political parties in the vast rural tracts of Bengal since the early years of LF rule. The principal LF partner, CPI(M), has become quite (in)famous for its hegemonic domination in the countryside that ensured it of resounding victories in one election after another.

One needs to study the style of domination being exercised by the present rulers of the state vis-à-vis the Maoist party to explore the possibility of the peace process initiated after the Assembly elections with so much fanfare. Has there been any fundamental change in the policy of area domination in the changed political scenario in Bengal? I shall try to examine the failed peace process in the background of the prevailing political practices of the contending parties that principally determines the future of a political process in this state.

The Politics of Area Domination

During the 34-year LF rule, the CPI(M) gained a kind of mastery in applying the policy of area domination, particularly in the rural areas. It applied its vast party machinery, skillfully combining it with the State machinery — over which it had established a vicious grip — to achieve its absolute supremacy over rural society. During its emergence, TMC waged a political battle against CPI(M) in the countryside of West Medinipur, Hooghly and Bankura districts from 1998 to 2001 to successfully bring substantial rural areas under its domination. The policy of area domination at that time found expression in the fight to physically capture villages after villages with marauding armed gangs attacking and counter-attacking each other's territory, burning and looting houses, killing and injuring people, thereby bringing immense misery to the people of the affected area.

Despite having having a completely different ideological make-up, the Maoists hardly lagged behind in this policy of area domination. One may recollect that about the same period the CPI(ML) People's War and MCC, the parties that later united to form the CPI((Maoist), fought bloody battles between themselves for area domination in the forest areas of Bengal. Such fratricidal fighting between various revolutionary parties continued for long in Andhra Pradesh, Bihar and Jharkhand. Interestingly, the Maoists (in their previous avatar as CPI(ML) People's War had intervened in that battle for area domination between the principal parliamentary parties of Bengal in the above mentioned districts, first against the domination of the TMC-BJP combine (TMC was then allied with BJP both at the state and national levels) and then against the aggressive CPI(M). That experience is worthy enough to be mentioned in this context.

In the aftermath of 1998 panchayat elections, the TMC-BJP combine made some gains at the expense of their rival, CPI(M), in some areas in West Medinipur, Hooghly and Bankura by capturing a number of panchayats and then eliminated CPI(M) activities from those areas to establish their exclusive domination. When the Maoists began organising people in Garbeta I and Garbeta II blocks of West Medinipur, their principal opposition came from forces loyal to the TMC-BJP combine, which had by then disbanded red flag from the entire area.

In 1999, the Maoists annihilated a local BJP leader in Sandhipur village of Garbeta I block in order to demoralise TMC-BJP workers, who in retaliation killed the brother of the local Maoist leader Asit

Sarkar, eliminated his nephew and blinded his brother-in-law. After these incidents, a series of clashes took place in Garbeta and its surrounding areas between the Maoists and TMC-BJP forces, with the former slowly gaining supremacy mainly because of their training in guerrilla warfare, including their skill in using long-range firearms. Notably, CPI(M) leaders of the area, cornered by the TMC-BJP forces, offered help to the Maoists in the form of food and shelter so that they could defeat their common enemy. The Maoists found the help convenient for their existence and battle for supremacy in the area. But things changed once the TMC-BJP combine began to retreat from the area in the face of the Maoists' attacks.

By then, CPI(M) had reorganised its forces in and around Garbeta after joining hands with the Maoists to oust the TMC-BJP forces. And once the latter began retreating from the area, CPI(M) forces immediately turned their guns on on the Maoists with a view to re-capture their lost territory. Ironically, some of the TMC-BJP supporters, evicted from their villages, then joined the Maoists in their bid to resist the aggressively expanding CPI(M) and return home. The Maoists, boosted by the support received this time from their 'yesterday's enemy', formed a bigger armed squad (platoon formation in Maoist parlance) to counter the CPI(M) attacks. But this time the Maoists did not get the crucial support of the SC-ST people that they had received while fighting against the TMC-BJP forces. In the ensuing fight between the Maoists and the CPI(M), the subaltern people in the war-zone of Garbeta became largely neutral and refused to provide shelter to the Maoists, which the radicals required badly to keep their hideouts secret from enemy forces.

In this situation, some TMC-turned-Maoist supporters offered the Maoists shelter in one of their villages, namely Chhoto Angaria. But the shelter was soon exposed to the CPI(M) which had already 'captured' that area. CPI(M) leaders soon gathered their forces and burnt the 'shelter' after killing at least five Maoist squad members. Interestingly, the panicked owner of the house fled to Kolkata to inform the state-level TMC leadership about the carnage, after which Mamata Banerjee promptly claimed that TMC supporters were killed by CPI(M) forces in Chhoto Angaria. After the gory incident, the Maoists retreated from the area once and for all, and instead concentrated their activities in the forest areas of south Bengal districts. That was their fast intervention in the battle for area domination of the parliamentary parties when the CPI(M) tactfully used their services to regain its domination over a certain area. But had the Maoists learnt any lesson from their bitter experience of allying with parliamentary parties in Garbeta?

The incidents unveiled in Junglemahal in the recent phase proved to the contrary. This time, the Maoist movement got a fillip with the outbreak of the Lalgarh movement that alienated almost the whole population from the state and consecutively from CPI(M), then principal ruling party. CPI(M), though maintaining a low profile in the initial period of the popular upsurge in the area, tried to re-establish its stranglehold over the area at a later stage by setting up a number of armed camps, bolstered and supported by the anti-Maoists operations of the joint forces. But remarkably, in this crucial period, the Maoists failed to mobilise the local people, estranged from the state and the CPI(M), to demonstrate popular anger against the atrocities of these forces, which had been a very common feature in the initial months of the Lalgarh movement. That people's mobilisation against armed camps was possible had been amply demonstrated by the Netai incident where CPI(M) gangs fired on agitating villagers, killing nine of them.

The Maoists instead concentrated on organising armed squads and conducting raids on the houses of CPI(M) cadres and supporters, and attacking the joint forces. In the offensive launched by them, scores of CPI(M) supporters, mostly poor and middle class villagers, and a number of state security personnel were killed. Junglemahal turned into a real war-zone where killings and counter-killings became the order of the day for quite some time.

Sleeping With the Enemy

After the announcement of Assembly elections, political equations began to change quickly with the entry of TMC as a contending power in battle-weary Junglemahal. A strange realignment of political forces began to take shape in the region with the Maoists and TMC coming to terms, though unofficially, in a desperate bid to defeat CPI(M) as the hustings. In the background of the fierce battle for area domination in Bengal's countryside, the compulsion for a political formation to maintain just its physical existence in a certain area often leads to a situation in which the enemy's enemy becomes a friend, thereby making strange bed-fellows that were seen earlier in the battle for Garbeta.

This time, the alignment of political forces in Junglemahal took a reverse shape as TMC was extended generous support by the Maoists, who even filled rally grounds with their supporters for TMC leaders' meetings. The declaration of top Maoist leader Kishenji that he wanted to see Mamata Banerjee as the chief minister of Bengal paved the way for the alliance in a pre-poll marriage of convenience. TMC that did not have substantial presence in Junglemahal earlier was quick to seize the opportunity and infiltrate in a big way the Maoist-dominated People's Committee against Police Atrocities (PCPA) and *Adivasi-Mulvasi Janaganer Committee* (AMJC). Later, PCPA and AMJC both became the targets of State repression. The Maoists contemplated that the presence of TMC supporters in these organisations would dissuade the government forces — at least to some extent — from attacking them and act as a safeguard for their own supporters working in these organisations. But in the tactical manoeuvre to use each other in the opportunist alliance, TMC ably organised its own organisational base cutting across the Maoists' support base throughout Junglemahal.

After the TMC-led alliance won the election with a thumping majority, the basis for the TMC-Maoist alliance suddenly evaporated and the ground was set for a new battle to establish supremacy in Junglemahal. For obvious reasons this time the battle line was drawn between TMC and the Maoists with each trying to consolidate and expand its base at the earliest lest the other take advantage of the changed situation was the result of the sudden end of CPI(M) domination. Not even an inch of land in Bengal's countryside is probably beyond the domination of one party or another and Junglemahal is no exception. It is also predictable that TMC would use the State forces at its disposal to suppress any resurgence of the Maoists. It was highly unlikely in such a situation that peace would be negotiated in true spirit between the two contending sides, one in state power and the other conducting insurgency against the State.

The Elusive Peace

People following the developments in Junglemahal closely should not have the illusion that the new government would negotiate peace with the Maoists in earnest. Negotiations between the State and insurgents materialise only when a insurgent group is too strong to be defeated by force and/or there is some room for the latter to be accommodated in the State set-up. Clearly, none of these factors exists in Bengal today. The first condition existed in Andhra Pradesh when the state government initiated discussions in 2004. But since the second condition did not exist, the state government used the facade of negotiations to unearth the Maoist network and then eliminate almost the entire Maoist force from the state.

No wonder then that peace talks between the Bengal government and the Maoists never materialized. In the game of one-upmanship, the new government put the agenda of peace talks by appointing interlocutors, but did not fulfil its pre-poll promise of withdrawal of joint forces and release of political prisoners (and withdrawal of previous political cases) that could have paved the way for peace negotiations. The anti-Maoist operations of the joint forces also continued to keep Maoist movements under check. On the ground a considerable number of leaders and activists of PCPA in West Medinipur and AMJC in Purulia were provoked and cajoled into joining TMC in the changed situation. Some of these forces were organised in resistance groups to thwart the movement of the Maoists in the villages.

This enraged the Maoists, who in retaliation once again resorted to individual killings to check the newly formed anti-Maoist formations. In one incident, a Maoist squad looking for an erstwhile leader of

AMJC in Purulia, who had joined TMC after the Assembly election, killed his brother and father when it did not find him. Such killings gave the government the required ground to restart full-fledged operations by the joint forces. Because of the substantial infiltration of TMC into the Maoist network, the Maoists became vulnerable to the joint forces' operations as never before.

The precision killing of top Maoist leader Kishenji raised questions about the extent of infiltration of the Maoists' ranks by the State intelligence network. The circumstances in which Kishenji was killed may remain a mystery, but the incident is probably an indication of the receding influence of the Maoists in Junglemahal. The new rulers of the state had strategically used the promise of joint forces' withdrawal and release of political prisoners to win the support of the Maoists in the crucial Assembly elections. Later, TMC leaders used the peace initiative along with several 'development' sops in order to divide and penetrate the Maoist ranks and extend their hegemony over the area.

The Maoists, in turn, seem to have become victims of their own politics by first forming an opportunistic alliance with a ruling class party, then misreading the ground situation in Junglemahal, probably lifting their guard for a while by over-emphasising the peace initiative and above all undermining, as always, the necessity to conduct political-ideological struggles to counter the influence of the State and the parliamentary parties and almost entirely replacing it by their brand of 'armed struggle', which principally took the form of annihilation.

Thus it seems that peace has not been a real issue of negotiation for either side, and they wanted to use the same tactics to gain the upper hand in Junglemahal. In the game of one-upmanship, the state government and the ruling party have scored over the Maoists at least for the time being. The principal problem for both sides seems to be their utter disrespect for democratic norms and aspirations of the people. The new ruling party went back on its own pre-poll promises of withdrawing the joint forces, releasing political prisoners and withdrawing political cases of the earlier regime. The new government resumed the policy of 'encounter' killings to physically eliminate the

Maoist threat. The Maoists, on their part, did not change their policy of killing individual political opponents. Both sides seemed more than eager to establish their exclusive domination over Junglemahal. Given such scanty regard to democracy, society cannot rid itself from the cycle of violence, and peace will hardly get a chance.

Maoists and the Indian State: Is Peace Possible?

Kunal Chattopadhyay

Two former fellow combatants, Debabrata Bandyopadhyay, now Trinamul Congress Rajya Sabha MP, and Sujato Bhadra, civil rights activist, have written articles, independently of each other. Bandyopadhyay[1] has accused CPI(Maoist) of using force and violence against ordinary people. Rather belatedly, he has also argued that they had been murdering CPI(M) members because of their hostile relation with that party. Supporters of CPI(Maoist) as well as those of TMC, along with many civil-social activists, had either been ignoring this angle in the past, or simply arguing, some directly, some obliquely, that all those 'sentenced to death' by so-called people's courts were invariably evil people deserving their fate. Bandyopadhyay's conclusion is simple — India has a functioning democracy for over six decades, so parties that do not agree to function within this democracy have no space in India. In a remarkable realignment of political voices, Bandyopadhyay, who was rooting for TMC and inveighing against the Left Front till the other day, now finds himself in good company with the latter. *Kalantar*, the CPI daily, reported the same day, with the writer scarcely concealing glee, that the state government was contemplating banning People's Committee against Police Atrocities (PCPA), *Matangini Mahila Samiti* and USDF, all of them allegedly fronts for CPI(Maoist).

Breakdown of an Opportunist United Front

Sujato Bhadra, probably the face most identified with the Association for Protection of Democratic Rights (APDR), regardless of whether he has been holding any executive post in that organisation, was also closely involved with anti-LF campaigns, to the extent that he decided, notwithstanding his widely known identity as a civil rights activist not aligned with any party, to throw his weight behind TMC's electoral campaigns during 2009-11. Bhadra feels, clearly, that the TMC-led government has greater commitment to democracy than the previous regime.

We thus read, in connection to the role Bhadra and a few others were asked to play as mediators: 'We had readily agreed to accept the assignment for three reasons — 1) this new government, being sincere to its electoral pledges, has clearly recognised the political nature of the conflict, which is a definite break from the past, 2) repeated insistence on opening of dialogue to end the killings and sufferings of the people of the area and bring peace, and 3) we fought against the misdeeds of the LF government to the best of our ability over the years, so it was our responsibility also to bring peace and help the new government build the infrastructure for development of the area.'[2]

Yet Bhadra, for all his contortions, has now to take a stance somewhat different from Bandyopadhyay's, if he wants to retain even a shred of his image and integrity. I begin with Bhadra and Bandyopadhyay, not because they are the principal actors, but because I want to emphasise that unless one recognises the basic issues in the conflict, one is apt to end up as either irrelevant or a fifth wheel in one or the other of the principals' cars. The second reason for placing them against each other is to argue that a united front very often begins to unravel at the moment of its victory and after the enemy who had brought such disparate forces together is routed, even if only for the moment, the erstwhile allies may fall out. But in an opportunistic united front, the nature of the alliance is not clearly explained, so its falling apart also comes as a curious process.

Indian State, Democracy and Capitalist Development

Bourgeois democracy is never what its starry eyed defenders think it to be, including those would-be Marxists who believe that there is some ideal bourgeois democracy in which people get plenty of rights, and by which standard they want to condemn existing bourgeois democracies, notably the one in India, as inadequate. The inadequacy is actually built into the very structures of bourgeois democracy. At least once in the 20th century there was a serious attempt to consolidate bourgeois democracy and to proceed further forward. It is only by thoroughly distorting the tragic Chilean experience, which confirmed so many previous lessons of history, that so-called communist parties in large parts of the world, including in India, as well as centrist formations and social democrats, push the strategy according to which the working class movement can fully attain its goals within the framework of bourgeois parliamentary institutions, through reliance on parliamentary elections and gradual conquest of 'positions of State power' within these institutions.

This has to be energetically opposed and denounced for what it is: a cover-up for abandonment of the struggle for the conquest of State power by the proletariat, of the struggle for the expropriation of the bourgeoisie, of a policy of consistent defence of the class interests of working people, a cover-up for substitution of ever-more systematic class collaboration with the bourgeoisie for the policy of consistent class struggle, for disarming of the proletariat in the face of violence unleashed by the capitalist class and, consequently, for a growing tendency to capitulate to the class interests of the bourgeoisie at moments of decisive economic, political and social crisis.

Far from reducing the 'costs of social transformation' or from ensuring a peaceful, albeit slower, transition to socialism, this policy, if it should decisively determine the political attitude of the toilers in a period of unavoidable overall class confrontation, can only lead to bloody defeats and mass slaughters of the German, Spanish, Indonesian, and Chilean kind (in the German case, additionally caused by the criminal ultra-left 'social-fascism' theory and practice of the Comintern).

The Indian State has not been a neutral umpire, not even merely an abstract entity which either side can tilt in its own direction at will. It has been a key element in the strategy of the Indian capitalist class since Independence. In this essay, we lack the space to examine all of this in detail. However, there is a need to discuss some of the issues.

From the late 1960s, the global economy has entered into the declining phase of a long wave that had seen, in the previous years, a spectacular boom. As part of that, the Indian capitalist class had organised its own growth using protectionism, even as it promised some types of State action, however limited, to some sections of the working people. But the downward phase of the long wave changed the situation drastically. The initial response of big capitalist powers to the crisis was to try and administer new doses of Keynesianism. But this proved unviable. Class struggle under these circumstances sharpened everywhere.

On the economic field, it was Paul Volcker, a Keynesian, but also a pragmatist, who administered the sharpest monetarist shock in his role as chief of the US Federal Reserve. Austerity was taken up by IMF and World Bank and became the global slogan. And this was done everywhere formally under the banner of free market but, in fact, through huge pro-capital State action, often coercive against workers. What is significant in the Indian case is that Indian capitalist class followed a closely parallel path. In 1974, the working class' combative mood in the country had reached the peak and the situation was fertile for an explosion of anger from below. Railway workers went on an all-out strike but the strikers' resolve was matched by government's determination to put the strike down with a heavy hand. Across the country, thousands of workers were arrested using draconian provisions of DIR and MISA even as BSF, CRPF and PAC personnel were deployed in labour townships. Victimisation of railway workers during the 1974 strike was quite ruthless — 46,000 dismissed, 9,000 suspended, 19,000 arrested and 863,000 of the over 15 lakhs who participated in the strike were served break-in-service notice.

Eight years later came the two-year-long struggle of Bombay textile workers. Like the railway workers, the textile workers, too, were disillusioned with the established unions and the strike was organised from below. Workers in factories and chawls set up committees, and debated and made policy decisions. The strike was eventually crushed because of continuous dithering by a leadership in friendly terms with those in power in Maharashtra. The defeats of 1974 and 1982-3 broke the moral of the working class for a considerable period. These struggles, in bourgeois historiography, when at all mentioned, are treated as pawns of high politics.

Thus, the railway strike is seen as part of the attempts by the opposition to weaken Indira Gandhi's government, refusing to accord agency to the workers. But it was as a result of these defeats that new forms of capital accumulation became easier. The final years of Indira Gandhi saw the beginning of a turn to economic liberalisation, an impetus strengthened by Rajiv Gandhi. And contrary to the traditional perception that Congress necessarily stood for a more State-controlled economy while it was Swatantra Party, Jan Sangh et al that were pro-free market, economic policy underwent a transformation in which Congress and the opposition had little difference.

In other words, lagging only slightly behind the major capitalist countries from the mid-1980s, the Indian capitalist class was, thus, orienting itself to neo-liberal policies. The defeats of earlier years, together with the paralysis of the left in the face of the collapse of the bureaucratised workers' States and their transformation into capitalism, meant very poor resistance from large sections of the organised blue-collar working class.

State Violence Not Limited to Marginals

I mentioned this history for three reasons. First, to negate the idea that violence and confrontations are restricted to 'marginal areas'. People like Bandyopadhyay, when arguing that there is ample democratic space and all you need is civil-social action to get redress for injustice, simply forget that their civil society excludes the working class. This came out very clearly in a recent incident. In the first working class action after the TMC-led government came to power, when Bhadra et al were enjoying their honeymoon with a 'government sincere to its electoral pledges', unorganised sector workers demanded improvements in their conditions through a three-day sit-in programme. Reporting on their programme, *The Telegraph*, the most important voice of the ruling class when talking to itself and its humble servants, headlined the news thus: 'Return of rally raj: City centre chokes, citizens suffer'. Workers not getting minimum wages are evidently not citizens. When workers go beyond mere sit-ins or deputations, violence is unleashed on them. And if they respond in kind, they alone are held responsible, as in the Manesar plant of Maruti Udyog Limited.

The second reason to mention this history is to argue that Indian capitalism has been transforming itself for a much longer time than the supposed sudden turn under Narasimha Rao and Manmohan Singh in 1991. And the third reason is to stress that capital accumulation in India, however, has a significantly different pattern, in as much as Indian capitalism cannot rely on any colonial exploitation for primary accumulation of capital. This is where *Adivasis* are slotted in. Relying on the ideological weaknesses of India's working class movement, the *Adivasis* have been successfully delinked from other workers. Exploitation, or rather super-exploitation, of the *Adivasis*, is a major factor, along with unequal town-countryside relationship, in ensuring primary accumulation of capital. The in-built two-stage theory of revolution within the bulk of the 'Marxist' left, one of the legacies of Stalinism, has meant that *Adivasis* are not seen as doubly exploited as community and as working class, but rather, are simply seen as exploited ethnic groups. The Indian State has brutalised and exploited *Adivasis* systematically, because, on one hand, as P. Chidambaram stated very bluntly recently, the elite wants to exploit natural resources, and on the other hand, because the *Adivasis* form a significant part of the large source of cheap labour.

Maoist Bogey and Repression of *Adivasis*

It is this reality that must be grasped when we talk about the responses of the Indian State to CPI(Maoist). For many a well-meaning Gandhian, political liberal, or civil-societarian, it is simply a failure of this or that government, a failure to recognise that certain issues are political and not just law and order issues, that has led to so much bloodshed. If only the issues were duly recognised as political issues, they sigh, there could be a dialogue between people of good faith. This overlooks that all talk of law and order is also, precisely, political talk. The repression of CPI(Maoist) is not just repression of a party. It enables the State to send in huge masses of paramilitary forces, terrorise the *Adivasis*, and try to push through the agenda of Indian and international big capital. Hence, for example, the difference between how Chidambaram and his fellow ministers handled Singur and how they handled Lalgarh: In the case of Singur, the Centre could afford to destabilise the state government headed by an opponent political group, since the outcome would not destabilise the system as a whole, but in the case of Lalgarh, by contrast, Chidambaram went out of his way to cooperate with Buddhadeb Bhattacharjee.

We also need to situate this in an all-India context. In Chhattisgarh or Madhya Pradesh, places where the left is not and has never been in power, the left parties have campaigned in support of the *Adivasis*. There, roles have been reversed. What is important is that while reformist ideology, populism or various factors may have led some parties, some politicians (CPI in Chattisgarh, Mamata in West Bengal) to declare seeming support for the exploited *Adivasis*, the State has, in all cases, been forthright in using violence. The incarceration of Binayak Sen, the utterly ludicrous charges against him and the way State agencies hounded Nandini Sundar when she went on a fact-finding mission to Chhattisgarh all show this.

Beyond the well-known hounding of reputed individuals, though, are the repressive measures on a far greater numbers of ordinary people. A statement issued on this subject by the Campaign for Survival and Dignity remarked: (I am providing only extracts, not a full, continuous quote) 'The government tells us that this offensive will make it possible for the 'state to function' in these areas and fill the 'vacuum of governance''. This is grossly misleading. The Indian state is very, very active in these areas, often in its most brutal and violent form ... vivid example is the illegal eviction of more than 300,000 families by the forest departments a few years ago ... This war is not about 'national security''; it is about 'securing' the interests of global and Indian capital and big business. Any government worried about security would send its troops against mining mafias, forest mafias, violent vigilante groups like the *Salwa Judum* and others. Rather than being curbed, these killers are, in fact, supported by the police. Have the security forces ever been deployed to defend the people struggling to protect themselves, their forests, their livelihoods and their futures? The answer is no. The notion of 'security' being advanced by the government clearly has nothing to do with the people ... Government knows perfectly well that it cannot destroy the CPI(Maoist), or any people's struggle, through military action. How can the armed forces identify who is a 'Maoist' and who is not? The use of brute military force will result in the slaughter of thousands of people in prolonged, bloody and brutal guerrilla warfare. This has been the result of every 'security offensive' in India's history, from Kashmir to Nagaland. So why do this? Why now? Unless the goal has nothing to do with 'wiping out the Maoists' and everything to do with having an excuse for the permanent presence of lakhs of troops, arms and equipment in these areas. To protect and serve whom?'[3]

The killing of Maoist politburo member Azad after initiating peace talks is evidence enough that the government is not interested in peace. As the above quoted statement shows, the government does not want peace with the Maoists. The CPI(Maoist) and its armed forces are the pretext for maintaining huge forces of repression across a big part of India, and forcing the toilers to obey the rulers, including the mafias, in the name of law and order. Naive people, or ex-Marxists who now desperately want to forget the reality of class struggle, can talk about sincerity of governments. The reality is, within bourgeois democracies, working people have won rights only when they have fought for those rights.

At the time when Azad was killed, there was a complexity. TMC, though a partner in the Central government, was in the opposition in Bengal. And Mamata had realised, through the experiences of past electoral battles, that neither aa alliance with BJP nor with Congress was adequate to topple CPI(M). She had turned her party into a populist party. And she was willing to form alliances with both dissident and extreme left as well as with others on the right. It is well-known that Kishenji, another top Maoist leader, had expressed hope that she would become chief minister of Bengal and that many of the

Sujato Bhadras had been gung-ho about supporting her at all cost.

Illusions about Mamata Banerjee and the Bhadras

The illusion had never been Ms Banerjee's. She had on one occasion said that she was using the 'brains of the Naxalites'. It was the dissident and extreme left, or large sections of it, which, as a result of the continued hold of Stalinist ideology, created illusions for itself. It, or sections of it, saw CPI(M) as 'social fascist' (a criminal theory that cast reformists as fascists and let real fascists off the hook, a theory originating with Stalin and resulting in the rejection of a working class united front against Hitler by the German Communist Party).[4]

It simultaneously accepted, in some form or the other, the ideology of popular front-ism according to which democratic or progressive bourgeois forces can be allies. TMC was cast into that role by SUCI(C), de facto also by CPI(Maoist), which declared that in areas where it was strong, TMC would be allowed to campaign but not the party of *harmads*. In 2006, when the Singur movement started, the picture had been very different. But forces on the radical left, with small exceptions, decided that they were tired of trying to build class struggle currents against CPI(M). Hatred of CPI(M), whose reformism had turned into social liberalism, a hatred, that in itself was a positive thing, slipped into the terrible error of anyhow toppling it. What this meant was that struggles where militant class struggle could have been built through patient work were given up and these forces ended up accepting the leadership of TMC. In these days of televised politics, this transformation was easy to see, with so many former radicals publicly taking stances that brought them within microscopic distance of TMC politics. Some ended up joining TMC, while others were content with being friends, hoping that they would remain friends ever after.

But the Maoist bogey was too good to let go. Mamata, both as chief and home minister, took full personal responsibility for what followed. Of course, it was dressed up as a sad but necessary action in view of the obduracy of CPI(Maoist). Paramilitary action was reintroduced. Even before the murder of Kishenji, the writing on the wall was clear. What is objectionable — not surprising, since he is trying to save his own reputation as well — is Sujato Bhadra's argument.

Even after the killing of Kishenji and Mamata's full-blown return to militaristic strategy, he argued: 'We have reasons to hold that attempts are on to impose the logic of the war economy forcibly on the newly born (state) government. The government has to overcome this pressure. The government has also to tackle effectively the potential spoilers — a part of the media which has been manufacturing public consent for declaring war on its own people, and a section of the police and bureaucrats, wich stand to gain from the war economy and war mentality. The people of the state know that this section of 'trigger-happy' police and bureaucrats was a part of the State terror during the LF regime. They have no experience of peace talks, and they, we are afraid, are not interested in taking lessons from history.'

Have we not met this rhetoric earlier, from soft critics of the LF, that it was not the government that was bad, but the rotten police and bureaucrats, the carryovers of the Siddhartha Sankar Ray era, and the Central government? To recollect what Marx once wrote, the second occurrence of this rank pathetic apologia is a low farce. Bhadra is, thereby, still exonerating the Mamata government and misleading his readers, using whatever remains of his reputation as a historic fighter for democratic rights. The Maoist bogey is now what is uniting the TMC-led government with all other governments. Ruling class needs are more significant here than any so-called goodwill.

CPI(Maoist) and Stalinist Mindset

Peace talks, in order to be serious, require two sides, both willing to be parties to the process. In the case of the Indian State, I have argued, using the pretext of CPI(Maoist) is necessary to carry out violence on *Adivasis*. That is why, it will not want any peace talks until its real strategic goals are met or until class struggles force its hands. CPI(Maoist), too, is not in a position to be very serious about peace talks. Built on solidly Stalinist-Maoist lines, it has no idea about socialist democracy.

Stalinist ideology was the ideology of the ruling bureaucracy of the

USSR and taken over by other ruling bureaucracies, including in the Peoples' Republic of China. This ideology of the bureaucracy — of which the key idea is the rule of the single party acting in the name of the working class — although not always explicitly formulated can be summarised in the following terms: a) The 'leading party' or even its central committee has a monopoly of political consciousness at the highest level, if not a monopoly of knowledge at least at the level of the social sciences. Hence, the party is always right. One is told to learn from the masses, but the learning is done by that very party leadership and no one else. b) The working class, and even more the toiling masses in general, are too backward politically, too much under the influence of bourgeois and petty-bourgeois ideology and 'imperialist propaganda', too much inclined to prefer immediate material advantages as against long-term historical interests, for any direct exercise of State power by democratically elected workers' councils to be tolerable from the point of view of 'the interests of socialism'. Genuine workers' democracy would lead to capitalist restoration or at least damage socialist construction. c) The dictatorship of the proletariat, therefore, can be exercised only by the 'leading party of the proletariat', i.e., the dictatorship of the proletariat is the dictatorship of the party, either representing an essentially passive working class, or actively basing itself on the 'class struggle of the masses', who are nevertheless considered unworthy, unwilling, or incapable of directly exercising State power through institutionalised organs of power.[5] d) Since the party, and the party alone, represents the interests of the working class, which are considered homogeneous in all situations and on all issues, the 'leading party' itself must be essentially monolithic. Any oppositional tendency necessarily reflects alien class pressures and alien class interests in one form or another (the struggle between 'two lines' is always a 'struggle between the proletariat and the bourgeoisie inside the party', the Maoists conclude). Monolithic control of all spheres of social life by the single party is the logical outcome of these concepts. Direct party control must be established over all sectors of 'civil society'. e) A further underlying assumption is that of an intensification of the class struggle in the period of building socialism. From that assumption is deduced the increasing danger of restoration of bourgeois power even long after private property has been abolished from the means of production and irrespective of the level of development of the productive forces. The threat of bourgeois restoration is often portrayed as a mechanical outcome of the victory of bourgeois ideology in this or that social, political, cultural, or even scientific field. In view of the extreme power thereby attributed to bourgeois ideas, the use of repression against those who are said to objectively represent these ideas becomes a corollary of the argument.

All these assumptions and dogmas are unscientific from a general Marxist point of view and are untenable in the light of real historical experience of class struggle during and after the overthrow of capitalist rule in the USSR and other countries. But they had become nearly universally accepted dogmas by communist parties in Stalin's time. And they have never been explicitly and thoroughly criticised and rejected by a communist party since then. These concepts continue to linger, at least partially, in the ideology of many leaders and cadres. They continue to constitute a conceptual source for the justification of various forms of curtailment of democratic rights of the toiling masses. CPI(Maoist), for example, has used force not against ruling class elements alone, but also against every attempt at independently organising the masses in areas where it is strong. Santosh Rana, for example, has spoken out publicly against this politics of violence over toiling masses.

Given its ideology, which involves the belief that any struggle other than 'armed struggle' (to be precise, struggle through armed combatant groups created by the party, not armed struggle as the result of the culmination of mass movements under certain circumstances) is revisionist, a sell-out to the rulers, CPI(Maoist) cannot engage in fruitful peace talks.

I reproduce here, as an example, an extract from a statement issued by the central military commission of CPI(Maoist): '... Thousands of people, particularly *Adivasi* peasantry are rallying into struggles with the aim of defeating the 'War on People' ... which was unleashed by the Central and state governments ... Maoists are not advocates of violence. In fact, they would be in the forefront among those who wish for peace. Do not believe a word of the vicious propaganda unleashed by the bourgeois media on Maoists! Stand firmly with the revolutionary movement! If we do not defeat this enemy offensive, if we do not defeat the conspiracy to wipe out the revolutionary movement, Maoist party, PLGA, alternate people's power organs and mass organisations, then all the valuable fruits won by the revolutionary movement would be destroyed ... Join the PLGA in huge numbers, increase its force manifold and strengthen it! Integrate with the deluge of mass movements rising in several areas in our country with the slogans land-power-democracy-building of people's army and self-reliance! Join hands with them! Stand shoulder to shoulder with the armed resistance struggles of PLGA! There can be no fundamental change without completely destroying the exploiting classes. The reforms thrown by them as bread crumbs are useless and would only destroy the lives of the people further. Let us advance for an alternative new democratic society by declaring that reforms are part of the conspiracy to damage the unity of the people and fight them back!'[6]

Readers should note the following: a) the statement is issued by the central military commission, and b) it states, for the record, that Maoists are not advocates of violence. But it also categorically states that the masses must not just wage class struggle, but also join the PLGA in large numbers. Democracy is supposedly being built by the people's army. Rosa Luxemburg said that while violence could not be ruled out as the ultimate law of class struggle, the struggle for reforms were, when carried out by revolutionaries, struggles that strengthened the proletariat. For CPI(Maoist), reforms are simply something granted from above, not a by-product of revolutionary mass struggles.

Peace to be Redefined to Make it Possible

I am not arguing that peace is impossible. But I do argue that the meaning of peace has to be redefined, and its contents examined closely. It is impossible to have peace between the Indian State and

CPI(Maoist), as if they alone are the principal players — the idea with which we started this essay, since that is the idea behind the current rhetoric on peace talks. At the same time, we cannot, of course, exclude these two from any idea of peace talks. As long as the ruling class is strong enough to impose its will without serious contestation, it will try to deepen primary accumulation of capital, and therefore it will require some kind of systematic violence on *Adivasis*, on whom CPI(Maoist), in turn, hopes to bank for that very reason.

So the first key to challenging the State, to forcing it to rethink its strategy, lies in developing mass workers' and toilers' struggles — both in those areas and elsewhere — so that the State is compelled to recognise the power of fighting workers and to negotiate with them. Only then would it be possible to force the State to move back from its open war against the people — at least for the time being the balance of forces is no longer favouring the rulers so blatantly. It is, therefore, unacceptable when someone claims, as Bhadra does, that '...we are optimistic. That is because all stakeholders, including the government, seem to have finally recognised the value of peace. However, we have miles to go before bringing the stakeholders to the negotiating table. We do hope that using the tools of patience and flexibility with unwavering determination, the government and Maoists can bring peace and development in Junglemahal. This example will surely inspire other states and peace-loving citizens of India to move forward with the slogan of peace.'

We, on the other hand, are optimistic, because workers across India are forging new instruments of struggle in place of the worn-out old instruments. Organisations like New Trade Union Initiative, National Forum of Forest People and Forest Workers, *Vangujjar Kalyan Samiti* and others have been replacing, though only partly, older, bureaucratised and co-opted unions and other mass organisations. It is their struggles, along with those by similar organisations of the oppressed and exploited, which will compel the State to move in the direction of peace. In the same way, any attempt to develop mass organisations of this kind, mass struggles conducted democratically, should they succeed, will sap the strength of Maoist politics with its commandist, authoritarian model of 'leading'-party and the 'led'-masses. To survive in a changed milieu, CPI(Maoist), too, would have to undergo a paradigm shift.

As long as we stick to the assumption that the State and CPI(Maoist) alone are the principal actors, the only other factor being a chorus of pious civil-social actors, we are condemning ourselves to futility. In its current state, the State wants and needs to use violence, and CPI(Maoist) believe in only the primacy of armed guerrilla warfare.

Notes

1. D. Bandyopadhyay: Mao and the Maoist depredation: A conscious deviation, *The Statesman*, 14 January 2012
2. Sujato Bhadra: Peace-talk process in Junglemahal, *Mainstream*, vol.L, no.1, 24 December 2011.
3. *http://www.forestrightsact.com/statements-and-news/69-a-pretext-for-brutal-repression*
4. On this, see my article, The Communist Party of Germany, the Comintern and Hitler's Rise to Power, *History*, Journal of the Department of History, Burdwan University, vol.1, 1997.
5. For a Marxist understanding of the dictatorship of the proletariat, see Soma Marik, Reinterrogating the Classical Marxist Discourses of Revolutionary Democracy, Aakar Books, Delhi, 2008, chapter 5. See also the document of the Fourth International, adopted in 1985, entitled The Dictatorship of the Proletariat and Socialist Democracy, at *http://www.radicalsocialist.in/articles/marxist-theory/67-1985-world-congress-of-fourth-international*, on which much of my argument is based.
6. Let us intensify People's War with the aim of defeating 'Operation Green Hunt' — *War on People! http://www.bannedthought.net/India/CPI(Maoist)-Docs/index.htm#2011.*

Failed Peace Process: A Postmortem

Biswajit Roy

'It began as a tenacious essay in political realism, entered a phase of sheer drama unbelievable in its unreality, and ended in the bitter rattle of gunfire. The reference is to the 'talks' between Y.S. Rajasekhara Reddy's government in Andhra Pradesh and the Naxalites (2004).' — K. Balagopal, *Economic and Political Weekly*, 26 March 2005.

With Maoist top gun Kishenji's killing in an encounter, fake or genuine, the peace process between CPI(Maoist) and Mamata Banerjee's government met the fate of the Andhra talks even before it could begin.

In November 2008, after the popular outburst against police repression on women and children following the rebels' bid to kill Buddhadeb Bhattacharjee, the Maoists were the main organisers of the People's Committee against Police Atrocities (PCPA), which spearheaded the movement against the LF government and CPI(M). TMC, then principal Opposition party, entered into an uneasy marriage of political convenience with the Maoists to transform public anger against the CPI(M) and the Centre-state joint forces into electoral gains.

But, unlike Singur and Nandigram, Mamata and her men failed to hegemonise the oppositional space in Junglemahal, because of armed Maoist resistance and lack of TMC's organisational base before the Assembly polls in May 2011. Simmering tension over the turf notwithstanding, both sides held together against their common enemy, the CPI(M), till the Assembly polls. After the TMC-Congress alliance assumed power with a sweeping mandate, some members of the pro-*Paribartan* civil society initiated the peace process with the blessings of Mamata the new chief minister. The Maoists, who had been friendly to Mamata despite misgivings, responded positively.

However, the outcome of the five-month-long peace parleys in Bengal were an exercise similar to that in Andhra in 2004. There was one crucial difference, though, as one of the government-appointed interlocutors said: the Bengal process died in the pre-talks stage. There were other similarities as well. The mutual mistrust between Mamata and the Maoists led to one-upmanship and brinkmanship with continued turf war at the ground level.

The conflicting signals about building mutual confidence and the growing trust deficit that resulted from it were palpable much before the Kishenji's killing. The aborted Bengal peace process, which could have opened a new chapter of political experiment, both in parliamentary democracy and revolutionary politics, ended in the victory of champions of competitive violence ensuring another spell of State terror, ruling party hegemony and sporadic reprisals by an underground armed group. Kishenji's killing is a 'huge success' for the government, for it would break the backbone of Maoist resistance in Bengal, at least, in the short term. But there will be no full stop in the violence in Junglemahal.

The avenging angels of the CPI(M), now in the Opposition, also belittled the peace initiative from the beginning and mounted pressure on Mamata to complete the unfinished agenda of the Bhattacharjee government on the Maoists. They swapped roles with Mamata after Kishenji's killing. Speaking at a public rally in Lalgarh in 2010 in the presence of Medha Patkar, Swami Agnivesh and others, the then Opposition supremo Mamata had condemned the killing of CPI(Maoist) politburo member Azad. But in her CM avatar, she has dismissed the complaints of CPI(Maoist) and human rights bodies that Kishenji was killed in a fake encounter.

On the other hand, CPI(M), which had virtually sided with P. Chidambaram in condoning Azad's murder when the party was in power, has 'questioned' Mamata's claims on the circumstances leading to Kishenji's death and accused her of influencing the CID probe into it. Nevertheless, the Marxists evidently enjoyed the irony of history. CPI(M) had widely used the the media reports on the slain leader's desire to see Mamata as the new CM to harp on the 'Maoist-Mamata nexus'. 'Kishenji got a befitting reward for his desire within six months of the new government (coming to power),' Bengal Opposition leader Surjyakanta Misra said after Kishenji's kiiling.

The media-friendly Maoist leader and the most televised guerrilla in the country, Kishenji was conspicuously silent on the Bengal peace process, fuelling media reports about his opposition to it and a possible friction among senior Maoist leaders on the issue. But the key mediators felt differently. Maoist representatives assured them that their leaders, including Kishenji, had been supportive of the peace initiative. According to one of them, he was waiting 2 km away from the place of the last rendezvous between the two sides. The Maoists had offered to take the mediators to him but they declined.

Cynics, of both revolutionary and establishment hues, have already started celebrating the failure of the process with their usual 'we-told-you-so' wisdom about the impracticality of the dialogue between an elected government and pople who want to overthrow the parliamentary system forcibly. The Maoists and their sympathisers in human rights groups as well as the Mamata camp dismiss the 'sandwich theory' as they claim complete identification of the local population with their respective causes and blame the rivals for the renewed bloodshed and terror. The blame-game notwithstanding, an unbiased examination of the ground reality will reveal that both the warring sides were responsible for vitiating the situation in the wake of the changed post-poll political equations and military balance.

Realpolitik and Lack of Vision

Despite the rhetoric of democracy and revolution, development and people's power, both sides played their part in the politics of opportunism. The replay of Andhra 2004 again cost the Maoists dearly. They supported the Y.S. Rajasekhara Reddy-led Congress in ousting the Chandrababu Naidu government following his vow to finish off the Maoists after they tried to blow up his motorcade. The peace talks failed after YSR demanded surrender of Maoists' weapons and the subsequent ruthless police onslaught wiped out a large number of Maoist rank and file who had exposed their hideouts during the talks.

In Bengal, the Kishenji-led CPI(ML)-People's War had entered into an understanding with TMC in the Garbeta-Keshpur zone after a brief bonhomie with the CPI(M) more than a decade earlier. Following the Maoist bid to do a 'Chandrababu' on Buddhadeb in 2008 in Junglemahal and the subsequent offensive by the joint forces and CPI(M)'s *Harmad Bahini*, the clandestine relationship strengthened despite mutual misgivings over the clash of interests. The anti-land grab movement in Singur and Nandigram witnessed Mamata's hegemonic politics as she occupied the entire Opposition space by elbowing out other mainstream anti-CPI(M) forces since the Lok Sabha polls in 2009. The rainbow coalition has faded further since then.

The Maoists, who had no direct electoral stakes in Singur or Nandigram, survived the clash of interests at that time. Given the importance of 14 Assembly seats in the heart of Junglemahal out of 40 in three districts, most of which the LF had retained in the 2009 parliamentary polls, Mamata kept the Maoists in good humour to get their covert support for TMC.

After her landslide victory in the Assembly polls, however, Mamata changed her tune. She demanded that the Maoists/PCPA be subservient to her changed political priorities and play second fiddle to TMC in Junglemahal. In return, she privately offered to restrain the Centre-state joint forces in their hot pursuit of armed Maoists (if they lied low) and hinted at a marginal role for PCPA leaders in her development scheme, albeit on her terms.

She refused to recognise the emerging political reality across the globe indicated by popular movements, from Occupy Wall Street to the Anna Hazare campaign at home, that democracy was no more only about elections and electoral victories. The widening gulf between the electoral parties, the democratic institutions that they dominate and the people they claim to represent has underlined the growing importance of non-elected voices and the need for new political paradigms and institutional experiments, particularly in grassroots democracy.

Her bragging about TMC's brute majority in the state Assembly reminded of arrogance and intolerance that Bhattacharjee had come to be known for.

On their part, the Maoists apparently expected a quid pro quo for their pre-poll support to TMC and insisted on maintaining their upper hand in Junglemahal in view of their strategic plan of creating guerrilla zones across the tribal hinterland. They refused to recognise Mamata's massive mandate and Junglemahal's expectations from the new government and people's willingness to give her time to deliver. Their armed squads-driven domination exercise, with little or no political control and lack of free interaction with the local people, prevented them from appreciating the shifting allegiance of the anti-CPI(M) forces that had flocked to PCPA and the changing public opinion. Wanton killing of rivals of all hues and suspected police moles, irrespective of their class background, only alienated their supporters and justified the State repression.

Even their worst critics cannot deny that the Maoists had gained popular support to a good extent by tapping the widespread and accumulated anger against CPI(M) apparatchiks and their government in Junglemahal by shedding sweat and blood for over a decade. But dealing with a newly installed populist government was a different ball game. They ignored the lessons from the new left-wing socio-political movements in South America and elsewhere that armed insurgents of all hues now need to contest the existing nation-states and their supporting parties through radical experiments in democracy even if they wanted to win popular support for their brand of revolution. Opportunist politics of making an enemy's enemy a friend at the time of the polls and hit-and-run actions from jungle hideouts are not all about the protracted people's war that Mao had waged.

In this scenario, we will try to draw some pertinent lessons for all from the aborted peace process in the light of the Andhra peace initiative in 2004. This postmortem is intended not to end in a blame game but to identify the still unresolved issues which need to be addressed.

Trajectory of the Peace Process: Conflicting Signals

The five-month-long peace initiative in Junglemahal formally began with a joint statement of the Mamata government and its team of six interlocutors on 7 July following a meeting of high-level officials, ministers and the go-betweens in presence of the chief minister. The team included well-known human rights activists Sujato Bhadra and Choton Das, senior journalist and former rights body leader Debasis Bhattacharya and three other pro-*Paribartan* civil society members, Asokendu Sengupta, Kalyan Rudra and Prasun Bhowmik. Mamata herself picked the team from among those who had been active in TMC-led pro-*Paribartan* campaign before the Assembly polls and also enjoyed the trust of the Maoists and rebel-controlled PCPA.

The statement conveyed the government's 'sincere interest in discussions for the peaceful solution of the problems of Junglemahal' and the appointment of the interlocutors. However, it did not mention the Maoists and PCPA as the partners in the peace process. Promising a special package for economic and social development of Junglemahal and rights to forest dwellers, the statement asked all sides to 'hold fire' while mentioning that the 'government would take legal steps to recover (illegal) weapons'. Appealing to the Maoists to hold talks 'to create a democratic atmosphere free of fear and terror', it reflected the government's strategy to entice potential prodigals from the Maoist rank and file. It promised not to be 'revengeful against those who would wish to surrender arms' and offered them 'financial package and social rehabilitation'.

Taking care of the Maoist/PCPA concerns, the statement said the administration would investigate the 'atrocities and injustice perpetrated during the earlier regime', albeit on the basis of 'specific complaints'. But on the more immediate and most contentious issues, the statement belied the hopes of the Maoists, most of the human rights organisations that are dominated by Naxalite groups and their civil society sympathisers. On the demand for the unconditional release of political prisoners, it merely asked the government-appointed separate review committee (which also included key peace negotiators) to 'expedite its work'. But on the other demand for withdrawal of the Centre-state joint forces, the statement said that they 'will be withdrawn (only) after Junglemahal becomes free of (illegal) weapons and peace returns there'. The message was clear: the forces would remain deployed as a deterrent against the Maoists' bid to regain the turf and their withdrawal would depend upon rebel violence.

But Bhadra and his teammates later argued that neither Maoists nor the interlocutors' detractors insist on making the acceptance of the two demands a precondition for the talks before the polls. But their critics described it as a deliberate violation of Mamata's poll manifesto, which had said that TMC 'does not believe in atrocities in the name of the joint forces' operation but wants to restore peace through humane steps and developmental work'. The statement reflected the complaints the government and TMC had against the Maoists as it asked all to 'maintain the democratic atmosphere, join developmental activities and stop threatening others who are involved in such works'.

Despite the misgivings and tension, a relaxed-looking and confident-sounding Mamata later briefed the media on the peace initiative. She addressed the Maoists as 'my brothers and sisters and comrades' and appealed to them to shun violence and join her development work in Junglemahal.

Mamata's Changed Priorities

But the feel-good vibes changed perceptibly within a week. In her first round of public meetings on July 12 in Junglemahal, Mamata did not delve into her peace initiative and kept mum on the release of political prisoners and withdrawal of the joint forces. She also chose to ignore the post-poll charter of PCPA, which included a judicial probe into the fake encounter deaths of its leaders, release of their jailed comrades and punishment of police officers who had committed atrocities on *Adivasi* women during the LF regime. The charter also listed the demands for genuine autonomy for the region, developmental priorities, people's vigilance on the flow of funds, freedom to continue the PCPA-led development activities as well as recovery of vested and tribal land allotted by the earlier government to the Jindal group for mega-steel plant at Salboni.

Instead of dealing with the socio-political aspects of Junglemahal's discontent, Mamata stressed on her sops to local voters in the form of subsidised rice for poor tribals and non-tribals, cycles for poor school-going girls and promises on development projects that included building roads, bridges, schools and colleges. As she harped on development and establishment of rule of law, and renewed interaction between the nearly defunct administration and the hoi polloi, the Maoists saw the announcements as her populist ploy to consolidate her support base in the contested zone at their cost. Despite her placatory messages that the Maoists should not 'misunderstand her', the tension between the two sides became evident as she publicly accused the rebels of obstructing the government's/TMC's move to distribute subsidised rice and other doles among the tribal poor through official channels. In an apparent retaliatory move, she declared the government's plan to distribute subsidised food from police stations and BDO offices and urged people 'not to listen to those who are stopping them'.

Mamata did not stop at giving an assurance on a rehabilitation package for those who would surrender, but she alarmed the Maoists further by exhorting local youths to 'take up arms for the government and the country'. She capped that call with her announcement to recruit 10,000 special police constables from Junglemahal. It later turned into a flashpoint as the Maoists and some civil society members took it as a clear move on her part to raise an anti-insurgent armed force on the lines of Chhattisgarh's infamous Special Police Officers, being absorbed in the regular police force after the Supreme Court disbanded the Centre-state sponsored SPO. Her ministers and civil society supporters justified the recruitment drive as a move to create jobs for the local youth.

Maoist Nod to Peace Process

The interlocutors met some of the jailed Maoists and key PCPA leader Chhatradhar Mahato between 22 July and 6 August 2011, and interacted with other 'stakeholders', including leaders of the *Jharkhand Samannay Mancha*, a forum of anti-Maoist Jharkhandi and Naxalite groups. Welcoming the peace initiative, the jailed leaders, too, demanded the release of political prisoners, withdrawal of the joint forces and an end to fresh arrests to facilitate the dialogue. Outside the jail, Maoist leader Vikram, in a statement on 20 July, asked the government to release 'senior leaders' and 'withdraw 90-95 per cent of the joint forces' from Junglemahal. In the meantime, Maoist state secretary Akash approached the key interlocutors to know 'Mamata's mind' and after a rendezvous between them on 28 August, he gave the green signal for talks. It prompted the government to assure safe passage to representatives of the underground. Subsequent developments, however, proved that both sides were suspicious about the real motives behind the other's peace gesture.

MAJOR HURDLES

The issues of unconditional release of political prisoners and immediate withdrawal of the joint forces were the major hurdles for the Bengal peace process from the beginning. Human rights groups got bitterly divided between the mediators and their supporters, who shared the government's concerns and preferred to give the six-month-old dispensation some more time, and their detractors, who accused them of condoning Mamata's post-poll volte-face. The spat between two sides made the anti-government camp indifferent and sceptical, if not openly hostile to the peace initiative.

The government-constituted review committee first recommended the release of 78 political prisoners but the government cut the number down to 52. The later list included two Maoists, with the 50 others belonging to two Rajbanshi community organisations that are demanding a separate state in the north Bengal districts close to Assam. But not a single Maoist has been released so far. Though the CM herself announced the release of 52 prisoners before Independence Day 2011, only about 30 non-Maoist prisoners have reportedly been freed so far. Of late, the review committee has recommended the release of some other prisoners and political status for Chhatradhar Mahato and his close comrades. But the government has not acted on it either.

Mamata's reluctance to act upon the review committee's recommendations only emboldened the critics of her government and the interlocutors who had described her decision to go for case-to-case review as 'dilly-dallying' tactics. The pro-government circles cited objections from the Union home ministry and procedural hassles over judicial recognition of the status of political prisoners as the major hindrances for their release. But their detractors accused them of speaking with a forked tongue by referring to the public prosecutors' opposition to the appeals for such a status by Maoist undertrials and convicts.

On the withdrawal of the joint forces, Mamata first tried to assure the underground forces through the interlocutors and later declared publicly that she had restrained the forces for four months to facilitate the talks. But the underground forces contested her claim by complaining about the atrocities committed by the men in uniform on ordinary villagers, which included rape, arbitrary arrests of suspected Maoists and PCPA leaders and hot pursuit of and firing on suspects.

The critics of the government also said that Mamata did not spell out her post-poll position on enforcement of the draconian Unlawful Activities Prevention Act under the new regime and the fate of the 90 detenues under UAPA, including Maoists and PCPA leaders. She tried to assure people through the interlocutors that no fresh arrests would be made under the UAPA. Nevertheless, the arrests of more PCPA leaders and suspected Maoist supporters, and people visiting Junglemahal from Kolkata and other parts, vitiated the atmosphere further. The blame game at the ground level turned ugly and violent rapidly between August and September 2011. Mamata toughened her stand in dealing with the Maoists and PCPA members and the release of their jailed comrades after receiving reports from intelligence and TMC sources on the Maoists' purported move to make peace with some of the *harmads*. The Maoists denied the charge and in turn accused the new ruling party of raising its own armed vigilante groups, *Bhairav Bahini* and *Jana Jagaran Mancha*, by co-opting *harmads* to enforce TMC's supremacy.

In the meantime, the government claimed to have asked the joint forces to move out from their camps 'on specific tip-off against the Maoists', which led to exchange of fire between the two sides. Raids on Maoist strongholds, intermittent clashes with motorcycle-borne armed *Bhairav Bahini* and joint forces engaged in 'area domination', and a poster war in which the newly formed anti-Maoist groups accused the Maoists of sexually exploiting village girls vitiated the fragile peace. Mamata, as the Opposition supremo, had accused CPI(M) cadres and uniformed forces of committing the worst sexual assaults on women in Singur, Nandigram and Junglemahal. She often flanked herself with rape victims at her public rallies. But as CM, she has dismissed complaints of rape victims in Junglemahal, rubbishing them as 'lies parroted by women under Maoist pressure to smear the government forces'. She rubbished other rape victims' complaints in Kolkata and elsewhere as 'fabricated stories'.

Maoists Resume Killings, Declare Ceasefire Later

The peace initiative suffered a huge blow when the Maoists resumed the killings after a lull since the Assembly polls. The renewed killings were aimed not at CPI(M) cadres but TMC leaders and supporters. The murders of key organisers of TMC's anti-Maoist resistance, especially Lalmohon Mahato and Rabindranath alias Babu Bose between August and September, incensed Mamata. Babu Bose was a CPI(M) cadre-turned-popular Jharkhandi faction leader. He fell out with the Maoists after the they hegemonised the anti-CPI(M) platform, PCPA. The Maoists first accused him of joining hands with the CPI(M)'s *harmads* and the joint forces to hunt down and kill their supporters and PCPA leaders. After the polls, TMC had roped in Bose to build up its resistance against the Maoists in the strategic Jhargram area. The Maoists claimed to have killed him to pre-empt that move. Sujato Bhadra condemned the two killings on behalf of his team and expressed fear that it could harm the peace initiative. His team again met Mamata, who vented her ire on the killings but apparently gave a nod to continue the peace efforts.

Within a few days of the two killings, on 3 October, Maoist leader Akash, in an apparent damage-control exercise, announced a conditional 'ceasefire' after meeting two key interlocutors, Sujato Bhadra and Choton Das, on 30 September. The announcement was 'countersigned' by both the negotiators. The statement said 'ceasefire' would be maintained 'for a month in letter and spirit if the government reciprocates the same by stopping the joint forces' crackdown during the period'. Maintaining that the 'government would have to take the initiative to disarm the various other armed groups, including the *harmads*, the Maoists gave an assurance to inform the government about the attacks by such groups through the interlocutors. 'The sincere fulfilment of these conditions would create an atmosphere conducive to talks,' it added. The supplementary press statement by Akash on the same day detailed the Maoists' demands and assurances as he wanted the government to strictly 'confine the joint forces to their camps, and stop patrols and arrests'. In exchange, he promised 'not to use arms and execute people's courts verdicts on punishment (to rivals)'.

But the damage was already done by the renewal of reckless killings by the Maoists.

Mamata's Outburst against Maoists

The CM and top state officials first denied having received the 'ceasefire' declaration in writing after the Maoists made it public through the media, and continued doing so for almost a fortnight. According to the interlocutors, despite being angry over the killings, Mamata had told them to continue their efforts and wanted them to come back with a written statement from the Maoists committing them to the ceasefire and peace talks. She reportedly sounded 'warm' after being informed about the 'positive outcome' of their second meeting with the Maoists. The mediators expected her to appreciate their 'achievement in terms of obtaining the ceasefire agreement' despite the killings by the Maoists, arguing that every peace process had suffered such jolts but resumed later in the larger public interest.

However, Mamata had a different reading of the situation because she used her public engagements to 'avoid' meeting the mediators. Her public reaction became known during her second round of public rallies in Junglemahal on 15 October. Holding the girl child of the slain Lalmohan Mahato in her lap and flanked by Bose and Mahato's widows, she trained her guns on the Maoists. Blasting the underground forces for their 'doublespeak in the name of peace talks'. She called them '*supari* (contract) killers and jungle mafia' and 'cowards who run away after killing people and live by issuing statements to the media'. Challenging the Maoists for a public face-off, she dared them to kill her at a place of their choice and set a weeklong deadline to decide whether 'they will shun violence' or face the music. While the threat of a full-scale security crackdown after the deadline was implicit in her warning, she insisted that the government had so far kept the joint forces on leash. 'Talks are still welcome. But killings and peace efforts can't go together,' she warned.

On 18 October, the interlocutors met Mamata at Writers Buildings for the fifth time but the bonhomie was clearly missing, as government officials later conveyed Mamata's 'dark mood' and 'stern message' to the Maoists through the mediators. The interlocutors offered to step down after a 'battle of nerves' with the government at the meeting. The CM asked them to continue the peace process, obviously because she did not want to take the responsibility for the failure of the talks. Bhadra disapproved the mamat's use of epithets against the Maoists and parried questions on her deadline.

Ground Rules for Truce

On 24 October 24, the interlocutors prepared a six-point note 'after consulting both sides' on the ground rules for maintaining truce before the talks. They asked all sides to hold fire — the Maoists to stop the killings, threats and display of arms, and the government to stop the joint forces' operations and raids on villages temporarily to ensure a congenial atmosphere for the peace talks. Other armed groups, forums and individuals, too, were asked to exercise restraint. This was in tune with a similar exercise during the Andhra talks.

The interlocutors hoped the Bengal talks would be a 'pioneering model for similar ventures in other states'. They invited opinions both from the government and the Maoists within a fortnight to finalise the guidelines and pave the way for a meeting between both sides. The government would have to ensure safe passage for Maoist representatives during the talks, their statement iterated.

Once again Mamata didn't react publicly. The note was 'leaked' to the media, as the interlocutors later complained, by the government. Top government officials conveyed to the media the CM's 'anger' over the 'interlocutors' treatment of Maoists at par with the legitimate government and its forces' and consequent suspicion about the 'neutrality' of the interlocutors. The mediators cited the Centre's talks with ULFA and Naga insurgents as well as the government-Maoist truce in the Philippines to argue for 'equal status' for the opposing sides as an essential precondition for successful peace talks.

But Mamata's next moves made it clear that she was not at all convinced. The interlocutors hoped that she would 'appreciate' their 'achievement of extracting a month-long ceasefire' from the Maoists and 'reciprocate' it by extending the period of restraint by the joint forces and TMC vigilante groups. But to their 'utter disappointment and dismay' they found Mamata 'increasingly cold' to the peace initiative.

Maoist Chargesheet against Mamata

The Maoists raised their pitch with a virtual chargesheet against Mamata's government and her party in an open letter addressed to Bhadra and other interlocutors on 26 October. Akash not only complained about the 'hellish State terror', including rapes but also described it as 'worse than the CPI(M) regime'. The Maoist leader found Mamata 'more eager than Chidambaram' to finish them off militarily. He blamed her for trying 'deceive the people of Junglemahal in the name of peace talks and developmental package'.

Castigating her for launching a 'Mamata-style *Salwa Judum*', Akash cited various atrocities of TMC's *Bhairav Bahini* under the joint forces' protection, and justified the killings of Mahato and Bose as retaliatory action. Claiming that the Maoists had maintained 'restraint since the political change in Bengal and did not kill anybody without reason and tried to avoid clashes', he blamed Mamata for 'trying to kill the Maoists, including him, despite the fact that he had been engaged in the peace talks'.

Nevertheless, Akash affirmed his party's 'sincere commitment to peace', put up a 13-point charter of demands, and asked for a 'direct and written communication from the CM on peace and development in clear terms' and an end to attacks by the government forces.

Making it clear that the issue of arms surrender would not be a part of the agenda for future talks, he suggested a mechanism to 'monitor the commitment of both sides to the peace process'. Reposing faith in the 'sincerity' of the interlocutors, the Maoist, however, rapped them too for failing to investigate their complaints against the joint forces' atrocities and prevail upon the government to stop the raids by those in uniform. It also castigated the mediators for keeping mum on Mamata's 'hidden agenda to prepare for a full-scale armed onslaught under the guise of peace talks'.

On 31 October, Akash issued a statement ending the ceasefire and reiterating his complaints. In a letter to Bhadra on the same day, he said their fight was against 'an unprincipled State' and warned that 'Mamata's model of *Salwa Judum* would not only liquidate us but you too if we can't stop it together'. However, on 6 November, he offered to extend the ceasefire for four months while asking for a monitoring committee for the period before the talks. The mediators viewed the new offer positively in the light of their note on the ground rules, which apparently did not reach Akash before his last letter. But the government took it as a 'Maoist' ploy to get a respite from the security crackdown during the winter when their jungle cover would be thin.

Spiral of Violence Escalated

The CM and her party responded by unleashing the joint forces and motorbike-borne TMC vigilante groups as well as holding public rallies against the Maoists and fresh arrests. The spiral of violence continued as the Maoists killed an old and poor tribal, allegedly a member of the TMC-led village-level anti-Maoist vigilante group, in

Purulia in the first week of November. Mamata reacted at a public meeting held close to the place of the killing by calling the Maoists 'coward killers and extortionists who speak of tribal interests but kill tribals when they refuse to serve their petty interests'. She said that henceforth the government would be stern after restraining the joint forces for four months in the hope of a negotiated peace.

Though Mamata did not announce the resumption of full-scale security crackdown publicly, she asked the Maoist-hit villagers across Junglemahal to organise *gram rakshi bahini*s or village protection guards to take on the insurgents. The joint forces arrested the underground spokesman for PCPA from a hideout along with two others in West Midnapore. In Purulia, the government side engineered desertion from the Maoist-backed *Banavasi-Mulavasi Janaganer Committee* (BMJC) to the TMC-backed *Maobadi Birodhi Unnayan Committee* (MBUC) and public disavowal of the Maoist violence by the converts. Both sides complained of atrocities committed on their supporters in both districts as well as parts of adjoining Bankura.

On 14 November, Maoists retaliated by killing the Maoist-turned-TMC leader Rajen Singh Sardar's father Ajit Singh Sardar and brother Baku Singh Sardar at Khuntar village, close to the Ayodhya Hills in Purulia. Being the secretary of the MBUC, Rajen was the main target of the raiding Maoist squad but he fled earlier. Revealing the shifting sands of the turf war in Junglemahal, Rajen said Maoist leader Vikram had told him as well as some other local youth to join TMC to facilitate their fight against CPI(M) before the polls. He said he was also associated with BMJC, and even served as the rebel squad member for some time before being arrested at Ghatshila. After being released, Vikram suspected him of having arranged his own release by bribing police and working as a police mole. The underground squad leader wanted to settle scores with him and asked his schoolmaster father to send him to their hideout.

In the meantime, equations between the Maoists TMC had changed and local TMC leaders roped in Rajen and his friends to join their anti-Maoist forum. The Maoists retaliated by killing his family members after failing to find him. Mamata described him and his slain family members as TMC workers and the latter's dead bodies were brought to Kolkata ostensibly to pay homage and launch a counter-campaign against the Maoists. Jitu Singh, in contrast, was a common villager belonging to the poorest of the poor. But he apparently earned the Maoist wrath as a suspected police mole like many other poor villagers.

In retaliation, the joint forces killed two local youth, described as members of the Maoist squad that reportedly had an encounter with government forces after raiding Rajen's home. The gun-battle claimed the life of a Naga jawan, too. The killing of the 'squad members' was the first such action of the government forces since the change of guard in Bengal.

Mamata also increased the monetary reward for surrendering every kind of illegal firearms and offered a better package to those who deserted the Maoists. As police showcased the deserters, the CM continued present high-profile surrendered Maoist couples at Writers' Buildings to highlight the success of the government's appeal to the prodigals. The increasing queue of local boys and girls applying for police jobs, with some family members of even Maoist squad members among them, unnerved the Maoists and emboldened the government.

The Endgame

The fast escalation in competitive violence put the peace process on the deathbed. On 16 November, the mediators wrote to Mamata requesting that they be 'released' from their responsibility in view of the worsening situation at the ground level. Mamata was non-committal but again did not want to take the blame for the breakdown. The mediators sent a letter on November 20 to the Maoists seeking contacts. But it could not 'reach the targeted recipients'.

The government geared up for a massive hunt-down of the Maoists in their in their jungle hideouts. The Bengal police intensified its co-ordination with the Andhra police and Central forces for a full-fledged crackdown on the Maoists. The guerrillas were on the run as the joint forces got tip-offs from their friends-turned-foes in the TMC camp, including some former insiders. It is during this time, 24 November to be precise, that Kishenji was killed in an 'encounter'. The Maoist central committee, which had not explicitly supported the Bengal peace initiative, announced the withdrawal from the initiative after calling the killing a cold-blooded murder. On 28 November, all the mediators, except Debasis Bhattacharya, resigned on grounds of their 'helplessness and inability' to 'carry forward' the peace process in view of the 'prevailing situation'.

What Went Wrong?

The interlocutors believed that peace was achievable, because Mamata had recognised 'the political nature of the Junglemahal problem', and given pre-poll assurances for and shown post-poll interest in holding dialogue. The distinctions that Maoists had made earlier between the CPI(M) and TMC also emboldened them. For them, Mamata could have broken the spiral of the government-Maoist competitive violence for the first time in India. Though the interlocutors felt let down by both sides, the key members blamed the CM and her higher officials more for the breakdown of the peace process. According to Bhadra, the government failed to 'seize the historic opportunity' created by the Maoist ceasefire and the halt in Maoist killings for the whole of October.

However, their understanding of Mamata's politics was unclear as contradictory assessments have revealed. Even though they privately insisted on her 'initial good intention', they blamed her 'knee-jerk reaction to Maoist violence, intemperate public outbursts and lack of understanding of radical politics and organisational structure' for the eventual breakdown. The 'pressure from P. Chidambaram, security and administrative mandarins and hawks among TMC ministers and party leaders also took its toll'.

A key mediator was wary of Mamata's 'real intention' after she asked the underground Maoist leaders to come out in public without their hoods, revealing their identities, and announce their commitment to peace talks. Mamata either did not understand the nuances of peace-making or she was trying to provoke the Maoists into armed hostility, he told me. In hindsight, some of the mediators privately felt that Mamata wanted to 'divide' civil society and 'neutralise the 'influential voices' by appointing them as peace-brokers. They suspected that Mamata wanted to turn them into the *Shikhandi* of *Mahabharat* to facilitate the joint forces' crackdown on the radicals. But their detractors accused them of 'belated wisdom and political opportunism at the cost of unity in the human rights movement'.

Interestingly, K.G. Kannabiran, the leading mediator in the failed Andhra talks, had also blamed the then Congress government in Andhra of 'skulduggery'. In an interview to *Deccan Herald* in 2006, he accused the YSR government of using the period of peace talks to 'go over the Nallamalla forests (the Maoist hideout) with a toothcomb'. He said: 'We (interlocutors) unwittingly played a treacherous role in believing the bona fide of the government.' Nevertheless, he did not consider the entire effort to be fruitless. 'I won't say we achieved nothing. It was the people's pressure that brought the government and the Maoists to the table to talk peace. That was a victory for democracy' (See Annexure I). Similar are the sentiments of the Bengal mediators.

The Mamata administration, however, denied any game plan but criticised the mediators for failing to contain the Maoist violence during the initiative. They defended the CM's public position that she could not shun her constitutional responsibility to act against the Maoist killings. The interlocutors' insistence on restraint in the joint forces' operation and their advocacy of equal status for the two sides further eroded the government's faith in them, TMC leaders complained.

The detractors of the government shot back by referring to the withdrawal of the ban on CPI(ML)-People's War, one of the major constituents of the CPI(Maoist), by the YSR government in Andhra and subsequent permission to the radicals to hold public meetings before and during the talks in 2004. According to them, though the Centre has banned CPI(Maoist), the Mamata government could have lifted the ban in Bengal and allowed the Maoists to propagate their politics if they had agreed to do it peacefully. Given her all-time-high clout in the Central government, she could also have released a few of the jailed state-level Maoist leaders and sympathisers as the party had expected. At least, efforts could have been made to facilitate their internal meeting to prepare the ground for talks with the government.

With the Supreme Court's clarification on what actually amounts to sedition and fresh demands to repeal the colonial sedition law, the the public criticism of Indian democracy and its mainstream participants by the Maoists would not have led to its fall but made it resilient, they argued. For them, withdrawal of UAPA cases against the Maoist and PCPA leaders and holding talks with them would have put her on a pedestal different from Buddhadeb Bhattacharjee. This was important in view of the decision of the Maoist leadership not to expose its underground top brass to intelligence surveillance and subsequent killings of its emissaries like the post-talk Nallamalla killings in Andhra and Azad's murder later. This gesture could have addressed the political issues that the Maoists-PCPA had been insisting on and, in turn, reduced tension.

Azad, in an interview to *The Hindu* before his murder, had referred to the 'rich experience and important lessons' of the Andhra 2004 talks. 'If at all a situation for talks arises once again ... we can instruct our leadership in various prisons to take the responsibility ... the mistakes committed in Andhra during the talks with the government will not be repeated." But the glitch in the formula, some people involved in the Bengal peace process said, was the Maoist organisational principle that forfeited the internal stature of leaders once they were jailed. Accordingly, a move to hold separate talks with the jailed leaders was discarded.

The Question of PCPA

Mamata failed to distinguish between the Maoists and PCPA members. She could not see PCPA's democratic character according to constitutional standards, at least for a considerable period. She declined to address the socio-political issues that the Lalgarh movement threw up. PCPA and its supporters both have prioritised the action against violation of human rights by police and healing of the injured 'dignity' of tribal and non-tribal women and poor as well as recognition of the political-cultural autonomy of the local communities. Mamata could have begun by announcing actions against the police officials who were accused of committing atrocities on tribal women in 2008, which triggered the movement.

But she tried to assuage the local feelings through a mere cosmetic move — financial compensation to the injured tribal women which some of them refused to accept. Similarly, she kept mum on the Maoist-PCPA demands for judicial enquiry into the fake encounter killings of several leaders of the Lalgarh movement. Though she has opened investigation into several massacres, including the 40-year-old Sainbari killing, her silence on the Junglemahal killings during the CPI(M) regime is presumably guided by her decision to keep the joint forces and Central government in good humour.

Her stubborn refusal to release the key PCPA leaders, including Chhatradhar Mahato, who is a Congress-turned-TMC leader, smacks of her brand of vindictive politics. Mahato contested the 2011 Assembly election from the Jhargram constituency against both TMC and CPI(M) candidates despite Mamata's request not to do so. Also, one of the peace negotiators was a TMC emissary during the failed talks on seat adjustments with Mahato, a leader close to him said.

According to TMC leaders and pro-PCPA activists, Mahato insisted on contesting because he wanted to underline his democratic credentials and PCPA's independent voice in the backdrop of the CPI(M) campaign accusing it of having a nexus with the Maoists and Mamata. Initially, TMC wanted him not to contest and later asked him to move away from the strategic Jhargram seat, which Mahato refused to do. A section of the Maoists opposed his decision and did not endorse his poorly run poll campaign, apparently sharing TMC fear of the division of the anti-CPI(M) votes.

Mahato finished a poor third by polling only 20,037 or 12.88 per cent of the total votes polled. The poll outcome greatly compromised his bargaining power with Mamata, who dismissed him and the PCPA as a spent force. TMC now reportedly asked Mahato to decide his future politics before his release. According to Mahato's wife Niyati, also a Congress-turned-TMC worker, her husband first wanted his and fellow leaders' release and a month's time to discuss with his followers before entering into talks. With no breakthrough, Niyati and others close to Mahato accused Mamata of a 'great betrayal'.

TMC leaders close to Mamata argued that Mahato and his men would create further trouble if freed now and the matter would have been considered only if the peace talks with his Maoist mentors had borne fruit. Clearly, she preferred to build up her party's organisation in a bid to consolidate her political base at the cost of the Maoists and PCPA. But she must learn from CPI(M), which could not hold its fiefdom despite denying the Opposition any space for three decades.

Maoists Must Stop Killings, Respect Others' Freedom

The Maoist killing of rivals in Junglemahal, particularly TMC leaders, damaged the peace process enormously. The PWG and its ally, CPI(ML)-Janashakti, did not indulge in killings after the ban was lifted and talks were on the cards in Andhra. Analysing the reasons for the failure of the Andhra talks, the late K. Balagopal blamed both the Maoists and the YSR government (See Section II of this book). Taking on the police raj, he said: 'The police should also agree not to kill a person taken into custody, nor hunt down militants and shoot them while eating, sleeping or bathing in a mountain stream as if they were wild game.' On the other hand, Balagopal asked for 'transparency' in the 'allegations that the revolutionaries make about people being police informers, anti-people elements, etc, and (be) fair in their modes of proof, before setting out to punish them'. He said (they should be) 'mindful of the person's social-economic background in deciding the punishment to be given. Indeed, this is perhaps the single most important demand that the people at large would place upon them.'

Disapproving the Maoist killing of political rivals, he said: 'The Naxalites on their part could agree not to harm any and every leader of the ruling party, however small or inconsequential, in retaliation to the state's repressive policies. That any and every policeman would not be killed in retaliation to "encounters".' Balagopal was also critical of the government and police for denying political rights to the Maoists and their mass organisations on the alibi that such lenience would 'tend to increase revolutionary violence'.

But he also pointed out the dichotomy in the Maoist position on political freedom as they considered it legitimate for them but refused to extend it to their rivals, including parliamentary parties. He referred to the Maoist logic that 'these parties tell lies and cheat the people, and allowing people to freely follow them would be tantamount to allowing the people in their innocence to offer themselves to the cheating'. He said: 'This objection too is not without basis, but nevertheless the revolutionaries must agree not to obstruct the freedom, *for truth can be realised only in freedom* (emphasis added), though they will, of course, be free to expose the lies and the cheating.'

The trajectory of the Lalgarh movement and PCPA is ample proof of the Maoist double standards on political freedom. They killed CPI(M) cadres, accusing them mostly of being police moles and *harmads*, irrespective of their class backgrounds, and forced other anti-CPI(M) Naxalite and Jharkhandi factions out of the movement. But substitution of one-party rule of the CPI(M) or TMC by a Maoist variety cannot be accepted as a notion of superior political legitimacy, despite the revolutionary claims over better representation of people's interests.

Despite the widespread dismay over the killings of 'moles' and political rivals, which many of Maoists' sympathisers also share, the Maoist leadership had justified such killings but its logic mirrored the logic of the State. For them, everything is justified during 'war', including booby-trapping the dead bodies of slain policemen or moles. The rotting of the body of murdered Salku Soren, a poor CPI(M) supporter in Lalgarh, at the height of the Maoist power was a grim reminder of this mindless cruelty. But their enemies, including the government forces, too believe in the same axiom. Together, both sides have left little room for democratic niceties in the killing fields across the country.

Like Andhra, the row over the rebels' right to display weapons clouded the peace process in Bengal. Akash not only made surrender of arms non-negotiable but insisted on the Maoist PLGA's right to carry and display weapons demanding equal status for the government and insurgent troops. But Balagopal had found a similar claim untenable in Andhra. According to him, this could be a realistic demand only when and where revolutionaries would be able to bring the government to its knees. But the ground reality in Andhra in 2004 and in Bengal in 2011 were far away from that.

Maoist Dichotomy on Conditions for Peace

Arguing a case for withdrawal of the ban on his party, Azad had told *The Hindu*: 'If peaceful legal work has to be done by Maoists as desired by several organisations and members of civil society, then lifting of ban becomes a prerequisite.' But did he or his party believe in peaceful movements? Here he had couched his reply in terms of people's immediate and ultimate level of consciousness as the key to the transition from one to the other. 'We believe that ultimately people have to take up armed struggle to seize power. But this does not mean we take up armed struggle at the cost of all other forms of struggle and thereby invite the state to unleash its brute force on the people.'

It's another matter when it comes to assessing the level of people's consciousness and whether the Maoists consult the people before changing the form of struggle. According to Azad, the Lalgarh movement was 'a stark example of the transformation of a peaceful mass movement into a violent armed struggle. Lalgarh's peaceful mass movement with simple demands for an apology from the police officials and an end to brutal police repression had transformed into a revolutionary armed struggle due to the brutal suppression campaign unleashed by the State and State-sponsored terrorists like the *Harmad Bahini*.'

But in an interview to *Tehelka* during the peace talks, Maoist state secretary Akash made it clear that the Lalgarh movement's metamorphosis was planned much earlier and executed accordingly. He said: 'Our long-term goal is to establish a people's government in Junglemahal through a process that leads to the establishment of liberated zones and seizure of political power through area-wise occupation. The 2007 all-India congress of our party has already given the guideline that we want to make Junglemahal a liberated zone. All our activities, mass, political and military, are actually aimed at this.'

Divided Civil Society and Hostile Media

The fragile peace initiative in Bengal lacked the wider popular constituency from the beginning. Compared to Andhra, the impact of the Maoist-government mutual violence on public life is still limited to a few blocks in Junglemahal. The hostility of a powerful section of the media in Bengal to the peace initiative and their campaign for a full-fledged security crackdown on the Maoists, even before the talks had failed, weakened the public opinion further. Unlike the positive role of a good section of the vernacular media in Andhra in 2004-05, the media in Bengal in 2011 did not care to build pubic opinion for peace through informed debates. Most of the local media have turned into weathercocks and become the mouthpiece of the government and new ruling party in tune with Mamata's soaring political fortune.

The bitter division in the pro-*Paribantan* civil society, particularly human rights groups, in pro-Mamata and anti-Mamata factions also confused the peace constituency. Unlike the Committee for Concerned Citizens, which had spearheaded the peace process in Andhra, a similar move in Bengal didn't evolve as an independent civil society initiative but a half-hearted move by some people who were close to the CM. The interlocutors' endorsement of the government's line of gradual and conditional release of political prisoners and their decision not to articulate their independent position in public in the initial phase of the peace initiative, also aided the split.

The public spat between these sections revealed the stereotyped nature of the discourses in the human rights movement and larger civil society circles in Bengal. They failed to encourage a fresh churning over of the issues in Junglemahal and attract new ideas and forces in the peace initiative that could have turned it into the beginning of a new politics. The refusal to oppose Maoist killings in unequivocal terms while condemning State terror and denial of the independent existence of the affected people caught in the crossfire in a conflict zone has only eroded the credibility of the human rights community as a non-partisan public watchdog.

True, human rights groups condemned some of the killings of civilians by the Maoists, apparently to be even-handed following criticism by governments and the media. The media, which had often ignored those statements, should be pulled up for their politics of suppression and playing up news, according to their editorial policy. But rights body insiders can themselves vouch for the fact that how much difficult these occasional acts of balancing are and how tentative is their limit. Pending the debates on legitimacy of revolutionary violence against structural violence and repressive State machinery, the campaign against killings of non-combatants — civilians, unarmed members of government and revolutionary forces including POWs and political rivals — is part of international conventions that guide global human rights bodies in conflict zones. But closer home, apologists of the government and insurgent groups both often turn a blind eye to the misdeeds of the side they support.

Many sympathisers of the Lalgarh movement had lamented in private about the derailment of a genuine and unique mass movement by the Maoists in pursuance of their blueprint. But they failed to come out with friendly criticisms, except airing feeble murmurs of disapproval as they feared it would help the 'enemy' — the CPI(M) and the government. Unfortunately, Bengal has no Balagopal that can be unflinchingly persistent in his public exposure of the competitive violence of the Indian State and its armed challengers, as well as its impact on the hapless hoi polloi, not as a politically correct exercise but for greater democratisation of the existing State, its partisans and those political forces who want to replace it with their cherished one. No claimant to the privilege of being the sole spokesman for the people or sole agency of public good and progress should go unexamined under the scanner of 'higher human standards', as K.G. Kannabiran had said in his letter to the Prime Minister after the collapse of the Andhra talks.

Is a Middle Ground Possible?

In our understanding, the vicious blame game may end and a reasonable middle ground can emerge only if the Central and state governments as well as the Maoists are ready to accept the ground reality that neither side can liquidate the other militarily, at least in the foreseeable future. Peace may have a chance if both sides prepare for major paradigm shifts, even for a mutually agreed period, in terms of the new economic and political vision for radical experiments in democracy and socialism, in this case, people's democracy, as the Maoists envisage it. This article is not aimed at exploring these possibilities and the minefields around them. Nevertheless, if we are to believe in the public vibes of the stakeholders in Bengal, a small beginning could have been made in that direction.

Mamata and the Maoists both claim to champion the cause of development and democracy in Junglemahal. Therefore, both could have set the legitimate agenda for the talks. In turn, it could have broken new ground in both terms of contest and engagement between parliamentary and non-parliamentary parties in a contested zone and the emergence of new grassroots politics. Azad had succinctly put up the Maoist opposition to the prevailing model of development. 'It is worthwhile to keep in mind that it is not the lack of development that has become the problem in the rural areas, particularly the *Adivasi*-inhabited areas. On the contrary, it is its imperialist-dictated anti-people development model that is driving them to displacement and deprivation, death and destitution, and extreme desperation.'

Mamata shared this criticism to some extent like some other Congress leaders thanks to her populist instincts and vote-bank calculations. She had championed the plight of the land-losers in Singur and Nandigram and opposed the corporate-propelled development discourse of the Buddhadeb government which endeared her to the Maoists. Her post-election administrative moves so far have largely been in tune with her electoral promises on the land question, despite pressure from the corporate bodies for government intervention in land acquisition and granting of SEZ status.

But the Maoists were not convinced about the development credentials of the Mamata government. In his interview to *Tehelka*, Akash said: 'As long as a government — it may be Mamata or XYZ — takes pro-people stands, we will not oppose it. But it is impossible for the new government to do this ... A white sari and Hawai slippers do not reveal the actual nature of the present government. We have to be conscious to understand how Mamata, despite (her) popular slogans, is actually working for imperial interests. Decline of the CPI(M) raj does not mean the eradication of social fascism.'

Development and Participatory Democracy

If the Maoists want to foil Mamata's political game to win over Maoists' support and pre-empt the corruption inherent in the administrative delivery mechanism, they can voice their opposition by demanding people's vigilance and control over the implementation of the projects, including rice distribution. A monitoring mechanism can be developed involving popularly elected village-level representatives of poor tribals and non-tribals and women that would supplement the panchayats and other elected but virtually defunct local bodies. Mamata's ministers had earlier indicated that she wouldn't mind if the the Maoists launched their own frontal outfit to join the implementation and monitoring mechanism.

On the other hand, Akash (and earlier Vikram, his comrade from the Purulia squad) had evinced his party's interest in overground development activities and grassroots politics. To prove their development credentials, the Maoists had invited journalists in their strongholds to visit medical dispensaries rainwater reservoirs, embankments, rural roads and drinking water supply and other such projects started by PCPA despite severe repression. The government and its joint forces tried to destroy such parallel development efforts to demolish the underground activists' popular support base.

If Akash was to be beileived, the Maoist rank and file were rethinking their role in development politics. 'Both tribal welfare and political power are our primary goals. But one thing has to be clarified here: We don't think tribal welfare will be obtained after achieving political power alone. It is not true that we are not participating in overground politics and we have never maintained that we will not do so. We address both the overground and underground process of politics,' he told *Tehelka*.

His subsequent words indicated further new possibilities. 'We are already opting for democratic participation. That is why we made an appeal to the past and present governments to come to the villages, the *gram sabhas*, then make their policies. If the government calls a meeting in these villages, the CPI(Maoist) will definitely participate.' Does it mean that Maoists will consider participating in panchayat polls which Mamata is likely to hold in 2012 instead of 2013 as scheduled? The key interlocutors believed so after their interaction with the Maoists and claimed to have tried to convince Mamata about this peace dividend.

Akash also indicated that the Maoist desired to monitor the huge funds that flow down to the panchayats. 'We demand an inquiry commission that will take detailed accounts of allocated funds in the Junglemahal area. The point is to find out where those crores of rupees are going ...'

But Maoists don't regard the prevailing self-governance institutions democratic and consider their armed squads, not the collective and pro-active vigilance by villagers, as the final defenders of the people's interests. Also, in the Maoist scheme, people's committees are both the panacea for participatory democracy illnessses and the organs of people's power. 'In our model of development, whether money is allotted by the Central and state governments or is the people's own initiative, everything will be guided, directed, collected and checked by the people's committee. We believe all this can be achieved only through armed struggle. This is because all institutions of the State, from the gram panchayat to Parliament, are hardly democratic,' Akash said.

Experiments in Grassroots Democracy

There is no denying that Panchayati Raj institutions, despite their initial potential, had largely become instruments of political control, domination of a new rural elite and appendage to state-party bureaucracy during the CPI(M)'s virtual one-party rule. As a result, people's participation in the *gram sansads* waned drastically. The situation hardly changed after TMC bagged a few *zilla parishads* and a large number of panchayats in 2008.

However, the question that remains is whether the Maoists would allow the non-Maoist parties to be part of their proposed people's committee or would they like to run it as their own fiefdom. If democracy means de facto Maoist rule through people's committees and people's courts, development through public participation in policy decisions, implementation and monitoring will never be accomplished. In popular imagination, the Maoist party, despite its claim of superior political morality and legitimacy, would in due course degenerate into another supremacy mongering political organisation, albeit of a non-parliamentary hue.

On the other hand, if Mamata thinks that she will hegemonise the entire political space in Junglemahal at the cost of all opposition forces, including the Maoists, and dictate the terms of contests and engagements in developmental politics, peace will continue to elude her despite her government's short-term military and political advantage.

* This is an edited version of the article originally published in the annual issue of *Mainstream* 2011.

Section II

Experiences in Andhra, Chhattisgarh and Elsewhere

Killing of Kishenji and Peace Talks

Varavara Rao

Has the killing of Kishenji dealt a death blow to peace efforts? This question has become a subject of discussion. But the moot question is who is responsible for this situation? Neither the Bengal government nor the Centre have ever been serious about talks. Some of the interlocutors had been desperately trying to make both sides to agree for talks. The Maoists cooperated with the interlocutors in creating a congenial atmosphere for talks. What they wanted was that both sides should observe simultaneous ceasefire. Aakash, the state secretary of CPI(Maoist), declared ceasefire for one month from 1 October 2011, asking the state government to reciprocate.

As Sujato Bhadra (one of the six interlocutors appointed by Mamata Banerjee to initiate peace talks with Maoists in Junglemahal) observed after a month that it was the state government which violated it. The government had not come forward to declare ceasefire simultaneously for one month. All the while Mamata Banerjee was insisting that the Maoists must give up arms, while the Central home minister Chidambaram, in September, said that Maoists must abjure violence, as if they are engaged in it.

It is the Centre-state joint action forces and the *Bhairav Bahini* which had indulged and perpetuated violence on the *Adivasis* of Junglemahal. I as part of a fact-finding team saw myself how these forces reigned terror on people. The team, which comprised intellectuals and writers of Bengal that included Prof. Saroj Giri of Delhi University, extensively toured Nayagram and Jhargram blocks for two days on September 20 and 21.

Before we left for Junglemahal on the fact-finding mission, I had asked the state government of Bengal to tell the Central government to withdraw the joint forces. Mamata herself had demanded the state and Centre to withdraw the forces several times before she came to power. She had alleged that the Left Front Government was misusing the joint forces to curb political dissent in the state. She had argued that on the pretext of tackling Maoists, the LF government was suppressing political opposition and other individuals who it thought were not with them. Mamata also had demanded the release of political prisoners unconditionally as all they stood and fought for genuine democratic demands, braving the fascist rule of LF. She alleged that the government put them behind bars, branding them as Maoists.

The Contrast Between Andhra and Bengal Initiatives

I am highlighting this point to compare the situation in Andhra Pradesh as it prepared for talks in 2004. The Congress Party had never asked the Centre to withdraw the paramilitary forces such as CPRF or BSF engaged in combing operations to eliminate Maoists. It had only promised to hold talks with Naxalites unconditionally if they came to power.

To give the devil its due, when the Congress in Andhra Pradesh came to power in May 2004, it took some measures conducive to talks: a) called back the Greyhounds (the special police force created exclusively to kill Maoists) from combing operations and confined them to barracks as long as first round of talks were over in October 2004, with minor exceptions; b) stopped encounter killings. There were some covert attempts, though; c) the Congress government had responded simultaneously to the declaration of ceasefire for six months from June to December 2004 with minor attempts on the part of government now and then; d) the government had let the ban on the party go on July 21 when the stipulated duration of the one-year ban was over. Finally, the Congress government in Andhra invited the CPI(Maoist) and CPI(ML)-Janashakti for talks on 14 October, facilitating safe passage for the whole contingent representing the two parties to reach Hyderabad for talks. They were to go to the state capital on 11 October and return to Nallamala forest on 21 October.

The team included Ramakrishna, central committee member and state secretary, and state committee leaders from both parties.

The government, however, did not keep its promise to invite the two parties for the second round of talks and violated the ceasefire on 8 January 2005, by killing Lakshmi, an executive member of *Andhra Pradesh Chaitanya Mahila Samakhya* in Kurnool. Lakshmi was running a tailoring training centre in Kurnool, leading a normal, legal life. She had gone to meet her husband Panduranga Reddy alias Sagar in Nallamala forest since there was no ban on the party. She also thought that since a ceasefire was in force there was no problem and harm in meeting her husband. She was brutally tortured and killed by Greyhounds forces. It was just a beginning. The state government went on a killing spree, violating the ceasefire agreement. On 10 January, it killed Raji Reddy of *Janasakthi* in Mulug forest of Warangal and on 14 and 15 January, it 'encountered' legal, mass organisation leaders in Karimnagar and Warangal and tribal women in Nallamala. CPI(Maoist) was left with no option but to withdraw its ceasefire offer from 17 January 2005.

The government had violated the ceasefire because it had scant respect for democratic rights (rule of law) and land reforms — the two main, broad demands put forth by not only the Naxalite parties but also the mediators. While this was the case with a Congress government in a state, its national parent acted no different in 2010. The TMC government in Bengal too behaved the same way later. Com. Azad, the then spokesman of CPI(Maoist), had offered for talks. Com. Kishenji and Aakash had offered for talks in Bengal. Both the governments never attempted to create any kind of atmosphere conducive for talks. They, in fact, were never in the mood to listen to public demand for talks.

Chidambaram, the Central home minister, had appointed Swamy Agnivesh as interlocutor and Mamata Banarjee appointed a full-fledged team. The Congress government in Andhra in 2004 had given a letter to Sri Sankaran, one of the six mediators suggested by the rebels to act as interlocutor for talks. The government in on its own did not appoint any interlocutor or mediator. It had accepted the mediators suggested by the two revolutionary parties and it had also accepted the modalities suggested by them. There was a dispute on one aspect; the Naxalite squads should not move in villages with arms. Both the parties, however, had agreed to discuss this issue along with the main agenda. This was not mentioned by the government during the four-day talks about in October. It was advantageous for CPI(Maoist) not to discuss this issue.

Six years later, Chidambaram invited Swamy Agnivesh to play the role of interlocutor and asked him to write a letter to the spokesman for CPI(Maoist). Com. Azad was picked up on 1 July 2010, at Nagpur, by anti-Naxalite intelligence force when he was going to Dandakaranya carrying that letter in order to discuss the proposal with the party leadership. He and the journalist Hemachandra Pande, who was also caught along with him, were killed the following day in Adilabad forests. Though the CBI conducted an enquiry on Supreme Court instructions, it 'found' out that the encounter was real. Everyone knows how real it was and that it was a murder.

Mamata Banerjee, in the six months of coming to power in 2011, did not show any inclination to withdraw the joint forces. Instead, she declared that she would arm ten thousand *Adivasis* to fight the Maoists in Junglemahal, announcing in ample words that she was ready to create a civil war. It was no less a crime than the creation of *Salwa Judum* by BJP government in Chhattisgarh, which was struck down by the Supreme Court. Mamata allowed her henchmen to create *Bhairab Bahini* replacing *Harmad Bahini*, the notorious private army of CPI (M) created during the LF rule to carry out attacks on people.

The fact-finding team listened to and talked to women raped by *Bhairab Bahini* in that area. We had seen houses burnt by that private army that had full backing of joint forces. When the interlocutors warned that they would withdraw if the government failed to create a congenial atmosphere, Mamata had persuaded them and promised that she would ask the joint forces to remain in barracks. This promise was made in the third week of November. Instead of creating conducive atmosphere for talks, she had let the CRPF forces of Vijay Kumar and Manoj Varma's anti-Maoist forces to surround Com.

Kishenji, take him into custody, brutally torture and kill him on 24 November 2011.

Murder of Kishenji

The forces must have taken him into custody at least on 23 November 2011, the day media carried news that Com. Kishenji was surrounded in Junglemahal area but managed to escape to Jharkhand. The state government deliberately leaked false news to buy time to torture him and kill him.

He was tortured so brutally that his body was mutilated. I have not seen such horrendous wounds standing testimony to torture in my 40 years of experience in claiming dead bodies of 'encountered' Maoist activists. There were three kinds of wounds on his body. His feet were burnt, resulting in the removal of the left foot. His right eye was removed and his right shoulder was broken into pieces. There was a deep cut in the throat. They had burnt his legs and body with an electric heater. And then they had cut his body at several places with rifle bayonets.

When he had become completely immobile, they shot six bullets into his body, including one in the mouth that smashed lower jaw and pierced through the back of brain. Though they had allowed us into mortuary and permitted to take photographs, the transparency ended there. While the photographs show the world that he was killed in a fake encounter, the post mortem report given by forensic doctors speaks about firing from a distance to make people believe that it was a real encounter.

The chief minister, who was in Delhi on 24 November 2011, first feigned ignorance about the encounter. Briefed by intelligence department on her return to Kolkata, she claimed that the encounter took place for three days, that he had refused to surrender and that one thousand bullets were exchanged. The security forces were left with no option but to kill him, she claimed. Her statement is a proof in itself that she and the Centre (since she was in Delhi at that time) knew for sure that Kishenji was in their custody when feigned ignorance about the encounter.

Kishenji on Mamata

Did Kishenji want to see Mamata Banerjee as chief minister of Bengal? Even if he wanted to see her as chief minister or not, it was writing on the wall during the elections that she would become one. Why, everyone, including the CPI(M) leadership itself, knew that they were going to be dumped. People were vexed with the 34-year-old fascist rule of LF. The democrats and intellectuals right from Mahasveta Devi to Sujato Bhadra thought that this unknown devil was better than the known demon. Did anyone hear Kishenji say that he wanted to see Mamata as CM? Did Bengali daily *Ananda Bazar Patrika* hear? Did 'intellectuals' in Delhi hear? If it were to be true, then why did she choose to kill him?

Far away from Kolkata, a Telugu paper (*Andhrajyothi*) published a letter written by Kishenji to his 85-year old mother Madhuramma, two years before Mamata became CM. He had put his heart out in the letter, relating the historic revolutionary struggles being waged in Bengal and other places. In that letter, written not long before Mamata became the chief minister, he had clearly expressed his opinions on Mamata.

I quote from his letter: ' ... This letter is incomplete if I do not write about Mamatamma, the Central railway minister. The struggles of Nandigram and Singur have brought *soubhagya* (wealth and prosperity and even womanhood) to her. But the people who have given her this *soubhagya* through their struggles and sacrifices are losing their *soubhagya*. Many women lost their husbands in these struggles. The land (given to the Tatas) at Singur has not been returned to the farmers yet. The chemical hub in Nandigram is only temporarily stopped. The government is making every effort to establish that hub at Nayachar. Joint scams and murders by CPI(M), Trinamul and the Congress have become a daily topic of discussion for people. In this (land) scam, 60 peasants were killed and 120 more are missing. Rajarhat has become a battlefield. Now the policy of acquiring 100 per cent land has come into force. This policy is being implemented in Rajarhat. It seems the elephant eater is coming (into power) in place of the goat eater. Mamata is waving a green flag to a new train every day. She is fully engaged in *iftaar* dinners. She is meeting the mother of Rizwan (ur-Rahman), the IT professional who died under mysterious circumstances after police and his in-laws forced him to leave his Hindu wife) and playing vote bank gimmicks. The Centre is implementing the anti-people policies, holding Mamata with its right hand and left parties with the left hand.

That's why, dear mother, it is clear that struggles alone will bring light into the lives of people. It is not festivals and feasts that bring cheer to people. Food, shelter, clothes and democratic rights in day-to-day life are possible only through struggles. To achieve their rights people are on the path of struggle.' (*Andhrajyothi*, 27 September 2009)

I have seen this letter written by him and not a composed one. Doesn't this show how he had estimated Mamata? Should I still believe Delhi intellectuals who argue that Kishenji wanted to see Mamata as chief minister and that's why he had become victim of his own choice? Is it not cruel, deceitful and treacherous to circulate such baseless views?

Evaluating Kishenji

Was Kishenji sectarian? Did he fail in bringing all democratic forces into a united front fold? This is yet another argument sans truth. If this argument is true, how do we understand his long march from Jagityal to Junglemahal from 1978 to 2011? His life was an awe-inspiring revolutionary life, organizing a wide variety of people from different walks of life and different economic, social and political levels. People who worked with him would still recall his extraordinary capacity to organize, inspire, grasp and explain things in a lucid way.

He participated and built a wide variety of struggles covering over three decades — Jagityal (1973-78), Karimnagar-Adilabad (1978-80), Andhra Pradesh, in general and Telangana in particular (1980-85 as People's War secretary), Dandakaranya (1985-90) and Bengal. Building a great movement in Bengal itself was a major contribution because it was an uphill task for real communist parties to go to people after the setback in Naxalbari and land reform laced with deceit in the name of 'Operation Barga'. Ruthless repression by the LF government too posed a challenge. Kishenji's role in building and gathering support to Nandigram and Singur movements was commendable. From lending support to PCPA in Junglemahal and alternative development model to building the *Sidhu-Kanhu Militia* to fight back State repression, he played a historic role.

Is it not true that Bengal could see unprecedented and widespread support and solidarity of intellectuals and democrats to Nandigram, Singur and Junglemahal movements that can only be compared with only Naxalbari? Junglemahal was seen as another Naxalbari by many with great expectations. He along with many others played their bit to revive revolutionary spirit in Bengal. But was it not his uniting, driving and leading role that made it possible? He used a variety of methods, including umpteen interactions with media, to ignite hopes in revolutionary masses and planted seeds of revolutionary dreams in intellectuals. He stood next only to Com. Charu Majumdar in building hope of revolution, particularly in Bengal. Kabir Suman and Nabarun Bhattacharya's songs and poems stood as testimony to his enormous contribution.

Were Peace Talks Suicidal?

Was peace talk or attempt to hold peace talk responsible for Kishenji's killing? Accepting proposal for talks proved suicidal after the Andhra Pradesh and Azad experiences? Who will judge — peace negotiators other than the people themselves? Naxalbari and Srikakulam setbacks had happened without any offer or attempt to hold peace talks. Even the setback in North Telangana had happened after it was declared as a special guerrilla zone. There was no talk of peace talks then too.

The Concerned Citizens Committee (CCC) in Andhra was formed in 1997, after an observation made by Justice M.N. Rao while delivering a judgment. 'All the while we are considering Naxalites as a problem and trying to find a solution. But it seems more and more people are looking at them rather as a solution not a problem,' he said. CCC had persistently asked the government to recognise Naxalites as a political party and to hold talks with them. APCLC, PUCL, and many democratic organisations and individuals along with the media in Andhra also supported the view that it was time for peace talks.

People, by and large, also were for peace talks, without giving up arms as in the times of Telangana Armed Struggle (1951). People wanted a respite. A revolutionary party is there to serve the people, obey the people and make struggles and sacrifices for the people. The three top leaders of Central Committee of CPI (ML-People's War) killed in a fake encounter on 2 December 1999. Two among them (Nalla Adi Reddy @ Shyam and Erramreddy Santhosh Reddy @ Mahesh) had given consent for talks with TDP government when CCC met them in forests and spent two days with them, discussing the issue.

Talks with the TDP government had taken place in June 2002 despite their killings. But the process could not progress much as ceasefire was observed only by CPI(ML)-People's War unilaterally and ended in deciding modalities and failed in paving way for the party leaders to come out of forests to take part in the talks. It is true that the party had suffered huge losses in Nallamala after the talks in 2004. It lost top leaders and several cadres. There were heavy losses in North Telangana, saving the leadership. But the movement in AOB (Andhra-Odisha border) is intact and progressed too. So the Andhra Pradesh talks experiment cannot be compared with the Srikakulam setback.

At the same time, one should also take notice of another positive development. During the AP talks only two main revolutionary parties in the country — CPI(ML)-People's War and MCC — had merged to form the united CPI (Maoist). The movement had spread to 14 states in the country. In spite of heavy losses, the united CPI(Maoist)) could hold its congress in March 2007 after a gap of 37 years. The last united congress was held in 1970.

The Maoist movement has become the 'greatest threat to the internal security' of the comprador ruling classes. The guerrilla war has reached the mobile warfare stage in Dandakaranya. The State declared a war on its own people in November 2007 in the name of 'Operation Green Hunt' and now we are witnessing heavy deployment of Army in Dandakaranya. The so-called democratic intellectuals — craving for peace in Kashmir, happy about the JKLF giving up armed struggle and citing Nepal as a model — are now saying that going for peace talks has turned suicidal for Maoists in India. Strange! A revolutionary party obliges wishes of the people. It will never discard any form of struggle in the interest of people. Dialogue is a respite in the long drawn people's war for new democratic revolution.

Joseph Stalin held talks with Hitler. Mao Zedong had shaken hands with Chiang Kai-Shek. And all through the Vietnam War for 20 years, talks were held in Paris now and then for peace. In principle no revolutionary party can reject an offer for peace talks if atmosphere conducive for talks is created more particularly so, when the people and democrats demand it. We may have to review the mistakes, drawbacks and losses in a comprehensive perspective. Going for talks alone cannot be taken as the cause for the losses of movement.

This criticism coming from the democratic intellectuals is more surprising than coming from other Marxist-Leninist parties. In principle, democratic intellectuals are expected to strive for a dialogue, as long as they do not claim themselves as guiding forces to revolutionary movement. There is no atmosphere conducive for peace talks or dialogue in any part of the country from January 2005. It is a reality that the country is in a civil war situation after the heavy deployment of army in Dandakaranya. But this bitter truth will not dismiss the revolutionary party's choice to go for talks if people thrust on it.

Peace Talks in Andhra and Bengal: Some Lessons

G. Haragopal

The peace talks between the Naxalite parties and the state of Andhra Pradesh in 2004 was perhaps one of the most significant experiments, if one can use that expression, in the history of revolutionary movement. The meeting of the radical parties, engaged in a protracted armed struggle to overthrow the Andhra government, and the Indian State, determined to put down the movement by fair or foul means, was an event one could never have imagined until it really happened. But now several questions are being raised: Whether such talks or experiments are desirable at all? Are such talks not responsible for the debacle of the movement in Andhra? What did the peace talks achieve at the end of the whole process? Did not civil society members who worked for it know the nature and character of the Indian State? Where did the parties involved in the dialogue draw confidence or hope from? These and several other questions are important and have to be addressed. But those who are raising these questions should be equally conscious that such a meaningful debate would have had no place if the experiment had not taken place. Assuming that the peace talks have failed completely and that such a possibility existed in the past are something that can be construed as a contribution of the experiment.

Is Peace Possible?

There has been continuous discussion at the national level over the possibility of peace dialogue. Union home minister P. Chidambaram, however deceptive and cunning he may be, continues to mention peace talks on different occasions for known and 'unknown' reasons. This has the Andhra peace talks in the backdrop. In Odisha in 2011, the CPI(Maoist) sought mediation in certain Adivasi-related issues in the wake of the abduction of a district collector and a junior engineer. It forced the plight of the *Adivasis* to become a part of the public debate and opposed the model of development that has no concern whatsoever for the *Adivasis*. The failure of the State to carry its minimum constitutional obligation towards the *Adivasis* exposed the so-called development projects. The Maoists' opposition to reckless mining by the companies and multinational corporations has been powerfully conveyed to the larger sections of society. Thanks to the dialogue, a couple of hundred tribals detained illegally were released as were five activists, who too had been detained unlawfully. If the process did not achieve any gains, at least it prevented loss of human lives for a brief period.

The third instance was of the West Bengal, where Trinamul Congress (TMC) made peace talks a part of its electoral mandate, raising high expectations. The point I am trying to make is that when we judge experiments of this kind, what is important is not the end product but the very process. After all, history is a process of crossing milestones and landmarks towards a destination that none of us is very clear about the blueprint. Many of us wish with all good intention that history ought to move in a particular direction, which it may or may not at a point of time. After all, Marx observed that people make history but not the way they choose to make it. Human beings' creative intervention is essentially exploring alternative possibilities in the womb of history and one may or may not be totally rational in selecting an alternative. Besides, the validity of the option is known only after the consequences fully manifest. One can only draw lessons and improve upon the experiment and its complex political dynamics of transformation. That is where the experiment of Andhra peace dialogue can be of great value and relevance to contemporary Indian society — and perhaps for a long time to come.

Role of Civil Society: The Andhra Experience

The peace dialogue in Andhra was a result of tireless work of the 15-member Committee of Concerned Citizens (CCC) for almost a decade. The members came from different walks of life — academic, law, journalism, civil service and public life. Each member had some public standing because of his/her contribution to their respective fields and public causes. This cumulative social credibility (social capital) was the initial resource which made it possible for them to initiate the process towards a dialogue, although the idea of a dialogue between the Naxalite parties and the state government was an after-thought or a by-product but not the end towards which the process began. The initial objective was to facilitate a dialogue or discussion within 'civil society' by drawing different sections with a primary goal to build public opinion in order to build public pressure on the then CPI(ML)-People's War and the Andhra government to contain, if not stop, the cycle of violence and counter-violence causing huge loss of human life — not only of the revolutionaries and police, but also some innocent people in the crossfire. The loss of human life on both sides is an issue around which it was possible to mobilize public opinion and muster the support of the print and electronic media. Thus the experiment began with a simple objective, but intrinsically it had a wider appeal.

CCC members started their work in the backdrop of an observation that a judge made while dealing with a case related to the Naxalite movement. He said: Can't these two parties at loggerheads explore the possibilities of putting an end to the spiral of violence and counter-violence? This was picked up by the media and some members of society, though it is not clear how the exact process began. It was S.R. Sankaran, a remarkable civil servant and an exceptional human being settled in Hyderabad after he retired as the government of India's rural development secretary, who took the initiative to rally around like-minded people to engage in reducing the violence in which the Andhra government and the Naxalite parties were ensnared. The committee commenced its efforts first by visiting villages in north Telangana, the site of an intense struggle from the late 1970s. Some of the districts of north Telangana like Karimnagar and Warangal were entrapped in deep feudal practices that continued, notwithstanding the historic Telangana armed struggle of the 1940s.

These practices were unbelievable in post-Independent India, supposedly governed by a democratic constitution and rule of law. The land ownership was so skewed that the labor class was helplessly dependent on feudals who exploited them to the tilt. These agrarian relations provided the objective condition for the people to organize, protest and demand change. These were met with stiff resistance from the landlord class, which deployed goons to intimidate the protesters and suppress the movement and gradually push the nature and form of the movement into an armed struggle.

With neither the feudal lords nor the oppressed amenable to any change and both sides determined to fight it out, violance mounted. This violent confrontation by the 1990s almost reached a point of no return resulting in enormous sacrifices of the Naxalite leaders and cadres. In the process of tackling the problem, the state police blatantly violated the spirit of rule of law and threw their entire might behind the landed gentry and thus exposed the true character of the State. This was buttressed by the repressive laws such as Disturbed Areas Act instead of dealing with the problem through agrarian changes and curtailing the power of the landlords. The social and economic power of the landed gentry, backed by the organised police force and the political party in power, closed the democratic space and widened and deepened the armed conflict. This resulted in the killing of political leaders and police personnel. This process reveals the very weak foundations of liberal democracy and limited scope for constitutional governance. The developments led to shrinking of role of democrats and societal organizations, reducing them to that of mere spectators. The State portrayed any social intervention or democratic initiative as aiding and abetting the Naxalite movement. The civil liberties movement, which insisted on observing the rule of law and constitutional norms, was condemned as a front organisation of the Naxalites and reached a point where the police started killing unarmed civil liberties leaders in retaliation to killing of police personnel or political leaders by the radicals. It is true that the civil rights movement has been sympathetic to the cause of such movements and people's sufferings. The organisation kept on telling political leaders and police officers to address the social base of the Naxlite movement and respect the rule of law, which is the source of State power and the only source of their legitimacy to govern. The parties in power never heeded this advice. Instead, they believed in brute force as a solution to the problem.

Civil Liberty Movement: Two Lines on Maoist Violence

The Andhra Pradesh Civil Liberties Committee (APCLC) was, of course, a product of the Naxalite movement. It is this birth that shaped the attitude of the State and opinion of a large section of the middle class which, ofcourse, are not deeply rooted in democratic culture. Consequently, the civil liberties movement which was essentially concerned with the excesses of State power like fake encounters, lock-up deaths and rapes had to seek wider social base and larger concerns with experiential understanding that the arbitrary State power had its social roots in caste violence, family violence and other structures of dominance in the societal order. Once this scope got enlarged, there were number of issues that it started fighting for. In the course of these changes, the organisation started facing criticism from the State, particularly the police, the media and the middle classes, which questioned why an organisation that condemns varied forms of violence does not look critically at Naxalite violence even in cases where their excesses have resulted in killing of innocent people or abduction of unarmed State officials or mutual killings between the Naxalile parties themselves. The civil liberties committee had to invariably to respond to this public or partisan criticism, departing from its initial understanding or mandate. It was in 1987 that the then APCLC president K.G. Kannabiran intervened in the kidnapping of S.R. Sankaran and seven serving IAS officers on the request of both Sankaran and the Andhra government. It was a fruitful intervention in the sense that the problem was solved without loss of human life on either side. This led to considerable criticism from APCLC members, who said it was an unwarranted intervention in revolutionary politics and went against the very mandate of the civil liberties movement. But given Kannabiran's contribution both to legal battles and civil liberties, his action was grudgingly accepted, paving the way for an intense debate in the late 1980s and early 1990s on the role of civil liberties in dealing with the State violence and revolutionary violence. This debate on two lines continued for six to seven years, leading to branching off of one section and the formation of the Human Rights Forum. It was K. Balagopal who not only essayed a long critique of the excesses of the Naxalite parties, but also conceptualised the need for intervention in political violence in the larger interest of democratic transformation of revolutionary politics and social change. The CPI(ML)-People's War responded to the critique in a comprehensive way, marking a significant development as it opened up possibilities of a dialogue between democratic and revolutionary. It is this ground that created the space for CCC and its intervention. In the absence of such social and democratic development, a peace initiative for dialogue might not have had a chance. The CCC member enjoyed unquestionable credibility both on the personal and public front. The anti-democratic forces could not question either the credentials of individuals or the credibility of the group. In a way that was the 'social capital' the democratic struggles of Andhra society accumulated over a period of time.

CCC started its work in 1996-97 visiting the villages and individual families affected by violence. This created an opportunity to understand the ground realities and confront the State and the Naxalite parties, particularly CPI(ML)-People's War. CCC wrote a letter to People's War giving its observations and seeking te radicals' point of view on the incidents and overall understanding of the situation. It was refreshing that People's War responded saying that CCC's understanding was conditioned by a liberal perspective which is in the habit of putting violence and counter-violence in the same bracket. People's War also said that its violence is counter-violence as part of people's resistance and inevitable in a situation where the ruling classes suppress people's movements through force. It cautioned CCC that the force used to maintain status quo should not be equated with forces of change. It conceded that there were some limitations which it was willing to debate and that it would clarify its stance on some of the issues even in a face-to-face interaction with the CCC members. This opened up a whole range of possibilities and scope of intervention for CCC.

CCC Initiative During TDP Regime

It is at this stage that CCC met Chandrababu Naidu, then Andhra chief minister and head of Telugu Desam Party (TDP), and briefed him of the committee's initiative and efforts to restore normalcy in which the State could address the basic issues of the rural people of Telangana region. Naidu appreciated CCC's work and promised his support for the committee's efforts, sauggesting that it could go ahead with its task. The assurance from the chief minister helped CCC to move forward, and it sought a face-to-face interaction with People's War, which responded positively. Some of the CCC members held discussions with three important and senior leaders of People's War for two days. The People's War leaders appreciated the CCC's initiative and clarified their stand on a number of issues, though they politely differed with the perceptions of the committee members. CCC shared its anguish and argued that the role of weapons seem to be overtaking politics. People's War maintained that its actions were determined more by the 'enemy' and it was the State which was pushing the confrontation towards a violent direction and that they were left with no option but to defend themselves, their party and the people. They further argued that their actions were more in self-defense and less as first strike. Braodly agreeing with CCC that violence should be contained, they said they were open to any peace initiative taken by the committee.

CCC again met the chief minister as well as the home minister and briefed them about the meeting with People's War leaders. The government responded favourably and promised to initiate necessary steps to take the peace process to a higher level. Encouraged by the response, CCC continued its pursuit of peace. In the course of its effort, CCC met a cross section of society — civil liberties' committee, trade unions, teachers' organisations, university teachers, liberal intellectuals and organisations sympathetic to people's movements. Opposition parties, including the Congress, welcomed the initiative and gave an assurance of their support. Support came forth from a section of the media, too. A daily newspaper, *Vaarta,* published the debate in its columns, particularly in the letters to the editor section. The debate broadly supported initiative and the letters ran into thousands. 'Civil society' got enlivened and the middle class became vibrant. This created huge public support and built a social environment that worked as an additional pressure both on People's War and the State. The response was very instructive and encouraging to CCC, which lacked organisational network, and political and even financial resources. The support of societal forces can always be a driving force of peace initiative.

CCC encouraged and supported by social, political and democratic forces continued its efforts to ensure that there was no loss of human life and peace prevailed in rural Telangana and to create conditions conducive to a meaningful debate between the revolutionary parties and the State. The second round saw a real breakthrough when People's War named two emissaries and the government two ministers as negotiators on condition that there would be no armed activity on either side. But it is sad that whenever dialogue between the negotiators was scheduled, there was some incident or the other on the part of police vitiating the climate. One can conjecture that those incidents of violence were not accidental but orchestrated. One can see, too, that police had a deep vested interest in the armed conflict for varied reasons, including discretionary powers to use force against citizens and accessibility to unaccountable money under the pretext of controlling the Naxalites. These are the inevitable conclusions one can draw from circumstantial evidence. The sad and most disturbing development was the encounter killings of some of the important People's War leaders, including those with whom CCC has held talks for two full days. This was a serious setback to the peace initiative.

The series of violence that followed resulted in the breakdown of the peace talks. In retaliation of killing of their top leaders, People's War, attacked the convoy of Chandrababu Naidu at Alipiri when he was proceeding to Tirupati temple. This altered the total political scenario. The attack led to the premature dissolution of the Assembly. TDP went to the polls seeking voters' mandate to crack down on the movement, while Congress promised peace talks. Apart from several issues that entangled TDP and its developmental model, Congress said that apart from initiating peace talks, it would also revisit the model of development and tilt it in favour of the agricultural sector. The electoral verdict was in favour of the peace talks. That, in a way, was respected by Congress and People's War, for both saw the verdict as people's mandate. It is this change of context that paved the way for the peace dialogue.

Talks between Maoists and the Andhra Government

As People's War and the Andhra government in agreed in principle for peace talks, CCC did all it could to facilitate the process. It rendered advice and gave suggestions to both sides on how to take the process forward. After Congress came to power, the Y.S. Rajasekhara Reddy government, particularly home minister Jana Reddy, was keen on carrying through the process, for which he he played a crucial role. In quick succession, the state government announced its decisions to lift the ban on People's War and declare 'ceasefire' for three months, allowed the radicals to organise public meetings. Jana Reddy sent a letter to People's War formally inviting it to talks. The state government also announced the names of its representatives who would negotiate on its behalf. People's War was equally forthcoming. In fact, it was the first to announce cessation of armed activity, and announced the name of five mediators and three representatives. The CPI(ML)-Jana Shakti, too, joined the process, by announcing its mediators and representatives. Several discussions were held to formulate the modalities for the talks. CCC contributed substantially and aided both sides to reach a mutual understanding on the modalities. As a part of the modalities, the following terms of the ceasefire agreement were to be observed for three months by the revolutionary parties and the Andhra government.

First, the ceasefire agreement between the state government and

Andhra Pradesh state committee of People's War (also representing the Andhra-Odisha Border special zonal committee and north Telangana special zonal committee of the party) and CPI(ML)-Janashakti Andhra Pradesh state committee will come into force from the day they are agreed to. Second, the agreement reached between both sides will be in force for three months. Third, the agreement will be applicable throughout Andhra Pradesh. Fourth, a monitoring committee has to be formed with mutual agreement to oversee the implementation of the terms of the agreement. If any side alleges that the terms have been violated, the monitoring committee will conduct an inquiry and place the facts before the people and suggest suitable action.

The terms of ceasefire agreement were accepted by both the sides except clause 7 (see appendix), which says: 'During the period of talks, with a view to ensure peaceful atmosphere, police should not obstruct the political campaign of any political party including People's War and Janashakthi.' This clause became controversial because the government felt the State cannot allow any party or group to move freely with arms, for it would send the wrong signal to anti-social elements and amount to abdication of the State's responsibility for law and order. The Naxalite said that telling them not to move with arms amounted to disarming their parties. They further argued that there were several mafia groups and Rayalaseema factions that moved freely with arms. They said arms should not be considered an issue as long as they were not used. Expressing concern, CCC communicated to People's War that arguing in favor of carrying arms openly would be a delicate issue for anybody. The party saw the point and agreed to consider asking its members to move without openly exhibiting their arms as long as they were allowed to campaign their politics.

After considerable grounds were prepared and mutual agreement between the negotiators, the dates for the talks were announced and People's War leaders emerged from Nallamalla forest in full public view handing over their weapons to their comrades. They addressed some meetings on their way and reached Hyderabad on 14 October, 2004 as official guests of the Andhra government and stayed in a government guest house. The agenda for the peace talks was mutually agreed upon. People's War and Janashakti responded to the government's invitation and agreed to participate in the talks. Ramakrishna (RK), People's War secretary, personally headed the team of three members, and two Janashakti leaders also joined the dialogue.

On the first day (15 October) of talks, People's War submitted a letter to the home minister that the name of their party has changed to CPI(Maoist) as a result of thye merger of PW and MCC merger, another Naxalite party, and requested that they should be addressed by this name during the deliberations. Exchange of pleasantries followed. The first issue discussed was the need for a formal ceasefire agreement, on which almost the entire day was spent. The Naxalite parties insisted on a formal agreement, and the government expressed its inability given its legal difficulties and potential public criticism for formally entering into a ceasefire with an armed revolutionary group. Several ways and means were thought of. The mediators expressed their views and maintained the talks could proceed on mutual trust that no side would resort to armed action. In fact, the issue of arms would continue to be a formidable challenge to any peace dialogue at in any part of India in future.

The second day's discussion centered on the need to create a democratic atmosphere in the state in terms of respecting democratic rights, controlling vigilante groups and free expression of political ideas. The deviations of the state government — violations of the rule of law, resorting to extra-judicial killings and encouraging anti-social elements — also came up for the discussion. The radicals demanded withdrawal of cases against political activists and release of political prisoners. The government complained that the movement had violated the rights of the people and attacked and killed political leaders, and the debate ended without any concrete outcome.

On the third day, the question of land reforms and agricultural development came up for discussion. The Naxalite parties highlighted the struggle of the landless people and the police repression they faced. The government representatives recounted the steps that the state had initiated for land reforms and their continued commitment to land distribution. The Naxalites asked why land reform legislations had not been enforced and wanted a white paper on the causes of the failure to implement land reforms. What obviously annoyed the government, particularly the chief minister, was the detailed list of people who were in possession of thousands of acres of land in and around the city of Hyderabad. The government side did not have a detailed record of land holdings, surplus land, land litigations and other details. It was apparent by the end of the day that the government had become impatient and wanted an escape route.

That became clear by the end of day, when no other point could be discussed. It was hinted that the items on the agenda would be taken up in the second round of talks, which was never to be held. The peace, in terms of cessation of armed action, lasted a brief while and the cycle of violence and counter-violence returned. The Congress chief minister kept repeating that laying down arms was a pre-condition for any further peace talks, which indicated his move to renege on the regime's earlier pronouncements and electoral promises. The Naxalite parties continued their resistance movement. The flashpoint came with the return of encounter killings and to which the Maoists retaliated by killing an MLA. At one point, the situation looked worse than the days of the Telugu Desam regime.

Failed Peace Initiatives: Lessons from Andhra & Bengal

The failures of the peace initiative in West Bengal and similar moves at the Central level earlier were largely because of the deceptive character of politics. The Andhra talks fructified, albeit for a brief period, because of a combination of several historical, social and political forces combined with a long democratic tradition laid down by a vibrant civil rights movement. There was such public pressure that the political party that rode to power had to take some steps towards the talks however unwilling it was. Similarly, TMC and its leader Mamata Banerjee are a product of misgovernance of CPI(M) for more than three decades and consequent negative politics. But these negative politics did not led to positive values nor was popular opinion in Bengal organised enough for TMC to be afraid of it.

It is equally clear that the middle class *bhadralok* (eduacted upper caste middle class) is tired and devoid of democratic energy. CPI(M) carried such an intensive propaganda against the Maoists in the name of Marxism that the mainstream middle class did not see Maoist movement as people's struggle as an alternative. The CPI(M)'s latest resolution on the Maoist movement makes one feel that it is worse than a resolution by the BJP. It was expected that after being out of power, CPI(M) leaders would now ask themselves why certain sections of the people support the Maoist movement. CPI(M) should have supported the peace initiative in the longer interest of the people of Bengal. This is the major objective limitations that impaired the Bengal peace initiative.

The second lesson to draw from the Bengal experience is that TMC has neither an ideology nor an economic policy of its own. It relies fully on the global model of development, which is evident in Mamata's choice of finance minister: former FICCI chief Amit Mitra. CPI(Maoist) and the other Naxalite parties are the only political force opposed to this path of development and are organising the people, particularly the *Adivasis*, for this purpose. Global capital in nexus with the Indian State is determined and willing to use means fair or foul (mostly foul) to put down the movement. The repeated statements of Union home minister P. Chidambaram and his pressure on the Indian Army, combined with the Prime Minister's statement that Naxalites are the greatest security threat to the nation, leave no space for any state government to maneuver power at the local level.

The third lesson that civil rights or democratic rights groups should learn is that they have to focus on and address civil society more than the State. In Bengal's case, people who worked for peace put too much hope in Mamata's rhetoric, instead of creating the necessary pressure on the administration from society. That is the reason why there was haste in completing, rather than strengthening the process. In fact, the citizens for peace initiative at the national level were seized of the issue and were planning to mobilize different sections and organise a march in Kolkata. Binayak Sen volunteered to take the responsibility and visited Kolkata twice for the purpose. The peace intiators in Bengal did not even try to communicate to other organisations to put together a concerted and coordinated action.

The fourth lesson is that CPI(Maoist) should recognise that while it defines the Indian States character in its own way, it does not reflect in its strategy or practice. After the Andhra experience one should know that the State forces, particularly police, take maximum advantage of any new party coming to power and use maximum force before the party in power loses its freshly acquired legitimacy. Police also ensure that the new political force depends on the coercive arm before it decides to take action against erring police officers of the previous regime.

The fifth lesson is that law and order, notwithstanding the fact that it continues to be a state subject, has been completely taken over by the Central home ministry. No government in a state where struggles are going on has the guts to tell the Centre not to transcend the limits of federal polity. The kiling of top Maoist leader Kishenji in a fake encounter by the joint forces — a total setback to the peace initiative — is a clear indication that that is where the real power of decision-making lies. India has perhaps reached a point where no state-level peace initiative has democratic space. The only option still open to peace initiatives is to mobilise democratic opinion at the national level.

And the last lesson is that a peace initiative is something that society cannot afford to give up under any condition. In fact, the State scuttled the last attempt of Azad, CPI(Maoist) politburo leader who too was killed in a fake encounter, to further the peace prospect. The emphasis put by Kobad Ghandy, another CPI(Maoist) politburo leader, on the urgent need of this initiative lies in the very historical context where neither the revolution is round the corner nor the State is in a position to put down the movement. Hence, several experiments to contain violence and bring about a radical transformation with minimum loss of human life are the need of the hour.

Naxalites in Andhra: Have We Heard the Last of the Peace Talks?

K. Balagopal

The government of Andhra Pradesh says it continues to be open to talks with the Naxalites and that it is the latter who have broken off negotiations. What the government does not say is that the Naxalites broke off talks only after it became clear that the government had no intention of stopping the killing of their cadre. To this extent, the Naxalites' decision to leave the table cannot be faulted and the principal responsibility for restarting the process would lie with the government. But the revolutionaries have an equal responsibility, namely, to ensure that the unreal tone and the drama of the first round is eschewed and the two sides conduct themselves with the degree of realism one supposes they are capable of.

It began as a tenacious essay in political realism, entered a phase of sheer drama unbelievable in its unreality, and ended in the bitter rattle of gunfire. The reference is to the 'talks' between Y.S. Rajasekhara Reddy's government in Andhra Pradesh and the Naxalites. To be fair to the devil, Rajasekhara Reddy never really believed in the talks and never joined the effort, nor the theatre that was enacted in Hyderabad for about a week ...

But if Rajasekhara Reddy (let us call him YSR hereafter) did not join the effort after becoming chief minister, he was complicit with it in its origins in the pre-election campaign ... In Telangana, he heard many complaints about police lawlessness. It was characteristic of the man that even in that most expansive pre-election mood the one thing he took care not to promise was relief from police harassment in case his party came to power ...

But what YSR did promise was that his government would initiate talks with the Naxalites to 'solve the long-standing problem' ... Getting elected was a very pleasant shock for Congressmen ... A certain humility is natural in such circumstances and so to begin with, steps were taken on various fronts to implement some of the promises. The talks with the Naxalites was the most high-profile of them.

The ban in force from 1992 against the CPI(ML)-People's War (as the party was called until September 2004) was lifted, and cessation of police operations against the Naxalites was announced in June 2004. The principal Naxalite parties, especially People's War, reciprocated by ceasing violence against instruments and partisans of the establishment. For a full six months there was practically no killing in police-Naxalite war, which is a record for the last decade and a half at least. The people living in the main areas of conflict had a taste of what they had long forgotten: life reasonably free of fear.

A more detailed code of conduct for the period of the talks needed to be agreed about before the dialogue could start. Would the police continue their search for underground cadre, and if so by what kind of means? Would they take lawful measures against armed cadre, such as, for instance, arresting them and seizing their weapons, or would the Naxalites have the run of the state? On their part, would the Naxalites indulge in violent forms of protest such as the burning of buses and blowing up of government buildings, and would they use force as an instrument of struggle, for instance, in land occupation? Or would they confine themselves to lawful means of agitation during the period of the talks? It would obviously be difficult to get the dialogue going without some agreement on these matters.

Need for Agenda

An agenda for the talks too needed to be agreed on, if possible. The People's War and the CPI(ML)-Janashakthi announced a team of representatives to talk to the government about the code of conduct (which came to be called the ceasefire agreement, though many in government claimed to be uncomfortable with the notion of a ceasefire, which in their understanding could apply only to two sovereign armies and not between a legitimate force and an illegitimate rebel group).

The People's War was the party that was mainly targeted for the talks for the obvious reason that it is far and away the strongest of the Naxalite groups. The CPI(ML)-Janashakthi got tagged along apparently because it was working together with the People's War on many issues. The other armed communist revolutionary groups — there are at least five more which can claim varying degrees of armed efficacy and popular support — were not sure whether they were invited, though some of them expressed willingness to join the talks if invited. At least two, the CPI(ML)-New Democracy and CPI(ML)-Unity Initiative, whose activities tend to be predominantly peaceful, showed no interest since it — probably rightly — saw the talks as a matter between the State and the more violently inclined Naxalite groups.

Interestingly, while sympathisers of the Naxalite movement outside Andhra Pradesh have been heard to express doubts about the desirability of the talks, practically no one in the radical left camp in the state saw the talks in themselves as undesirable. Left to themselves, the normal reaction of the average radical intellectual or activist in the state would have been to ridicule the notion of the talks, and indeed one prominent writer who is generally left to herself did ridicule the process, but the rest sensed that there was a strong current of public opinion cutting across class and region favouring some kind of dialogue between the revolutionaries and the State, and sensibly bowed to it.

It was realised by the two sides that talks require mediation, and so a committee of mediators was agreed upon. In this as in much of the first round of the talks, the Naxalites practically had their way: the mediators were essentially their choice. In the heady months of June-October 2004 there was an air of the return of the prodigal child in all official response to the Naxalites. The only thing missing was the fatted calf. This strange pampering, which the uncommonly benign air the home minister perfectly sported, was merely one moment of the unreality of those days. The mediators and the representatives of the Naxalites discussed the matter of the code of conduct with the government and a draft of the terms of ceasefire took shape by the end of July. The ceasefire agreement had eight clauses. All of them amounted to only one thing: that the two sides would, for the duration of the talks, refrain from the acts of violence that had permeated revolution and counter-revolution during the last decade. Clause 1 committed the two sides to non-use of firearms and any and every means of destruction of life. Clauses 2, 3 and 6 set out the various acts of violence the People's War had habitually committing in the course of its fight against the State, and committed that party to abjure the lot for the duration of the talks. Clauses 4, 5 and 8 similarly listed the repressive acts the police had been habitually committing in the course of their counter-insurgency operations and committed them to abjuring the lot too.

Clause 7

That leaves out Clause 7, which has become historic in a manner of speaking. The issue this clause addressed was whether the Naxalites would go around sporting weapons in public view during the period of the talks. From the beginning, it was clear to all (or so we thought) what unlike the previous dispensation of Chandrababu Naidu, this government would not insist as a pre-condition to the talks: that the Naxalites put down their weapons, that is to say give up armed struggle altogether. The issue for the code of conduct was only this: during the period of talks, when the Naxalites were free to move around spreading their political message of revolution and organising people on issues would they keep their firearms in some hideout, or go around with the guns slinging from their shoulders? The government insisted that they refrained from moving around with weapons. Clause 7 as proposed read: 'During the period of talks the People's War as well as other political parties will be free to undertake propagation of their politics without carrying weapons, in a manner that will preserve the atmosphere of peace.' The wording was somewhat elliptic but the intent was clear.

Hazy Controversy

There has been some hazy controversy regarding the incorporation of and assent to this clause, with trading of charges of bad faith on both sides. The fact perhaps is that it was initially not seen by the revolutionaries as involving any major compromise, but they had second thoughts later. In fact, their first response was the right one, but soon rhetoric took over and there could be no going back thereafter. It is obvious that while a government working under a rule of law regime can in public interest very well open talks with armed groups that reject its law without making it a precondition that they give up armed struggle, it cannot assure them that they can freely move around with weapons and the police will look the other way. It is no answer to this to say that a lot of ruling party men have unlicensed weapons and the police do look the other way when they take them out. They do, but the point is that the State cannot and does not on paper commit itself to such licence. Perhaps, if the revolutionaries — or rather, their intellectual sympathisers, who can never have enough of blood and gore — had not taken off at a tangent and messed up the matter with uncalled for rhetoric, Clause 7 could have been approved as proposed by the government, with an unwritten understanding that in areas where the revolutionaries faced danger from renegades or other criminal counter-insurgents, they could carry unostentatious weapons of defence, and the police would not interfere.

But any such possibility was foreclosed by radical ideologues of various kinds who quickly got into the act. It was said that the people had a right to carry weapons so long as the State in the form of its police and armed forces did, and any view to the contrary was an ideological surrender to the hegemony of law as an instrument of the State. More earthily, it was said that the oppressed people could no more be asked to abjure weapons than cattle could be asked to give up their horns, or tigers their claws (if claws are what tigers have). Along a different ideological trajectory, it was said that when the gods of brahminical Hinduism were all armed to the teeth, the Dalit-Bahujan masses had every right to arm themselves. Radical theories of political violence had a field day, as they would, since Andhra Pradesh is unfortunately full of pen-pushers whose capacity to withstand the reality of a violent conflict is untested but are fascinated by violence in ink.

Anyone hearing the discussion would have thought that the very justification of armed struggle was in question, and that the government was going back to Chandrababu Naidu's position: that the government will talk to the revolutionaries only if they give up armed struggle. By and by YSR would start saying that, but that was not the issue when disagreement initially cropped up concerning Clause 7 of the ceasefire agreement. Indeed the way that innocuous term of the ceasefire agreement was made to look like total surrender of weapons for good and all not only physically, but ideologically as well, has resulted in an obfuscation of the issue that enabled YSR to talk of total disarming as a pre-condition for talks and yet give the impression that he was insisting only on having his way with Clause 7.

At that time, however, the strong public mood in favour of talks saved the situation. It was suggested by well-wishers of the talks, and accepted by both sides, that the disagreement over Clause 7 would not be allowed to become an obstacle to the talks. The rest of the ceasefire agreement would be finalised and talks initiated, with the controversial clause itself being an item on the agenda of the talks. This, of course, put the revolutionaries in a happy position, for until the time there was some agreement on Clause 7, they would go around the countryside with weapons, notwithstanding the ceasefire and the dialogue. That the government knowingly countenanced this is of a piece with the prodigal child syndrome referred to above. Or perhaps it was the long rope syndrome: it is a little difficult to be certain. For soon the press started publishing news — with telling photographs of armed squads of the People's War and Janashakthi going around villages, holding meetings, occupying lands, issuing warnings and threats to people accused of harassing or cheating the people or informing the police about the movements of the revolutionaries, ordering externment of some of them from villages, and so on. While this state of affairs caused understandable disquiet in more than one quarter, the police started expressing disquiet about collection of large amounts of money by the revolutionaries 'taking advantage of the freedom given to them'. There is no evidence that even the worst kind of repression had ever diminished the capacity of the revolutionaries to collect such money as they wanted, and at will at that, and the police knew this better than any one. That nevertheless they chose to make a big issue of it is probably because they thought they could use it to disturb the popular mood which had turned very friendly towards the revolutionaries. The most attractive thing about revolution is its deep moral tone, and extortion ill becomes it. But there could be another reason: the police in general — and this has nothing to do with the presence or absence of militancy in the area — tolerate extortion the least among all offences; in fact, it enrages them, because they dislike competition. There are no greater organised extortionists than the police, and they do not like anybody cutting into their business.

But popular mood remained friendly, in fact hugely so, and the talks did start. Nobody had any notion what the agenda could be. Many among the public seem to have thought that the ultimate agenda was the establishment of peace, which can only mean that armed struggle would be given up by the revolutionaries. In tune with this, the talks were frequently described as 'peace talks'. This expectation, which had no basis in any fact, is probably one reason for the enthusiastic reception the talks got from quarters normally quite unfriendly towards any suggestion of a civilised response to the Naxalites. Equally surprising is the belief entertained by many otherwise intelligent persons, including some known as competent social analysts, that the government and the revolutionaries would sit across the table and discuss how best to solve the problems of poverty, untouchability, dowry, drought and so on. They should have known that no government sanctified as lawfully elected will accord that degree of respect to an armed group that is a law unto itself, unless the group is either ready to lay down arms if some policy changes are agreed upon, or has reached a degree of strength that makes normal governance impossible.

That the Naxalites are in no mood to disarm themselves is a well known fact. And it can be nobody's case that they have the kind of strength that makes normal governance impossible in Andhra Pradesh. That they are capable of causing substantial degree of inconvenience to the administration in its routine functioning in areas of their strength and influence is true. But by no stretch of imagination can it be said that administration has been crippled to a degree that it makes it impossible for the government of the state to function without letting the revolutionaries into the privilege of policy-making, even as they are free in the interregnum between one round of the talks and the next, and permanently thereafter, to carry on armed revolution. This should have been obvious but was apparently thought irrelevant by many quite intelligent people. The amount of wool that flew around Hyderabad in those heady weeks could have clothed a sizeable Arctic expedition.

Give and Take

In the realm of practical politics, dialogue can only be on the basis of give and take, unless one side has made life truly impossible for the other. One area where give and take was possible was in the matter of the forms of violence and counter-violence that the two sides have developed over the years. The police could agree to stop torturing the kith and kin of a militant to reveal his/her whereabouts, or to put pressure upon the family to make the militant surrender. They could agree to see provision of food or shelter to militants as a matter of political sympathy or social empathy and not a crime. They could agree therefore not to harass people who do so. They could agree not to see the encouragement of the Naxalites behind every protest movement in the areas of their activity, nor to construe such encouragement, if true, as in itself criminal, so long as the grievance was just. They could agree not to obstruct any social or economic benefit obtained by the people with the help or assistance of Naxalite activity. In plain terms, to agree not to punish political and social activism in the name of preventing violence. This would be a difficult decision to take, but it would have to be taken ... The State must agree not to suppress political aspirations and their peaceful expression in the name of the revolution that lurks behind it, even if we all know that it does. The police should also agree not to kill a person taken into custody, nor hunt down militants and shoot them while eating, sleeping or bathing in a mountain stream as if they were wild game. And not to corrupt militants and create covert operatives inside the revolutionary ranks.

The Naxalites on their part could agree not to harm any and every leader of the ruling party, however small or inconsequential, in retaliation to the State's repressive policies. That any and every policeman would not be killed in retaliation to 'encounters'. That the routine political-administrative activity of the establishment would not be forcibly prevented. That elections and election campaigns would be allowed unhindered and people's freedom to choose to be followers of the Congress, Telugu Desam Party or BJP would not be curtailed. It would be objected to on the ground that as we all know, these parties tell lies and cheat the people, and allowing people to freely follow them would tantamount to allowing the people in their innocence to offer themselves to the cheating. This objection too is not without basis, but nevertheless the revolutionaries must agree not to obstruct the freedom, for truth can be realised only in freedom, though they will, of course, be free to expose the lies and the cheating. The revolutionaries should also agree to be transparent in the allegations they make about persons being police informers, anti-people elements, etc, and fair in their modes of proof, before setting out to punish them. And mindful of the person's social-economic background in deciding the punishment to be given. Indeed, this is perhaps the single most important demand that the people at large would place upon them.

Distribution of Fallow Land

The amount of violence the two sides have subjected to each other is such that the mutuality implied by such an agreement would be attractive to both. And the people living in the affected areas would be immeasurably happy with it. It could, therefore, be a fruitful agenda for the talks. Some other issues could be added to it, without transgressing the limits of plain realism. There are some thousands of acres of fallow land, mostly in the districts of Warangal, Karimnagar and Adilabad, which were occupied forcibly by the revolutionaries.

They intended that the poor should cultivate it but the police would not allow that. With the original landholder scared of the Naxalites and the poor scared of the police, the land remains fallow. There could be some agreement beneficial to the poor about the disposal of the land. Not all the original landholders were landlords. Some were merely political enemies of the Naxalites or their cadre, and otherwise ordinary farmers ...

There is another important matter that both sides could fruitfully come to an agreement on. This is the mutual obstruction of political freedom. Whether legally banned or not, the Naxalite parties and their mass organisations face tremendous obstruction from the police. They are not permitted to hold meetings, distribute pamphlets, stage cultural programmes, etc. For offences of violence committed by the underground radicals, the activists of the mass organisations suffer terrible police retaliation. They have not infrequently been killed as surrogates for the underground. In turn, they — especially the CPI(Maoist) as the People's War is now called — have made life quite miserable for the local supporters and leaders of the TDP and Congress (indeed all the parliamentary parties) in the areas of their influence. Election time can be pretty bad, but even normal times are not altogether safe for them. The elected representatives in the local bodies are especially vulnerable. They can be killed, maimed, their property set on fire, the land planted with red flags, etc, for no greater reason than that they represent the repressive regime at Hyderabad. The Maoists, at any rate, have never made a secret of the logic of retaliation: when these parties, in power or in opposition, deny us our political freedom, why should we respect theirs? It is precisely because of their logic that a fruitful agreement that will permit both sides to exercise their political freedom — from participation in polls to publication of pamphlets — would be of value to both.

We have already seen the likely objection — especially from the police — that political freedom for the revolutionary point of view will tend to increase revolutionary violence. If revolutionary violence is found attractive by significant numbers of the people, and will grow at the first opportunity, then that says something about the existing state of affairs, and whatever any one may think about such a state of affairs, shutting it out forcibly from society's sight is no response. This far, the dialogue could reasonably have gone. Since an extended ceasefire with armed rebels is unlikely to be acceptable to any government in the absence of the disarming of the rebels on the agenda of the talks, the proper thing would have been to fix a brief agenda as outlined above, get down to the nuts and bolts of it, and conclude it as fast as possible. Indeed, if the dialogue had been understood as a brief and pointed matter, the 'controversial Clause 7' could have been simply ignored.

Resemblance to Theatre

But that is not what happened. The closer the situation came to the actual beginning of talks, the more unreal it became. The government never spelt out any agenda, and the revolutionaries, for their part, seemed to have thought of it as some sort of a public debate between ruling class politics and revolutionary politics. Indeed, a large number of their followers too appear to have thought so, and were quite happy about it, for if it was to be a debate, it was a foregone conclusion which side would win. There was, for instance, a proposal that the talks should take place by turns at Hyderabad, and three towns in the three regions of Andhra, Telangana and Rayalaseema. The resemblance to theatre is unmistakable. The resemblance survived the prologue and extended to the first act too. When the time came for the revolutionary delegation to emerge from the underground for the talks, the delegation of five (at least two of whom are known mostly to live in Hyderabad) went from their normal places of activity to the Nallamalai forests, and then emerged in the full glare of television cameras. They could well have left their weapons somewhere and come down to Hyderabad if they were not already there. Instead, they came out of the forests weapons in hand, followed by their comrades to whom they then handed over their weapons. Turning their backs on the jungle they walked weaponless into the 'mainstream' as their comrades disappeared into the forests, arms and all, camera bulbs flashing furiously.

At Hyderabad, the government put them up at one of its guest houses, arranged police security and let them interact freely with the public. The media and public attention they received was stupendous. Any unsuspecting stranger walking into Hyderabad in those days could well have thought that they were leaders of a victorious rebel army, come to receive the sceptre and the crown at the defeated capital. The chief minister vanished from the TV screen, and it was the revolutionaries all the way. Delegation upon delegation from different walks of life, political persuasions and ideological inclinations called upon them. Problems of various sections of society were taken to them and they were asked to raise them with the government in the course of the talks. Even prominent Ambedkarites who had on more than one occasion accused the revolutionaries of not comprehending caste and not fighting for its annihilation for the reason that their leadership at the top is upper caste, attended the durbar of the revolutionary delegation, whose main spokesman Akkiraju Haragopal also known as Ramakrishna was a brahmin by birth, to suggest an agenda for the talks that would take in the components of social revolution.

Disquieting Phenomenon

Forgetting the ideologues, in the minds of the literally hundreds of ordinary people and activists who thronged the Manjira Guest House, there was this assumption, perhaps, that the government had called the revolutionaries to Hyderabad to discuss intractable social issues and people's problems with them, and so it made sense to add their problems to the agenda. It did not occur to any one to ask themselves why the government would want the advice of the revolutionaries, for it is nobody's guess that the government does not solve people's problems not because it is not aware of them or because it has no in-house experts in its secretariat who can advise it as well. Nor did anyone ask why all problems of society should be discussed with the Maoists, whose programmatic concern — and certainly their comprehension — had always been confined to only a few. Perhaps the less innocent assumption was that the government would sense the threat of violence behind the issues raised for discussion by the revolutionaries, and resolve them in the manner suggested by them. Indeed, this undercurrent of faith in the efficacy of the gun over persuasion or democratic pressure was the most disquieting thing about the otherwise quite charming adulation the revolutionaries received in those few days.

Most of those who visited them — delegations of the physically disabled, *Adivasis*, hutment dwellers, etc — certainly knew much more about the issues they had been fighting for than the revolutionaries did, and they knew that the government had never deigned to send any delegation other than the police to answer their agitation. In normal circumstances, any suggestion that the government discusses their issues with some other party or organisation would have given rise to understandable resentment at the usurpation of their agenda, but now they themselves voluntarily invited the usurpation. It is not that overnight they had acquired faith in Maoism. They were merely expressing the cynical faith that lurks under the democratic skin, that the gun is a more effective political weapon than any devised by democracy.

The revolutionaries rose to the dramatic occasion and promised to talk of everything with the government — land, caste, gender, the World Bank, globalisation, minority rights, etc. To what effect, no one knew. And no one asked, for it was a grand show that no one wanted to spoil. And to give them their due the revolutionaries handled their role with poise and dignity. They avoided the usual radical habit of construing all dialogue as an exercise in putting the interlocutor in his/her place. They of course made it a point to tell people that the solution to all problems lay in their leadership. They meant their political leadership but those who had come to them had already accepted that at a more cynical level.

And on this note the talks started. Some one should have taken things in hand at this stage, made the two sides see sense, and pared down the agenda to the politically feasible — and saw to it that the talks would be a quiet face-to-face affair with no more than two or three on either side, give or take a mediator.

That is how all serious dialogue between governments and rebels takes place anywhere in the world. But not in Hyderabad. In retrospect one wonders whether the radicals and the government both were not laughing up their sleeves. On the government's side, to declare an agenda would be to give legitimacy to the notion that there was something the government should discuss with the revolutionaries. To just sit across the table and listen to them hector the establishment without committing itself to anything in particular would belong to the genre of humouring the prodigals, and that the government had no objection to doing.

The revolutionaries, for their part, even as they were talking to the government, were in fact addressing the public behind it. For about a decade if not more, they were known to the public outside their areas of activity through news of death — death at their hands or their deaths. Intelligent people would often pose the question whether there was nothing more to revolution than killing and getting killed.

Now the revolutionaries had a good chance to tell the public that they cared for a wide range of issues of justice. Intentionally or otherwise the revolutionaries utilised the first round of talks to address the public and answer the questions often flung at them. In this they succeeded. They also held a series of well-attended public meetings in various corners of the state, spreading the more usual kind of fire and brimstone message and giving heart to their followers who had grown tired over the years of talking of nothing but police repression.

The only concrete decision that came out of the first round of talks that were held from 15 to 18 October 2004 was that a commission of sorts would be constituted to go into the question of distributing land to the landless. The People's War which had in the meanwhile become the CPI(Maoist) after merging with the MCC of Bihar, insisted that the commission should not consist only of government officials but also include persons with a history of involvement in agitation of land to the poor. The government agreed, but nothing was put on paper, and soon enough the government forgot about it. It was said that the second round of talks would take place by and by but neither a date nor any more concrete agenda than in the first round was agreed upon.

At that time, it was generally expected that there would be a second round, though any one with any political intelligence must have realised that the government could not go on playing the benign host for ever. The ceasefire was effectively used by the Maoists and all the revolutionaries to re-enter areas that they had practically vacated for quite a few years. With 'Clause 7' undecided, they were going about with weapons, planting red flags in lands, issuing orders to all and sundry, holding public meetings disseminating the idea of armed struggle. And they had from the beginning made it clear that there would be no surrender of arms and abandonment of their armed struggle at the end of the talks. Any indefinite continuation of this state of affairs would evidently be unacceptable to the government. It would, quite likely, insist on more purposeful talks in the second round, namely, some bargain that would make life easier for its rural representatives and administrators while conceding something by way of freedom and relaxation of repression in return. This is what was generally expected.

Now YSR started speaking as if he had been asleep all these days and had suddenly woken up. Where is the question of talking about people's problems with the Naxalites, he asked. He would talk to them about the modalities of their surrender, if they wished. And of course there would be no toleration of armed men and women moving around. The police would have to act. The DGP, taking the cue, expressed the point of view of perhaps the majority of the policemen, that is, any talks other than for the final surrender of the revolutionaries would only strengthen revolution. If governance had consisted of nothing but policing, this is of course a perfectly sensible view. And indeed it was the view that prevailed with Chandrababu Naidu's government.

But the whole point in seeking a different approach from the government was that revolution being a socio-political process, looking at it exclusively from the point of its containment made no sense even to the rulers, let alone the ruled. If there is an armed revolution going on and if it has proved its staying power, it makes little sense even for the purpose of administration to think exclusively in terms of its containment and extermination ... But of course there was little possibility of YSR seeing things this way. The only hope for the talks lay in his continued non-involvement in the process. And so the moment he opened his mouth about it, all possibility of a second round came to an end ...

Tough Talk

The tough cop started talking tough and the police started killing. The ceasefire, that is to say the mutual agreement not to kill each other, had stood quite firm for six full months by the end of 2004 ... On December 16, when the ceasefire was due to be extended, the state cabinet met but said nothing. It neither extended the ceasefire nor did it declare that there would be no further extension. Some ministers pretended that they were not aware of any ceasefire agreement, and some said that no statement was needed to extend it since it was an informal agreement. Hypocritical noises were however made about continuing the talks with the Naxalites, without getting down to anything specific, and without in plain terms extending the cessation of killing. Indeed, the chief minister, ever since he broke his silence in the matter, consistently talked in a manner calculated to knock down the very basic of the talks by saying that the Naxalites would have to give up arms as a precondition ...

Aggressive Police

Once the signal was given from above, the police became quite aggressive. They started going quite deep into the forests to hunt and kill armed cadre of the Naxalites, in particular CPI(Maoist) cadre. For many years, they had been regularly getting a lot of information about the movements of the armed squads, a fact that reflects the increasing organizational brittleness of the Naxalites from about the mid-1990s, and so if they decided to hunt and kill, it was a matter of time before they started hitting the target ... YSR did not leave any doubt in any one's mind. He publicly defended the killings, saying that so long as the Naxalites were armed, there would be encounters, and there was no need of any enquiry because the police, he somehow knew, had acted out of lawful necessity. Once it became clear that the action of the police had the sanction of the government, the Naxalites declared that they were withdrawing from the talks, and they too started killing. About 60 lives were lost in the first two months of 2005, and things were back to normal.

On the possibility of resuming the talks, YSR and his cabinet colleagues indulged in the most reprehensible doubletalk, which appeared to have been taken at face value outside the state. The government continues to be open to talks, they said, and it is the Naxalites who broke off. What they do not add is that the Naxalites broke off only after it became clear that the government had no intention of stopping the killing of their cadre. And after YSR reneged on the basic point which the government had accepted at the very beginning of the whole process, namely, that the Naxalites giving up armed struggle would not be a pre-condition for the talks. To this extent their decision to leave the dialogue table cannot be faulted and the principal responsibility for restarting the process would lie with the government. But an equal responsibility lies on the revolutionaries namely, to ensure that the unreal tone and the drama of the first round is eschewed, and the two sides conduct themselves with the degree of realism one supposes they are capable of.

This is a slightly abridged version of the original article published in *Economic and Political Weekly*, March 26, 2005. Courtesy: Human Rights Forum, Andhra Pradesh, Balagopal Memorial Trust and EPW

Manmohan to Mamata: Doublespeak Continues

Swami Agnivesh

I returned from Raipur-to-Dantewada 'Peace and Justice March' on 10 May 2010 after exhorting both the Maoists and the government to abjure the spiral of violence and counter-violence, and to seek solution through dialogue. The slogan we had raised was '*Goli se Nahi Boli se* (not through bullets but dialogue)'. Therefore, when on 11 May, Union home minister P. Chidambaram gave me a letter asking me to take the initiative for peace talks, I felt happy. And as soon as we took the initial steps we found that the Maoists were prepared for a negotiated peace. Both sides put forward certain conditions for ceasefire. This development encouraged me, and I felt that at long last there would be some solution to this problem. While the situation was expected to ripen for talks, what happened was just the opposite. Suddenly, I came to know the shocking news of the killing of CPI(Maoist) politburo member Azad's who was interacting with me to facilitate the talks. It vitiated the situation. The mysterious situation in which Azad was killed itself created antagonism. Both sides were taking a rigid stand. The Maoists said it was a cold-blooded murder, but the authorities claimed it was a genuine encounter. So, I demanded an inquiry. The government was not inclined to institute one. If the government had nothing to hide, it should have agreed to hold a free and fair inquiry. Even the National Human Rights Commission has said that every incident of encounter killing should be inquired.

Prime Minister Did Nothing

When it was evident that the home minister of the country was not in favour of any investigation, I met the Prime Minister. He requested me to give him five days. Days became months, but the PM did nothing. I met Rahul Gandhi then; he too gave me an assurance of action. I met Salman Khurshid, too. I even met the Opposition leaders. I told them that they should come forward so that I could continue with the peace initiative. To create a favourable condition for peace talks, it was necessary to win the confidence of the Maoists afresh. It could be won only by instituting a free and fair inquiry on the encounter to find out whether it was genuine or fake. When nothing happened, we moved the Supreme Court. On 14 May 2011, the apex court ordered to institute a CBI inquiry. Justice Aftab Alam ordered to produce an interim report in six weeks and the final report by three months. When even the interim report did not come after six months, I knocked the door of the Supreme Court again.

What I have learnt is even more disappointing. The interim report has tentatively established that it was a genuine encounter. But it has asked for more time to look into the Central Forensic Scientific Laboratory report. The Supreme Court has now given the CBI time till the end of March. Let us hope that the CBI will at long last look into the very basic material of the Central Forensic Scientific Laboratory report — hopefully again, without any influence from its political bosses. My experience of working with the government is not good. I feel it did not stand by what it commits. It do not even have the deftness to carry out a great task. The Maoists were ready for talks even after Azad's killing but they were given a short shrift.

Mamata Banerjee: Before and After Assembly Polls

I went to Lalgarh on 9 August 2010. I addressed a rally there with Mamata Banerjee and I supported her. There I described the Azad incident as a fake encounter. But Mamta went further and described it as murder. It was heartening for me as Mamata, a leading member of the ruling UPA at the Centre, attached so much importance to it. I hoped she would win. Rather I was confident that she would win and form a government in Bengal. I said that in my speech there. That is exactly what happened later. After Mamata formed a government, I asked her and her partymen to take the initiative so that peace negotiations with the Maoists could start afresh. At that juncture, only she could do it, both at the state and the national level. Her party has significant presence in the Union cabinet as the Railway ministry is still with it. She is in power in the state, too. She has the required strength to do it even now. Then she formed a committee of interlocutors to negotiate with the Maoists. I was not a member of that committee. But Sujato Bhadra and my other friends were there. I do not know what transpired between them and the Maoists, but the initiative did not succeed. Then Mamata Banerjee started saying that she had given enough space to the Maoists, but they had not responded. She said it was time for police action. I felt sad when I came to know about it.

When I got the news of Kishenji's death in an 'encounter', I felt very sad. Because even after Azad's death, Maoist leaders Kishenji and his party's state secretary Akash issued a press statement that if Swami Agnivesh continued as mediator they would be ready for talks. This statement was carried in the front page of *The Economic Times*. They showed their sincerity about talks. I am not aware of the reasons of failure of peace initiative in Bengal. But when the Bengal government hardened its stand, I felt they too were having the attitude similar to the Central government. Kishenji's death has dealt a body blow to the peace process. Who is responsible for this? Only Mamata Banerjee and Sujato Bhadro and his fellow interlocutors can say that.

But I may share what my experience of working as a negotiator was. I have found that the Maoists stood by whatever they promised through their sources. They took away five jawans of the Chhattisgarh Armed Forces and kept them hostage. After 18 days, they freed all of them, unharmed, before the media. The family members of the five jawans went to the jungles along with me. They were all happy. The next day at a press conference, Chhattisgarh chief minister Raman Singh, thanked me for my effort. There I proposed that the state government also release five of the many *Adivasis* in jail as a return gesture, for that would send a very good message for peace initiative.

Raman Singh promised to do so, but he never kept his word. The Prime Minister had earlier promised, and did not keep his. Rahul Gandhi, too, had promised to take an initiative but never did so. Mamata Banerjee supported the demand for investigation into Azad's death. But when her government assumed office, she changed her stance. I demanded an inquiry into Kishenji's killing. Thereafter, I tried to meet her — in Kolkata, when I had gone there, and in Delhi when she visited it. But I was not given an appointment.

I do not know why. I firmly believe that that the governments, both at the Centre and the states, will never be able to eliminate the Maoists through arms and armed personnel. For that they must, keeping in view the demand of the *Adivasis* for their right to *jal-jangal-zameen*, look at why Fifth Schedule of the Constitution of India, PESA Act and Forest Rights Act were not implemented. They will have to find out which forces were responsible for it. Without solving this, one cannot expect to find a solution to the Maoist problem. Of late, the present Union minister for rural development Jairam Ramesh has been saying the same thing. But I do not know how far his government is sincere on that.

As far I understand, the Maoists have taken up arms to resist the exploitation of the *Adivasis* and bring an end to the injustice done to them. To find a real solution to this the leaders of the Central and state governments will have to talk to the Maoists. To initiate the talks, the government should release some of the jailed top Maoist leaders like Kobad Ghandy and Narayan Sanyal for a limited period so that they can formalise things. Every discussion and negotiation should be recorded so that later it can be verified who said what. There should be a committee of prominent citizens and human rights workers to monitor whether agreed conditions are being observed on the ground. This committee should have to be neutral, so that it can fix the blame of any violation, irrespective of whether the violator is the government or the Maoist. Operations by the joint forces or *Salwa Judum* and the Koya commandoes will never find a lasting solution.

Finally, a word of unsolicited advice to the Maoists leaders: please never lower your guard at the first glimpse of an olive branch from the governments, however keen they may appear for a negotiated settlement or ceasefire.

* As told to Diptendra Raychoudhuri

An Open Letter to the Prime Minister

Himanshu Kumar

DEAR HONOURABLE MANMOHAN SINGHJI,

I am writing this open letter to you so that this country knows who is responsible for fomenting war in tribal areas, and how your government has swindled this country. Any attempt by social activists to broker peace between Naxalites and the State has been subverted by your regime. P Chidamabaram, the home minister in your government, who has consistently fought cases for corporates and against the government, was a board member of the notorious Vedanta company.

The same Chidambaram assured the people of this country in an interview given to *Tehelka* in 2009: 'Yes, if any Dantewada organisation arranges a public hearing, I am ready to go there and listen to their problems.' After his pronouncement, I met Chidamabaram in 2009 at his home in New Delhi, where we talked for approximately 45 minutes. During the conversation, he had promised me that if I organised a public hearing in Dantewada on 7 January 2010, where *Adivasi* victims of violence would detail their heartrending stories, he would come and listen to their grievances.

HOME MINISTER: HUNTING WITH THE HOUNDS ...

During that meeting, I also handed Chidamabaram a CD which contained testimonies of girls who had been gang-raped by police officers, along with the shocking picture of a one-and-half-year-old child whose fingers were chopped off by CRPF and the description of the incident by the child's grandmother.

After this, I asked Chidambaram to send me a letter informing me that he would attend the public hearing (organised by the author's organisation Vanvasi Chetna Ashram). He assured me over the phone that he would definitely come. But he did not send me any official letter. Meanwhile, the government threw Kopa Kunjam, a senior worker of our organisation in prison, because he was visiting villages exhorting villagers to come to this public hearing. After that, police abducted the abovementioned girls (who had been gang-raped), and the child whose fingers were chopped off by the Cobra battalion of the CRPF, and whose CD I had given to Chidambaram.

I cannot understand till today why police abducted the victims of the heinous crimes, victims for whom I had organised a public hearing. Other than me, only Chidambaram had prior knowledge of the hearing. The natural question that arises in this context is who ordered the abduction of the victims. The court proceedings of the case concerning the gang-raped girls were ongoing. The government was consistently and brazenly lying that the accused police officers were absconding. In fact, they were doing regular duty at the Dornapal police station and receiving their regular salaries. With the support of the entire State machinery, the rapist police officers, along with 400 other policemen, abducted the *Adivasi* girls. They took them to the Dornapal police station, kept them hungry for five days and beat them up mercilessly for daring to file a case in the court accusing them.

I informed P. Chidambaram, Union home secretary G.K. Pillai, Chhattisgarh's chief secretary P. Joy Oomen, Chhattisgarh DGP Vishwa Ranjan, and Dantewada collector Rina Kangale and SP Amresh Mishra of this horrifying incident. But not one of them stepped forward to help the girls. After beating up the girls incessantly for five days, the rapist police officers dumped them in the vicinity of their villages. They warned the villagers that if any of them ever dared to even talk to me again, their whole village would be burnt down as a consequence.

Please remember that just four months after this heinous crime was committed, 76 CRPF personnel were killed in this area. If you care to analyse the cause of this vicious cycle of violence, you will find that whenever government forces perpetrate one injustice after another, considering that people are weak and cannot fight back, the consequence have been terrible. When all democratic options for seeking justice are denied to the oppressed people, horrifying violence is met with unspeakable counter-violence. After this incident, it was reported in the newspapers that the Chhattisgarh governor had written to you asking you to dissuade Chidambaram from going to the public hearing in Dantewada.

Thereafter, *The Indian Express* reported that Chidambaram had been stopped from attending the public hearing. Meanwhile, I called Chidambaram and asked him why he had not sent any information in writing that he would be attending the public hearing. He responded that it would be impossible for him to attend in view of the changed political situation. In the meantime, the officials of the state administration threatened most of the activists of our organisation with dire consequences. They arrested the *Adivasis* whose cases we had filed in court. The police surrounded me from all sides. Neither could I meet any of the *Adivasis* nor could any one of them come and meet me. Finally, on 2 January 2010, we were escorting an *Adivasi* woman Sodi Sambo — who was shot in the foot by the Cobra battalion of the CRPF — from Dantewada to the Supreme Court in Delhi. The police kidnapped her and brazenly filed a case against me for abducting her.

Government Broke the Bridge

I realised that under these circumstances, I could not do anything for the *Adivasis*. Hence, I was forced to leave Chhattisgarh in order to expose this vicious cycle of repression by the Chhattisgarh government. It is clear that we had tried to facilitate the Indian State an opportunity to talk to the *Adivasis* who support the Naxalites. We had hoped that the government would try to fathom the anger and anguish of the victims of the atrocities unleashed by its forces. We thought that the government would listen to the victims' grievances in order to win their hearts and minds so that they started believing in the democratic institutions of the country. But your home minister and you have lost that last sliver of opportunity. Now you can try your utmost, but the *Adivasis* who feel alienated from the Indian State will never talk to you again. We were the last bridge to reach those *Adivasis*, but your government deliberately ruined that bridge.

Naxalites have two different strategies to deal with different situations: a military strategy and a peacetime strategy. If they carry a gun on one shoulder, they have a bag of books by Marx and Mao on the other. When the enemy moves in, they take up their guns to face them. On the other hand, in peacetime, they uncock their guns and open their bag of books to teach and train people about the ideologies of Marxism and Maoism. I had told Chidambaram that the Indian State had a military strategy only; no ideological strategy was in place. The Indian State and its defenders know only how to shoot and kill. They have no strategy to win the hearts and minds of the people.

We had proposed that we would give you the opportunity to implement this strategy. Listen to *Adivasis*' grievances, deliver them justice and instill confidence in them that the Indian State is capable of bequeathing justice to them. But alas, you lost that opportunity. You sent them a curt message that the Indian State is not on the side of suffering *Adivasis*. It is on the side of rapist police officers. It is on the side of the CRPF, which chops off the fingers of a one-and-half-year-old boy. Adivasis understand perfectly which side are you on. But the middle and upper middle classes of the country should also understand that it is not the much-maligned Naxalites who are responsible for the pervasive violence in our country, but the Indian State itself, and at present, Chidambaram and Manmohan Singh.

Costly Betrayals Leading to Civil War

I was not the only one you betrayed. Under the pretext of holding peace talks with him, your regime invited CPI(Maoist) spokesman Azad, with Swami Aginvesh acting as a mediator, and then killed Azad. Similarly, you trapped Kishenji and murdered him. History will decide who was wrong and who was right in this struggle. But at least the people of this country should understand that your government is responsible for pushing the country into a civil war.

The industrious and hardworking people of this land are facing mass starvation. But you do not care about this grave situation. All you care about is GDP. And GDP grows only by selling minerals to foreigners, but that does not improve the condition of the poor and working people of the country. By continuously harping on GDP growth, you are instigating a civil war in the *Adivasi* regions of the country.

It is difficult to believe that you do not know how 15,000 *Adivasi* and Dalit women have been crammed into prisons in the Kaimur region of the Hindi heartland. Don't you know that in order to acquire land on behalf of the London-based company Vedanta, police has registered false cases against each and every *Adivasi* living in the Niyamgiri mountains in Odisha? These *Adivasis* are too mortified to come out of the forests, and the government hopes that with no access to medicines, they would die in the forests, after which the government could acquire the land without much resistance.

Don't you know that the women and children of Jagatsinghpur in Odisha tried to resist forcible acquisition of their land for the South Korean company POSCO by lying prostrate on hot sands, that the police slapped false cases against men and women of the three villages, and that as I write, those women cannot go to hospital even for childbirth?

Don't you know that it is under your rule that the biggest genocide was perpetrated on the *Adivasis* of India when a brutal vigilante army called *Salwa Judum* was unleashed on them in Chhattisgarh in active collaboration with the state government led by your main Parliamentary opposition, the BJP? Is this what freedom means? Would the martyrs who sacrificed everything, even smilingly embraced death, for India's freedom from British rule have ever imagined that the country would become a slave to foreign corporations within 65 years of its Independence? People do not see any avenue through which they can achieve justice.

The chairperson of the National Human Rights Commission, who has several cases of corruption against him, openly says: 'At times, encounters are unavoidable.' The National Commission for Protection of Child Rights did not think that the CRPF had violated any children's rights by chopping off the fingers of a one-and-half-year-old child. An SP of a district inserts pebbles into the private parts of an *Adivasi* teacher Soni Sori, but the National Commission for Women does nothing.

While the hardworking people of the country live a precarious and famished existence, a tiny fraction of rich and upper class parasites shamelessly enjoy obscene wealth. Your government dubs criminals people criminal who dare to raise their voice in support of the millions of toiling masses. Who suffers indignity and privation in this country? The industrious labourer, the farmer who breaks his back to produce the food we all eat, the Dalit who produces most of the goods we use and the forest-dwelling *Adivasis.* Don't ever forget that these people are poor not because they do not work hard. They are poor because the political, economic and social forces keep them poor. And you call the revolutionaries who want to change this perverse, upside down and unjust system criminals.

This country's prisons are filled with people who dared to raise their voices against the pervasive injustice of our society. These are frightful times. You are snatching the life-sustaining resources of the poor and giving them away to rich transnational corporations at throwaway prices, and then sending security forces to brutally crush even the slightest resistance to this daylight robbery. The irony is that under the Indian Constitution, these security forces are supposed to protect and defend the poor against depredations of the powerful.

This situation cannot last long. People will destroy a system that caters to every opulent whim of the minuscule rich and their henchmen in governments who force the rest of their compatriots to struggle for their survival. And this is their natural right, regardless of how many aristocratic laws created by the rich are invoked to declare such resistance criminal.

The Path to a Conflict-free State

Nandini Sundar

Contrary to the dominant narrative that areas where Naxalites are strong are where the State has been absent, for the last 100-150 years, there has been a gradual expansion of the State in tribal areas regardless of whether the people want it or not. However, the state has been expanding in the wrong areas. You have an extension of the forest department, the bureaucracy, the *patwari* and the forest guard. But at the same time there is no State presence in the form of school teachers, health-care workers and other services.

The problem here is that the State only wants to take a military approach towards ending Naxalism. This will not work as it has been proven in the case of Kashmir and the Northeast. It may have 'worked' in Punjab, but that was because the people were already alienated from the militants. The criterion of success is also debatable because of the grave violations of human rights. In terms of a constitutional approach to conflict resolution, I wouldn't say that was an approach that worked.

This attitude (of the government) is reflected in the CRPF (Central Reserve Police Force) programme of winning the hearts and minds of the people, as part of which the paramilitary gifts people *lungis* and *saris.* Ironically, CRPF personnel beat up people if they don't accept the gifts and people laugh as they recount this.

In Chhattisgarh, in the areas where Maoists are strong, there is no voting in the villages, and many of the *sarpanch*es have joined the *Salwa Judum.* So, when development work is routed through the *sarpanch*es, it has no relationship to anything on the ground. The *sarpanches* don't even live in the villages, and invent paper schemes in collusion with the block officer. It's a fantasy of development where the paperwork looks good, but no one's heart or mind is being won. Much of this is also being shown for roadside villages which were never *Salwa Judum*-affected or Maoist-influenced in the first place, so that the figures look good. But the real areas that are affected remain unaddressed.

The only way to proceed towards establishing peace in Chhattisgarh is to start on the plank of justice. Three villages were torched last year and in 2007. The interesting part here is that in 2007, the average losses (claimed by the tribals) per household was around Rs 1 lakh, but due to the recent incidents (attacks on the tribals by the paramilitary), in many households, the figure is as low as Rs 20,000 per household. It is evident that the *Adivasis* are not only under relentless attack, but are also becoming paupers.

In this context, it is not clear what role the integrated action plan announced by (Union minister for rural development) Jairam Ramesh will play. Where people have been killed and raped and houses burnt and they get no justice, will their hearts and minds be won through roads and panchayat *bhavans*? For their part, the villagers will accept *State* intervention if it is seen as part of a justice package and not as part of counter-insurgency. We [activists fighting on behalf of the tribals in Chhattisgarh] had submitted a rehabilitation plan that ensured precisely this — through an enumeration of what had happened in each village and a transparent compensation and criminal registration process with an appropriate monitoring committee. But the central as well as the state governments have kept stalling. If the Centre is serious about bettering the situation in Chhattisgarh, first it needs to withdraw troops to the barracks and hold peace talks with the Naxalites.

But that seems unlikely as they have killed [Maoist leader] Kishenji. The Maoists, for their part, must stop initiating attacks and renew expressions of interest in peace talks. As unlikely as the prospect seems, there is no other way, but talks. As for other steps, the onus lies on the government alone. The second thing that the Chhattisgarh government needs to do is to implement the Supreme Court order disbanding Special Police Officers in its spirit. The state government has recruited the SPOs into the Chhattisgarh Armed Auxiliary Force and they continue to threaten the people even today.

The SPOs are allowed a free run by the police. Today, the SPOs who have been recruited into the auxiliary force earn four times the salary they used to draw earlier. While they were paid Rs 1,500 a month as SPOs, today they earn about Rs 7,000. They are the ones to benefit the most out of our petition. This would have been fine in terms of giving them security, but to make it constitutional, the guilty ones among them have to be taken to task. Otherwise, what you have is regularisation of criminals.

The government needs to ensure that justice is delivered to the people of Chhattisgarh. It also needs to implement our rehabilitation plan and file criminal cases. Today, you can be a mass murderer and get away with it whether in Gujarat in 2002 or 2005 onwards in Chhattisgarh. Unless there is an end to impunity, and a movement for this, just like the movement against corruption, we will never see a conflict-free country.

What needs to be done:

n End military approach towards Naxalism;

n Start on the plank of justice and begin peace talks to establish true peace; and

n Disband Special Police Officers who still threaten locals with impunity.

As told to K.P. Narayana Kumar.

Jan 26, 2012.

* This article was first published in Forbes India news magazine on 3 February, 2012. We have reproduced it with the author's permission.

An Appeal for Peace in South Bastar: Need for Political Engagement

Binayak Sen

The present situation in South Bastar is characterised by an infinitude of chronic deprivation, along with a complete absence of political discourse. Instead, we have on the one hand, the remnants of the *Salwa Judum*, which the government dishonestly tried to characterise as a 'peoples' response to Maoism', and on the other, a purely military engagement between the State forces and the Maoists, which acts as a proxy to a political discourse. The deadlock can be appreciated when we note that even when the Supreme Court judgment of Justices Sudarshan Reddy and S.S. Nijjhar ruled in 2011 that the *Salwa Judum* cadres be disbanded forthwith, the state government responded with legislative steps to absorb the former members of the *Salwa Judum* into the regular police force. Both parties to this engagement deliberately ignore the fact that a purely military solution, imposed by either party, even if it were possible, would neither be valid nor sustainable.

PHASE I

Any quest for a resolution of this situation cannot start by addressing the humanitarian problem on the ground alone, catastrophic as that no doubt is. The humanitarian situation in South Bastar today, is both the end product as well as the precipitating factor behind the current impasse. Any standard appeal for peace would begin with an agenda for the resolution of the humanitarian situation, but given the total breakdown of societal mechanisms in the area, this might have limited possibilities for success. Instead, the first and most urgent necessity is the establishment of an institutional forum for political engagement without preconditions. The purpose of this forum would not be to search for solutions, but rather to concentrate on the identification and recognition of participants in the forum, and the elaboration of an agenda as well as the guarantees necessary for the forum to conduct its business, i.e. talks about talks.

Essentially this proposal resembles that suggested on certain occasions for the resolution of the current situation in Jammu and Kashmir. The identification of members of the forum must be an inclusive process, and must include, apart from the government and the Maoists, representatives of political parties as well as civil society in the area concerned, i.e., South Bastar.

Phase II

Once this institutional mechanism is in place, it would undertake, within its overall supervision, a specific series of measures directed at relieving the humanitarian situation on the ground. As an immediate priority, the problems to be addressed would include:

- Food and Water;
- Shelter and Livelihood;
- Health care; and
- Transport and infrastructure.

Education is a more contentious subject and may be addressed once we move beyond the preliminary stages.

Food and Water

For all intents and purposes, the entire region is a famine-stricken area and should be treated as such. The indigenous systems of food production and livelihood have been destroyed. A universal public distribution system, at zero cost to the identified card-bearing consumers, needs to be put in place as an immediate priority. The identification of consumer households should be through electronic ration cards which can be redeemed at any geographical location throughout the affected area. This will leave the option open for households and household members to either return to their villages or continue to reside at whichever/camp or other place they may have relocated to. The PDS should supply, in addition to cereals, pulses and oil. Adequate locally relevant measures to obtain potable, safe drinking water should be put in place.

Shelter

Village homes which have remained unoccupied for months will need repair and reconditioning to make them habitable. Help should be at hand to enable returning families to rebuild their homes.

Livelihoods

The NREGA should be extensively implemented over the entire area to secure a minimum livelihood for all returning families. It is only once guaranteed livelihoods are effectively in place that people would enjoy some degree of autonomous control over their own lives. The issue of *pattas* to revenue lands abandoned for lengths of time, and cultivation of what are technically forest lands, is also extremely complex, and, in view of the new Act for granting land rights to families cultivating these lands, should be handled with extreme sensitivity. Pending the reclamation and recording of the land rights of people, implementation of all existing decisions for land acquisition must be put in abeyance.

Health Care

Adequate, accessible health-care facilities, universally accessible to all, on a cashless basis must be put in place as soon as possible. This should include supplies of drugs and other necessary equipment. No discrimination should be there between different population groups with respect to access to basic health facilities. In case State-sponsored facilities are not available, non-state providers who fulfill the above criteria should be welcomed.

Transport and Infrastructure

The network of weekly markets must be restored on a priority basis. The minimum infrastructure for resumption of agriculture, including animal husbandry, would also need to be out in place.

CITIZENSHIP RECORDS AND VOTER RIGHTS

Widespread displacement and population dislocations have made this a critical issue at this particular time. Transparent mechanisms must be put in place to ensure that citizenship rights are preserved and entitlements to democratic decision-making ensured.

DEMILITARISATION

It would not be possible or practicable to wait until full restoration of normalcy in all the above parameters. However, significant progress in a forward direction that demonstrates the bona fides of all parties as far as their commitment to peace and political discourse is concerned, will have to precede the negotiations and move for full demilitarisation. It is our belief that significant progress towards a ceasefire and eventual demilitarisation can only take place when the ordinary people have a stake in the maintenance of the peace.

ISSUE OF PEACE CAN BE BASED ON FOLLOWING PEMISES:

- Peace is a matter of concern for all the people;
- It is not an issue only between the contenders on either side;
- Peace cannot be restored through force of arms; and
- Legitimacy of dissent is of utmost importance for the resumption of dialogue and open communication.

The original version of this appeal was issued by the author from jail. It has been slightly modified and updated by him to accommodate present realities. ♦

Initiatives for Peace and Justice: Need for a Fresh Perspective

Manoranjan Mohanty

Rulers: Before and After

West Bengal chief minister Mamata Bannerjee's abandonment of her pre-election promises of pursuing peace talks with the Maoists is the latest in a series of such policy reversals by other political leaders. N T Rama Rao and Biju Patnaik in their days started with much nicer words for the Maoists describing them as fighters for the poor people's rights. Yet repression had gathered momentum during their regimes. Andhra chief minister Rajshekhar Reddy had carried out peace talks only to see its failure and follow it with massive wave of killings of Maoist leaders and cadres in AP. Odisha chief minister Naveen Patnaik frequently announced his commitment to the cause of the *Adivasis* and the rural poor during his first term in office. He often met representatives of *Adivasi* organisations and civil liberty activists and promised concrete measures to address the problems of the tribal areas. But in the recent years Odisha has seen intensive operations by the security forces. Even the fourteen point agreement that was announced by the mediators to secure the release of Malkangiri Collector Vineel Krishna in February 2011 was not implemented and instead mopping up operations and killings in false encounters were increased.

Some committees of the Indian government have occasionally talked of treating the Maoist movement as a 'political and developmental challenge'. But in practice, the Central government has led the states in increasing the coordinated drive to liquidate the Maoists and their support base. Thus the resort to a strategy of maximum coercion has emerged as the preferred line of action of all the ruling forces.

However, this strategy has failed to curb the spread of the Maoist movement and its political strength. The Union home ministry has identified 83 districts in nine states as affected areas. Other estimates mention as many as 150 districts in 13 States. At the current moment there are three major factors which need to be taken into account. Firstly, there is an escalation of the coercive strategy combined with a set of infrastructure-building plans launched as Integrated Action Plan (IAP) in the Maoist movement areas which the government calls left-wing extremism (LWE) areas.

Besides giving sophisticated weapons and new training in jungle warfare and deploying additional forces, the Centre continues to add new techniques to anti-Naxalite operations. On 7 February 2012, for example, Home minister Chidambaram inaugurated a new CRPF Intelligence School in Gurgaon and said: 'Counter-insurgency and countering LWE require a very different strategy and approach. It is not intervening and setting things right in a few days and returning to your group centre or your headquarters. It is remaining deployed for a long time to take on the adversary such as the CPI(Maoist) which is organised as a regular fighting army.'

The IAP was introduced in 60 Maoist movement districts in nine states where the *Adivasi* population is more than 25 per cent, forest areas over 30 per cent and poverty ratio is at least 50 per cent. The Rs-25-crore budget, mostly for infrastructure building, is managed by three officials, the collector, the superintendent of police and the district forest officer. Union rural development minister Jairam Ramesh is the public face of the Indian government pushing for the implementation of IAP as the development response of the 'two-pronged strategy' — the other being the law and order measure — to meet the Maoist challenge. In fact, in certain areas there are special plans in operation as the Saranda Development Strategy in Jharkhand. But it is very clear that this one-year-old intervention has not made any difference on the ground. The new infrastructure-building and beneficiary-listing effort is seen mainly as aiding the security operations and partly as recruiting supporters for the government initiatives. The Chidambaram line of 'first clearing the areas of the Maoists, so that civil administration can exercise its authority and then implement development plans' remains the dominant response of the Indian State.

The Corporates and Primitive Dispossession

The second trend is the open alliance of the Indian and foreign capital backed by the Indian State, in the determined drive to clear the Central Indian tribal belt of the rebels so that mining and other industrial development can take place. The FICCI report on the Naxalite challenge came out clearly advocating this line of thought. During the past decade and more the movements against mega mining projects in Odisha, Chhatishgarh, Jharkhand and West Bengal have created hurdles for the multinational companies such as POSCO, Vedanta, TiSCO, Jindal and Mittal to proceed with their steel, aluminium and power projects. Even though the Maoists did not launch or lead these movements, the many streams of resistance got linked because the peaceful movements of local people against displacement and in defence of livelihood were subjected to severe repression.

The third trend is equally significant, though of a different kind. The public opinion in the country is deeply disenchanted with the government policy on the Naxalites. Even though government of every major political party has fallen in line with the strategy of maximum coercion against the Maoists there are sections in practically each and every party which ask for a different approach. In some cases many of their local leaders have to depend on the local Maoists to enter their areas. Even in the police and para-military forces there are sections which are fed up with the failure of the prevailing line and privately complain against their assignments. The Army has been formally kept out of the operations, but in reality it performs crucial support functions in critical situations. But the army leadership has rejected suggestions to play an active counter-insurgency role in Naxalite areas. Of course, the experience from the Northeast and

Kashmir has guided its thinking in this, for here too it would have had to deal with a rebellious and hostile population.

Role of the Democratic Forces and Public Opinion

The work of the civil liberty groups has contributed significantly to the making of the public opinion. They have documented atrocities committed by security forces, approached human rights commissions and courts and the media. Some judgements like the one by the Supreme Court on *Salwa Judum* in July 2011 has persuaded many ordinary citizens to condemn the paramilitary operations in the *Adivasi* areas where innocent people have been killed, tortured, women raped, schools destroyed and so on. The public demand to investigate every case of encounter death has become stronger day by day. There is a much greater public appreciation of the reasons which drive masses of *Adivasis* and peasants to join the Maoist ranks.

For example, how a peaceful mass movement of the *Adivasis* to reclaim tribal land under law in Odisha's Narayanpatna was subjected to severe repression paving the way for the spread of the Maoist movement to that area is a well-known story. The public also is shocked by the many instances of killings by Maoists in the name of punishing police informers and has condemned them. In some cases the Maoist leadership has explained or regretted many such incidents. There is a much greater public engagement with the government and the Maoists today than ever before. Thus there is ample evidence of a public opinion favouring an alternative to the current strategy of maximum coercion by the government.

All three developments : the escalated coercive action plan of the GOI which is failing to achieve its ends, the determined drive to locate mega plants in the tribal areas which is facing firm resistance from people and the increasing disillusionment about the government's approach present a qualitatively new situation for taking peace initiatives.

Anti-Neo-Liberal Movement and Fight for Peace & Justice

The new initiatives have to learn from the earlier efforts such as the momentous initiative of the CCC (Committee of Concerned Citizens) in Andhra Pradesh in 2004 and the other attempts in different parts of the country. The Citizens Initiative for Peace functioning from Delhi in 2009-2010 also gives us some lessons. At the same time the initiatives have to respond to the new situation existing today.

The first element of the new initiative has to carry the common orientation of all the earlier peace efforts, namely, linking peace with justmce. Justice involves two components. One is the concrete problems of livelihood and dignity faced by the *Adivasis* and peasants, their right to land, forest and natural resources which are under attack. The other is the enforcement of right to life and civil liberties guaranteed under the Indian Constitution. The demand that all the projects that are planned to be located in tribal areas must have transparency of their MOU is still not accepted by the authorities. Forest Rights Act and the proposed Land Acquisition Bill leave much to be desired to respond to the *Adivasis'* right to self-determination.

As for respecting the right to life, the government's strategy of maximum coercion comprehensively violates it, often by staged encounters and sometimes under draconian laws. Every effort has to clearly negotiate the terms of peace and justice as the first premise. That follows from the Constitution of India, its chapters on fundamental rights and directive principles.

The second aspect of the peace effort has to be a call to prepare physical conditions for face-to-face dialogue. The earlier attempts pleaded for ceasefire by the government and the Maoists. Now new methods have to be found out. The government's call to the Maoists 'to abjure violence' has been a non-starter as it amounts to giving up their ideology of revolution. Making surrender of arms a precondition is yet another presumptuous demand, for without the armed strength of the Maoists the government would not have taken them seriously.

One has to recognise that in vast areas of central India the Maoist Army operates with mass support and people feel a sense of dignity in such conditions that has freed them from the oppression of the forest guards, mining mafia and the police. The Maoist Army is also accused of many criminal abuses. But there is a vast zone of Maoist base where the government authority does not hold firm. At the same time the government cannot let that condition persist. In this situation conditions have to be created for talking about the agenda of peace and justice so that the actual problems of people can be addressed. That is possible only if organs of people's power are created and respected at the grassroots level to manage their political economy.

This is the third and the new element of the present situation. Forces of peace and justice must address the society to pursue the new initiatives rather than plead with the government and the Maoists. The broad masses of the peasants, *Adivasis*, Dalits, unorganised workers, lower middle classes who are suffering the consequences of the present-day neo-liberal economic policies and the democratic rights groups , liberal intellectuals and independent thinkers who side with the common people in their struggle for an alternative development strategy should be drawn into the movement for peace and justice.

Earlier peace initiatives have been mediations between government and the Maoists. The new initiative should be a mass movement in all parts of the country to defend the endangered rights given by the Indian Constitution. It should be a part of the new mass awakening for democratic transformation in contemporary India rather than securing peace and order for the ruling elite's growth strategy.

'War for Peace' to 'Peace as War': Lessons from Northeast

Samir Kumar Das

I confess my knowledge of West Bengal is poor and that of the recent peace initiatives in the state that ended in a fiasco even poorer. This brief note is more of a reflection on the lessons that I have drawn from my research on peace processes in the India's Northeast and the bearing that it may have on any possible peace talks with the Maoists in future. As we reflect on the lessons from the Northeast, we also seek to demystify some of the commonplace beliefs and assumptions that are associated with our understanding of peace and peace talks.

Pacification or Peace?

In common parlance, war and peace are usually held as binaries. Peace, according to this view, is what brings an end to war and insofar as war breaks out it is believed to have clearly disrupted peace. This brief note prepared to contest this line of argument — not so much by arguing that war is intrinsically 'bad' or for that matter peace per se is 'good' but very much by arguing that peace unlike the commonplace view is 'war by other means' and peace is a war — winning of which is as much difficult as winning a military war. Many victors of war in history have lost the battle of peace that inevitably followed it. Peace in my view has to be waged as much as — though not in the same way — war is waged.[1]

I am not for a moment arguing that peace is desirable for it is an end in itself knowing fully well that the Maoists do not regard peace per se as a virtue — but that peace too is a form of war that many of us simply do not think will have to be won. My interviews, particularly in recent years, with many former rebel leaders of the Northeast[2] actually involved in peace negotiations with the government of India bear ample testimony to this: Rather than the war they fought against it, they feared the government of India most when they were in peace with it. They were completely baffled and outwitted by the Indian political elite in course of peace negotiations. Almost all of them have told me that they knew how to fight wars. But what they did not know was how to win peace talks.

The entire Northeast is now in a peace mode. The Indian government has been involved in peace negotiations with the Isaak-Muivah faction of the National Socialist Council of Nagalim (NSCN-IM) since 1997 without any visible sign of solution in the near future. The pro-talks faction of the United Liberation Front of Asom (ULFA) seems to be hopeful about the progress made during this short span of time. In both cases, the rival factions (NSCN-Khaplang and the anti-talks facton of ULFA) although not directly involved in talks, chose by and large not to disturb, let alone derail, the peace process and promised to wait till some concrete outcome was achieved by the groups directly engaged in the talks. The peace that has been established in the region — variously described by such military terminologies as 'suspension of operations', 'ceasefire', etc — is through pacification, that is to say, by conducting massive counter-insurgency operations. The kind of peace that prevails in the Northeast, whether in Nagaland or in Assam, is seldom accompanied by even the semblance of a solution to the problems that insurgencies in the two states have highlighted and brought to the centre of public agenda.

This compels me to propose a distinction between peace and pacification. Pacification is also peace but peace that is established by way of substantially weakening, if not completely eliminating, the adversary, thereby marking an end to war. I reserve the term 'peace' to refer to an outcome that culminates or at least promises to culminate in the realisation of such values as rights, justice and democracy. The challenge now is to turn peace by pacification into peace that is infused with the triadic values as rights, justice and democracy. No war in history has ended by winning everything for the winner; it cannot.

It leaves the unfinished agenda of war for peace to take care of.

The Peloponnesian War. world's first recorded war, also could not mark any decisive win, as Thucydides wrote. Great revolutions in history left certain things unachieved. What cannot be won in war has to be negotiated, if not won, in peace talks. Peace talks, in simple terms, provide another enduring battlefront that the adversaries are called upon to fight and win — ironically after the war comes to an end. In other words, peace does not necessarily mean surrender, far less an end to war. It is important that peace talks are taken as seriously as war.

Inroads into State Power

There is the commonplace belief that this is the most opportune moment for peace talks to be conducted because the Indian State over the years has morphed substantially in the sense of becoming increasingly accommodative. In the specific context of Bengal there was definitely the expectation that the change of government would pave the way for peace talks in right earnest. I argue that if at all there has been any change in the Indian State's attitude towards the radical movements, it has less to do with any change of heart on its part and more to do with the changing profile of people's movements over the years, particularly since the 1990s. It has its obvious implications for the nature of State power.

During the last two decades, a series of people's struggles has been going on in different parts of India, affecting them widely, though not uniformly, over such largely overlapping issues as gender, land and livelihood, ownership and control of resources, starvation and hunger, minority and *Adivasi* rights, corruption and graft, so on and so forth. If India is called democratic, it is regardless of whether the Indian Constitution in its Preamble declares the Indian State as democratic or not. It is precisely because these movements have over the years been slowly successful in creating a democratic space well beyond the ambit of State institutions — yet exercising hitherto unprecedented influence on them. Never before in India's post-colonial history has this democratic power of people's movements exerted so much influence on the Indian State as it does now.[2]

The influence is sometimes strong enough to prevail over the will of the 'elected majorities' — whether it is in Singur, Nandigram, Niyamgiri or elsewhere. Who could envisage that Singur and Nandigram would have happened so soon after the resounding victory of the Left Front in 2006 and that too in such quick succession? I happen to have publicly interviewed a former LF minister on the day the election results were declared, who told me categorically that the thumping majority they had mustered should be taken as a mandate for industrialisation and land acquisition. The rest is history. One has to understand that of late a divergence has developed between the 'elected majority' and what may for want of a better term be called 'social majority'. Does this happen because people who vote apparently with their feet up in the air do not vote all that seriously and have reduced expectations from their elected representatives?

Those who theorise truly in the liberal mould that people vote with their expectations from their representatives are sure to make a fetish of the electoral process under these changed circumstances. Had the official argument that parliamentarians being people's representatives should be free to make laws for the people and not be put under any kind of pressure been true, Singur and Nandigram would not have happened at all. Democracy in simple terms shows signs of being dis-embedded from the established democratic institutions. Otherwise, how does one explain the enormous difficulties that the elected majorities — everywhere, not just in Bengal — face while carrying out land acquisition and similar neo-liberal policies. This only shows that the fulcrum of democracy has been imperceptibly shifting away from the established parliamentary institutions that the constitutional fathers once so fondly cherished. Democratic power of people's movements has definitely slowed down, if not in some cases successfully stalled, the otherwise furious pace with which the State had initially started implementing the neo-liberal policies in the early 1990s.

Quite ironically, it has its positive implications too. It is for instance found that structural adjustment in India has not been associated with what is otherwise known as the 'the retreat' of the State from welfare activities. Quite the contrary, it has actually meant the return of the 'welfare state' in its new avatar, in the form of such social policies as MGNREGA, ICDS, etc, and the Indian State's 'welfare' expenses instead of coming down have shot up under conditions of liberalisation — whether or not these have actually benefited the poor and the underclass is an altogether different question. Of course, I am aware that this is not the same kind of welfare that John Maynard Keynes or, in our country, Jawaharlal Nehru had envisaged. Now welfare is couched in the idea that people should not be kept idly on cash doles; they too must bear at least part of a responsibility for whatever they enjoy as welfare benefits. There is nothing like 'free lunch'.

The 'democratic' state that once was inspired by the vision of 'democratising' the society is now increasingly being engulfed by a vast democratic space brought into existence by a series of people's movements. The democratic power of the people has the potential of democratising the State itself. Unlike in the immediate aftermath of Independence when a democratic State was believed to have been encircled by a vast 'undemocratic' society, today it is the other way round: it is the democratic society that fights the battle of further democratising the State. It is not to be taken as a paradigmatic shift whereby a totally undemocratic State turns into an equally totally democratic one.

It is the continuous sedimentation of democracy that historically takes place thanks to the persistent struggles of the people for their rights in a variety of forms, some of which have already been mentioned here. Some struggles do not leave any impact — sometimes they fall victims to unbearable State repression; sometimes repression by peoples' leaders is no less unbearable — they are the movements that are easily forgotten without leaving any lasting impact. Many of them are appropriated by what an eminent scholar rather tragically describes as 'strategic politics' of the modern State and civil society. But there is no denying that many of these movements do leave their mark on the character of the State without however changing the latter's lock, stock and barrel.

This kind of democratisation of the State burrows the State from within and cannot give unto itself any mega history whereby the 'undemocratic' State gets transformed into a democratic State by a magician's wand, an historian's pen, a constitutional claim or even a great revolution; it involves those micro-processes that suddenly turn against the grain of mega history or borrowing the phrase that Michel Foucault has famously used — 'against its birth' on 26 November 1949 — the day when 'we, the people of India' gave unto ourselves the Constitution. In other words, the series of people's struggles does not lie outside the State, but is implicated in it. In today's world there has been a certain enmeshing of the State and people's struggles in each other.

We are standing witness to a series of people's struggles that refuses to end and be bound by the rigours of a discourse. Thus to cite an instance, if the minorities fight for their rights, the minority women have to fight afresh against the patriarchy that exists within their communities. Do the feminists who evidently fight for women's rights also fight for the rights of the lesbians and turn against a section of women themselves?[3] In one of my papers, I pointed out that the process that generates 'minorities within minorities' is infinitely regressive. In other words, people's movements under present circumstances have been self-spiralling and the liberal or even the radical plea for tying them up and bringing them under one single discourse simply refuses to acknowledge the irreducibly multiple character of these struggles.[4]

It is of course a difficult choice that we have to make now. Do we need to re-institute a State that will by definition exist as a monolith and impose its will on one and all in society, thereby muzzling and numbing the endless heterogeneity that confronts us? Or do we create a democratic space that is based on the principle of irreducible multiplicity and will eventually render the State increasingly irrelevant in our social life? There is a strong Indian tradition — nevertheless radical and therefore completely discarded — that argues along this line. A good part of the people of India anyway remains outside the State's ambit — living in remote jungles or hills or river islands — having nothing to do with it. They live at a distance, perhaps mastering the 'art of not being governed'.

These two alternatives will call for two different kinds of struggles: one for re-instituting the State, maybe reinforcing it in its new incarnation, and another for wresting away spheres of social life from the control of the State and subjecting these spheres to autonomous self-governance. Drawing from my experience of the Northeast, I seek to normatively redefine 'autonomy' not so much as one that is carved out within the State following its rules — the Constitution and law of the land — but as one that forces a change of rules without necessarily severing from the State. Autonomy, understood in this sense, has to be differentiated from secession per se. For, secession and establishment of another State do not necessarily act as a game-changer. It is likely to be ensconced in the modern State system.

As I redefine peace as 'war continued through other means', I mean not playing the same game that denies freedom to us but changing the very rules of the game. Peace talks therefore are not intended to talk peace that exists, in our case largely through pacification and negotiating a space within it. They rather aim at changing the rules of the game with the promise of delivering rights, justice and democracy. My experience with the autonomy experiments in the Northeast leads me to conclude that autonomy within the existing State (or maybe without) may not necessarily entitle people to enjoy of rights, justice and democracy. Increasing federalization does not necessarily mean greater enjoyment of rights by the indigenous people. For, federalization or secession could hardly change the game.

Civil Societies in Contest

According to Sumanta Banerjee, 'Maoist violence' — now more than 40 years old — differs from other insurrectionary movements in the sense that it instead of aiming at secession from the Indian State, it intends to change the political system of the country and transform its socio-economic structure. Because of this wider class and all-India perspective, it has been able to avoid inter-ethnic and communal or religious feuds (like Naga-Kuki, Bodo-Santhal, Karbi-Dimasa, Hindu-Muslim, Hindu-Sikh conflicts), which mar many other insurrections. The point can hardly be exaggerated.

However, in one my recently published essays, I have reflected on the ethnic divide that has historically marked the society of Bengal since the early 19th century, implicitly keeping the domanation of civil society in the hands of the upper-caste, Western-educated Bengali middle class elite, and denying the *Adivasis* and the underclass who also live in the state any say. Few of us take notice of the fact that the civil society that has grown in Kolkata is highly ethnicised and the ethnic divide that lies at its core is too implicit to be visible. In our amnesia of the implicit ethnic divide, we often do not take notice of what I call 'Bengali imperialism' that Kolkata-based public intellectuals have sought to establish in the countryside, in Barak Valley, Tripura and elsewhere. This is unlike in the Northeast. Much, though not all, of civil society in the Northeast acts as a civic representative of any particular ethnic community or nationality.

Of late, only some political commentators have started reflecting on the implicit nature of the ethnic divide and why the Bengali middle class has been in some kind of a self-denial mode. I am not for a moment arguing that the entire Bengali middle class remains on the wrong side of the divide. Interestingly, there are very few public intellectuals who make attempts at crossing the divide while trying to de-intellectualize themselves (déclassé). But they do not or sometimes are not allowed to play any role in the civil-social sphere. Civil society seems to have either boycotted them or revered them as 'gods and goddesses', too distant to be its own. The latter will remain as the 'voice of conscience' for the Bengalis — to be listened to — but meant only to be ignored by ordinary mortals who are not known to have the moral resources to live their daily life 'conscientiously'.

As I pointed out, civil society in Kolkata continues to look upon the Maoist violence as 'uncivil war'. That is why I argue although the dichotomy between ethnic insurgencies and class insurgencies is often blown out of proportion, they may not be paradigmatically different.

For, much depends on how the ethnic divide is addressed. To say that it does not exist or will not have its ramifications for society and politics of Bengal will be like suffering from self-delusion.

In other words, civil society activism that one notices in West Bengal is likely to push the *Adivasis* and the underclass out of the public agenda farther into the margins — though it will conveniently need them for appropriation.[5] The pre-election composition of civil society that developed in Bengal around such issues as land acquisition, police atrocities and party regimentation, Rizwan-ur-Rahman's controversial death or Taslima Nasreen's ouster started disintegrating (though not decaying) as the state moved towards the Assembly elections in 2011. The public agenda of civil society today hardly refers to the *Adivasis* and their rights, poverty and starvation, peasant suicides and other burning issues. An eminent MP recently said that Parliament has time for everything, including not doing anything for days together — but hardly has time to deliberate on the issues of the poor and poverty.

The choice again is difficult: Do we call for radicalisation of civil society in Bengal? Or do we think in terms of wresting away what I called the democratic space from the clutches of civil society? In a society where the ethnic divide remains implicit, the need for radicalization is unlikely to be felt — unlike in the Northeast where ethnic divide is too explicit to be ignored thereby producing challenges from ever-smaller ethnic communities. Is not 'Bengal Renaissance' part of the problem, for it made us forget that ethnicities and castes do exist in the society of Bengal and Bengal too has a nationality question?

The Dalit intellectuals perhaps have been the pioneers in arguing for not one but many civil societies and the contest between them as a means of combating upper-caste hegemony. They claim that Dalit civil society is as much civil as mainstream civil society. It is only by contesting the dominant notion of civility that the other civil societies may emerge and make their voices heard. This is again a power game. Do women need to have a separate civil society of their own? Since making these voices heard presupposes the presence of the other being a partner in the democratic space, and by hearing other voices out, it implies that another war has to be waged — not a war for peace but peace as a 'war continued through other means'.

Endnotes:

1. Rajni Kothari took strong exception to my use of the phrase 'waging peace' when I precisely made this argument while interacting with an international audience way back in 1999. Kothari's was obviously a pacifist line of argument informed by strong traces of Gandhism. Priyankar Upadhyay albeit in a different context jokingly describes it as the *Om Shanti*-kind of argument' referring to the belief that mere chanting of peace — without actually making an effort for it — will bring about peace. But Upadhyay will not agree with my view of peace as war carried out by other means.
2. An ex-Naxalite leader from the Northeast actually maintains this.
3. One of my students, who seemed eager to find out the link — if there is any between feminism and lesbianism — went to interview a top-ranking leader of an established left party. As soon as she explained to her the research problem, she was turned out of the party's office.
4. Manoranjan Mohanty for instance makes such a plea.
5. Interestingly an eminent CPI(M) leader describes it as *matabbari* (uncalled-for interference).

Maoists Gaining Global Support

Anirban Roy

New Delhi's carrot-and-stick approach in handling the Maoist issue is all set to entangle India in a major embarrassment in the global theatre. While the UPA government always claims to be 'keen' in initiating a peace agreement with the red insurgents, its aggressive counter-insurgency actions, in the form of Operation Green Hunt, has transformed some of the areas in the states of Chhattisgarh, Odisha, Jharkhand and Andhra Pradesh into battlefields.

It is acknowledged that poverty and backwardness in the tribal areas of central India are the cause of the Maoist upsurge. Still the state governments, as well as the Centre, even after 65 years of Independence, are not ashamed of the underdevelopment. Instead, they are pushing the anti-Maoist operations forward with zeal. After all, Prime Minister Manmohan Singh describes the Maoist upsurge as 'the single biggest internal security challenge ever faced by India'. So the peace initiative with the Maoists, has now taken a back-seat.

Killings Subverted Peace Efforts

The first initiative of peace with the Maoists suffered a major jolt with the killing of top Maoist leader and peace interlocutor, Cherukuri Rajkumar, alias Comrade Azad, on 1 July 2010 by the Andhra Pradesh police. Azad was apparently engaged in a dialogue with New Delhi's peace emissary Swami Agnivesh and was exploring the possibilities of opening the first channel of peace talks. The Arya Samaj rector was appointed by none other than the home minister of India, P. Chidambaram, to broker peace with the Maoists.

The next possibility of peace talks with the Maoists, initiated in West Bengal, also came to a grinding halt with the killing of Mallojula

Koteswar Rao, alias Comrade Kishenji, in West Midnapore district in November 2011, a stronghold of the radicals. The government denies it was a staged killing. Still, in a knee-jerk reaction, the mediators' group resigned and refused to push forward the peace agenda.

As New Delhi's peace agenda with the Maoists is under serious question, the CPI(Maoist) would now shy away from the path of peace and try to push its people's war with a vengeance. As a result, the states where the Maoists have a strong presence will remain trouble-torn for at least a few more years with killings and counter-killings. The poor tribals will now have to bear the brunt of the ruthless counter-insurgency operations, which is aimed at eroding the ongoing people's war.

Waging the people's war, the CPI(Maoist) may not be in its best shape and command because six of its politburo members have been killed and four other politburo members, including Kobad Ghandy, arrested during the last five years. CPI(Maoist) general secretary Muppala Lakshmana Rao, alias Ganapathy, is running the organisation with active support and advice of two other politburo leaders — Prashant Bose, alias Kishanda, and Katakam Sudarshan, alias Anand. Still, the barefoot rebels of central India have succeeded in transforming their cause as a 'global political issue'.

Global Solidarity With Maoists

On 4 February 2012, a non-descript organisation, India Solidarity, staged a demonstration before the Indian embassy in Oslo, Norway, in support of the people's war waged by the CPI(Maoist) and the poor peasants against the Indian ruling classes and the Central government. The organisation was founded on 7 December 2011 in Norway by a group of anti-imperialists. It plans to hold open meetings on the people's war in India, and is organising a series of demonstrations against Operation Green Hunt.

The Maoist movement has support in Sweden as well. On 1 February 2012, a lecture on 'Imperialist War on Indian Masses, Challenges before Revolutionary Movemen't organised at the Press Club of Hyderabad, was attended by Swedish journalist and author

Jan Myrdal. The Stockholm-based author and journalist, who had interviewed Ganapathy in 2010, was the chief guest at the programme. During the last couple of years, Myrdal has been doing a series of writings on the Maoist movement in different publications in Europe.

Being an active member of the Co-ordination Committee of Maoist Parties and Organisations of South Asia and because of its close association with some of the members of the defunct Revolutionary Internationalist Movement, the CPI(Maoist) has started getting active support from fraternal organisations across the globe. Several other organisations like the Internationalist Proletarian Committee (IPC) have launched a massive campaign across the globe as well as on the Internet to portray New Delhi's image as a repressive administration.

Even as the CPI(Maoist) campaigns against granting mining rights to multinational giants, solidarity messages pour in everyday from Italy, France, Germany, Spain, Sweden, Canada and the Philippines. In one of the recent letters, the IPC's unit in Spain said that the struggle in India by the CPI(Maoist) actually represents one of the spearheads of the proletarian world revolution. 'The revolution in India is overcoming all odds and difficulties imposed by the Indian State and the imperialists, marching on victoriously,' the letter says.

Most of the global radical communist fraternal organisations adviced the CPI(Maoist) not to follow in the footsteps of the Unified Communist Party of Nepal (Maoist) or UCPN-M, which joined the political mainstream in 2006, and subsequently took active part in the electoral process of the Himalayan nation. 'For the international communist movement, triumph of people's war in India would mean the triumph of a revolutionary line over the revisionist and conciliatory thesis, promoted, for example, by the UCPN-M or the Revolutionary Communist Party (of the US), on a global basis,' the IPC says.

Global proletarian organisations are now making the best use of the social networking sites to campaign for the people's war in India. The international campaign on the Maoist issue is likely to catch New

Delhi on the wrong foot. Though it claims to be a torchbearer of 'democratic values' and emerging superpower, India has been ravaged by neo-liberalism and increasingly getting divided between the rich and the poor.

The Northeast Connection

In addition to the 'international lobbying', the barefoot Maoists have now started widening the ambit of their area of operation even to the insurgency-ravaged Northeast. The CPI(Maoist) has established tactical understanding with the separatist outfits in Manipur and Assam. Traditionally, the Maoists are known to be active in the Pashupati-Tirupati corridor. This 'tactical understanding' can now be dangerous for India because almost all the top insurgent outfits in the Northeast have strong links with the Chinese, Pakistani and Burmese agencies. And a section of Naga insurgents have reportedly been supplying arms and ammunition to the Maoists.

A stronger operational understanding between the Maoists and the insurgents in the Northeast may add to New Delhi's troubles. Departing from its traditional carrot-and-stick approach on the Maoist issue, the Union ministry of home affairs should now look for a long-term solution to tackle the radical communist insurgency and win back the confidence of tribal people in the Maoist strongholds. Otherwise, internationalisation of the issue will continue to show India in poor light.

Section III

State and Non-state Violence and Politics of Peace-making

People's War as Strategy and Peace Talks as Tactics

Gautam Navlakha

On the face of it, it appears as though a movement which hit the headlines with an abortive attempt on the life of former West Bengal chief minister Buddhadeb Bhattcharjee on 2 November 2008 met its waterloo with the custodial killing of Kishenji, the politburo member of the CPI(Maoist) and in-charge of the eastern regional bureau of the party, on 24 November 2011. But that would be glib talk for the simple reason that the movement neither began in 2008 nor has ended with the setback suffered by the party in recent times.

However, to understand the current disarray one has to explore where the Maoists went wrong in order for them to move ahead because, despite killings, arrests and enforced surrender of Maoist cadres, the fact remains that a new generation of cadres from the oppressed classes had emerged in Junglemahal and still exists — depletion in their ranks notwithstanding.

It is my understanding that the people's war being waged by the CPI(Maoist) provides the critical cutting edge without which it is well nigh impossible to imagine a revolutionary transformation in India. Without their revolutionary warfare we cannot meet the propensity of the Indian State to carry out military suppression nor be able to focus on seizure of power. But I do not believe revolution in contemporary India can be brought about through single party hegemony. Not in contemporary India with its social diversity and political plurality. Therefore, while the carping critics of the CPI(Maoist) ought to know that their resistance using constitutional means acquires its political edge from the people's war and indeed their proclivity to lapse into legalism and reform is kept in check by their presence. The Maoists, too, have to realise, in view of actual restrictions and impediments in their path and the social reality of overground resistance being offered by a wide spectrum of revolutionary and reformist formations acts as a force multiplier for their people's war. It is their complementary roles that I believe needs to be looked into.[1]

A spate of crackdowns and arrests made by the security agencies in the last two years (2009-2010) in Uttar Pradesh, Bihar, Haryana, Gujarat, Maharashtra, Odisha and West Bengal does suggest that the Maoists have suffered setback. But it also shows how rapidly the Maoists had spread in different parts of India! Their critics were proved wrong in claiming that the Maoist strategy was leading nowhere. In Bengal's Junglemahal region, they had managed to break the shackles and managed to emerge as a strong fighting force of the people just as they did in Dumka (Jharkhand). In purely politico-military terms, the meticulously planned looting of armouries as well as jail raids showed that they were capable of moving a force of 200-500 across a large territory, something not possible without a social base in those territories, to carry out operations. No longer were they a rag-tag guerrilla band, the irregular or partisan of the yore, but an army in the making. In all these areas, they have been actively engaged in building public assets such as ponds, roads, and work teams to develop agriculture, provide elementary health care and education to the people. And this did help place the likelihood of revolutionary transformation back on the agenda. But the setback suffered by them needs to be explained. Given that we do not have access to their assessment of such losses, we have to rely on information available in the public domain. And this itself has its problem of reliability. These caveats ought to be kept in mind. It is my conviction that more than holding 'peace' talks what matters is how the Maoists wage their people's war, because 'peace' talks are a matter of tactics, while waging people's war is the strategy for successful consummation of revolution. It is their people's war, which informs their tactics of talks.

Fight for Alternative Development and Dignity

The Maoists had been working among the tribals in Junglemahal since 1994. The area, in fact, has also been the scene of a celebrated peasant uprising in early 1970s. A number of revolutionary parties were active here. The struggle for a separate Jharkhand state picked up by 1980s and found some resonance here, boosting identity politics. Some revolutionary formation, working here for several decades spearheaded the demand for an autonomous council for Junglemahal after the emergence of Jharkhand state in 2000. The Maoist Coordination Centre (MCC) had had a presence in Purulia since the mid-1960's or rather the group within the Communist Party of India (Marxist) which then spun off into MCC. By the 1990s, CPI(ML)-People's War activities also picked up. The administration began to take notice of this and conducted raids in 2002 to 'nip the People's War-MCC in the bud'. Arrest and sexual exploitation of *Adivasis* was common in the name of hunting PW-MCC (*The Times of India*, 10 October 2002). It was reported that people were told to join either the ruling CPI(M) or the Jharkhand Party or else they would be seen as PW-MCC supporters. On 9 October 2002, the same newspaper quoted an old man as complaining: 'We are being punished for demanding development. If one had to do *janayuddha* (people's war) for a health centre, one might as well as do it.' The use of *janayudha* is a sure sign that the Maoists had been working there and this keyword had became part of the common language.

By 2003, it was also being reported by Kolkata newspapers that the Maoists were running schools for children of the *Adivasis*. Though the Maoists had emerged as a key player with the Nandigram and Singur struggle, it was the movement in Junglemahal that catapulted them to prominence. The IED attack on Buddhadeb Bhattacharjee on 2 November 2008 was meant to do that, which evoked a police crackdown on tribal villagers that led to the birth of the People's Committee against Police Atrocities (PCPA), represented by a number of radical and pro-people forces. When the *Bharat Jakat Majhi Marwa* (All India Association of *Majhis* or traditional chiefs) negotiated, unilaterally, an agreement with the local administration in November 2008, its principal demands of the people were rejected. As a result, the younger section of the tribals refused to accept the terms and withdraw the blockade they had set up. The demand for police personnel to come before the tribal assembly and beg forgiveness for the crimes they had committed against the people acquired life of its own with the expulsion of police and administration from Lalgarh area and with PCPA running the administration. Also, the CPI(Maoist), it appears, was clear that the struggle in Jungalmahal was a struggle of the general people, initiated by the tribals and not a tribal identity struggle, as some revolutionary groups insisted. The combined Scheduled Caste-Scheduled Tribe population in Lalgarh and Belpahari blocks, the area of struggle, is 55% and 58% of the total. This meant that more than 40% of the people did not think of themselves as or were tribals, and it was necessary to unite them.

It is worth noting that the Maoist's criticism of Santosh Rana led the CPI(ML)-PCC [Letter of CPI(Maoist) to Santosh Rana and reply from the CPI(ML)-PCC, 29 October 2009] for pushing ahead with the demand for an autonomous council for Junglemahal within the state of West Bengal and characterizing it as promoting tribal identity politics or playing into the hands of Left Front government did not mean that the Maoists were opposed to identity struggles such as the Kamatapuri and Gorkhaland movements. Moreover, the 'tactics and strategy of Indian revolution' of the CPI(Maoist) states that 'the party should organise *Adivasis*' with the slogans — 'Right over the forest belongs to people and Adivasis', 'Political autonomy to *Adivasi* territories' and transform the territory as exploitation-free territory, that is, 'red land', 'Don't be divided, be united', 'Unite the real friends against the real enemies', 'Right over all resources, including water and forest', 'Right for protecting their own culture and development' — and draw up a specific plan for work among them to 'mobilise them against economic, political, social and cultural oppression ...' Yet the Maoists were right in emphasising that the 'divisions' in the *Adivasi* could neither be lost sight of nor it would be correct to essentialise tribal identity and underplay class divisions and struggle. The lessons of Dandakaranya tend to confirm the correctness of this approach. After all, revolutionary movements are not wedded just to the issue of forest rights and opposed to land grab by corporations and displacement of people and loss of livelihood. They go beyond, by turning the focus on the issue of political power and work for a socialist planned economy. Unlike in Dandakaranya where the earliest struggles were based on mobilisation of the masses to increase *tendu* leaf collection rates, in Junglemahal, the rates were increased by a fiat of Maoist armed squads and not by people's struggle. The fight against police atrocity attracted large number of people, but there is little information about how large plots of land were occupied. Apart from sporadic redistribution of the land under occupation of corrupt CPI(M) leaders, a political programme based on primary demands like land, water, forest rights and employment, and mass struggle to implement them, which might have been more effective in exposing and isolating the CPI(M) was also missing. In its absence, the killing of CPI(M) cadres of other parties' supporters was deeply flawed.

Tactical Blunder: Maoist Control of PCPA

The mass front in the shape of PCPA had created a favourable ground for further expansion and consolidation of the Maoists. In Maoist parlance, Junglemahal was a guerrilla zone, meaning that it was an area of contention between the forces of the State and the revolutionaries. But there were confusion over Maoists' role in PCPA. On 15 June 2009, Maoist leader Bikash said at a press conference that the CPI(Maoist) had built the movement and was directing it. He thereby denied direct political space to the people and other political groups. Whereas in an interview with *Frontline* (October 24-November 6, 2009), Kishenji had said that not only were the PCPA and the Maoist movement 'not the same', but also 'it would be incorrect to say that the people of the region have been influenced only by the Maoists; they have been very much influenced by the PCPA also.' But it does appear that after the initial period when PCPA was formed and replaced the traditional *Adivasi* chiefs, the control passed into the hands of the Maoists. This coincided with the start of joint forces operation 9 June 2009 onwards. Taking credit for the movement in Junglemahal and declaring that they control it in the midst of a war made sense only if PCPA was really controlled by them. The way news spread, it became a political miscalculation and undercut PCPA's emergence as a mass movement, one with people's own creative endeavors and representing diverse political forces, even when the Maoists were the dominant force in this coalition. What it also did was push the CPI(Maoist) into the forefront.

The emergence of PCPA was no doubt a great achievement. Influenced as it was by the Maoist movement, the work carried out by PCPA in the field of health and education, their small irrigation projects to benefit peasants and help provided to small and marginal farmers, and the participation of women were remarkable contributions in a short span of time. They were remarkable also because they came in face of all-out efforts by the LF-led state administration and security forces to physically close the health centres and schools or simply interdict doctors and teachers from entering these areas.

All the work being done held out the promise of providing the Maoists with a mass organisation for a mass front and effectively getting around the proscription imposed on them that banned them from mass political work. So the urge to take credit and claim leadership of and control the movement widened the rift in the united effort of diverse political persuasions in Junglemahal and made the control of PCPA by the Maoists a divisive issue.

A comparison between with write-ups on Junglemahal between November 2008 and June 2009 and thereafter shows that. The Maoists' claim also lent weight to the propaganda of the CPI(M)-led Bengal government and the UPA government at the Centre that PCPA was nothing but a Maoist outfit. After its control became a divisive issue, PCPA helped the way for the joint forces' operation. Knowing fully well that such an offensive was imminent as soon as the elections to the 15th Parliament (May 2009) were over (and to keep the united front intact), the Maoists ought not to have sent conflicting signals about the nature of their relationship with PCPA.

By the time the 2011 elections to the state Assembly dawned, the situation had altered, which was revealed when the Maoists movement differed over the polls. But before that, let us consider another tactical blunder.

Tactical Blunder II: Killing of Political Opponents

In response to Sujato Bhadra's criticism of the Maoists for taking recourse to violence, Kishenji justified the spurt in killings, saying that these are not normal conditions but conditions of war where rules are different. He also said: 'In order to tire out informers, the people are adopting a number of methods. On the other side, the State is also trying everything in its power to whet their greed. Thus the number of informers being killed is also mounting. Had there been some proper system in Jungalmahal today, the number of informers getting killed would have been far less. In different parts of Dandakaranya, informers are being detained in people's prisons.' (http://sanhati.com/excerpted/18730). It is true that in conditions of war, the difference between combatants and non-combatants become decisive and informer or couriers are counted as combatants. When one condemns the Maoists for the killings it is not as though they alone are responsible for them. The large-scale killings by members or goons of CPI(M), Congress, BJP, Trinamul, etc, as well as the killings undertaken by the security forces at the behest of these parties and other, smaller anti-Maoist formations should not be ignored.

Nevertheless, revolutionaries fighting a war cannot adopt the same approach as counter-revolutionaries. Indeed, the rules of war adopted by revolutionaries are also meant to enhance their political appeal and rally those sections of people that are considered friends or allies. Besides, absence of jails is not as important a factor because their control of the area is far less effective than — in the case of CPI(Maoist) — in Dandakaranya. And the increase in the killing of 'informers' was linked to the increase in the number of 'informers' which, not in small measure, was the result of the diktat issued to CPI(M) members or their supporters in Junglemahal to leave the party or face social boycott or even death. CPI(M), then ruling party in Bengal, and the security forces both found in this a useful way of infiltrating PCPA. This, I believe, contributed to the increase in the number of informers.

Furthermore, without politically isolating CPI(M) through a popular political campaign, the increased killings actually eroded the

Maoist appeal and hghlighted the political consequences of such killings. Equally wrong were killings of people who belonged to another political formation such as Sudhir Mandi, chairman of Binpur II *panchayat samiti* from 2003 to 2008 who owned no more than 1 acre of land and lived in a thatched house, for being a member of what was an anti-Maoist vigilante group. Be that as it may, in his interview to *Frontline* (October 26-November 6, 2009), Kishenji said that 'in the last seven months 52 CPI(M) members were killed by them'. The total number of killings varies from 75 to 400 for 2009-2011. While not all killings can be attributed to the Maoists, they were responsible for a large number of them. The eastern regional bureau of the Maoists was reportedly criticized by the CPI(Maoist) central committee for 'un-necessary killings' (*The Indian Express*, 14 November 2011).

Tacit Support to TMC: Major Political Blunder

But by far the major political blunder was the Maoists' tacit support for TMC in the 2011 Assembly elections. This was reflected in the confusion within PCPA and the CPI(Maoist) over whether to participate in the polls, support TMC in the elections or boycott the polls. These divisions and confusion helped TMC, which won four of the five Assembly seats in Junglemahal. Thus, whereas voting was less than 10% in the 2009 the parliamentary elections, it crossed 60% in the 2011 May Assembly elections. What does this imply? That, unlike the 2009 parliamentary elections, there was no poll boycott campaign by the Maoists in 2011. The question is: Did the Maoists encourage people to vote for TMC? Another implication could be that the Maoists had lost ground since their heydays of 2009-10? The lack of clarity in 2011 about the elections was also the result of tactical decisions taken in 2009-10 when repression was severe and PCPA members were told to join TMC in order to protect them.

Through this period leading up to the Assembly elections in 2011, calculated ambiguity seemed to have been the buzz word in so far as Maoist support for TMC was concerned. Thus when the *Anand Bazar Patrika* (largest circulating Bangla newspaper) claimed in February 2011 that Kishenji had said that his party would like to see Mamata

Banerjee as the chief minister of West Bengal, the news got widespread coverage. Now it is a known that this was an invention of the newspaper and not the exact words of Kishenji. But what is intriguing is despite the deliberate distortion and misrepresentation by the newspaper, the CPI(Maoist) did not issue a denial immediately. Why did it not do so and set the record straight?

Without issuing a denial, the Maoists leaders gave life to the claim that they favoured TMC, which confused their own rank and file as well as the ordinary voters. Such was the level of confusion within the CPI(Maoist) that when the jailed PCPA president Chhatradhar Mahato decided in April 2011 to contest the elections, one section of the Maoists supported him, while another opposed his candidature. Many of his own followers demanded to know why they were asked to gravitate towards TMC when they faced attacks from the *Harmad Bahini* (private army of the then ruling CPI(M)). If the Maoists' strategy was to use the contradiction within the ruling classes to their advantage, in reality they were the ones who to be used and disadvantaged. If talks are a tactical issue then tactical ambiguity over elections can be a dangerous game and, as happened later, even have a great impact on the people. Significantly, no sooner did TMC came to power in Bengal than it began propagating that the Maoists and CPI(M) were allies. TMC replaced CPI(M)'s *Harmad Bahini* with its own *Bhairav Bahini.* And unlike the CPI(M)-led government, which after coming to power in 1977 released all political prisoners unconditionally, the TMC-led government decided to delay the process and impose conditions for the release of political prisoners. The prospects of peace talks, already floundering, were finally dashed with the custodial killing of Kishenji on 24 November 2011.

Thus, when the talks with interlocutors began, the Maoists were already on the back foot. They were coming under attack from the joint forces as well as TMC's private army in the area. Indeed post-elections, TMC moved in quickly to fill the vacuum left by CPI(M). The explanation offered above is sketchy because few are privy to tyhe Maoists' assessment of what went wrong there. But recalling what happened in Andhra Pradesh in 2004, if one tries to search for a possible parallel we come across the same problem that we do not become wiser. For instance, the political report of the Unity Congress in 2007, says that those who were in favour of talks in Andhra in 2004 had argued that '(t)he question of going for talks is an issue related to political tactics and utilization of the contradictions within the ruling classes. Ever since the ... declaration of Naxalism as the principal agenda in its election manifesto by the TDP (Telugu Desam Party) the political situation in the state had taken a significant turn and issue of talks came prominently to the forefront ... It was thus an outcome of public pressure ... and in such a situation our party would only have been isolated if it did not go for talks ...' They argued that 'we were clear in our assessment that the period of ceasefire would not last for more than six months and that there will not be any substantial outcome from the talks, the short period of relaxation would also be used to some extent for conducting revolutionary propaganda The current losses in AP are not related to talks but are a result of our overall weak subjective strength as well as some long term weaknesses.'

However, those who were critical of this line felt differently: 'The demand of the then existing concrete objective condition was to utilize the relaxation in the enemy's repression in order to complete the preparation for confronting future offensive and for advancing the war and thereby strengthening our subjective forces. The tactics of talks was in no way in accordance with this demand.' They also pointed out that '(at) that time our underground Party structure, secret functioning and our armed strength were weak'. The report then noted that 'by a majority vote the Congress expressed the opinion that 'taking into consideration the concrete objective situation in AP and the concrete subjective condition of our Party at that time' it was not correct to go for talks with the AP government.' Note the difference in emphasis on preparing for the offensive in the making and opposition to across the table talks. This leaves us with tantalising questions. What were the subjective weaknesses that are being alluded to? What were the 'long term weaknesses'? If the talks had to be pursued and the Maoists' assessment was that they would not last beyond six months, why did they expose their rank and file by organizing mass meetings in full glare of intelligence agencies who meticulously video-graphed them and used it to track down underground members later? Knowing their own 'long-term weaknesses' and erosion of subjective factors what did the CPI(Maoist) stand to gain from entering into talks?

Bengal Peace Process In the light of Andhra Experience

Given the Andhra experience, questions are naturally being raised after the failure of the recent 'peace initiative' in Bengal. These questions become all the more alarming if the account provided by one of the interlocutor, Sujato Bhadra, is to be taken at face value. [Peace Talk Process in Junglemahal; *Mainstream* Vol. L, No. 1 24 December 2011 (annual 2011)]. Caution is necessary and we should accept what Bhadra says with a pinch of salt, because there is no authoritative statement from the Maoists' side. Also, it is much too laudatory of TMC to the point that its treacherous role, including in the custodial killing of Kishenji, is something that does not find a word of condemnation. Indeed, he ignores the dastardly role of TMC.

That TMC was using the security forces' might to carry out the dirty task of murders, rapes and forced surrenders finds no reference in this account. But more startling are Bhadra's claim that the Maoists had stopped insisting on withdrawal of the joint forces and in fact, contrary to public statements, were privately in agreement with the interlocutors that the joint forces' activities had reduced or that the release of political prisoners was not an issue for the Maoists are astounding claims. One has to wait for the CPI(Maoist) to respond and clarify its stance.

So What Are We to Make of This?

In war as in politics, choosing strategic friends and allies as well as fighting the main enemy is of decisive significance. Carl Schmitt says: 'War finds its meaning in enmity. Because it is continuation of politics, politics too always involves an element of enmity, at least potentially; and if peace contains within itself the possibility of war — something that by the standards of experience has unfortunately proved to be true — peace too contains a moment of potential enmity.' The question, however, is whether the enmity can be contained and regulated, that is, whether it represents relative or absolute enmity.[2]

United Front: Needed More During Enemy Offensive

When military offensive is imminent, dividing the enemy is a tactical need. But PCPA was a coalition of class friends and allies. There were others who were earlier part of the struggle but had parted ways. They were political opponents and certainly part of the broad coalition of pro-revolutionary bent. Not keeping doors open for them and resolving political battles through annihilation (such as that of Sudhir Mandi, chief of Binpur II *panchayat* from 2003 to 2008, killed in November 2008) was simply wrong if not a criminal. In an interview that the CPI(Maoist) general secretary gave in January 2010, he made an observation about the importance of 'partial' victories or reforms, even when the CPI(Maoist) is committed for total revolution. This is part of the Maoists' practice and evident in areas where they are present where they encourage people to fight for various entitlements and welfare projects. Thus the CPI(Maoist) is aware of the need for some relief, some respite for the people. However, what has not been understood is that to fight for their rights people need mobilisation and an organisation. Since the Maoists' party is banned and their open activities are prohibited, its overt presence is a difficult proposition. The absence of mass fronts apart, there is very little mass work going on outside struggle zones. All this demands a relook at the pro-people forces that are working overground and at the likelihood of working with and not against each other. Trying to establish the CPI(Maoist)'s hegemony with the help of its guns is negation of revolutionary politics. In the interview to *The Hindu* (14 April 2010), Cherukuri Rajkumar, alias Azad, said that actually '(t)he Party and leadership will grow rapidly in times of war ... War is giving birth to new generals and commanders, which we never anticipated in normal times. While it took several years to produce a leader of caliber in relatively peaceful times, it is taking a fraction of that time in the midst of the war situation.' This happened also during the two previous operations launched against the Maoists in Dandakranya, in 1991 and 1997. How realistic is this assessment? Wars do sharpen people's powers of comprehension, and they also help spread their political appeal not only in areas where they dominate but also amongst those whose imagination is stirred by the Maoist movement. But it is equally true that civil wars which tend to be 'dirty wars' can alienate sections of the people because of needless blood-letting, conflicting loyalties and absence of mass political mobilisations.

Revolutionary War Does Not Mean Reckless Killings

The killing of CPI(M) activists, too, does not escape this criticism. By Kishenji's own account, 52 CPI(M) members were killed in just seven months of 2009. What were the charges against each of them? The failure to provide any information on each of these killings means we have only anecdotal explanations that they were all cruel and corrupt people, but there is no documented account available in the public domain. So how do we know if the killings of CPI(M) members were annihilation of political opponents or of 'informers' who had committed heinous crimes? I am against death penalty as such. But those who do subscribe to it, as the CPI(Maoist) does, are obligated to share the evidence if they want to convince people that those were not arbitrary acts or use of force to settle political scores. For Kishenji to have suggested that one of the factors contributing to the killings was the lack of jails in Junglemahal unlike in Dandakaranya is unfortunate. But it also points to the fact that while the Maoists did expand politically and geographically (an essential feature of area-wise seizure of power) in these new areas, they made up for absence of their political hegemony in the contentious zone with use of force. Their control was not just contentious but also politically weak. Also, they did not follow their own constitutional principle and practices of Dandakranya here. The actual practice of Dandakranya is that the death sentence is not necessarily given even in cases where an informer had brought about physical harm to people or the Maoist party. Also, in cases where the death sentence has been awarded, it has had to be approved by the higher instance. This is aimed at discouraging arbitrary acts as well as needless killings.

I am also of the view that had the Maoists encouraged democratic rights organisations to investigate such cases it would have brought out the facts related to the killings and helped silence the revulsion caused among many democratic-minded people, particularly in Bengal. This is necessary to keep in mind because there is a vocal opinion in the country that accepts the legitimacy and strategic importance of armed struggle for revolutionary transformation but does not condone or accept reckless killings and arbitrary acts or use of force to resolve political battles. Just as we do not condemn lynching of rapists, murderers, extortionists by women of a *chawl* in Nagpur but regard as bestial the massacres carried out by the Hindutva brigade, we mourn the death of our heroes such as Azad and Kishenji, but we do not mourn for Indira Gandhi.

These differences are grounded in political ethics. For people to be able to distinguish killings requires the Maoist movement to make itself accountable, not just to its own rank and file, but also to those whom it wants to or is trying to win over, because when we start looking into such killings we discover that there have been far too many of them that were abhorrent to revolutionary practice. Carl Schmitt reminds us: 'That heart of political is not enmity per se but the distinction of friends and enemy.' To treat as enemy an ideological opponent while enhancing the importance of tactical ally in the shape of a ruling class formation such as TMC is to devalue the significance of revolutionary politics. It is certainly true that many Maoists and PCPA members, too, were killed. But revolutionary warfare is not based on principle of reciprocity. Mao's admonition that 'revolution is not a tea party' is not to be taken literally. It was meant to draw attention to the fact that it involves bloody engagement and not a call to commit brutal acts. While war is a continuation of politics by other means, Mao also pointed out that war is politics, meaning thereby that the practice of revolutionary warfare is intrinsically political. If this is so then revolutionary warfare sets itself apart by the conduct of its warfare. While the pent-up fury of the oppressed, as Azad had said in his interview, is at times difficult to contain[3], he also accepted that the urban middle class perception could vary from that of the oppressed and exploited with their suppressed rage at gross injustice to which they are subjected. But the killings point to a more critical lapse. While the footprint of guerilla is large, the political presence of the CPI(Maoist) does not necessarily match this. The absence of Maoist party units at the village level in some areas was observed by the CPI(Maoist)'s 9th congress.

The presence or absence of the Maoist party unit is not a mechanical thing. It is, in fact, of political significance, because the tasks of mobilizing people, carrying on work designed to help a 'people's economy', ensuring participation of people in the goal of improving their economy and inspiring them to join the Maoist party and become a guerrilla, etc, are not possible without this. Wars, in particular civil wars, are brutal and cruel. Experience shows that 'goodness', is not reciprocated by government forces and agencies. Thus when one pushes the Maoists to accept the Geneva Convention — especially its Article 3 and Protocol II — which applies to the conduct of wars that are not international in nature, could one be exposing them to the 'venomous bites' of the State? Or actually encouraging them to acknowledge the importance of fighting their revolutionary war honorably as behoves a pro-people movement.

Maoist Dilemma over Chhatradhar Mahato

Finally, it is intriguing why there was divided opinion within the CPI(Maoist) over Chhatradhar Mahato's decision to contest the Assembly elections. What does this signify? Some objected and asked people not to vote for him, whereas others lent him support. Should not the entire CPI(Maoist) have supported his candidature? So a larger issue stares at us. For instance, the charge and counter-charge against the Maoists for having supported TMC to the extent that they campaigned even against the jailed PCPA leader Chhatradhar Mahato, brings to the fore an old problem which confronts them.

What should be the approach towards elections during protracted people's war and if they bend their own rules, what course of action would be a better option: to support one ruling class formation against another or encourage those who are part of a mass movement to contest? In the 2004 elections in Andhra Pradesh, the then CPI(ML)-People's War was accused of carrying out a lukewarm election boycott campaign that ended up helping Congress sweep the polls.

Remarkably, neither in Andhra in 2004 nor in Bengal in 2011, were talks contingent upon Maoists' backing Congress or TMC, respectively, in the elections. It was the Maoists' own calculations which pushed them, tacitly if not overtly, to support one ruling class party over another. Considering the decimation of the rank and file of the Maoists in Andhra in 2004-05 at the hands of the very same Congress whom they had tacitly supported, it is intriguing that the CPI(Maoist) adopted a course that helped TMC in areas where the radicals were strong. Indeed in Junglemahal, it is more than likely that the easy arrests and killings of Maoists could be traced to their easy identification by the TMC members. Both situations bring out the need for the Maoists to relook at their election policy. In Bengal, between 2008 and 2011, the Maoists could have encouraged PCPA to put up candidates as a way of enhancing their own political appeal.

This is all the more important if talks with the government are seen as being a tactical issue. If tactical, then there was nothing to be gained from backing TMC, rather the Maoists should have worked to ensure that TMC did not replace CPI(M) and allowed to consolidate their hold. Bernard De'Mello has said: 'What makes the implementation of mass line even more difficult is Article 59 of the constitution of the (Maoist) party that directs the party fraction in the mass organization to dictate terms thereby encouraging 'commandism' which can lead to 'isolationism'', i.e. the party ultimately failing to gain the support of the non-party leaders of its mass organisations.'[4]

Maoist Leadership Should Clear Its Stand on Talks

It remains to be seen whether the Maoist party will remove the confusion that prevails over its stance on talks in the light of the experience in Andhra in 2004, custodial killing of Azad in 2010 by using the Union home ministry-appointed mediator to track him, and the most recent custodial torture and killing of Kishenji while interlocutors were employed to ostensibly explore the possibility of talks. Whether these major setbacks of mediated talks would compel the CPI(Maoist) to revert to its earlier stance enunciated by its central committee remains to be seen.

The importance of this lies in asking the government to talk to jailed Maoist leaders to work out the modalities, a task currently done by mediators/interlocutors, with such disastrous outcome. Also if holding talks in Andhra was wrong, then did the CPI(Maoist) approach the talks in Bengal along the majority line at the Unity Congress 2007 on the issue of talks in Andhra Pradesh, that is, 'to utilise the relaxation in the enemy's repression in order to complete the preparation for confronting future offensive to utilise the relaxation in the enemy's repression in order to complete the preparation for confronting future offensive ...'?

What explains the deviation from the majority line of the Maoist party's congress? Does it mean that the party's state committee and/or the eastern regional bureau went beyond this in agreeing to whittle down its demand on the issue of unconditional release of political prisoners and withdrawal of the joint forces from Junglemahal? We can only make an educated guess, but the last has not been heard on this. nevertheless, the movement which leaders like Kishenji built is still alive, battered and bruised no doubt. The Maoist movement did strike roots. This is the great contribution of Kishenji, a Maoist revolutionary.

To serve the cause of the revolution for the emancipation of our people is the mark of greatness. To live and work among the people, without the comfort of being in one place constantly and yet to retain the focus and not waver, is not a simple thing. It takes courage and conviction. It would take mortals like me ten lives to achieve what Kishenji left behind for us to emulate. It is this commitment and integrity which will endure, many tactical blunders and strategic mistakes notwithstanding.

Notes:

1. Such is the confidence in the role of the revolutionary party that even the general secretary of Communist Party of India told the presss on 17 October 2011, referring to the large rally held in November 2007 at Jagdalpur in Chhattisgarh: 'I was amazed to see such huge participation of people in the rally. Neither my party nor I had any influence in Bastar. Hence, it was not possible for us to mobilise such large number of people. The rally was a success because it had the backing of Naxals.' (*The Times of India,* 17 December 2010). The local CPI leader in Bastar had earlier pointed out that 'Naxalite position at this moment is so strong among the *Adivasis* that they can, through dialogue bargain ... for strong measures that would protect the *Adivasis*, their culture and their national right over their land and forest ... ' *The Asian Age*, 18 October 2011.
2. *The Theory of Partisans: A Commentary/Remark on the Concept of the Political;* Michigan State University Press 2004]
3. Interview of CPI(Maoist) politburo member Cherukuri Rajkumar @ Azad by Siddartha Vardarajan in *The Hindu*, 14 April 2010.
4. Bernard D'Mello, *Insurgent Comrades: Maoist Learnings-by doing in India, 1967-2010* (unpublished). Article 59 of the CPI(Maoist)'s constitution says: 'The party fractions shall be formed in the executive committees of mass organizations. Party fractions will guide the executive committees of the mass organizations adopting suitable method in accordance with the correct concrete situation. Fraction will function secretly. The opinions of party committee/member guiding the fraction shall be considered as final opinion. If fraction committee members have any difference of opinion, they will send their opinions in writing to the concerned party committee/higher committee. The concerned party committees shall guide fraction committees of different mass organizations at their own level.'

The Maoist Dilemma

Dipankar Bhattacharya

The unfolding trajectory of the much-hyped 'peace initiative' of Mamata Banerjee ran perilously similar to what we had witnessed in Andhra Pradesh a few years ago. In Andhra, the Maoists had helped Congress return to power in 2004, openly calling upon the people to vote for it. The Y.S. Rajasekhara Reddy government duly launched a 'peace offensive', inviting the Maoist leadership to talks in Hyderabad. This gave the Maoists some sort of a breathing space and enormous publicity. But the negotiations between the state government and the Maoist leadership were over almost as soon as they had begun. We heard some noise about the state 'completing land reforms on a war-footing', but nothing of that sort happened on the ground. Instead, the state was seen unleashing a targeted campaign to exterminate the Maoist leadership.

In Bengal too, the Maoists had backed Mamata in no uncertain terms. On her part, Mamata too seemed quite responsive, lending vocal support to the demand for a judicial inquiry into the killing of Azad in an Andhra jungle and the call for release of political prisoners, including Maoist leaders and supporters, languishing in various Bengal jails. But once she rode the *Paribartan* wave to power it became increasingly clear that the issue of release of political prisoners or negotiations with the Maoists or the Junglemahal/PCPA leadership was not really on her agenda. Her government began to distance itself even from the limited recommendations made by concerned committees of reviewers and interlocutors.

Mamata's changing stance should not have come as a surprise to the discerning political observer, though. She had never called for an end to the Centre-state joint security forces' campaign or withdrawal of Central paramilitary troops — her objection was only to the state component [because Bengal still had a CPI(M)-led government]. Also, she never really expressed any particular sympathy for the Maoists, rather she always tended to attribute the entire Maoist phenomenon to CPI(M), often equating in her characteristic style of sweeping generalisation all variants and shades of red in Bengal politics. Once ensconced in power, she has quite seamlessly and naturally extended her 'oust CPI(M)' campaign to target every inconvenient political voice and every shade of independent social protest.

At a time when the Central government has repeatedly and categorically branded Maoists/Naxalites/left-wing extremists as the single biggest threat to internal security, it is difficult or rather impossible to expect any chief minister or state government not to comply with this doctrine. As far as the State is concerned, the politics of peace or the tactic of talks can only be subservient to this overarching strategy of 'war on Maoism/Naxalism/left-wing extremism'. This has been borne out by the experience of both Andhra, where talks had actually been initiated, and Bengal, where talks were only expected to be held. No 'civil society' stream that seeks to facilitate talks between the State and the Maoists can do so by ignoring, and certainly not by legitimising, this hard political reality.

Maoists Read Mamata Wrong

Ironically, the Maoists too had made a major mistake in reading the politics of Mamata. Thanks to her populist rhetoric and strong individualist streak, they had expected her to defy the strategic parameters of the Indian ruling classes. Kishenji had even said that parties led by dominating individual leaders could transcend the class dictates of bourgeois politics.

But for all her pronounced individualism and mercurial temperament, Mamata has already proved to be a ruthless practitioner of bourgeois politics; and none but Kishenji has become the first victim of a fake encounter in Mamata's regime. Quite unmistakably, Mamata's gospel of 'peace' has begun resembling the infamous autocratic order epitomised by Indira Gandhi in the 1970s.

Anybody having a stake in the rule of law and constitutional democracy cannot but feel concerned. A determined battle will have to be waged in Mamata-ruled Bengal to rescue and reclaim democracy on every front, whether to save the land of sharecroppers and peasants threatened with eviction and dispossession, or the democratic rights of students and workers whose unions are being forcibly taken over by TMC storm-troopers. Sections of civil society and left intelligentsia who had rather uncritically endorsed Mamata as the icon and instrument of *Paribartan* in Bengal to end CPI(M)'s seemingly interminable hold on state power will surely have a lot of rethinking to do in the coming days.

PEOPLE'S WAR AND PEACE TALKS

The Maoists too have a lot to rethink. They resent the revolutionary criticism that they have been rejecting politics and moving in an essentially anarchist direction. They would like us to believe that they are very much intervening in the political process — call it 'political intervention by military means' if you will. Their ideologues and propagandists would cite the ruling class doctrine identifying 'Maoism' as the biggest threat to internal security as an incontrovertible proof of their political success. They also claim that simultaneously they are ready for talks to explore the possibilities of a just and democratic peace. But the developments in Bengal have once again showed that much as they may claim to be powerful on the military front, in the political arena they remain as helpless and bankrupt as ever.

The crux of the problem facing the Maoists is how they really go about the whole process of talks. Even if the State agrees to hold talks without stipulating preconditions like making the Maoists lay down arms (as had actually happened in Andhra), the question remains as to what the Maoists really talk about. Evidently, the Maoists are not in a position of strength where they can force the State to make any strategic concession or agree to a calibrated transition to some new order preferred by them. The talks will invariably have to focus on specific issues like release of political prisoners, implementation of land reforms, issues of rural development, cancellation of specific projects and so on. But even if the Maoists succeed in securing some assurance or agreement from the State, how would they ensure the implementation of what the State promises?

If the Maoists are to pin the State down on specific issues of policy or implementation of government schemes and policies, they will have to enter the arena of politics that deals with bourgeois reforms and calls for everyday mass practice, something which continues to remain alien to the Maoist scheme of things. Lalgarh is a tragic example of the Maoists intervening in a powerful mass movement and ending up handing over the initiative to the State, both militarily and politically. Only time will tell if Indian Maoists who express all readiness to help bourgeois parties come to power are ready to rethink their own strategy and proceed towards any kind of independent political articulation following their disastrous experience first in Andhra and now in Bengal.

Peace is a Red Herring, Dignity and Prosperity are Real Issues

Diptendra Raychaudhuri

The Maoists have disturbed 'peace' in a large swathe of land lying between the north and southernmost parts of India. They have killed a lot of people and established a sort of 'reign of red terror' over the areas they control. However, within and around the liberated or semi-liberated territories, they have a very strong support base among the poorer people, particularly the tribal and backward population.

But the Indian ruling elite feel the Maoists should be crushed anyhow, the sooner the better, and often they are not prepared to bother about the collateral damage. At least seven state governments, aided and often guided by the sovereign federal government, have been trying for last two decades to re-establish 'peace, law and order' by reclaiming the land lost to the rebels. State forces and their proxies ranging from the *Ranbir Sena* to *Salwa Judum* have killed, tortured and raped a large number of people, mostly unarmed civilians.

Such 'operations' have actually helped the Maoists to prove their point before their support base, that the agents of the State — civil and forest administrators, police and politicians — are all and sundry enemy of the deprived and underprivileged people. There is no doubt, though, that the governments too have the support of the larger population living in territories beyond the control of the Maoists or where the rebels have no significant presence. The State forces believe they draw legitimacy from the fact that they are on the side of a democratic State and elected governments. It gives them license to be ruthless. If the Maoists blow up a bus carrying civilians and SPOs both, righteous condemnation is hurled on them from every side. If State or State-sponsored forces torture, rape or kill poor and weak people, the media seldom carry stories exposing the atrocities unequivocally, thus blotting out the possibility of larger public condemnation pouring in. The Supreme Court has banned *Salwa Judum*, but the concerned state governments and the media show no sign of remorse for glorifying that private militia (and thereby acting against the spirit of law) for more than half a decade.

Amidst such an environment of treachery, violence and ruthlessness, we have heard of peace initiatives many times in the last two decades. Various state governments have appealed for peace talks, and even Union home minister P. Chidambaram has echoed it. Such talks were held earlier, and conditions for holding another round have been considered by both the sides. Keeping in mind that the Maoist rebellion is totally different from other insurgencies based on fundamentalist and secessionist thoughts, and that the Maoists aim at radical socio-economic changes, utterly unacceptable to the ruling elite, it is not understandable what purpose talks will serve. They can at best lead to a truce, and nothing more.

Peace without Dignity is Nothing

In reality, the war between the Maoists and the State has turned out to be a free-for-all, and the mantra is *jo jita wohi Sikander*. Each side is trying to establish its domination for furthering the causes for which it stands. Ironically, both sides believe the causes they propagate are noble. However, it is essentially a battle for the mind of millions of people, and no side has a chance of winning it with weapons. Yet both sides dream of winning it exactly through weapons. More shockingly, neither side is serious about changing its approach towards the people who are victims of innumerable eviction notices, deprivation, torture and *dadagiri* (rule of might).

Under the circumstances, the word 'peace' becomes deceptive. Peace without dignity is just a prelude to another, often bigger, confrontation. That is why each time State forces are believed to have weeded out Naxalites from a particular zone, the rebels have risen like the proverbial phoenix in other areas. Rather, in last four decades, they have spread from a few districts to almost one-third of the country.

From the time of the great epics to recent days, we have innumerable examples when 'peace' has been disturbed deliberately by the gods and demigods whom people worship. *Kali* and *Durga* fought battles to break the status quo. *Rama* could have bought peace with *Ravana* by sacrificing his wife but he chose to wage a war. Despite being attacked, the US could have maintained peace. Instead, Washington waged a grammatically wrong 'war on terror' that only brought disaster and death to countries it invaded as well as to its own people. Most of such deliberate efforts to break peace have created various and often totally opposing reactions. *Asura* tribesmen till today avoid the vicinity of any *Durga-puja pandal*, because for them those are symbols of the wrong done to their ancient great king *Mahisasura*. Similarly, many people like to equate George W. Bush's war with Christianity's attempt to wipe out Islam.

So, it is less important whether peace is maintained; what is important is whether peace is justified. Breaking peace to end colonial exploitation is justified. Maintaining peace by carrying out a Jaliwanwallah Bag-type massacre is not justified. Thus, the important question is not whether it will be 'all quiet on the western front' of Bengal, or in Chhattisgarh, Jharkhand and other states. The question is whether the Junglemahals in the country will be living in signs of prosperity with dignity. Prosperity is important, particularly for those who still live in abject poverty and turn old much before time, but equally important is dignity. When, after a failed attack on former Bengal chief minister Buddhadeb Bhattacharjee's convoy, the goons in uniform unleashed brutality on the *Adivasis* of Lalgarh, the dignity of those people took a severe beating.

Those goons of CPI(M) and Bengal government cannot even imagine doing the same with the people of Kolkata or Mumbai. This very attitude of the police can be the nemesis of a democratic State. As far I know, none of those policemen have been punished even after the regime change in Bengal. And there are hundreds of instances of such brutality in states where the the Maoists have gained strong ground.

In fact, such attitude of governments of various hues gives the ordinary policeman the feeling of being above law. Ironically, except for the majority of IPS officers who themselves enjoy their role of being mightier-than-thou, as an individual most policemen are just common folk like us. The paramilitary *jawans* are our boys. They work in the way their bosses want them to do. This is mostly true about the officers as well. We hardly come across an E. Rammohan who will ignore the diktat of a chief minister and decline to kill anyone who is ready to surrender. When the police or paramilitary personnel go unpunished for their illegal acts, it sends a message that the government wants it to act in only that way. It paves the way for alienation of ever larger number of people.

So, the question of dignity will surely hang fire for a long time. Peace will bear no meaning in jungles spread over Gadchiroli to Lalgarh till the collective hurt of the tribals and non-tribal poor is assuaged.

It seems that, like all other state governments, the new government in Bengal too is quite oblivious about the social aspect behind disturbances in the heartland of India, the extension of which has reached uo to Junglemahal. Though such ignorance is potentially dangerous, for a short period Union rural development minister Jairam Ramesh's initiatives or Mamata Banerjee's appeal for giving development a chance may turn out to be good, only if it is implemented properly. The problem is, development does not depend upon a Central minister or CM's honest intention; it depends on the attitude of lower-level bureaucracy and other related sections.

In fact, it is intertwined with the concept of dignity. For ages, the rulers, their lower-level representatives, and traders have treated our *Adivasi* and *Dalit* and OBC populations as groups of gullible people who could be deceived, tortured, raped and killed with impunity. Rulers have changed, but this rotten attitude has not changed for centuries, nay, millennia. Every development effort will be usurped by these classes even now.

It is against this oppressive system that the mainland *Adivasi* population (and occasionally *Dalits* and backwards) have rebelled hundreds of times in known history. Now, the latest form of this rebellion has assumed a Maoist cover. Since I have traveled extensively through the 'Maoist' land for writing a novel keeping the rebellion as the backdrop, I can say one thing definitely: The leaders of the movement are concerned with Maoism or Mao's thoughts, but not the cadre or supporters. The leaders abide by a dogmatic and dangerous ideology, whose followers have killed innumerable people all over the world, while China, the country of its birth, has taken a U-turn to take the path of capitalism. The Maoists' ideology is dangerous, their modus operendi is fraught with grave consequences for local people, but the lower-level comrades have nothing to do with it. They fight for their own rights.

This assertion is inevitable in independent India where the dream of a less unfair society has receded farther and farther. A corrupt, headstrong and ignorant (about the reality of this country) political class and its cohorts (like middle and upper middle classes) have succeeded in making some 2-3 per cent of the population obscenely rich while providing scope to another 15-20 per cent to try and climb up the ladder. All this has taken place at the cost of 70 per cent of population whom we, the intellectual class, wished away during since the 1990s. A black lie about Manmohonomics blinded all critical faculties of a vast number intellectuals, and a selfish middle class decided to forget the vast majority.

The Maoists have come up stronger as an answer to that attitude. But it is not only the Maoists who have done so. A section of intellectuals and dedicated social workers have also emerged and taken up cudgels against the insensitiveness of the ruling elite and its cohorts. Probably, a young middle class is also emerging, prepared to fight this insensitiveness. The Maoists, because of their fanatic faith in guns and obsolete books, have failed to notice the burgeoning protest all over this country.

Kishenji: Not a Black and White Legacy

Truth is seldom etched in black and white. Most often it is all grey. It is more so in a zone of confrontation. The attitude towards recently-killed Maoist leader Kishenji, and the works he carried out throughout his life, stands testimony to this. While to many he was a villain, to others he was a hero, a character whom they saluted for the last time with the words, *amar rahe*. His body was cremated on a Sunday after it was handed to his family by the Bengal government. This is what *Hindustan Times* wrote about the cremation day: 'The small town of Peddapalli in Karimnagar district was chock-a-block on Sunday as thousands made their way there to catch a glimpse of slain Maoist leader Mallojula Koteswara Rao alias Kishenji. Since morning, people started pouring in from places as far as Nizamabad, Adilabad and Visakhapatnam. A serpentine queue could be seen at Kishenji's house at Brahmana Veedhi (street), where his body was kept. Intelligence officials said there could have been above 5,000 people. The district saw a larger turnout only during the funeral of another Maoist leader, Nalla Adi Reddy, in 1999.' (27 November 2011)

In fact, his funeral also witnessed the reading out of a statement of 'Abhay' (believed to be Kishenji's brother Mallajola Venugopal), the spokesperson for CPI(Maoist). It was read out by poet Varavara Rao who, according to *India Today*, said: 'Kishenji's death was a political murder in the name of Operation Green Hunt. But it will not demoralise the Maoist movement, which will continue.'

Kishenji was an outlaw, and still more than 5,000 people showed the temerity to attend his funeral! Such was the popular pull that the local Congress MP and *Telangana Rashtriya Samiti* legislators had to turn up there, even though they did so to show respect to a man who at a very young age had also fought for the cause of separate Telangana.

All these simply show that the government is not winning the battle for the mind. If more than 5,000 attended the funeral in that small town, one can easily imagine the magnitude of undercurrent of support for the Maoists in the Telangana region. This despite the fact that the armed movement has almost been wiped out again from the whole region. In fact, one survey published in *The Times of India* a couple of years ago stood testimony to this. The majority of the respondents in that survey conducted in five districts of Andhra, which earlier were strongholds of the Maoists, not only said they were better off when the Maoists were there, but also supported the 'means' the rebels adopted. The respondents of the survey, as well as the people who attended Kishenji's funeral, belong to the underprivileged section of our society.

It is equally true that for many people Kishenji was a villain. The families of the police or paramilitary personnel he and his People's Liberation Guerilla Army killed will always shudder at the very mention of his name. The same would be the reaction of the families of the political workers (mostly of CPI-M) who were killed by the Maoists in Bengal before the Assembly polls. This, in fact, shows that the path the Maoists are following is only dividing the poor of the country.

The 'Encounter' Killings and Mamata

There are many unanswered questions about the killing of Kishenji. Unless one gets a clear answer to the questions, the social divide will only widen. What is important is to convey a clear message to the mass base of the Maoists that the country is gradually becoming civilised and the nation will not continue to fail them.

We must never forget that the police or other security forces have no right to kill anyone after they have captured him/her. Killing someone after taking him in custody is simply a murder, both according to national law and international convention. This is as true about Kishenji as it is about the unarmed supporters of the Maoists. In Kishenji's case, there are too many holes in the story. His body was lying on the ground with the AK-47 he carried lying beside him. We have seen similar photographs hundreds of times, sometimes in Andhra, sometimes in Chhattisgarh and Gujarat, and often in Kashmir. Many cases with similar photographs have later faced flak, and in some cases truth was ripped open from heaps of lies. In some cases it has come to light that after killing innocent people, the police or the army had put the weapons beside them. So the photograph with Kishenji proves nothing.

Again, just after the 'encounter', Mamata Banerjee said she had heard '(the Maoists) have fired 1,000 rounds'. Strange! Were the

Maoists firing at the sky? The question is: If the Maoists had fired 1,000 rounds at the security forces, why not a single one of them had received any serious injury. And how in the vicinity of a village could such a marathon encounter take place?

Politicians often change their stands on the Naxalites dramatically after coming to power. We have many examples of this: N.T. Rama Rao, Janardhana Reddy, Laloo Prasad, Shibu Soren and so on. Almost every political party, except BJP, has tried to take advantage of the Maoists' presence to win a few more seats and has turned against them after coming to power. Mamata is the latest addition to the list. But, probably, there is no point in blaming politicians for this, for they don't have the option of allowing the Maoists to challenge the writ of the State by violent means. But it was Mamata who had raised questions over the killing of Azad [a CPI(Maoist) politburo member], supposedly nabbed in Chhattisgarh and executed in Andhra.

When Mamata was the minister, she had raised questions about the suspected summary execution of Azad and supported the demand for a probe into his death. Then it seemed she was an exceptional politician who cared for democracy. What was needed was a fair judicial inquiry to bring out the truth about the killings of Azad and Kishenji in 'encounters'. It was expected that Mamata, as Bengal chief minister, would order such inquiry into Kishenji's controversial death. There was no reason whatsoever why she should have two different yardsticks for two men killed in similar and controversial conditions. But her refusal to accept the same in case of Kishenji's death proved that she had swung 180 degrees since her coronation as Bengal CM.

The problem is, for millions of people Kishenji will remain a 'martyr', and his killing will stoke the sentiment that the rulers are still killing those who stand by (and for) the poor.

But it is also true that the Maoists themselves are votaries of violence. About Maoist violence, one does not need to write much, for almost everyday newspapers report it. It seems that by killing poor constables, or paramilitary *jawans* who join the security force only because they are poor, the Maoists get a strange sort of joy. Kondapalli Seetharamaiah, the founder general secretary of People's

War, was against this attitude, and for that he was thrown out of the organisation. A bitter power struggle continued within the organisation from 1987 to 1992, and finally Ganapathy took over the its leadership. It marked the end of the possibility of organising open mass movements and the beginning of isolationist arms-dependent politics. The fact that the Maoists execute people for being suspected police informers speaks volumes of heinous tendencies in them.

Thus, at the end of the day, we face a strange situation. One side has risked the lives of paramilitary *jawans* and the people to create opportunities for the super-rich to earn tens of thousands of crores ruppes more by establishing private mining fields and industries, while the other side is using those very people as canon fodder to establish its supremacy.

Every act of violence or killing is condemnable, irrespective of who the perpetrator is. The life of every individual is precious. As we are still in a lower stage of civilisation, we try to impose concepts of legality or morality on the acts of violence. That, in fact, helps both sides, in our case the Maoists and the governments, to justify their acts of violence. Common people remain sandwiched between the Maoists and the State forces, between dreams and harsh realities, between aspirations and indignity.

In Search of Lasting Solutions

The question is: Do we have any chance of finding a lasting solution. Of course, we have. But for that both sides will have to change their attitudes towards the society. The middle and upper middle class intellectuals must learn to respect the assertion of the lower 70 per cent for a socially and economically dignified life. And the Maoists will have to understand that the age of totalitarian regime they want to establish is long over. If they believe in brute force, they will be answered by brute force. It will be a never-ending war.

If the two sides do not understand what compromises they will have to make, the lives of tens of millions will be at stake for, maybe, many decades. The people who have rebelled are simple men and women, and the most deprived lot. And that is why the elite like us assume that they will tolerate everything. On the contrary, in reality dignity is as important for these men and women, either in the forests of Abhujmad or Lalgarh. Yet they are simple folk and can settle issues with utmost simplicity and magnanimity. We stand witness to their magnanimity in Lalgarh. Despite being savagely beaten up by the goons in uniform, they only demanded apology from the perpetrators of the crime. In any civilised society, those criminals should have been behind the bar.

But our ruling elite never do anything like that, because they need the forces by their side. The arrogance of the elite manifested itself in turning down the proposal of tendering 'apology'. This arrogance that essentially betrays anti-democratic, anti-poor mindset of our political class is not only enemy to peace, but has generated strong reaction against the present elite rule.

And such reaction is getting stronger among a wider mass. In Bengal, intellectuals and civil society failed to raise a strong voice supporting the demand for apology from the police to the people of Junglemahal. But in Andhra, the voice of civil society was often effective. Since the inception of simultaneous operations by the joint forces in several states under the aegis of an over-enthusiastic P. Chidambaram (who started his stint in the home ministry like a BJP jingoist), we have seen a major role played by the intellectuals. It has compelled Chidambaram to change, and even to admit the axiom that enough intelligence does not emerge out of the Maoist areas as the locals have more faith in the Maoists than the institutions of the State.

Ruling Elites and Maoists Need to Rethink

But it is high-time that the Maoists gave their politics a rethink. Azad's and Kishenji's death should lead them to some serious introspection. They have not achieved much by their over-dependence on arms. They have a large support base in the central and central-eastern part of the country, but they cannot protect their supporters. The guerrilla war they are waging will kill many of them, many dedicated workers, who could be assets in our political system. The recent arrest of Soni Sori and her nephew Lingaram Kodopi (a quiet-type whom I have met several times in the Jantar Mantar Road office of Swami Agnivesh) for being a conduit between the Essar and the Maoists in Chhattisgarh shows the pathetic condition of the local people. An article in *Frontline* (Nov 5-18, 2011) noted the most crucial fact: 'Last year, when Soni and Lingaram were accused of being party to the attack on Avdhesh Gautam, a local Congress leader and wealthy contractor, Madru Ram went to meet S.R.P. Kalluri, then Dantewada's senior superintendent of police. According to a newspaper account, when Kalluri asked Madru Ram why Soni lived and worked in an interior area, he replied that she needed the job to feed her three children. To this, Kalluri responded that she must be going to the meetings of the Maoists and giving them supplies. Madru Ram's riposte was: "Sir, doesn't everybody?" The SSP then asked, "Do you?" He replied, "No, but then I am an old man, I can afford to die." What could be more tragic than this?'

This is the reality that puts both the government forces and the Maoists in equally poor light. It is known that the agents of the State often turn notorious when they face weaker people. The IAS and IPS officers who wag their tails before the ministers turn into rogue elephants when they face the poor. Of course, there are exceptions, and such exceptions are increasing, but this is generally true. The Naxalites are no better with poor men who are not ready to nod at their whims all the time. In all the areas they dominate they torture people who are not with them. Their world, like that of all the communists of different shades all over the world, is divided between comrades and enemies. Like the elite and their cohorts, they and their sympathisers have scant regard for individual freedom. They cry hoarse about human rights after every killing by the government forces, but we all know the day they come to power, they will leave us only with the epitaph of human rights. Their respected leader Mao Zedong has shown them this path.

The tragedy for them is that they will not come to power in India ever, unless they change themselves to inculcate basic human values like individual freedom and dignity. They must understand that democratic institutions of election and multi-party system are means only, and by themselves value-neutral; the end depends on the character of the ruling class. Democracy can be used for the uplift of the poorest, it can be used for serving the rich, or else it can be used for anything lying in between the two extremes. The fighters in the jungles who are waging people's war must admit that their founder general secretary was right: Military activities are much, much less important than organising mass movements.

There is a great opportunity waiting for them, if only they accept open politics. This is so because the other side is crowded with petty narrow-minded people who are there to serve the interests of the rich. The vast majority of the country already knows it. For 75 per cent of the population, all hopes flickered by Independence have got extinguished in the six decades marked by self-aggrandisement, corruption and pretence of the elite. About 90 per cent of the mainstream politicians stand morally low, which is true also for the IAS, IPS and other service officers.

In contrast, the Maoists, at least many of them, stand tall as adherents of an ideology of sacrifice. They have followed, in different degrees, an ideology of 'forget your narrow interest and think of others'. In that sense, there is not much difference between honest Gandhians such as Baba Amte on one hand and Kobad Ghandy [CPI(Maoist) politburo member under arrest], Azad or Kishenji on the other. What makes the Maoists different is their staunch adherence to a totalitarian ideology and over-dependence on arms.

Different political parties in different parts of the country depend on arms to have their way. CPI(M), another communist outfit, used arms to create terror in the minds of the people in some districts of Bengal (and is now facing a bleak future as the people got rid of the fear-factor). Violence was the instrument of the BJP in Gujarat to gain the support of the people. But, these parties do so while remaining within 'mainstream' politics. Following the cue, the Maoists may keep their arms secretly, and come out to participate in open politics. The Maoists may decide whether or not to participate in electoral politics later. They can come out in the open and campaign among people to boycott votes, and preach against the ideology of self-aggrandisement and other vices. By organising a mass movement, they can go a long way in protecting the interests of the poor of the country. This is the only way the Maoists can someday come to power, or play a meaningful role. True, democracy in our country has failed the majority of the people, but it is the only system through which we can change the situation.

Maoist Mistakes

Kishenji made a shameful mistake when he sabotaged a glorious people's movement in Lalgarh by converting it into a typical armed Maoist rebellion. Had the Maoists not lost the chance the Lalgarh movement had offered them, Kishenji would have been alive today. India needs politicians like Kobad Ghandy. India needs organisers like Ganapathy or Kishan-da (Prasanta Bose, former head of the MCC). It is high time they accepted the fact that mainstream politics does not necessarily mean politics of self-aggrandisement or service for the rich. It can also include present-day rebels who will work for the underprivileged. The sooner the Maoists realise this, the better it would be for the country. A combined movement of democratic Maoists and all well-meaning people can bring an end to the era of Manmohonomics and perform a real miracle. Armed struggle only weakens the cause as it cannot gain the legitimacy a democratically elected leader has.

Unless bpth warring sides accept the reality and amend their courses, the casualty will be dignity of the poor. Even if one side wins without amending itself, there will be no change in the casualty.

* This is a reconstructed and edited version of the author's two articles published earlier in *Mainstream* and *Frontier* weeklies.

Maoists, Radical Intellectuals and Peace Talks

Aditya Nigam

With the debate on Maoist violence, Operation Green Hunt and Peace Talks hotting up, things are taking a disturbing turn. The danger really is that all spaces of radical political movements and indeed the entire space of the left, part of it gradually vacated by the parliamentary 'left' in recent decades and finally completely abandoned in the last few years, will now be virtually erased. In its place will be installed the phantom of an 'armed struggle' that threatens to completely swallow up the spaces once occupied by different shades of the CPI(ML) and the Naxalite movement and other left-of-CPI(M) groups and movements.

The Maoist Myth and Game of the Indian State

It all began, of course, with the declaration of the Prime Minister some years ago, that Maoism (which is used interchangeably, sometimes out of ignorance and often with deliberation, with Naxalism) was 'the single biggest security threat to the country' — a highly exaggerated claim but entirely understandable in retrospect. Understandable because, by reducing the entire spectrum of the non-parliamentary left and all shades of Naxalism — and more importantly all big anti-corporate mass struggles — to 'Maoism', he was deligitimising the very idea of the left, as it were. This was the best bet of the fanatically neo-liberal Manhohan-Chidambaram-Montek group — the middle digit of this triumvirate also being more than just an 'ideological' neo-liberal; after all, he is known to have actual stakes in the well-being of the corporate marauders of Niyamgiri/Lanjigarh, Goa and other places. Manmohan Singh's identification of 'Naxalites' and 'left-wing extremism' as the 'number one security threat' makes eminent sense then, for it is only when all these struggles against corporate plunder of the forest and mining areas are defeated can the neo-liberal dream be realised.

It is well known that for quite sometime now state, district and local level administrations in different parts of the country have found it truly rewarding to brand all local activists — even those like the Gandhian Himanshu Kumar or Sandeep Pandey — Maoists. A case of calling a dog mad before killing it, one might say. Thus when there was a popular rebellion in Nandigram, we saw state CPI(M) leaders allege a 'Maoist plot' with a politburo member of the party even alleging that 'they' were coming by the sea-route to Nandigram! It did not work that time. But by the time Lalgarh happened, it did. More often than not, this strategy works wonders. And it is employed by administrations and governments irrespective of whether they are run by the BJP, the Congress or the CPI(M).

This strategy suits the intentions and plans of corporate plunderers, the ruling coterie and their cheer-leaders in the media. Thus, the effort to relentlessly reduce every voice of protest to 'Maoism' continues. It is here that the symbiosis between the State and its mimicry — in the form of the 'state-to-be' (codenamed 'Maoism/Maoist') — becomes most evident. Each needs the other. A pervasive myth is manufactured through this symbiosis — a myth that has lately found expression through some very articulate and high-profile voices among sections of the radical intelligentsia: The myth of the Maoist as the answer to Special Economic Zones (SEZs) and corporate designs in the forest and mining areas. This myth goes hand in hand with another: that the Maoists only take up arms and kill because they (or their loved ones) is being killed and raped day in and day out. This is a story that has been endlessly retailed over the past few months and seems to be fast becoming some kind of common sense.

The Sleight of Hand

And yet, there is a sleight of hand involved here. In the first place, this myth deliberately screens out the fact that nowhere have the really powerful resistances to corporate and neo-liberal designs been more effective than where these resistances were actual mass movements. From Singur and Nandigram to Pen Raigad and Goa, to the various unreported and 'unspectacular' struggles in Jharkhand and Odisha, every struggle that has succeeded in rolling back such designs has been a mass struggle. There have, in fact, been even much older struggles like the Koel Karo struggle that have succeeded in stalling the dam project without ever picking up the gun. This is not to say that these are non-violent Gandhian struggles. Yes, there was violence in Kalinganagar, Singur and Nandigram. In Kalinganagar, it was the naked violence of the State that came into full view and put a huge question mark over the ethics of the 'Development' neo-liberal style. In Singur, too, it was the violence of the police against the unarmed peasants that was on display. It was different in Nandigram — but there it was not really violence against a particular set of people (at least initially) but a kind of symbolic violence against the CPI(M) offices that gave vent to the anger that had boiled over once the information of impending land acquisition leaked out. It was only when the party-State violence began to be unleashed on the rebellion that more direct bloodshed took place. At any rate, the violence there had a close connection with the breakdown of the long reign of unspoken terror in rural Bengal.

The struggles that followed Nandigram — the Nandigram effect — in other parts of the country, or struggles that acquired a new legitimacy after it, put the State on the backfoot. Violence in all these cases was exercised at the limit point, or not at all. At any rate, it was more a consequence of mass anger, not the premeditated terroristic attack of a force armed to the teeth.

It can be argued, in fact, that violence may at times become necessary in the course of an otherwise non-violent mass movement. In a country like India, it may be difficult to even contest a *panchayat* election, let alone win it, if the force of upper caste landlords' armed might is not met with a deterrent — a possibility of retaliation. Such violence, or simply a threat of violence, is very different from the cult of the gun that has now become part and parcel of a celebratory rhetoric of the Maoists and their intellectual supporters.

The sleight of hand is also apparent at another level. It lies in the representation of the 'Maoist' as someone forced to resort to arms under threat of his/her life and honour. This representation obliterates the distinction that is most crucial here: The Maoist — as in the party and its leadership — is a worshipper of violence independent of any contingency and needs to be discussed separately from those hundreds of others who might be attracted towards it in specific circumstances as the armed might of the Maoists seems to provide them with some security against the violence of the State.

Talks: What About?

A quick glance at the history of the People's War and the MCC should be enough to convince anyone that their attachment to violence is independent of everything else. Violence is to them not merely legitimate but a necessary means of achieving political ends, that is, 'capture of State power'. Thus when sections of the radical intelligentsia demand that the government hold 'unconditional talks with the Maoists', one is not quite sure what the talks are supposed to be about. Will they be talks to negotiate something specific, say the several MOUs that have been signed between the government and the corporations? If that is the case, will the Maoists give up their arms or armed struggle in the event of the MOUs being scrapped? Clearly not. The Maoists are fighting for State power and have made no bones about it. Then what are the talks meant to be — except as a ruse to buy time strategically, in order to regroup and reorganise?

It is true that in the aftermath of the final defeat of the *Narmada Bachao Andolan* — where every effort by the movement to seek redressal within the framework of the State's institutions, its judiciary and its political process was met with cynical disregard — the Maoist option did begin to seem attractive to some people. Even leaders like Medha Patkar and B.D. Sharma began to express doubts about what signals the State was sending and whether allying with the Maoists was not something to be seriously considered.

Needless to say, such a feeling of desperation among these stalwarts of people's movements says more about the State than about military violence as a strategic option. As a matter of fact, it is well known that in many places where the Maoists hold sway, their extortion economy functions by making peace with contractors and corporations and with the local development bureaucracy. So clearly, the mere fact that at some point the Maoist option can seem attractive to some people is not argument enough, either about its ethicality or indeed, its efficacy.

At any rate, we know that the historical destiny of all twentieth century revolutions has been to simply 'build capitalism': armed struggle or no armed struggle, no 'socialist' experiment has produced anything but a more ruthless capitalism and even more ruthelss modernity at the end of the day. Even Prachanda, at the end of a decade-long Maoist insurgency in Nepal, after he assumed power, had to assure the Nepal Chamber of Commerce and Industry not to be frightened, for the Maoists only wanted to build capitalism.

This article was first published on *kafila.org* as an intervention in the ongoing debate on Maoism. We reproduce it here with some minor editing.

Maoist Proto-state, Violence and Democracy

Nivedita Menon

Thinking About Violence

There is over a century of discussion on political violence within the Marxist tradition and outside, but that is not my focus here. I also set aside arguments that condemn all violence as morally unacceptable, except to note that these do not always address the fact that the modern State has monopoly over legitimate means of coercion, thus establishing a visible horizon of violence within which we live.

Here I will quickly outline my own views on violence in order to reflect on the possibilities for democratic politics today.

At the most obvious level, violence is associated with physical coercion and injury. Even here I distinguish between violence against a person and against property, and within this, between violence against private property and State-owned property, placing on a descending scale of magnitude, physical violence against a person, against private property and against State property.

We move now to the understanding that structures of capitalist property, patriarchy or caste ensure that physical violence is not required to maintain inequality and injustice on a day-to-day basis, because they successfully hegemonise public notions of morality. Thus, the violence carried out on the sense of self and against the bodies of the powerless in these structures and through these discourses, is invisible, while acts of resistance or counter-formations appear to be violent because they threaten the stability of the social order.

Michel Foucault might say that the very production of subjectivity through various discourses and practices of governmentality, renders actual violence unnecessary unless faced with counter-formations of self — the feminist within patriarchy, the non-heterosexual within heteronormativity, the indisciplined body within capitalist work practices, the militant *Dalit* within caste practices.

Such an understanding of structural violence underlies B.R. Ambedkar's support in 1951, to the amendment to Article 19 limiting the right to freedom of expression. In this debate over the first amendment to the Constitution, Ambedkar argued that calls for social boycott of the Scheduled Castes by caste Hindus, or campaigns to prevent them from using wells, constituted 'incitement to violence', and should not be protected under freedom of speech and expression.

An understanding of structural arrangements that leave some sections permanently empowered, and others permanently weak, would recognise that violent acts by the latter are unavoidable, and therefore tries to outline the kinds of violence that are morally justified, 'self-defence' being the simplest of these. It is within this framework that the term 'political violence' arises, as distinguished from criminal acts of violence. However, this distinction is impossible to sustain, beyond a point.

Take household theft by a person employed as a domestic servant, who may injure someone in the process. Is this simply a 'criminal' act within the broad understanding of structural violence? Not if you place it within the violence involved in the very institution of 'domestic servants', rooted in feudal relations of power and patriarchal sexual division of labour. Nevertheless, 'political violence' continues to be a useful conceptual device to differentiate an act of violence arising from a structure of violence that pre-exists and frames the act. A parallel distinction is often made that accepts the greater morality of violence of the weak against the strong.

The Structural Violence of Property Relations

Anarchist thinker Proudhon refers to the structural violence underlying property ownership in his claim 'Property is theft'. He argued that originally all things were common and undivided, property ownership comes about with war and conquest, followed by treaties that distributed property unequally; possession of property breeds more property, and so 'we live in a permanent condition of iniquity and fraud'. To Proudhon, all property is illegitimate, all acts of violence against property are acts of political violence, and therefore property must be abolished altogether.

Marx develops another kind of argument about property that is more useful to understand what is happening in India today. In *Capital* he demonstrates how in England over the 16th to 18th centuries, common property was privatized by a section of the nobility/landlords, dispossessing peasants and artisans and transforming them into impoverished wage labourers who were then made available to future capitalist employers. Thus by the 18th century 'the law itself became the instrument of the theft of people's land'. In other words, it is possible to read in Marx a distinction between non-capitalist forms of ownership and property in its capitalist form. While Marx sees the transformation of the first to the second as historically progressive ultimately, no 21st century Marxist can afford not to be critical of this progressivist account, especially in view of ecological critiques of capitalist development. The blind acceptance of this progressivism is largely responsible for CPI(M)'s role in advancing corporate interests in West Bengal.

In India then, we can see from the late 20th century onwards, this theft of people's land being carried out by corporate capitalist interests aided by the State, whatever the party in power.

Thus — spontaneous violence against the structural violence of the state and of capitalist property, violence in self-defence, even pre-planned violence as an act of desperation — these possibilities always seethe just below the skin of normal society, and must be understood within the context of unrelenting, never-addressed injustice. Such acts are justifiable political violence — from the long history of *Adivasi* uprisings against State power, to violence against property during strikes, to the battered wife with an endlessly abusive husband, waiting for him to fall into a drunken sleep before stabbing him to death.

Political assassinations and executions would not be part of this range — the crucial distinction I make here is between a) violence arising in the course of a political movement or in the course of everyday life, and b) violence as integral to the revolutionary consciousness (a la Fanon) and as strategy (a la revolutionary vanguards). Such an integration of violence into the heart of an institution or movement mimics the modern State, with its monopoly over legitimate violence. The challenge to the State offered by this position is limited to challenging this monopoly, offering in turn a counter-violence that becomes equally institutionalised.

Armed Revolution Towards Becoming The State

Parties like the CPI(Maoist) are based on armed revolution as a strategy to overthrow State power, which involves a) working towards becoming the State, b) intense, paranoid secrecy, and c) the normalisation of a wartime mentality in which loss of non-combatant lives is taken to be unavoidable collateral damage. All three tendencies are inherently anti-democratic.

The CPI(Maoist) document, Urban Perspective, available freely on the Web, outlines its strategy of using 'broad mass organisations' in order to work under cover for a long time and accumulate strength'. This work 'of course' has to be conducted under 'the strictest methods of secrecy'. Such organisations 'can and must be utilised' in the periods of legal opportunities. The party must also engage in 'fractional work' — here it 'works through the numerous mass organisations that operate in the urban areas ... penetrates such organisations without exposing any links with the party'. It then 'strives to achieve a leading position in it ... the important point in fractional work is the skillful exposure of the reactionaries and reformists leading or participating within these organisations. This exposure is essential to draw the masses away from their influence.' Within existing legal democratic organisations, such as the coalitions and alliances formed against repression, globalisation, Hindutva, anti-capitalism or people's struggles, the aim is to work with them while 'we concentrate simultaneously on developing the secret Party core within it'.

In short, take over existing mass organisations when you cannot set them up, work towards subverting their existing processes by producing propaganda about those who are influential in it, always utilise movements towards a secret end that you know if you reveal, very few will be with you.

Like all States, it cannot permit competitive centres of power. The case of Lalgarh is illustrative. Santosh Rana, a veteran leader of the Naxalite revolt in 1967 and leader of one of the important CPI(ML) groups active in the Jharkhand region today, says about the CPI(Maoist) role in the context of the mass uprising: 'After the withdrawal of police camps ... the movement was spreading to new areas. An opportunity was found where the awakened masses could be mobilised to establish organs of self-rule on the basis of a democratic principle ... But the Maoists operating in the area ... wanted to utilise the uprising to create an area where the rule of the Maoist party ... would be established, an area where there would be no opposition, not even any differing voices. So they attempted to abolish all other party and social organisations ... The differences with the *Majhi Marwa* was objectively not such as could not be resolved within a democratic framework. This is an association of *Majhis* (traditional village headmen among Santhals). There are no landlords or even rich peasants among them. When the CPI(M) had tried to impose its one-party rule in nearby Jamboni a few years back, the *Majhis* played an important role in mobilising the masses in their fight for democracy. But the Maoists wanted to abolish all social and political organisations that would not abide by their diktat. The PCPA led by the Maoists issued a leaflet announcing the trial of Nityananda Hembrom, the head of *Majhi Marwa* in 'people's courts' ... They issued orders that everybody living in their area of influence would have to join processions called by them. Some people under the influence of *Majhi Marwas* defied this order. Many of them were beaten (up) and some were killed. The murder of Sudhir Mandi in the last week of November by the Maoists created a major split among the masses. He belonged to the Jharkhand Party. He was a poor peasant having one acre of *dahi* (highly infertile land) ... Even after remaining chairman of *Panchayat Samiti* for five years, he lived in his traditional mud-house with thatched roof ... But to the Maoists ... (a) poor tribal is a class-enemy simply because he refused to carry out their order ...' (kafila.org)

The experience of Himanshu Kumar in Chhattisgarh is equally revealing. A Gandhian who had worked for years in the area, running an NGO called *Vanvasi Chetna Ashram*, his attempt in September 2008 to enable *Adivasis* caught between the CPI(Maoist) and the *Salwa Judum* to return to their villages was cut short at the diktat of the party. In an open letter to the CPI(Maoist) in the EPW (October 4, 2008) he said: 'In an attempt to restore peace in these areas, the *Vanvasi Chetna Ashram* (VCA) adopted a village called Nendra and decided to rebuild the lives and livelihoods of tribals of the village. The VCA deputed a 'Human Shield Team' to Nendra that stayed there and supported the tribals who were willing to resettle ... The tribals ... ...of many other villages approached the VCA and its Human Shield Team to support their return and to help rebuild their homes where their old houses were burnt by the *Salwa Judum*. In response I and my team of eight tribal boys and four tribal girls began a 12-day *padayatra* ... to spread the important message that the time has also come to end this division of tribals into two 'groups' ... (On the fourth day of the *yatra*) we were surrounded by a group of Maoists ... they retorted that they could not allow us to continue as they had orders from their 'seniors' to prevent us from completing the *yatra*. Then they took our mobiles, clothes, bags, food and medicines and the bicycle carrying these provisions ... (T)he woman commander of the Maoist group told us that now they would see to it that the VCA was not allowed into Nendra ... If we had been stopped by the police or *Salwa Judum* we would have been angry, but having been stopped by the Maoists we feel hurt and insulted ... '

In May 2009, the *Vanvasi Chetna Ashram* was demolished by the local authorities, Himanshu Kumar made peace with the CPI(Maoist), and the 'other' politics he was trying to maintain, between the Indian State and the CPI(Maoist), was thus wiped out by the parallel operations of both.

Parties like the CPI(Maoist) require secrecy not just from the State, but also to penetrate democratic mass movements. A secret core has to commit the movement to courses of action dictated by the party from afar, not emerging from the situation on the ground. The secrecy is thus directed at the mass movement and to its subversion as much as it is to the State. And the ultimate aim of this party and others like it is to become the State itself. This vanguardism is what many in other mass movements oppose.

Similarly, its violence too is directed against the people, whether through bomb blasts, during enforcement of poll boycott or through killing of 'police informers'. This last is routine and well publicised, as a deterrent, by the Maoist party itself — these are usually poor people, *chowkidars*, auto rickshaw-drivers, caught helplessly in the pincer-grip of police brutality and the CPI(Maoist) proto-state.

Death, Displacement & Deprivation: The War in Dantewada

A Report (2006) by the Human Rights Forum (HRF, with K. Balagopal as secretary), while being scathing about the violence of the State and supportive of the Maoist party, said about the village administration set up by the Maoists: 'While the *sangham*'s internal functioning may well be democratic, in the sense that airing of different views is permitted before any decision is taken, there is no freedom to set up a rival organisation or to practice one's dissent after a decision has been taken. Any one practicing alternative politics of any kind runs the risk of being dubbed an agent of the State, and dealt with accordingly.' (p.13)

This report records widespread resentment among the forest-dwellers with the Maoist party's destruction of existing roads to prevent troop movement and destruction of school buildings: 'the (Party's) rationale is that there should be no pucca buildings in villages that the paramilitary could use as shelter or for setting up camps. This is symptomatic of how the working out of the Maoist strategy of guerrilla struggle against the State creates needs for the organisation that are not congruent with the needs of the people, and could in fact be against the interests of the people. It is for this reason that democratic activists should be cautious in identifying all the needs of the guerrilla struggle as the 'interests of the people".' (p.17)

The point about the aspiration to become the State is that we don't have to wait for some future time to see how the Maoist party will operate if it comes to power. It is already behaving like a State — imposing taxes, taking to itself monopoly over means of coercion, and so on. In a recent interview with *Mint*, Kishenji had said that the Maoists take 'contributions' from everyone in the area, but not from those whose earnings come from NREGA — imagine what this means. The party keeps track of the source of every household's earnings, decides whom to spare and whom not to. The HRF report says that the forcible recruitment of youth into Maoist organisations was a complaint they heard from many. However, since the Maoists denied this, the report leaves this as an unverified fact (p.19). However, this complaint is heard by many visitors to these areas, for example, students on NREGA survey teams — we must assume the people are lying and the Maoist party is telling the truth?

When a small armed group declares war on the State, it does not do so after conducting a referendum involving the people of the area that will be affected. It starts its operations and expects that return pressure from the State will drive more and more people into its fold helplessly. If you take up arms against the State, you are prepared for the State to hunt you out. There is no middle point, you are not asking for self-determination, you are not demanding the rolling back of some policy. Your objective is to overthrow the State and become the State. The point is that when you do this, you (the committed party members) are ready for this. But not every *Adivasi*, not even most *Adivasis*, in the region.

On the question of the undifferentiated *Adivasi*-Maoist, there is much dissembling among middle-class supporters of the CPI(Maoist). They say simultaneously that the State is using the 'Maoist menace' as an 'excuse' to attack resource-rich tribal areas (that is, the party is small and no real threat to the State), but also that there is no difference between the Maoist party and the *Adivasis*, (that is, there are no 'innocent' people, no civilians in this war). And yet, despite all this, my democratic instincts insist, even the CPI(Maoist) must be given its place within the spectrum of political dissent. As one element of the spectrum.

CONFRONTING THE STATE-CORPORATE NEXUS

There are other voices in India militating against corporate greed in partnership with institutions masquerading under the cover of democracy. We must insist on the legitimacy of dissenting voices within the dissent to the State.

It is in the interest of the Indian State and the CPI(Maoist) both to claim that all resistance to corporate marauders comes from this one single entity, thus delegitimising all the shades of opposition in the spectrum of dissent to the State. A pernicious conflation carried out by the mass media and the government-and unknowingly by intellectuals of integrity — which suits the CPI(Maoist) very well — is the complete non-differentiation between tribals taking up arms, 'Naxalites' and the CPI(Maoist). The same tactic is followed by local administrations and the Indian State, and all activists are branded Maoists. Following the militant land struggle of *Dalits* in Chengara (Kerala), an organisation called Dalit Human Rights Movement has been accused of acts of murder and 'anti-mainstream propaganda' and nearly 200 *Dalits* have been put behind bars; part of the media campaign against the DMHR is that it is linked to 'Maoists'.

The myth of the composite *Adivasi*-Maoist obscures the fact that the really powerful resistances to corporate and neo-liberal designs have been most effective where they were militant mass movements. On the contrary, where the CPI(Maoist) is established in its role as proto-State or State-in-waiting, it is well known to permit corporate interests and local state bureaucracy to operate peacefully on payment of extortion rates.

It is of course no coincidence that the greatest turmoil is currently in tribal regions, areas rich in natural resources in the process of being appropriated by corporate interests aided by the State. However, what has halted their rampant progress is the spectacular success of militant mass struggles — whether in Goa where the government was forced to scrap 12 SEZ's, denotify three where construction had already started, and announce the review of the whole policy in February this year, or Nandigram and Singur. In Jharkand, over 50 MOUs signed by the BJP government remained unimplemented till 2006 due to sustained resistance from local people. Recently, ArcelorMittal announced it is on the verge of leaving Jharkand due to this resistance, although the movement here is now split, with one section breaking away to come under the leadership of the CPI(Maoist). So what the future holds, we cannot say. In Pen *tehsil* of Raigarh, large-scale agitation by farmers forced the district administration to hold a referendum on a proposed Reliance venture, and in a massive turnout, 82 percent of the farmers voted against it.

What we see in such struggles is spontaneous resistance coalescing into broad coalitions of local interests, held together by a common minimum programme set collectively by the forum even though serious differences on other issues may continue to exist. These coalitions include affected villagers and tribal people, religious groupings (the Church in Goa, *Jamat Ulema-i-Hind* in Nandigram), leftists of various hues including the CPI(Maoist), middle class intelligentsia, Gandhians, the range can be very wide. These movements are not necessarily non-violent at all times, and involve as in Nandigram, serious challenges to the authority of the State. However, they are not (at least initially and for some time) led by or influenced by the ideology of the CPI(Maoist) or any other party, though local parties, (including Trinamul and even the CPI(M) outside West Bengal and Kerala), are part of these coalitions. This is the pattern of non-party non-funded citizens' initiatives of the 1990s in many cities in India, coming together on issues like secularism, workers' rights and anti-nuclear platform. These had period of quite effective intervention for some years, and started fading out after that. However, from my experience in such forums, I know that at least some of them broke up due to 'fractional work' by front organizations of the CPI(Maoist).

A now familiar trajectory is of State-corporate appropriation of local resources, popular resistance followed by State repression, and the branding of a mass movement as 'Maoist', thus increasing the possibility of its actually coming under the control of the CPI(Maoist), as we saw with PCPA in Lalgarh.

Of course, I denounce 'Operation Green Hunt' as another

manifestation of the Indian State's violence towards its citizens. But the CPI(Maoist) is as little concerned about the lives of non-combatants as is the State. What we see in 'Operation Green Hunt' is the crushing of an unarmed non-combatant population between two armies — the mighty army of the Indian State and the less mighty army, but equally deadly as far as civilian populations are concerned, of the CPI(Maoist). The Maoist party have declared war on the State, so it cannot possibly enter into any dialogue with the government.

We now hear that the CPI(Maoist) is ready for talks, whatever that means, because its official line in its document Urban Perspective is: 'The line of protracted people's war, the liberation of urban areas, will be possible only in the last stage of the revolution.' As the HRF report said: 'The Maoist movement is not a movement for economic benefits to the poor that uses violent methods for better results ... It is a political movement that hopes to smash the existing State structure and establish a new State to herald a new society.' (p.12)

Thus, the very idea of talks is actually ruled out, but the Maoists periodically agree to talks in order to gain time through the ceasefire that will be effected. They will use the time to re-group and prepare for the 'next stage'.

On the other hand, what message is the Indian State sending out when it offers to hold talks to those brandishing guns, but not to those who do not?

Militancy, Violence, Democratic Dissent

As State repression of non-violent struggles continues — for instance on 30 October 2009, police cracked down brutally on *Narmada Bachao Andolan* activists following the demonstration in Madhya Pradesh of about 10,000 people affected by the Indira Sagar and Omkareshwar dams, demanding that the State fulfil its promise of 5 acres of land to each oustee — one might reflect on the NBA's experience of reposing inordinate faith in institutions of the State for far too long, endless appeals to the courts, for example. If the NBA were to 'take up arms' I would support it, because it would have a specific limited goal in mind.

This is very different from the CPI(Maoist) war on the State, directed towards its capture. This paradigm of capture of State power that dominated revolutionary thought for more than a century has failed. The reform/revolution debate has proved to be limiting and misleading. As we have seen during the 20th century, this model has been nothing but a painful transition from 'revolutionary socialism' to capitalism, whether in Vietnam or Nepal, given Prachanda's statement on building capitalism.

John Holloway says that Marxist revolutionary movements have persisted in seeing the State as an instrument that can be wielded in the interests of the people. But 'such a view reproduces the autonomization of the State from its social environment, the critique of which is the starting point of revolutionary politics ... The mistake of Marxist revolutionary movements has been ... to misunderstand the degree of integration of the State into the network of capitalist social relations' (Holloway 2002: 13-14)

The only successful confrontation today of the contemporary forms of capital and State will be through genuine mass movements with alternative visions of power, a radically different conception of nature that rejects altogether its framing as a 'resource' to be used, and of alternative democratic communities.

These will also be local and differentiated, not fitting into one model of revolutionary transformation.

If the Indian State ever retreats from its policy of facilitating corporate loot of tribal areas and ecologically unsustainable development, it will be due to the pressure of mass movements. The CPI(Maoist) on the contrary, offers the State the best possible escape route from sustained and sharp criticism on democratic grounds, enabling it to lauch war-like retaliations in response to the Maoists' unilateral 'declaration of revolutionary violence', and offering it a justification unavailable to it in Kalinganagar and Nandigram.

In conclusion, let me draw your attention to the Chiapas region of Mexico, under the armed occupation of the Zapatista Army of National Liberation, an organization of Mexican Indians, since 1994. According to its representative, the masked Subcomandante Marcos, six individuals who came to the Chiapas to propagate Marxist-Leninist theory found that the 'absurdities' they had come with — 'imperialism, social crisis' — was a rhetoric that did not ring true for the Indians. So, abandoning the classic and familiar project of 'correctly explaining social reality to the masses', they unlearnt their theory. Marcos calls the difficult process that began 'a process of cultural contamination' — the non-Indian Zapatistas learnt to listen to and learnt from the Indians. The lasting transformation that took place was 'socialism in broad brush-strokes, but enriched with ethics, morals, more than simply indigenous' (Higgins 2004: 159-167).

Low-intensity warfare continues to this day, but their democratic, radically other transformative practices are what make the Zapatista revolution unique. Their battle is against capitalism and the Mexican State, but while they want to remake the world to create a world of dignity and humanity, they are doing so without taking over the State.

Romanticism? Well, if I have to choose between the romanticism of martyrdom and images of lonely, courageous, armed squads holed up in jungles, and the counter-romanticism involved in the image of a whole community rising, posing radical alternatives to dominant common sense about work, nature, sexuality, social organisation, defiantly operating outside the legibility zones of the State, refusing to set up a counter-State, evolving new ways of democratic self-governing, remaining permanently open to criticism and transformation — then I choose the latter.

Balagopal, that visionary of extraordinary integrity, had, in his reflections on violence, *Beyond Violence and Non-violence*, said that neither 40 years of the Naxalite movement nor the longer history of non-violent civil disobedience in India had been effective in terms of reversing structural trends, though each has had small successes. This is what 'tempts honest activists', he said, to 'look for short cuts, ranging from armed action to PILs. But there are no short cuts.'

This is a remarkable insight, that both reform and revolution are 'short cuts' caught within the ambit of the state. Short cuts to mass democratic transformation.

After all, if Naxalite struggles and democratic mass mobilization both have been limited in terms of 'success', at least mass mobilisation has the advantage of involving the larger number of people, allowing for the possibility of learning from mistakes and changing course — and most importantly, of learning to live and engage with differences within the spectrum of dissent to State and corporate power.

In a recent interview to *Tehelka*, Union home minister P. Chidambaram said that SEZs are falling by the wayside anyway due to global recession, and that he is open to both licensed SEZs and MoUs being comprehensively reviewed. But, he added: 'The starting point of that dialogue is that the violence must stop.'

The NAPM has been militating against the Land Acquisition (Amendment) Bill and Rehabilitation and Resettlement Bill which will further concretize the dispossession of people from their land and natural resources. How about holding talks with them? Or will they have to start violence for Chidambaram to listen?

Thus, by the logic of operation of the State, the Indian State has recognized its mirror-image, the CPI(Maoist). When did this one party become the representative of all the movements in the country today resisting the onslaught of corporate capital in alliance with the State?

The Indian State with all its powers and resources — ministers with corporate links, judges owning shares in companies plundering people's wealth, brutal paramilitary forces — still flounders in the implementation of the SEZ policy, which began in 2000. The stark immorality and indefensibility of this policy can no longer be ignored, with its despicable 'MoUs' that have passed into everyday language — 'memoranda of understanding' between State and corporations, haunted by the spectre of the people forcibly expelled from them, a people whose audacity and defiance are stamped on every landscape in India today.

The SEZ Act must be repealed. Every MoU already signed must be opened up to referendum involving the affected communities. The government has no option but to talk — to people's movements all over the country.

References

Higgins, Nicholas P. (2004) *Understanding the Chiapas Rebellion. Modernist Visions and the Invisible Indian,* University of Texas Press, Austin.

Holloway, John (2002) *Change the World without taking power. The Meaning of revolution today,* Pluto press, London

Since 'anarchism' is a term of abuse from the organized left, posing as it does, a threat to legitimate centres of power, and since the CPI(Maoist) has therefore been castigated as 'anarchist' by Prakash Karat, I want to reclaim here the meaning of anarchism as anti-statism, anti-power centres, and standing for recognition of power as productive and multi-focal. Anarchism thus, is as far from the CPI(Maoist) as it is from the CPI(M).

* This article, originally published in *Economic and Political Weekly* on 12 December 2009. is reproduced here with minor editing and changed title.

Debate on Lalgarh Movement: Violence, Class Struggle and Human Rights

The Lalgarh movement in Bengal has accomplished many things. It has taken people's movement to a higher stage where resistance against State repression in various forms is tied up with the struggle for the development of the *Adivasi* languages and script, a new pro-people model of development and a determined fight against handing over the region's natural resources to foreign and domestic big capital for plunder in the name of 'industrialization'. The historic movement's nature has led to controversy over the nature of Maoists' involvement in it, the relation between PCPA and the Maoists, and the problems faced by civil rights bodies and different sections of people in responding to the movement in different stages of its development. Since the debate is rich in content, we felt the arguments and counter-arguments should reach as many people as possible. Such debates are good for the functioning of democracy — to dispel wrong notions and to help form/change/modify/strengthen one's opinion. We have selected three articles — all written as open letters — for the purpose.

The first article, *An Open Letter to the Maoists, is* by Sujato Bhadra, a well-known civil rights activist from West Bengal. The second and third are in response to Bhadra's 'letter'. *Response from Junglemahal* was penned by Kishenji, the well-known and much-talked-about Maoist leader, before he was killed by security forces in November 2011. And *Violence and Non-violence* is written by Amit Bhattacharyya, professor of History, Jadavpur University, Kolkata, and human rights activist. The three articles were published in Bengali daily *Dainik Statesman,* the first on 26 September 2009, and the second and third on 10 October 2009. The following is a free translation from the Bengali originals.

— *Radicalnotes team*

An Open Letter to the Maoists

Sujato Bhadra

The present writer is an Indian citizen, associated with the civil rights/human rights movement in West Bengal for some decades. You are probably aware of the fact that recently in this state your armed activities and the more violent and more cruel repression subsequently adopted by the state by making your activities a pretext has given rise to a debate. As you know, civil society became vocal in its criticism of police repression and terror in the Junglemahal area, including Lalgarh, in November (2008). The charter of demands placed by PCPA got the wholehearted support of civil society and many organisations. Civil society was conscious about the happenings that had taken place since 18 June; it raised its voice time and again against the repression perpetrated by the joint forces, stuck to the demand for the withdrawal of the joint forces and called upon the government to hold a dialogue with all the parties. We have strongly opposed the 'terrorist' tag affixed to your organization (by the State). The dissident part of civil society was much vocal, too, in demanding the repeal of UAPA. In a nutshell, the position of civil society against State repression and terror is zero tolerance. Many of us are in no way subscribers to the 'ticking bomb situation' model.

The basis of our protest is our adherence to democratic values, consciousness emanating from humanitarianism and morality. Such elements, we feel, should also become part and parcel of politics guided by class outlook. It is these thoughts that have made me feel that some of your activities suffer from lack of logical thinking. Some events even severely hurt out consciousness and caused us pain. Your party has been confronted with such questions earlier, too. You have replied to an open letter from the 'Concerned Citizens Committee' of

Andhra Pradesh, and I have gone through your reply to the questions (centring round Chhattisgarh) raised by some eminent persons (Ramchandra Guha and others). At that time you worked as an underground party. Recently, after yoiu were banned and the draconian black law was promulgatede, the situation, no doubt, has become more difficult for you. Now there is no legal avenue for us to know your views and to respond to them from our side. We appreciate the fact that you have to carry on in the face of such a suffocating atmosphere and State terror. While sharing your anguish, I bear doubts about some of your activities. I am placing those doubts before you, keeping in mind the difficult situation you are in. My request to you is to give these (critical observations) some consideration. In one of your leaflets on 'Maoist violence', the following is stated: ' ... violence has a class-orientation, it is never neutral ... only armed struggle and people's war would develop and spread people's democratic struggles ... our work is not violent, it is people's violence to get rid of violence, which is part of people's war' (dt. 18 July 2009).

I do not subscribe to this political view. I am not opposing this standpoint from an alternative political outlook. On the contrary, I would raise questions by keeping myself within your logical structure: one can talk about the notion of violence and deal with it at the theoretical plane — problems crop up at the time implementation and the social impact that necessarily follows from it. It is related to the intense reaction that has been generated within the supporters of Lalgarh and other democratic movements. Not only you, many philosophers throughout ages have clearly said that justice could be established through violence only. For example, Sartre has written: 'Violence is acceptable because all great changes are based on violence.' (*The Aftermath of War* p.35). He forgot to add that history itself had shown that a society created through violent means could not live for long. Whether anything good can be achieved through violence is also very much doubtful. The concept 'end justifying the means' rejects the notion of justice and morality. And the result is that 'the means outweigh the end'. You have declared in quite unequivocal terms that the heroic people of the area (Junglemahal) under the leadership of the CPI(Maoist) held trials in people's courts and meted out to the lumpens [*harmads* of the CPI(M))] the punishment they deserved for being police informers (Press Release, dt. 16 September 2009). Our opposition is over the question of this capital punishment. Many people and civil rights bodies throughout the world, including India, have gathered public opinion for the final abolition of capital punishment (legalised murder).

As a result, the majority of the countries in the world (224 countries) have abolished the death sentence. The reason is that as a form of punishment, this practice is barbarous and cruel. Over and above, it also does not act as a deterrent. Beheading does not allow the victim any chance to rectify himself/herself. Not only that, there is also the possibility of error in judgement. After carrying out the capital punishment, if it is found that the condemned person was innocent, no one can return his life. On the contrary, such a violent punishment makes society more inhuman and more violent. Tom Paine has said: 'The people by nature are not violent, they only reproduce the cruel methods used by the State.' We strongly oppose this cruel method/means adopted by the State. Side by side, we also hold that if notions such as 'eye for an eye' or 'life for a life' take root in the minds of the oppressed people in this unequal and deprived society, then there will be an outburst of violent mentality from the people, which is happening now.

You represent the advanced elements striving for social transformation. What should be your role as the vanguard? Will you submit to that violent emotion, or will you uphold advanced democratic values and guide the people under your influence along that path? What is the organisational structure of the 'people's courts'? Are the accusers themselves the judges and the butchers? It is important to remember that in the judicial system set up by the State, there are certain recognized stages — judicial procedure, regular and separate judicial structure, a higher court of appeal and the right to clemency at the hands of a country's President. Despite all these, we demand abolition of the system of legalised killing. How can we thus

— and from what democratic, human rights or values of just trial — accept trials in such 'people's courts' and the subsequent meting out of punishment?

The armed forces deployed in Jammu and Kashmir and the Northeast think that all the people living there are 'suspects'; they put up big hoardings to declare 'Suspect all'. Are you not acting in the same way? In your judgement, each and every CPI(M) supporter or individual is part of the *Harmad Bahini* and engaged in spying for the police, and unless they surrender to the people, they would be given death sentence. Such a method could be the manifestation of your power, but it is devoid of a sense of values. You have already handed down death sentence to many 'informers'. Nobody knows how many more will have to meet the same fate before the rest of the lumpens surrender to the people. This is because everything depends on what you think about it. You have stated: 'To set those lumpens free would mean handing over the struggling and revolutionary masses to the joint forces' (Press Release, dt. 16 August 2009).

Psychologist Christopher Bolas has said: 'Every time the killer strikes, it is his own death that he avoids.' It means that such attacks come from a sense of fear and apprehension. If you have a social base in the area, then it is possible for you to socially isolate the informers. On the other hand, if your political opponents carry on an ideological struggle, and they are physically liquidated after being branded informers, then it will appear that some type of acute 'irrationality' pervades throughout your activities. In reality, Lalgarh has become a valley of death, and from there the message of death is travelling around. Is there no way to combat espionage other than liquidating the 'informers'? Could not the people adopt the method of exposing those informers under your leadership? Marx had to close down his *Das Kapital* to write an entire book, *Herr Vogt,* in order to expose espionage. And Mao was in favour of beheading only a few. In that case, propaganda and exposure will, on the one hand, not exert any negative social reaction and, on the other, the State will not be able to get any illegal but apparently social sanction to 'liquidate' you. If espionage cannot be combatted without 'liquidating' informers, then we will be faced with a terrible situation: unmoved, indifferent human mass. In a situation attended with violence, counter-violence, repression and counter-attack, it will not be possible to mobilize democratic people and raise the voice of protest. We who belong to the third force (those who are neither with the State nor with you ideologically) would find ourselves in a helpless situation. Had we been able, as an alternative, to unite and create a tide of democratic movement against the ruthless State repression in Lalgarh, then we would have found in our ranks the civil society that was imbued with democratic values and inspired by the teachings of Singur and Nandigram, and thus would have ensured the victory of the weak over the strong. In the initial period (November 2008 to June 2009), it was in fact achieved.

You have passed your judgement on some eminent persons and decided to hand them down the death sentence because, as you said, it is the demand of the people. There was an attempt on the life of the (former) chief minister (Buddhadeb Bhattacharjee) through the Salboni blast. It is true that the (former) chief minister has been accused of committing genocide. It is also true that after the 14 March massacre in Nandigram, posters and placards, screaming 'Hang the chief minister' were put up. But all of us realized that such outbursts were the manifestation of immediate intense emotion. But if that (to kill him) is interpreted as the serious, logical demand of the people then I am forced to say that it is totally childish. To brand someone 'authoritarian' and then to try to kill him is equally ludicrous and a manifestation of anarchist philosophy. Let us remember that Marxist philosophy was established in the world by negating anarchist philosophy. Whether there is any philosophical or theoretical recognition of such individual-centric attack from Marxism to Maoism is not known to me. Mao Zedong's favourite military strategist Karl von Clausewitz wrote that like politics, war also has a specific aim, but war at the same time negates that politics — the contending parties get busy parading their forces. War and annihilation bring destruction to the enemy, but they also inflict severe damage to your own side. Also, there is no end to this war. Friends and foes act always by treating each other as a 'unholy forces'. The fact is, that while getting rid of the unholy, we ourselves are getting influenced by that force.

We should not forget that great note of caution: 'Whoever fights monsters should see to it that in the process he does not become a monster. And when you look long into an abyss, the abyss also looks into you.' (*Beyond Good and Evil*). Counter-violence, counter-attack — these are the natural reactions of human beings. That does not require any special kind of philosophy. Philosophy, on the other hand, can control that reaction with logical thinking, can make human values and notions about morality indispensable elements in formulating policies. I feel that you suffer from serious limitations on this issue.

In the recent past, the police arrested two of your important members, but did not produce them in the court in time. Through your press release, you had quite rightly claimed that the police had violated the law by not producing them in court within 24 hours and appealed to civil rights bodies for intervention, and you rightly thought about fake encounters. In the face of a public outcry, the police were forced to produce them in court. Before that, you also made appeals to intellectuals to visit Lalgarh to see with their own eyes the barbarity perpetrated by the joint forces there. By doing so, you admitted that if, even within this structure, the process of 'rule of law' is kept operative in the proper manner and if democratic voices are raised in its support, then it is possible to resist in some cases the illegal, anti-human rights activities and bad intentions of the State. Should it not be our task to strengthen all democratic forums of this type so that it is possible to ensure the implementation of State-declared commitments to safeguard civil rights of the people? The more such space widens, the more will it be possible to prevent fake encounters, killings of the struggling masses and to isolate and defeat the 'culture of impunity'. Instead of doing so, if we kidnap someone, torture him and then kill him and throw his body in a street, then we become oppressors like the State. You will have to accept responsibility for the trauma that children undergo when murders take place before their very eyes. Murder can never be accepted by sensitive people. How can then we be able to enable people to dream of a society based on human values in place of the ugly face of the State? How can that dream be fulfilled by following the same condemnable, mean method? You have claimed that Junglemahal has posed the questions to everyone: 'Would you support the repression by the joint forces in Lalgarh, or would you support the resistance and protest movement of the heroic people under the leadership of PCPA against the joint armed forces and other forces, including the *harmads*?' (Statement dt. 16 August 2009).

You have appealed to one and all to stand by the side of the Lalgarh movement. Many of us have consistently been supporting the movement against police atrocities and Lalgarh people's demands unconditionally. That is not the question. Many of us also do not consider your extension of support to that movement to be unjust. The problem started with the transformation in the character of the movement. It relates to your practice of violence. Needless to say, you have been using the typical Marxist 'binary' model of seeing it as a contradiction between the two — either one is on this side or on that, that is, the side of the enemy. None among you is prepared to accept the fact that there could also be a third, fourth or fifth position in which a person can be and still stand by the movement. Scholars have written so many things on this 'history of seeing'.

We condemn the continuous State violence and the repression perpetrated by the main ruling party in this state. Along with it, we also feel that your declared presence has pushed into the background the focus of the direction of people's upsurge and movement under the leadership of the people's committee. On the other hand, there are some negative elements inherent in the armed resistance under your leadership that stand in the way of getting mass support against State violence. Whether you realize it or not, we do not know. The 21st century is an era of human rights consciousness, and in any resistance movement, particularly those with arms, certain universal unchallengeable notions, which we may call 'minimal absolutist view', will have to be recognized. Discarding those notions as 'bourgeois' at the time of principles' formulation would only be suicidal.

Response from Junglemahal

Kishenji

The human rights movement in Bengal started in the early 1970s after the setback of the Naxalbari movement. The next few decades were one of vacuum in the revolutionary movement; it was in that context that human rights movement developed. The human rights movement played a glorious role for four decades, standing by the side of the oppressed masses. In those days, Sujatobabu (Sujato Bhadra) stood in the forefront of that struggle. Civil rights movement in those decades took some shape. That model was the model of standing by the side of the oppressed masses.

However, as there was a resurgence of revolutionary movements in Andhra Pradesh and (undivided) Bihar in the 1980s, the civil rights movement, by degrees, was beset with a crisis. That was the time when the masses rose to shake off the image of 'oppressed masses' and asserted their identity as the 'resisting warrior masses'. Thus the old model of the civil rights movement could not fit in the new situation. Besides, the State started clamping down on human rights activists to keep the movement within specified limits, which gave rise to debate and contradiction within human rights movement. The glorious representative of human rights movement at that stage in Andhra Pradesh was Ramanathan R. Purushottam. The human rights movement in Bengal still remained untouched by that crisis. This is because the revolutionary movement in Bengal, as yet, had not regained its relevance in the political scenario. Today, the movement in Lalgarh-Junglemahal has raised a question before the human rights movement. Will the civil rights activists, who are accustomed to stand by the side of the 'oppressed masses', will not be equally be successful in standing by the side of the 'resisting warrior masses'? The movement in Lalgarh-Junglemahal has brought to the fore two main questions: 1) Should the people's movement, in the last analysis, be allowed to be exploited to make room for mainstream leaders/woman leaders? Or will the people be able to channelise it in a way that helps the resurgence of the people? 2) Should the people fighting against fascist rule be satisfied with saving their skin by holding the hands of leaders/woman leaders along the constitutional path? Or will the people protect themselves by destroying the fascist fortresses like that of Bastille?

Violence or non-violence? This had never been an 'issue' in Indian politics. In what is called 'democratic politics', the practice of violence — in that mainstream constitutional politics — far surpasses the practice of violence in revolutionary politics. Thus in the language of law, this is a 'non-issue'. It is to bury the two main issues raised by the Lalgarh movement that the State policymakers have put forward this 'non-issue'. The right to self-defence is recognized even in bourgeois law. The right to kill the attacker in self-defence is recognized, though that right is used as a pretext by the State to kill the revolutionary masses and revolutionaries. But when the oppressed masses turn into resisting warrior masses and come forward to exercise that right, the whole context changes. What is meant by fascist rule? It is a rule by a coterie of a handful of political leaders and bureaucrats. At the grassroots level, it takes the form of combined terror perpetrated by State forces and 'Gestapo' forces of the party. Let us keep in mind that fascism is a well-organized centralized system. Even if there is a tiny loophole, the fascist system will penetrate through that it into villages and bring with it murder, rape and arson.

The right of self-defence of the masses demands that no shadow of the *harmads* exist in the villages, no loophole is allowed to develop through which they can penetrate any time. Today, we are witness to the hair-raising serials associated with genocide, terror, rape and torching of houses of Hitler's Gestapo after the emergence of *Salwa Judum* in Chhattisgarh, *Nagarik Suraksha Samiti* in Jharkhand, and *Harmad Bahini*, *Ghoskar Bahini* and *Santras Protirodh Committee* in the Junglemahal area of Bengal. These are part of everyday life — the operation by the joint forces, the setting up 80 to 90 bunkers, big *harmad* camps, with modern weapons like LMGs under police protection around Keshpur and Garbeta to recapture Junglemahal. All these are known thanks to the media. On the other hand, the State is moving with moneybags from one village to another to create an informer and covert network, the police forces are creating terror by beating up people indiscriminately, all the schools have been converted into police camps and thereby a war-like situation is being created. In such a situation, can the yardsticks of just principles remain the same? Can the yardstick be the same for a normal situation and a situation when fascism rules? Civil war and fascism bring changes in human lives. The notions and yardsticks about just principles also undergo changes temporarily. In order to tire out informers, the people are adopting a number of methods.

On the other side, the State is also trying everything in its power to whet their greed. Thus the number of informers being killed is also mounting. Had there been some proper system in Junglemahal today, the number of informers getting killed would have been far less. In different parts of Dandakaranya, informers are being detained in people's prisons. As long as the joint forces did not enter the area, no need was felt to liquidate the spies in such a large number. After the intrusion of the joint forces, the situation has changed. Likewise, the notion of self-defence has also changed. We are also opposed to the death sentence. However, the notion of just principle in a normal situation is different from that a war-like situation. During war, freedom of thought, consciousness, initiative and innovation is much limited in scope.

Sujatobabu has observed: 'Your pronounced and armed presence has pushed the focus of the speed and movement of people's upsurge led by the PCPA to the background.' Sujatobabu, the State has snatched your right to openly enter Junglemahal area with only one objective: that is, to indulge in disinformation campaign. Had it been otherwise, you would have been able to see that everyday thousands of people have been taking part in processions, mass gatherings, gheraos and demonstrations in every nook and corner of

Junglemahal. Despite the repression by the joint forces, the system initiated by PCPA is inspiring the people. The creativity of the masses has increased even after the arrest of Chhatradhar Mahato. You would have seen how irresistible the people's movement has become. The inherent strength of the people's movement and people's initiative, and people's intense consciousness have truly been instrumental in writing the epic of struggle. If you are willing, we are ready to arrange everything for your visit to Junglemahal and provide security. Come, see with your own eyes, put them in writing, change your outlook. And turn upside down the frontier of human rights movement.

When the decision to form a central coordination committee to take steps to curb Maoists' movement and to silence their top 100 leaders is taken and when retired DG of BSF Prakash Singh openly expresses his displeasure with such a move, it shows that the State has been waging a war, and a war has to be fought in a particular way. In order to counter the decision of the State to silence the top 100 revolutionary leaders (Prakash Singh himself has explained what it means in police parlance to make one fall 'silent'), does the need to take military action against top leaders of the State arise. Sujatobabu has stated that no change achieved through violent means has ever been long-lasting. We are not giving his remark much importance. We do not feel that he himself seriously believes in it. Most of the epochal changes in history could not have been accomplished without violence. It was through violence that the ruling dynasties of the Medieval Age came to an end. Let me conclude by citing one example, that of slave Dred Scott against American slavery, the defeat in which made the American Civil War inevitable. It is the lust for power and property that has made violence inevitable in all ages.

Violence and Non-violence

Amit Bhattacharyya

In his letter of 26 September (2009), *An Open Letter to the Maoists,* human rights activist Sujato Bhadra has completely messed up the cause and effect of the Lalgarh movement. In Lalgarh or Junglemahal, State repression was not the outcome of the 'armed activities' of the Maoists, rather, it is State repression, deprivation and sense of humiliation and years of pain and exploitation that has forced the people to support the 'jungle party', to become Maoists and to adopt 'armed activities' as the means of resistance and the realization of demands. What is actually implied in Bhadra's statement is that since armed resistance or counter-attack would invite more severe State repression, it is better not to get armed at all. Bhadra then refers to the application of violence and the meting out of death penalty through trials in people's courts. Here, he harps on several issues. What transpires from his statement — and that is also the view of many others — is that 'democratic' struggle should be peaceful, and, if takes a 'violent' turn or gets 'armed', then it would lose its 'democratic' character and become an undemocratic one. The question is: Is it a fact that only peaceful movements are 'democratic'? And does a movement that is 'armed' and 'violent' necessarily become 'undemocratic'? What do history and practical experience tell us? Generally, every person (barring the ruling clique and their faithful servants) wants peace, wants to have food and clothing and live in dignity; nobody wants violence or bloodshed. It is the repressive State that forces them to take up arms.

One of the main features of the Lalgarh movement is armed resistance (with firearms and traditional weapons) in the face of violent attacks launched by the State. There the State is waging a war against the people and the people in their turn are keeping up the resistance to the best of their ability. Some CPI(M) cadres and *harmads* have been killed, and the Maoists declared that all of them were police 'informers' — that they were warned before but did not listen, so they were given the death sentence in people's courts. Whether they were police 'informers' is not known to the writer.

However, what is quite clear is that during the past 32 years, the gap between the ruling CPI(M) and the police administration has vanished into thin air. Two years ago, when members of the *Nari Mukti Sangha* (Women's Liberation Committee) had been putting up posters at Bagha Jatin railway station in Kolkata, they were encircled by CITU/CPI(M) cadres, taken to the 'party' office and then handed over to the police. During the same period, members of the women's wing of the CPI(M) and some cadres tried to hand over five members of the *Matangini Mahila Samiti,* who were living in Jadavpur, Kolkata, to the police. These mean attempts prove that CPI(M) cadres were playing the role of police informers. Bhadra is against the death sentence. I believe, not only he but many peoplein general are against the death sentence. Bhadra's question is: As 224 countries have abolished the death sentence, why should the Maoists still keep it as a form of punishment? Here Bhadra has committed a major error. This question is reasonable if it is addressed to countries and established governments. But how can it be applicable to those who neither run a country nor have an established government? I am in total agreement with Bhadra on one point: there should be thorough investigation before making any move — the loss of lives on the part of and damage to innocent people is totally undesirable.

In Bhadra's opinion: 'A society formed through violent means is short-lasting'. My question to him is: Where at all has fundamental social transformation taken place and that too become long-lasting? Granted that in countries like Russia and China, where society was changed through violent means, there was change in colour. However, was the application of violent means responsible for those societies being short-lasting? Or was it due to the inherent contradictions in the new societies? History teaches us that fundamental social transformation did never take place without war and armed uprisings. Bhadra has raised the question of the social impact of violence. Why should he speak here only of some urban intellectuals who are detached from the struggle? What about the impact on the people of Junglemahal, for instance, the *Adivasi* students who have been subjected to State violence daily? Why doesn't he talk also about the resistance struggle by the people, the people of the area who, like the people of Nandigram, have been spending sleepless nights and standing up to the challenge of the *harmads* and the joint forces? The problem with the human rights activists is that they never challenge the existence of the State. On the contrary, they accept its legitimacy and demand that it should 'put into practice its declared commitment'. Influenced by post-modernist thinking, they see only the tree, but fail to see the forest. To them, the Lalgarh movement is just a conflict between State repression and counter-violence perpetrated by the 'armed opposition group'.

But the Lagarh movement is at the same time a struggle against the plunder of India's natural resources by foreign capital and domestic comprador capital, a struggle for attaining pro-people development (setting up of health centres, building of roads, dams and water reservoirs, implementation of land-to-the-tiller programme, etc, through people's initiative and voluntary labour). On 16 September (2009), *The Statesman* organised a discussion on 'Surely the Maoist is Not One of Us'. Speaking on the occasion, Prof. G. Hargopal said: 'When a landlord takes away a villager's wife, keeps her in his house to sexually abuse her and orders the husband to go away when he pleads with him for returning his wife to him and his two children, what is he supposed to do? Mouth platitudes about non-violence and peace? Or take up arms against a sea of troubles and by opposing end them? In one such case, a youth in Andhra Pradesh went straight into the jungle, organised a group of about 25,000 people, killed the landlord and ended up being Maoist.' (*The Statesman*, 17 September 2009). History teaches us that violence and murder have existed in the past and will continue to exist in the present. All of us individually want peace; nobody wants violence or murder. But they will continue to stay, irrespective of our wishes and will influence the direction of history, leaving behind their negative or positive imprint on the way.

* Source: Radicalnotes.com. Posted on October 24, 2009. The articles are being reproduced with some minor editing.

Section IV

Voices from Junglemahal and Accounts of Activists'

Whither Junglemahal!

Sumit Chowdhury

'Those who created the world did so by "walking while asking questions".'

Sub-Commandante Marcos

On 25 November 2011 newspapers splashed a gruesome picture on their first pages: a middle-aged man, with partially blown-up jaw and a deep gash across the only eye visible, his rather mundane clothes grubby with blood, lying face somewhat up but sideways on the ground, dead as dead can be. The big headlines accompanying the picture were brazenly euphoric, perhaps to drive home that the dead man in the picture didn't even deserve the respect normally accorded to the dead. After all, he was one of the top guns of left extremist insurgents who constitute, in the oft-repeated words of our Prime Minister and echoed by media and political go-getters of every hue, 'the biggest threat to our internal security.'

The dead man in the picture, Mallojula Koteswara Rao aka Kishenji, happened to be, the contempt shown by newspapers notwithstanding, a citizen of this country, a 'child of the Republic,' who according to the same country's apex court, 'the State cannot kill.' 'Killed,' in of course, he was — that is what the cheering in newspapers and news-channels was all about. But 'how,' 'when' and 'where' were the ugly questions, destined to raise their heads. Did he really die in a gun-battle, euphemistically put as an 'encounter?' Or, was he captured earlier, tortured in custody and then murdered in cold blood, his body later dumped in the forest for news-gatherers to click their Nikons.

The paramilitary, sent by state and Central governments together to nab him and his armed comrades, Claimed, as they have always claimed, that they had to spray him with bullets and mortars in self-defence since the man was firing a flurry of shots at them. Bengal's brand new chief minister — who the dead man had wished to see as the CM when she led the opposition in the state — even went to the extent of saying, almost by way of an explanation, that for three whole days Kishenji was repeatedly asked over microphones to surrender but he just wouldn't and kept firing. 'He fired a thousand rounds,' she added to impress upon her audience how dangerous or what a lunatic the dead man was.

Holes in Mamata's Story

The deceased's kin, the political setup he belonged to, upholders of civil liberties and democratic rights as well as several left parties, fact-finding teams and even a few columnists, however, cried foul. How it was that Kishenji, commander-in-chief, People's Liberation Guerilla Army (PLGA) — was the lone person to be knocked out while none of those deputed to provide him security cover was as much as spotted in the battle arena, let alone killed or injured? How come not a single of the 800-1000 jawans engaged in the high-profile operation was hit at least by a stray bullet, given that, if paramilitary and cm Mamata Banerjee were to be believed, Kishenji was shooting from his AK—47 like a man possessed? Wasn't it odd that the termite hill behind which his body lay didn't have a single bullet mark? Why had villagers around Burishole forest not heard anything when for three whole days microphones were supposedly blaring appeals to give up? Why did they hear gunshots only in the afternoon of that day, and for a mere twenty odd minutes, a time span in which it was impossible to fire a thousand rounds even from the fastest automatic? And, finally, what caused the slashes and burns on his body that Kishenji's niece, who had come all the way from Andhra to identify the dead, found?

A spicy yarn regarding the circumstances of his killing was also doing the rounds, floated by paramilitary, administration and TRP-seeking media in concert. Suchitra Mahato, guerilla commander and widow of Sashadhar Mahato — who, too, was killed under similar circumstances some eight months before — was, as the story goes, beside Kishenji during his last moments. Jawans taking part in the operation apparently saw her carrying her newborn and firing incessantly from her rifle. She, however, managed to escape to Jharkhand despite receiving a gunshot wound in her abdomen. How did a bleeding Suchitra, baby in arm, walk 20km to the inter-state border and across dodging the most stringent security cordon was anybody's guess. What was she doing in the battlefield with her baby? Where were the other members of her squad or did she and Kishenji have a date without the knowledge of any of their comrades?

Questions there were many but answers government was not inclined to provide and media bound to ignore. Mamata stopped journalists from asking Suchitra questions about the last hours of Kishenji when she presented the fugitive guerrilla at the state secretariat after her surrender. Post-mortem, ballistic and forensic reports, it could safely be assumed, would get a dusty burial in one of the messy filing cabinets in a messy office in either South Block or Bhawani Bhaban. The State reserved the sole right to information on 'encounter deaths.'

However, human rights principles demanded that every 'encounter death' be probed by a judicial or independent body and the investigation should begin by filing murder charge against the armed arm of the State. In a bid to pre-empt public suspicion and possible outrage, West Bengal CM did order a CID probe; but CID was directly under her wings and, thus, couldn't, by any stretch of imagination, be impartial. Mamata had herself doubted the even-handedness of CID and demanded instead a CBI investigation when Tapasi Malik was battered and burnt to death in Singur and the dastardly carnage was perpetrated in Nandigram. At that time, she was in the Opposition and her arch enemy was the LF government ; but now that she was ensconced in CM's chair, the same CID, she indicated, had overnight shed its baggage of bias.

Meanwhile, three months have gone by. With new leaves appearing on dry Sal and Mahul branches, the forests are preparing to put behind yet another winter of terror and bloodshed, misery and discontent. Kishenji, now a part of Junglemahal myth, has already faded from media's memory; and ordinary folk didn't know him. Maybe, there are still those in the forests fired by his revolutionary ideals, others who will remember him with a drop of tear and yet others who will judge him by his defeat or the futility of his political persuasion; but the circumstances of his macabre end will forever remain a mystery. We've seen that happen over and again — will we ever know precisely how Cherukeri Rajkumar aka Azad and so many others among Kishenji's comrades or fellow-travellers died in 'encounters' with police? Will truth ever come out?

Remembering Azad while writing about Kishenji comes almost involuntarily. Not only did they come from the same region and speak the same language, but they also were very senior leaders of the same political party, CPI(Maoist), and harboured the same political belief. Both of them were 'killed' in ostensible 'encounters' by armed mercenaries of the State.There was, however, a paradox glossed over by many among the far left as well as the selectively forgetful media: Kishenji died in the hands of a government whose supreme administrator had once — when she was not in government but trying every means to oust Left Frond government — condemned the killing of Azad, and demanded an appropriate investigation.

Bonhomie and Betrayal

Years before the Assembly polls in Bengal, there was a certain bonhomie prevailing between the two widely divergent, even antagonistic, political forces. Kishenji's party, there're good reasons to believe, were sincere about that relationship. For her, on the other hand, it was simply a matter of vote-catching expediency. The rapport had inevitably to break in a betrayal.

Mamata-CPI(Maoist) ties had begun in Keshpur at the turn of the millennium and was re-established during the historic people's struggle in Nandigram. In that creek-laden estuarine land, a few of Kishenji's men and women, though they arrived on the scene rather late, had battled the *harmads* arms for arms, allowing Mamata, then in Opposition, to easily expand her vote-base. In Lalgarh's red and rocky soil, on the contrary, the disposition of the people's uprising was such that sowing electoral seeds was not at all a realistic idea and she had to let the insurgents have a free run. The trade-off — 'you take Nandigram, I take Lalgarh' — worked fairly well until Maoists, perhaps considering the overall political equation in the state and unnerved by merciless onslaught of joint forces, made a tactical blunder by overtly rooting for her. The mole-killing spree that Kishenji's cohorts had indulged in further weakened their position by alienating their support base among the villagers and their sympathisers in urban areas.

In all likelihood, Maoist soft spot for Mamata came from their veiled admiration of her mass appeal and her relentless line of attack in taking on their common enemy, CPI(M). 'Enemy's enemy is my friend,' maybe it was their premise. She, on her part, made excellent use of this covert friendship, bagging in the Assembly polls half the seats in Junglemahal where earlier she didn't even have a toehold. Maoists were so enamoured of her that they stayed dormant even after Chhatradhar Mahato, the most known face and voice of the Lalgarh movement, decided to contest independently from jail. Mamata took advantage of this, using Maoists to serve her own end; Maoists, on the other hand, served none, not even themselves. Consequently, Mamata came out all winners and Maoists lost everything. Maoists' was the stupidity of ideological bankruptcy, hers was the ingenuity of pragmatic opportunism.

Mamata's terrific performance in the elections, the massive mandate she received from the people of West Bengal, changed the Junglemahal scenario dramatically. As she moved from street-power to state-power, she reneged on all that she had promised before. Not only she refused to pull out the paramilitary and release the hundreds of activists and ordinary folk rotting in jail, she also let loose her fearsome goon gangs, *Bhairab Bahini*, to make quick inroads into the forest-dotted territory. Kishenji's forces, who had already crumbled under the security operation launched by previous regime, were caught unawares and faced absolute demolition. His sudden but inevitable death made the picture complete.

Where Kishenji's party and many of our friends in civil society erred was their inability to comprehend the eruption in recent years of a series of astounding people's movements in West Bengal, which had been quite sedate until then. Maoists imagined that people in the state were fed up with over three decades of tyranny and misrule, stranglehold of the ruling party in every sphere of, and stifling of every voice of democratic dissent and increasing use of violence. True, those issues were at the back of people's minds, and sometimes they took centrestage. But Singur and Nandigram happened not because people were venting their anger at an authoritarian regime but to save their land and livelihood from the aggressive paws of ever-hungry corporate lions. To put it in a macro perspective, the turbulence in West Bengal was the fallout of the neoliberal policies which Bretton Woods institutions had been imposing on our people through a submissive State. All the power-greedy political formations, Mamata included, were zealously pursuing that agenda whenever and wherever they wielded power. Instead of countering the offensive by global financial capital, targeting the 34-year-old regime and befriending Mamata to boot them out was like missing the woods for the trees.

Mass Movement and Political Control

Lalgarh movement certainly was a major challenge to the Indian State, since it dwelt on police atrocities. It, nonetheless, was not aiming at destroying or uprooting the State machinery or the existing political system. Spearheaded by People's Committee against Police Atrocities (PCPA), it was purely a mass democratic movement seeking justice and dignity for an oppressed and deprived people. From its spontaneous inception, PCPA had put up a 'no entry' sign for party banners; activists and supporters from a whole range of political formations, discarding their affiliations and loyalties, took an active part in its functioning; meetings were held in open fields, under trees where thousands, carrying bows and arrows and thumping dhamsa-madal, took part in debates, discussions and decision-making, almost in festive mood.

Under these conditions, no mainstream electoral party could influence the course of the movement or use it to their advantage. That is how CPI(Maoist), being a clandestine setup, could steal a march over all the others who had worked explicitly within the recognised political arrangement. Within a few months, Maoists established their hegemony over the movement and took full control of PCPA.

What Kishenji & Co did in Lalgarh, Mamata had done it in Singur and Nandigram. Whereas Maoist agenda was setting up a people's State under their patronage after pulling down the existing repressive one, Mamata sought her share in the affairs of the state already on hand. Both snatched the reins of autonomous people's movements from the people in their bids to accessing political power, the former through bullets and the latter by way of ballots. Is that why they came together?

Peace is the Other Name of War?

Azad, it was said, was picked up on his way to meet the official peace mediator appointed by Central government and, thereafter, shot at point blank. Though the mediator had no hand in it — he was, obviously, taken for a ride by the Union home minister — the State's peace initiatives had become suspect. A point to note, in this context, is that the peace process was undertaken almost at the same time as the most vicious war was being carried out by the Indian State on a section of our own people. Was 'peace' then the other name for war, one supplementing the other? Was 'peace' a weapon of war?

These questions would be logical to ask if one was to observe Mamata's Junglemahal policy. Soon after assuming power, she launched the peace offensive by appointing a set of six mediators to open the gates for talks without making a single move to removing the main obstacles blocking that gate. Paramilitary operations — accompanied by raids in villages, indiscriminate beatings, arrests and tortures, even rapes — continued as before, caught considerably less by prying media eyes; and none of the prisoners were given any hope of being free in the near future. Who were they going to talk to, if the leaders of the movement were confined to dark and danky cells in Medinipur jail? How would state government's peace efforts be trusted when violence was being unleashed by its own forces?

Did such questions never occur to the dear mediators before accepting the appointment? Were they blind to the reality of Junglemahal, so anxious they were on ushering in peace in those unquiet woods? If they were so serious about opening dialogues between the conflicting sides, shouldn't they have delved into what transpired in the talks held before? The last talk between government and PCPA took place on 13 June 2009, which this writer attended as representing *Lalgarh Andolan Sanhati Mancha* (LASM) — Solidarity Forum for Lalgarh Movement. In that meeting, held amicably and government accepting all the temporary demands made by PCPA — a written agreement was signed which stated the next round would be held exactly a month after on 14 July. Five days later, on 18 June, joint forces moved into Lalgarh and nothing ever was heard about the agreement. Why didn't our mediators insist that Mamata's government abide by the spirit of that written piece of paper? It could've acted as the 'open sesame' for peace talks. PCPA, it need be told, had been keen on 'talks' right from the beginning. Even when roads were being blockaded and police PCPA was interacting with police and administration at various levels. Negotiations, Chhatradhar Mahato said, were also a form of struggle.

Let us be fair, Maoists, too, had shown their interest in talks time and again. A few hours before PCPA president, Lalmohan Tudu, was brutally annihilated by security forces, Kishenji had, in a fax to news-channels, declared 72 days' ceasefire in response to the Union home minister's offer of 72 hours. The only reaction received till now from government was Lalmohan's corpse. If the State was not desirous of peace, peaceniks had to hit the dead end. And, so they did.

Maoists were in a quandary. They wanted to participate in the talks — without, of course, giving up arms — but were not ready with a plan of action; so, they could make only half-hearted pokes at 'peace.' Their confusion were further confounded by their own doing when they killed two of Mamata's men — one of thme a well-known

Jharkhand activist in the region. It was yet another example of the opportunism of adventurism. Eventually, Kishenji had to pay with his life the price for his inconsistency. With his killing, the peace process was dispatched to oblivion.

Mamata, in the meantime, has been winning kudos from every quarter for the slew of development projects she announced for Junglemahal every time she went there. Without going into merits of her packages or whether they would ever be implemented in letter and spirit, one may well ask a basic question: Did the Lalgarh uprising take place because those projects were lacking? Did the quiet woods turn unquiet because a bridge was not constructed over Kangsabati or a polytechnic missing in Binpur? What about the original demand that the police officers who took Chhitamoni's eyes come to Dalilpur Chowk and apologise in public?

Actually, the packages are an extension of the war against people. What else is 'development' but war in another name, when its impact leads to displacement, deprivation and destruction of ways of life? Our Prime Minister and political leaders have been harping on a 'twin strategy, that is, security offensive and development, to tackle 'the menace of left extremism'. In effect, it works like a double-barreled gun — shots from either barrel wreak havoc on people's lives. The peaceniks have no hope of preventing the bloodshed, violence and destruction that awaits Junglemahal. The only way is to intensify the people's struggle.

Chronicles of a Death Foretold?

Saswati Ghosh

Death of what! A person, a leader, or a movement! With Kishenji aka Mallojula Koteswara Rao's death in an 'encounter' (as claimed by security forces) in Junglemahal, one may jump to the conclusion that I'm referring to the death of the Maoist leader. But in these uncertain times, words lose certainty, and with Kishenji's death in a 'fake encounter' (as claimed by his niece and civil rights activists), death of a people's movement may also be signified. This is a personal chronicle, based on witnessing the transformation and eventual demise of a people's movement, when hijacked by a political group.

Since I'm presenting a personal chronicle of the events I've witnessed and participated in to some extent, perhaps a few words about me will not be out of place. During my campus days, I had been actively involved with a far-left student organisation but left dissatisfied that gender issues were not being adequately addressed. Later in life, I became active with non-party political women's groups, which raised their voices against State repression and took up rights-based issues. My academic upbringing also led to an interest in tribal communities, their social-economic segregation and backwardness. Naturally, when the Lalgarh upsurge hogged headlines in newspapers, I enthusiastically joined the solidarity campaigns organised from my city

The police raid in the villages, the assault on women and children, and the unique resistance based on a unique demand and the mass participation of women in the movement had inspired a large number of urban activists including me. I was even part of groups that kept going to Junglemahal to express support and feel the pulse of the extraordinary movement. We saw an incomparable mass movement far beyond leftism in both theory and practice.

Chronicle 1: Amlashole Didn't Make Us Furious

In June 2006, the media was full of news about deaths in tribal families due to hunger. A correspondent reported, 'five tribals had recently died because of lack of food in Amlashole village in Belpahari block in West Midnapore district. An allegation not heard of since the 1942 Bengal famine, the report of starvation deaths seems to falsify official boasts of great success with agrarian reforms, agricultural boom in the state and equal success with the public distribution system.'[1]

The news did make some noise, but couldn't raise the level of anger to what Singur-Nandigram-Lalgarh would later generate. A research study carried out in a village in Medinipur (then undivided) — first survey in 1993 and repeat surveys in 1995 and 1998 — revealed a food calendar — should we call it 'hunger calendar'— which showed that the time-span of tribal people going hungry had been increasing rather dangerously. Earlier it used to be seven months, and now it was extended to practically nine months of the year. With more and more community land being acquired by government for social forestry, increasing government restrictions on collection of twigs, fruits, leaves and other minor forest produce in government land and rapid dwindling of aquatic livestock like small fish due to increasing use of pesticides had largely contributed to the extension of the season of hunger.

The calendar, I wrote in an article,[2] is analogous to the one described in the medieval Bengali classic *Chandimangal* by poet Mukundaram (circa 1579), an analogy still valid after 435 years. Mukundaram portrayed the hunger calendar of Kalketu and Phullara, the animal-trapper couple and their mother Nidaya. Animal-trappers were typically tribal people who remained geographically isolated from the mainstream. Usually, SCs and STs are clubbed together to describe the 'marginal' population. It disregards the spatial isolation of the tribal people, which is the major contributor to their deprivation.

The SCs, living on the fringes of upper-caste Hindu society, could become conscious of their deprivation and unite to raise voices, but such awareness took a much longer time for the tribal population. Perhaps, that's why extremist politics found a fertile ground among them. But the point to note is that while Amlashole failed to unleash public anger, police excesses in Lalgarh did.

Chronicle 2: for Lalgarh

24 April, 2009. We walked proudly in the streets of Kolkata, We walked in support of Chhatradhar Mahato, the leader of the People's Committee against Police Atrocities (PCPA) and the people of Lalgarh for resolutely continuing with police boycott. We greeted them because what we dreamt of doing ourselves, the remote villagers had actually done. As someone said, 'They've taught the police the right lesson!'

Chronicle 3: in Lalgarh

In Lalgarh Andolan Sanhati Mancha (LASM), we came together believing that PCPA was truly a unique peoples' organisation, though rapidly coming under the Maoist influence. When, in April-May 2009, reports of serial killings of CPI(M) workers, summary trial and punishment in so-called 'people's court' and extortion in Lalgarh and other pockets of Junglemahal started appearing in the media, intense debates broke out amongst us. A large number of LASM activists made it clear that they were expressing solidarity with a unique people's movement not the political agenda or strategy of a political party or group. A team was constituted to visit the area and assess the situation.

We found PCPA — to be truly a broad-based organisation, as even BJP supporters were active part of it. In fact, that was the uniting plank of PCPA — anyone could join it but without any party banner or affiliation. That, to some extent, explained why they had refused CPIML(ND) and Santosh Rana's group. Rana, of course, has a different version for the turn of events. PCPA, according to him, was the outcome of a joint effort by *Bharat Jakat Majhi Marwa,* a group of tribal heads, and various Jharkhand Party and CPI(ML) factions; later, Maoists took control and created a totalitarian atmosphere in which no other political organisation could function.

We visited some of the families who had faced trials in a people's court. When asked whether they could accept the trial in and the verdict of the peoples' court, one the respondents retorted, 'Did ever an accused accept punishment?' Another respondent lamented that the only 'sin' his son performed was to cast false votes during elections, and for, that he was driven out of the village. When we asked PCPA leaders, Chhatradhar Mahato and Lalmohan Tudu about such complaints, they assured us that in the people's courts, the majority opinion was not in favour of capital or any other violent forms of punishment but sometimes excesses did happen. Newspapers reported that Gopinath Murmu was beaten to death since he refused to participate in the PCPA rally in Kolkata. We talked to Gopinath's widow, who claimed that her husband died of excessive drinking.

At night, we used to walk up to Kantapahari to sleep in a building meant clearly to be a police barrack but now turned into a hospital managed by PCPA. From early morning, patients from far — mothers with their babies — crowded its tiny rooms for free treatment and medicines. A couple of local women had picked up nursing and basic medical aid from the doctors coming from Kolkata and other places. We also witnessed a 3-km road being built by villagers with voluntary labour. When asked why they were not asking the administration to pay wages under NREGS for such labour, Chhatradhar looked indifferent saying the people were fed up and had no faith in the administration.

Regarding media stories about extortion, PCPA leaders were quite categorical that officers at BDO and SDO offices, with whom they maintained regular liaison, could ever complain about them demanding ransom. Perhaps, miscreants were using PCPA's name.

We saw quite a lot of wall-writings calling for election boycott. As all the Lok Sabha seats in Junglemahal had been won by Left Front in the elections held a month ago, the then Opposition accused 'Maoists and Mahatos' of aiding the left victory through their poll boycott call. Chhatradhar, however, denied the charges saying PCPA was never opposed to elections; in fact, it'd itself have contested in the polls had all the opposition parties agreed on a common candidate. At the end, there were eight candidates against CPI(M) which got the villagers annoyed and confused; and, they opted to abstain from voting. Besides, the Election Commission failed to provide adequate transport for the voters while the pick-up points were too far away from many villages; it also didn't inform the voters about the location of the booths. All these were agreed upon during talks with the Commission a week before the polling day.

The LASM team ended up a divided lot. There was no single opinion on Maoist-PCPA relationship or the mindless violence frequently being resorted to in the name of the movement. Some of us began to feel choked by the contraction of democratic space such violence always brings about. Even Chhatradhar & Co's explanations, at times, sounded like justifications.

Chronicle 4: Shrinking Democratic Space

Maybe Chhatradhar was right — media was out to malign PCPA and the Lalgarh movement. But as stories of more and more violent actions in Junglemahal filled the news-pages, Maoist take-over of the movement seemed imminent.

A particular incident was shocking: a little girl, daughter of a CPI(M) functionary, was forced to beg for her father's life by writing a poster that he would have no further track with the party. When the picture of that girl writing that poster appeared in the newspapers, we were shamed. I wrote a piece slamming the intolerance of dogmatic ideology and expressing concern over the shrinking of democratic space and the shutting up of pluralism[3]. I asked whether one couldn't belong to a political party of one's own choice. Yes, CPI(M) had been making armed attacks on people but silencing their voices by force would lead to a grave situation. What was to be noted was that in these cases both the perpetrators and the victims of violent action belonged to the poorest of the poor.

My article angered some of my fellow-travellers in LASM. *Ganapratirodh*[4] dubbed my emotions to be bourgeois and lambasted me for eschewing the class angle and hiding the oppressive nature of the Indian State. It even threatened the writer that people would settle scores once the right time arrived. And yet, I was invited as a speaker to a PCPA mass rally in Belpahari.

Debates within LASM over Maoist violence intensified after they openly boasted that they were behind the Lalgarh upsurge and now leading the movement. One view was that Maoist violence would only aggravate the State's counter-violence. But those sympathetic to the Maoist cause were not prepared to concede an inch and a stalemate ensued. Soon after, to broaden the solidarity campaign, make it more inclusive and break out of the Maoist domination, the idea of Lalgarh Mancha (LM) was floated.

A booklet published at that time[5], angered those in LASM who supported PCPA but not Maoists. Stating that those objecting to the use of violence couldn't follow the class nature of violence, it added, 'And these people do not find any regular forum to give vent to their feelings and political opinion, they try to utilisze these broad forums to air their feelings.' This was clearly hitting below the belt! The fact was that activists who came together to uphold the Lalgarh struggle were not mere 'forum-seekers' but were prepared to go to any length and make any number of sacrifices. Since they came from a diverse range of backgrounds, accommodating every view and uniting on the basis of a common perception would have strengthened the movement. Sadly, such wisdom was missing on those whose sole argument was arrogance.

It was said that in Jungelmahal, because the State had declared war on the people, the people had no option but put up an armed resistance. Many of us, however, felt that it had eventually get ordinary villagers caught in crossfire between the State and Maoist squads. While the squads would be able to protect themselves, villagers would have to bear the brunt of the State's violence. But those endorsing armed resistance were not willing to listen; so, we who joined LASM/LM out of conscience, held independent views and had no armed vanguard' to defend the solidarity movement out of sheer frustration.

Some of us proposed that while speaking from a public platform, we should be free to air our views — some views might be critical of the violence, some would defend. The proposal was rejected as it was felt that diversity of views would 'confuse' the audience. People, of course, see various channels, read a multiplicity of newspapers, and yet form their own opinion — this argument, too, was lost on those who championed armed, and only armed, resistance.

Meanwhile, violence kept escalating in Junglemahal. And the movement's support base kept dwindling at a rapid pace.

Chronicle 5: Ignored Ethnicity

The jungle corridor from Maharashtra's Gadchiroli to West Bengal's Junglemahal (and including vast stretches of Chhatisgarh, Andhra Pradesh, Odisha and Jharkhand), where Maoists mainly operate in, is the tribal heartland of the country. Addressing ethnicity issues in these areas is as vital as dealing with issues of poverty and deprivation. That Maoist politics never seriously took up the question of ethnic identity came to surface when Jalamsai Sadmek of Gadchiroli, Hemal Mandi of West Medinipur or Gurucharan Kisku of Purulia, all Maoists, slammed the leadership for ignoring their cultural identity.

They felt that urban, educated Maoists, mostly from Andhra, were actually in control and they were insensitive to the tribal concerns. It's curious that Maoists, like the conventional left, are unwilling to take up any other identity but 'class.' Religion, gender, race, region or culture rarely finds place in their theories of emancipation. Naturally, Maoists passed it off as ranting of expelled cadres turned police spies. We, on the other hand, were pleased that someone, police spy or not, had spoken the truth.

Of the printed material produced during this period, none touched upon the distinctive needs of the tribal population. Only a leaflet brought out by the *Jharkhand Andolan Samanway Mancha* or Jharkhand Movement Coordination Forum (JASM) — raised certain specific demands : Santhali, Kurmali and Mundari language as medium of teaching in primary schools; 75 percent of forest revenue to Forest Committees and free auction of forest produce; forest rights for tribal communities; filling up ST vacancies in higher education; ST status for Mahatos and Bagals; and so on.

Babu Bose, one of the most respected leaders of Junglemahal and the leading light of JASM, was killed by Maoists on September 25, 2011.

Chronicle 6: Discontinued Talks

Once Lok Sabha elections were over in April — May 2009, state government invited the PCPA leadership for talks to find ways to end the police boycott. The first and the only round - there had been talks with EC as well as several rounds at block or district levels before — in which I represented LASM, took place on 13 June at Medinipur circuit house. The discussion was quite amicable, government accepted the immediate five-point demands and, therefore, road blockades were lifted. It was decided to resume the talks a month later.

Five days later, state police and Central paramilitary forces were sent to Lalgarh.

Chronicle 7: People's Festival Brings Joint Forces

June 14: people switched on television to find the people of Lalgarh in a state of fury. Hundreds had taken over and were demolishing the palatial building in Dharampur Anuj Pandey, CPI(M) local committee secretary, lived in. Several news channel OB vans were there to record the historic event.

Though we all felt good at what we saw, we were apprehensive of how the State would respond. We feared a bloodbath. A few amongst us did disapprove of the act but their feeble voice got submerged under the strident rejoicing of the others. A 'peoples' festival' was how we looked at it.

On 18 June, joint forces arrived and 'Operation Black Soil' was launched with great intent. One wondered whether it was meant to pre-empt a mass movement from earning the path-breaker's identity.

Chronicle 8: Arrests under UAPA

On 26 September, during *Durga Puja*, CID detectives who posed as media persons arrested Chhatradhar Mahato. There were instant protests, despite the festival mood. Questions were asked, even by Left Front partners, about the method of arrest and the ethics of it. The then Director General of West Bengal Police, Bhupinder Singh accused Chhatradhar of being a Maoist and LASM a Maoist front. In a press briefing, he named 'one university professor and one lady college teacher' as Maoist associates. My friends, those who were at the press briefing, told me that my name was mentioned. As a precautionary measure, I went into hiding for a couple of days.

A few days later, Raja Sarkhel, Prasun Chatterjee of GPM and Swapan Dasgupta, editor, People's March, were picked up from their homes. Gour Chakrabarty, Maoist spokesperson in the state, had been picked up from a television studio earlier. All four of them were charged under the Unlawful Activities (Prevention) Act (UAPA). While Raja, Prasun and Gourda are still languishing in jail, Swapan Dasgupta died in custody from lack of medical care.

All these arrests were a big blow to Maoist organisational efforts and fissures surfaced within.

Chronicle 9: Media's Kishenji

A few days before the arrival of joint forces, Maoists had come overground in full glare of the media. After Chhatradhar was sent behind bars, Kishenji hogged the limelight. The Maoist leader's *gamchha*-covered face and his beloved expression '*jenegen*' (meaning '*janagan*', the masses) in Telugu-ised Bengali became a hit with the media. But we helplessly searched for answers to several questions. Some of us re-read K. Balagopal's articles, who had felt the same dilemma when confronted with the question of violence as a revolutionary strategy. Through Kishenji, the experience of Andhra seemed to be replicating in Bengal.

We continued with our search for a path other than what was to be violent. Balagopal's writings didn't give us an alternative but helped us take a distinctive stand against the use of guns. Others like us found the answers in Himanshu Kumar, the Gandhian, whose *Vanavasi Chetana Ashram* in Bastar was demolished not by Maoists but the Indian State.

Chronicle 10: Brutalisation of Junglemahal

There has been too much bloodshed in Junglemahal since the area had come under paramilitary operations. If the State has been engaged in cruel repression, Maoists have been continuing with sabotage, mine-blasts and unnecessary killings. The Gynaswari derailment which killed and maimed hundreds, the massacre in Shilda, the killing of Lalmohan Tudu, Sidho Soren and Sasadhar Mahato, Umakanta Mahato in so-called 'encounters', the death of Swapan Dasgupta and continuing incarceration of Chhatradhar and so many ordinary folk go to show that Junglemahal is bleeding.

When will all these end?

Chronicle 11: Candidate from Jail

May 2011: when the time came for holding elections to the state Assembly, Chhatradhar Mahato decided to fight from jail, not as a PCPA candidate but representing a new forum[6] formed in Medinipur jail. A whole lot of us decided to support his candidature. Expectedly, debates broke out over whether Chhatradhar had done the right thing. I accepted it as an oft-used valid strategy. We decided to go to Lalgarh to campaign for him. Some well-known personalities also extended their wholehearted support. 'It proves,' they said, 'Chhatradhar has faith in the Indian Constitution.' There were unconfirmed reports that some people, known as champions of human rights, had approached him in jail to withdraw his candidature in favour of the TMC candidate. So much for human rights neutrality!

Chhatradhar polled 20,000-plus votes. It was a considerable figure, particularly when TMC storm was sweeping across the length and breadth of the state. Chhatradhar is still languishing in jail, in spite of pre-poll promises of release by those who are now in power.

Chronicle 12: An Inevitable Death

CP(M) regime has gone and TMC is now in power. Chhatradhar, Raja, Prasun et al continue to be in jail while joint forces are continuing with their raids, arrests and 'encounter' killings. There are also reports that PCPA, USDF and MMS will be banned as Maoist setups. The new government had appointed a group of civil rights activists as interlocutors who would work for peace in Junglemahal by persuading Maoists to lay down arms and come for talks. One was perplexed, because where was the credibility of the interlocuters? Whom did they represent? Did they forget how Azad was killed? Government was never serious about peace. How serious Maoists were, we don't know.

That Kishenji would be killed in 'encounter' was, therefore, a foregone conclusion.

Who actually died — PCPA, a unique peoples' movement or Kishenji?

Notes

1. http ://www.indiarightsonline.com/Sabrang/dalit.nsf/38b852a8345861dd65256a980059289d/fcdca31b075df5b965256ec3001e5b7b?OpenDocument)
2. See my article on food deprivation, *Ananda Bazaar Patrika*, 28 September, 2006
3. *Ananda Bazaar Patrika*, 5 May, 2009
4. Organ of *Gana Pratirodh Mancha,* a constituent of LASM
5. *Singur to Lalgarh via Nandigram* by Amit Bhattacharya, *Visthapan Virodhi Jan Vikash Andolan* (August 2009)
6. *Durniti, Santras O Samrajyabadi Agrasion Birodhi Janaganer Ganatantrik Mancha* — People's Democratic Forum Against Corruption, Terror and Imperialist Aggression

Role of Civil Society: Stand by the People's Struggle

Premangsu Dasgupta

Winter in Kolkata is a festive season. Tens of thousands of people throng the Zoological Garden every day, crowds collect in front of circus tents, the Maidan turns into a veritable fair ground for cricket enthusiasts even as the mild sun makes for golfers' delight. Winter in Kolkata is also the harbinger of annual trysts with fairs. From films to books, whatever the urban populace gets excited about. This winter has been no exception. While life in the city gets festive, our co-citizens in another part of the state live in a situation that can best be described as terror-stricken. They go to bed with fear and wake up with fear. For, the State has declared a vicious war against the people there. Those people, after all, have committed a serious crime. They want the State to apologise for the terrible atrocities its police have perpetrated on them. Peace, thus, has fled from their lives. In Junglemahal, it is the winter of continuing terror and elusive peace.

Dignity First, Development alongside

The restoration of peace in Junglemahal that is being bandied about nowadays may not hold. Sufferings of the people there have to take its toll today or tomorrow. Justice has been denied to the people there. So, they have raised the banner of revolt demanding the right to live with dignity. 'Development,' or the lack of it, is, not the reason for this rebellion, as is being presumed in policy-making circles. The area, no doubt, is underdeveloped, but there are so many areas which are similarly deprived of minimum living conditions. Everywhere people are complaining about lack of development and the indifferent attitude of the government. Junglemahal is no exception but it is not the prototype of all that discontent. 'Development packages' will, therefore, not assuage the feeling of deep hurt the people there are holding in their hearts. Economic measures alone are not enough to heal the wounds. The people's movement that has rocked Junglemahal for the past three years assumes an extraordinary dimension because it has been galvanized by issues beyond the economic. Civil society, mustering all its sensitivity, needs to comprehend this.

The state's 34-years-old previous regime never accepted that Junglemahal was a neglected area. Their prolonged reign and pro-poor image would have then been put to question. They were, however, not off the mark in diagnosing what the problem is not about. For, as we have argued, the upsurge in Junglemahal was not due to absence of developmental endeavours. The regime, nevertheless, failed to or did not want to understand that Junglemahal's principal demand was that the people there be treated as human beings, their culture and way of life given the respect they deserve. The past rulers, self-serving as they were, refused to look objectively at the chain of events in the wake of the blast on the then chief minister's convoy.

A Moderate Response

In November 2008, Lalgarh in Junglemahal rose like a volcanic eruption protesting the brutal police action following the attempt on the chief minister's life. Their main demand was public apology from the police officers responsible for the crime. The suddenness, spread and intensity of the upheaval caught the administrative system and political practioners off guard. Many an eyebrow was raised by the privileged elite. The State considered the people's demand as blasphemy. The vast masses of the urban poor, though poorly informed, were enthusiastically drawn to the uprising. Civil society, unused to reaching out, failed to mobilise their support.

After Singur and Nandigram, the term 'civil society' has become part of the common vocabulary. During the forcible acquisition of prime agricultural land in Singur for Tata Motors' Nano venture, several action groups sprung up within urban communities in solidarity with the peasant agitation. Among them was a committee of so-called 'intellectuals.' These intellectuals and some known faces of the cultural world were made out to be the main pillars of 'civil society.' Though classically Hegel and Gramsci had meant something else for the term, here it came to represent the section of urban society opposed to the government's policy of land grab for industrialisation. Under such circumstances, civil society in West Bengal consisted typically of the educated middle class, cultural activists, students and such other groups. True to its character, West Bengal's civil society has played contradictory, even dubious, roles in different episodes of contemporary history. It had a major hand in the defeat of Indira Gandhi in 1977 and in the next decades formed a strong support base for the CPI(M)-dominated Left Front government. In this period, civil society turned its eyes the other way whenever grave injustices were perpetrated by the administration and the coalition in power. It fell for the CPI(M) propaganda that opposition to their government would strengthen Congress which promulgated the Emergency.

Singur and Nandigram changed that perception. A vast section of the same civil society was awakened from decades-old slumber. Those historic movements drilled into its head fundamental questions regarding the paradigm of 'development'. But more importantly, because of the ruthless manner in which these people's movements were suppressed, the democratic and progressive mask was ripped off the face of self-styled left parties and their government. It also appeared that the Left Front government was no less zealous than the Congress-led UPA and the BJP-led NDA in pursuing the neoliberal policies prescribed by global financial institutions.

Civil society trained its guns particularly on the SEZ Act after Nandigram. The heroic people's resistance there inspired to break the silence of 30 long years. The protesting voices grew in volume with every passing day and began to be raised on almost every issue that reeked of neoliberal injustice. When the people's uprising took place in Lalgarh, it added further fuel to the already burning West Bengal. The police action made the government lose its credibility to such an extent that that even the much-decried assault on the CM receded into the background. Like they had done during the Singur and Nandigram agitations, civil society and rights activists began to frequent the forest land tucked away in a far corner of West Medinipur district along the borders of Jharkhand and Odisha. *Pulishi Santras Birodhi Janasadharaner Committee* — People's Committee against Police Atrocities (PCPA) — spearheading the Lalgarh movement, received active support from a host of urban activist groups. The slogan '*Singur-Nandigramer par, path dekhachbhe Lalgarh*', — After Singur and Nandigram, Lalgarh shows the way — said it all. Several mass organisations expressed solidarity with the Lalgarh struggle. *Lalgarh Andolan Sanhati Mancha* — Solidarity Forum for the Lalgarh Movement — came into being. It later became *Lalgarh Mancha* — Lalgarh Forum — to broaden its base.

Twist in the Tale

Then, a twist in the tale cropped up. All of a sudden, CPI(Maoist) openly claimed credit for the Lalgarh movement. The unique demands and features of the movement had even drawn independent political opinion. The appearance of Maoists on the scene and the violence they indulged in upset the scenario. It paved the way for alienation of a huge section of the movement's civil society support.

The declared political agenda of Maoists is the capture of State power through armed struggle. But PCPA neither wished to capture State power nor did they believe in the power of guns. Not a single killing was recorded in the area as long as PCPA held the reins of the movement. With Maoist intervention, a peaceful, democratic struggle against police terror transformed itself into an armed struggle for power. Chhatradhar Mahato always stood for peace and negotiations. Like a true democrat he defended the Maoist presence in the movement but was quite openly apprehensive of a Maoist take-over. For Maoists, their party's interests and recognition of them leading the movement were more important than the movement itself. It is the natural outcome of middle-class vanguardism.

Maoist appropriation of the Lalgarh movement provided the state government with an excuse to shut out the ongoing dialogue with PCPA. Instead, it dispatched its police and paramilitary forces eagerly sent by the Central Government. Security operation launched by the joint forces was an extension of 'Green Hunt,' which the Indian State launched against the Maoists but actually for handing over the country's resource-rich forest corridor to mining multinationals. 'Maoist' is a good tag to use to break people's resistances. In Junglemahal, Maoists, by their own action, made it easy for the State use the tag.

Maoist sympathisers argue that the autocratic State do not need an excuse for unleashing its repressive machinery. The question is, why then did the USA try to convince the world about the existence of weapons of mass destruction (WMD) before their war offensive in Iraq? Why did Indira Gandhi project the threat to her personal standing as a threat to India's security for imposing the Emergency? The reality is that aggressors do need pretexts, particularly in today's world, to carry out their heinous activities. And we, in our naivety, present those excuses in a platter stupidly hoping to satisfy our egos. Lalgarh paid the price for this. As much by the rapes, killings and indiscriminate arrests by the security forces as by the loss of support from ordinary citizens.

Petering out

Civil society, during this time, lost the initiative, will and force to stage strong protests against the joint forces' onslaught. They failed to distinguish or make ordinary folk distinguish between Maoist violence and PCPA-led people's upsurge. It was an irritating and helpless phase for a great number of urban activists who had pinned their hope on PCPA and the extraordinary movement it conducted. The result was there for everyone to see. When Chhatradhar was arrested or Lalmohan Tudu and Sidho Soren were killed in fake encounters or women were raped by security forces in Sonamukhi, civil society could respond with only token protests. Their voice got feebler with every subsequent repressive act. A large number of activists got steadily disillusioned. Even the broad-based *Lalgarh Mancha* found its support-base rapidly dwindling. Maoists never learnt any lesson from all these. Many among civil society activists simply kept waiting for the elections to the state Assembly. Almost all activities were concentrated on teaching CPI(M) a lesson at the polls. The assumption was that ousting the ruling regime from power would bring back normalcy in Junglemahal and elsewhere in the state. The demands of the people, the crying need for dialogue and restoration of peace were all but given a quiet burial.

No *Paribartan* after *Paribartan*

As anticipated, CPI(M)-led Left Front received a drubbing in the polls. Sailing the gusty winds of '*paribartan*' — change — a new regime has been installed on the throne of power. During the election campaign, Trinamul Congress (TMC), supposedly the chief agent of paribartan, called for the withdrawal of joint forces from Junglemahal and made vague promises that they would release all political prisoners. All that was quietly forgotten once they formed the government in coalition with Congress and its supreme leader assumed the CM's office. Ten months have gone by since the new alliance has taken charge of the state's administration. Chhatradhar Mahato and others are still rotting in jail and paramilitary operations are continuing as before. Arrests, killings in fake encounters and even sexual assaults are showing little respite.

The new government, like the previous one, is bypassing the real issue in Junglemahal. It is desperately making every effort to win over the people there by announcing — and may be sincerely trying to implement — a slew of development projects. At the same time, it is not only continuing with the security offensive but, more dangerously, trying to raise a *Salwa Judum* type force in the guise of recruiting thousands of special police personnel. Also, since CPI(M) *harmads* are on the run, they are being replaced by TMC-backed *Bhairav Bahini.* Clearly, the new regime is slipping into the shoes of its predecessor. Except that, they are using a double-edged sword. One cuts with repressive action in the name of maintaining law and order and the other with globilisation in the name of development.

Peace in a Blind Alley

The new government, perhaps to pacify civil society, started the so-called 'peace process' with great fanfare. Some of the civil society stalwarts were given the job of parleying with Maoists. It is strange that they accepted the assignment without demanding that paramilitary forces be withdrawn and those in jail unconditionally released first. Peace, they should have known, cannot take off with arms in one hand and the carrot of development in the other. The initiative was bound to end as a sop story. And so it did after Kishenji was annihilated in what appears to be a fake encounter. By agreeing to talk primarily to Maoists, the interlocutors also fell for the State's projection of Junglemahal as a purely Maoist issue. They might have forgotten that civil society activists had been in solidarity not so much with Maoists as with the people's movement in Lalgarh. So, to put the government on the right track, they should have put greater stress on the demands the movement had based itself upon. PCPA is what they should have insisted the government talked to.

Struggle for Peace

Civil society activists still have a significant role to play in erecting the peace edifice in Junglemahal. It has to acknowledge that peace cannot be achieved by working as interlocutors. Mass opinion must be built to pressurise the government to look honestly at the real issue. There is no way out but restart the unfinished dialogue initiated since almost the beginning of the Lalgarh uprising. The foremost task is to remove the sword hanging over the head of the people of Junglemahal. Joint forces will have to be withdrawn without further delay and the release of political prisoners cannot be kept hanging in the balance. The ball is in the government's court. It will have to be reminded with a very strong voice of its election promises.

In order to bring peace, civil society has to stand steadfastly by the people's struggle in Junglemahal. It must ensure that the people there do get the justice they have been fighting for. Will civil society rise to the occasion and perform its historic duties?

Learning from Their Mistakes: Sidho-Kanhu's Descendants Will Rise Again

Amrit Paira

After the killing of Kishenji, many people wanted to know: 'Will Maoists be able to turn around?' Others have quipped: 'It must have been a senior leader of their party who betrayed him, for how could Kishenji, alone, like this ...?' '*Arre*, where's the forest in Burishole? Must have been indoors in a meeting, they just nabbed and killed him.' A friend of mine (an ordinary left-leaning individual) asked me in a low voice: 'Did so-and-so (a member of the mediators' team) inform on Kishenji?'

Thousands of similar questions and comments are being heard in Junglemahal. Perhaps not openly as yet, but people do open their mouths to trusted friends. The questions indicate that the people of Junglemahal have begun to dissect Maoist politics. Though not a political commentator, as a resident of Junglemahal, it is quite natural and typical of me to participate in this discussion.

Let's take the first question: 'Will Maoists be able to turn around?' 'Turn around' in what sense? Kill a few CPI(M) or Trinamul Congress workers, or 'police informers,' or engage in some petty armed action — is that turning around? Maoists can do that even now or will be able to do it in a while. Maoists have that capability at the all-India level. But if this turnaround is seen in the perspective of the Lalgarh movement, it has to be said that Maoists have lost that capability in Junglemahal; and this situation has been created quite some time before Kishenji's killing. I experienced this through a few small incidents.

After the Assembly elections — the new government had been in power for quite a few days by then — I took a journalist friend to visit

Chhitamoni Murmu, one of the victims of police atrocities following Maoist bid on Buddhadeb Bhattacharjee's life in November 2008. Disgruntled and angry Chhitamoni didn't even want to meet the journalist. With great difficulty when her whereabouts were found out, she was adamant about not speaking to? the camera. The journalist's question was: 'the movement that you were conducting against police atrocities, has the coming of new government changed the situation in any way?' After repeated requests, her response was brief but telling: 'ask Mamata *Ma* to come once and see how we are.' Chhitamoni is not a leader but she is a symbol of the Lalgarh movement. Any woman can call Mamata Bannerjee '*Ma*' but on Chitamoni's lips it indicated to me a perilous political weakness of the Maoists.

This weakness I had felt even before the elections. I've heard that there was a difference of opinion among the Maoists over Chhatradhar's contesting in the election. Ultimately when Chhatradhar did contest, there was almost no campaign by People's Committee against Police Atrocities that he had virtually headed. I had thought then that it might be because of fear of police. Not that the fear was absent, but there was another reason: through a campaign in the entire Lalgarh area, the voters had already been exhorted to vote for TMC. Chhatradhar gathered very few votes from Lalgarh; among the areas from where he got the most votes, one was the Sapdhara area close to Jhargram.

This area is known as an old Jharkhandi stronghold and the people here had joined PCPA. But after their Pradhan was killed by Maoists, the people of the entire area, especially Santhals, went against Maoists. Post-elections, a divide was created once between Santhals and Mahatos of the area. Even though this divide did not lead to an inter-community conflagration, it did deepen into a permanent chasm. At present, the entire area is under the control of a force calling itself *Janajagaran Mancha* — Forum for Mass Awakening. It is the armed wing of this body that is being called *Bhairab Bahini*. Its members have close ties with TMC's Subhendu Adhikary group; the administration, too, is helping them. The administration did not stop them when in broad daylight, they rode, faces covered, on motorbikes through Jhargram town. Villagers say some of them are seen openly carrying arms.

Over a long time, one faction of CPI(ML) had great influence in the south-eastern area of Jhargram, (which falls under Gopiballabhpur Assembly constituency). The present MLA, Churamoni Mahato, is close to this faction. At present, this faction is very close to TMC. Churamoni won the elections on a TMC ticket. Maoists also supported his candidature. This faction's member-supporters were in PCPA.

Though Maoists had overall control over PCPA, at the local level, the Committee's character used to be different in various areas. The political character of PCPA units in Lalgarh, or Sapdhara, or Lodhashuli or Belebara areas is not the same. Maoists in some places, the Jharkhandis in some other places, TMC or Naxalites in other places and even CPI(M) dissidents in some areas were in the leadership of such units. As long as Left Front was in power, these groups had a common identity — they were all in the 'opposition.' But after TMC has come to power, there have been significant changes in the political equation.

Clever politician Mamata Bannerjee had well intuited the situation. By demanding a judicial enquiry into Maoist leader Azad's death, by talking about the freeing of political prisoners, she lured the Maoists. Before elections, she addressed a meeting in Lalgarh together with intellectuals and activists close to the Naxalites. Seduced by these moves, the Maoists issued a call to make '*Didi's* rally' a success. In village after village, they issued fatwas against working for any other group except PCPA or TMC; they talked of voting for TMC in the elections. From the time People's Committee transformed into *Gana Militia* — Mass Militia — and effectively turned into a secret and illegal organisation, it lost its mass character. For mass gatherings, Maoists then became dependent on TMC rallies. Leaders like Sido Soren, Lalmohan Tudu, Chhatradhar Mahato and others were forced to go underground. Government, too, perhaps wanted this. Sido and Lalmohan were killed by police, Chhatradhar was arrested.

Taking advantage of this situation, TMC entered the arena and succeeded in establishing its political leadership over the entire Junglemahal area. After the elections and the formation of a new government, Mamata, despite making a gesture of peace talks through intermediaries or release of political prisoners, in reality, took all steps to drive out the Maoists.

Aiming to create ruptures in the Maoist ranks and make police sources among Maoists, she dangled police jobs and financial packages for those who would surrender with arms as enticement while promising no-holds-barred 'development' to the locals. On the other hand, she appointed mediators to confuse Maoist or PCPA leaders —this was Mamata's strategy; she was never eager to establish peace through political dialogue with Maoists or PCPA.

The Maoists either did not comprehend the political situation, or because of their internal debates, were unable to adopt an anti-TMC political stand. Even when they did take somewhat of a stand, one section was asking the mediators to carry on with the peace talks. Perhaps, they had to pay for this political blunder with Kishenji's life. Not just losing a life, the way they lost their base in Junglemahal, perhaps, cost them much more.

There are, of course, questions also about the real picture of this Maoist mass base. Some believe Maoists had no mass base in Junglemahal; whatever was there was entirely based on terror. This view is an exaggerated one. Even to conduct terror over an extensive area continuously for two-three years requires some kind of mass base. But again, there is some truth in this view.

It is true that in the beginning, the anger of the *Adivasi-mulbasi* — tribal and original — people against police terror in Lalgarh erupted in a massive explosion. This struggle was seen, especially by *Adivasi* society, as their social rebellion. It was like another *hul* — rebellion. Then the organisation of the struggle, *Bharat Jakat Majhi Maroa*, was broadened and transformed into *Pulishi Santrash Birodhi Janasadharaner Committee* — the PCPA in English — to give political character to a social movement. The people also welcomed this. Even though they knew 'this is a Maoist organisation,' people accepted it as a mass political platform for anti-CPI(M) forces.

But the Maoist leadership of this organisation wanted to wage 'war against the State.' They believed that 'revolution has begun' and *Adivasis* of Junglemahal were ready for this revolutionary war. So, 'terror is a revolutionary weapon.' And, so, many ordinary CPI(M) workers were killed for being 'police spies'. The Maoist leaders provided journalists with photo ops carrying arms. The PCPA was turned into a 'mass militia.' Gradually, the role of the armed cadres became important in this movement, while the role of ordinary people declined. The youths of Junglemahal were picked up and given training in using weapons, but most probably, they were not given any revolutionary politics. Close observers have said of these local leaders: 'they themselves don't know what they want.'

In many instances, there was no sign of any class outlook behind the killings. *Bandhs* were called day after day, but MPS or factories belonging to the Patwaris, were merrily open. Funds were collected by force. These incidents drove the ordinary people away, made them suspicious of Maoist politics Together with these, people were forced to attend meetings at night and all odd hours, women made to walk in rallies for miles. Such incidents for day after day irritated the villagers. People can make many sacrifices for a greater ideal, but the Maoist leadership was not able to present any such ideal, any such culture to the people through the activities of their rank and file. In fact, in many instances, the reverse picture became prominent.

Different sections of the people of Junglemahal lost respect for Maoists following incidents of coersion and highhandedness. But as long as there was military control of the Maoists in the villages, people accepted them quietly. In Maoist politics, there is no means of listening to criticisms by the people. Locals, for that matter, anybody thought of criticising them ran the risk of severe beating even, loss of life. Consequently, fear sealed the lips of the people. After the elections, when the Maoist military control loosened, people, too, moved away.

In reality, people of Junglemahal were genuinely keen on protesting the State's exploitation and deprivation. After the fracture and fall of the Jharkhandi parties and factions in Bengal's marginal politics, people were in search of a genuine alternative leadership. In the initial phases of the Lalgarh movement, people had accepted the leadership of PCPA and wanted to move forward. But the people of Junglemahal were unable to step together with Maoist politics. This does not mean that Junglemahal people have become TMC supporters. Shattered by the monstrous and relentless State terror, they do not, at this moment, have the strength to oppose TMC and counter another bout of State terror. People are tired. Besides the boom of guns is still reverberating in Junglemahal. Only the hands wielding the guns have changed.

Junglemahal will overcome its temporary fatigue and awaken again. The descendants of Sidho-Kanhu are still there. A new generation will learn from the failure. Let reactionary forces cheer as much as they want now; struggling, rebellious people will have the last word.

(Translated from Bangla by Aditi Chowdhury)

Women's Power Vs State Power

Krishna Bandopadhyay

The history of Junglemahal's *Adivasi* people is strewn with narratives of long periods of neglect, torture and humiliation and the never-ending fight against such oppression. Not delving too far back in time, I will strive to describe in bits and pieces the horrible State-sponsored terror activities, which started on 4 November 2008, and the tremendous courage exhibited by *Adivasi* people, especially their women, during this period. In the process, I shall also discuss the relative 'peace' residing in Junglemahal area after the 'change' in West Bengal's administration.

On 2 November 2008, former chief minister of West Bengal, Buddhadeb Bhattacharjee, accompanied by the then central minister for iron and steel, Ram Vilas Paswan et. al, had gone to Salboni to inaugurate the steel plant project of the Jindal Group in the usual convoy of police vehicles. On the way back, a police jeep was severely damaged in a land-mine explosion and a couple of policemen suffered minor injuries. Following this incident, a huge battalion of police led by district SP and IC Lalgarh PS raided and wreaked havoc on 35 villages in the Lalgarh-Kantapahari area. In the wee hours of 5 November, police entered Chhotopelia village and launched a brutal assault on the village women. Chhitamoni Murmu woke up in the middle of the night to discover that police were dragging her husband away from their hut. When she tried to rescue him, police thrashed her, and in the process, she ended up losing her left eye following a vicious blow of the rifle butt. More than fourteen women of the village were seriously injured in this attack. Likewise, in Bansberia village, when police tried arresting Dipak Pratihar, his pregnant wife, Lakshmi, came to his rescue but the cops dragged her onto the road and beat her so badly that she suffered a miscarriage.

All these incidents took place in an area almost 40km from the site of the land-mine explosion. Reacting to such police barbarity, the humiliated and agitated people of the area decided to organise themselves. On 8 November, People's Committee against Police Atrocities (PCPA) was formed with representatives from 19 villages. PCPA started the Lalgarh agitation with the demand that the police officers responsible for the assault on women and children come to Dalilpur Chowk at Kantapahari and apologise in public. The demand was that the errant policemen would have to seek the affected people's pardon in accordance with *Adivasi* tradition — by holding ears and doing sit-ups and by rubbing noses on the ground. All roads were blocked by felling trees and police boycotted till their demands were met with. In no time the Lalgarh people's movement spread like a prairie fire to far corners of Junglemahal and generated a great deal of passion and interest in the entire country.

Women in the Uprising

Life is harsh in the forest and the women of Junglemahal have always been very hard-working. Here the land is fertile but the lack of proper irrigation results in poor harvest. The people of this region are, thus, dependent mainly on forest resources along with little patches of cultivable land they possess. Collection of leaves, Sal and Kendu, from the forest is traditionally done by the women; and they make plates with Sal and *bidis* with Kendu leaves. They also make ropes with Babui grass, which, too is gathered from the forest. Firewood comes from the forest but water has to be fetched from great distances. Besides, the women help their men in agricultural work. It was these women who have had to bear the brunt of police atrocities; and that's precisely why it was the women of Junglemahal who first rose up in protest against the violence. People in Junglemahal, too, realised at the very beginning that it was extremely crucial to acknowledge the role of their women as the real leaders of the movement. Hence, it was decided that every village unit of PCPA would have 50 per cent women representatives. It is important to note here that in

Chhattisgarh *Salwa Judum* was initially sponsored by the Tatas and the Essar group to evacuate six villages. But owing to the carnages carried out by *Salwa Judum*, at least 664 villages have now been deserted and occupied by those corporate giants. According to the official report titled 'State Agrarian Relations and Unfinished Task of Land Reform', 'till date it is the largest land robbery.' The then ruling party, police and administrators in Junglemahal have had taken a leaf out of the *Salwa Judum* book. Here they floated *Maobadi Daman Sena, Gana Pratirodh Committee,* so on which were tacitly backed by the Jindals, who have already been given 5,000 acres of forestland by state government for their so-called steel plant. Bengal's *Salwa Judum* since then had gone on a criminal onslaught on the agitating, protesting people of the region, killing, raping, looting and setting fire to villages. On 2 February, 2009, three PCPA supporters were killed when these armed groups, the *harmads*, fired on a mass rally. The brutal action was overseen by Anuj Pandey, one of the most notorious local leaders of CPI(M). On 4 February, a man and a woman were attacked by the same *harmads*. They were admitted to hospital with bullet injuries. On 26 February, with active support of police, almost 200 *harmads* launched an attack on Madhupur in Salboni. Women were beaten and almost all homes in the village ransacked. To resist such merciless attacks, women in village after village came forward to join the PCPA-led people's movement. On 8 March, International Women's Day, the 'women's wing' of PCPA was formed.

Women in Development

The women of Junglemahal had been seeing how the moral fibre of their men was being affected by alcohol abuse. They decided to take a firm stand against this and launched a movement to stop selling of hooch in the area. However, local merchants, helped by CPI(M) leaders, managed to maintain the supply chain for the willing. The women started a massive local campaign to destroy this set-up. They also took the lead role in people's active and participatory endeavours in building essential infrastructural facilities like community health centres and basic irrigation facilities. These measures forced government to stand up and pay attention to the voices of the movement.

Women under Attack

On June 13, 2009, the then Left Front government invited PCPA to a high-level meeting with top administrators and police officials at Medinipur Circuit House. The meeting ended amicably with government representatives promising to sympathetically consider all the PCPA demands and the latter agreeing to lift the road blockades straightway. It was also decided to have another round of discussions on 14 July. Chhatradhar Mahato, the then PCPA spokesperson, also assured government representatives that they had no intention of continuing with police boycott. Just five days later, the joint forces' operation began.

People's anger at and mistrust of those in power had been growing steadily as economic and social disparity escalated massively over three long decades of LF rule and three long decades of Congress rule before that. During the movement, the rage came to the fore and took an ugly turn when the palatial residence of Anuj Pandey, Secretary, Lalgarh unit of CPI(M) and a corrupt and vicious political worker, was torched down by the people. State administration, instead of investigating the huge revenue source of a full-time party worker, seemed keener on maintaining a stranglehold over the poor. After the joint forces' operation was launched in Junglemahal, men, particularly the youth had to flee or were arrested. In the absence of earning members, women had to take up the responsibility of running the household. But they couldn't go to the forest to collect fuel, fodder, leaves and other subsistence items for their family for fear of the forces. Administration had, by then, clamped down an iron curtain around the area by promulgating section 144 CrPC that made any gathering unlawful and daily chores difficult for the locals. The health clinics and local schools were turned into paramilitary camps, thereby jeopardising the education and health care requirements of the villagers. School boys were regularly frisked and harassed by the forces, and girls were forced to strip down to determine their gender.

On one such day, a local school student was taken into police custody for extraction of 'information' and was severely beaten up. The villagers reacted furiously and next day, a large rally, comprising mostly of women from adjoining villages, gathered around the SDO office to demand the boy's freedom. Police and paramilitary forces used lathis and rifle butts to disperse the crowd. Repeated requests by the injured women to take them to hospital for treatment fell on deaf ears. Fourteen women, 40-70 years old, were also picked up by the police and kept in police custody for several days without producing them in court; later, they were sent to jail. That, of course, has been the way administration maintains 'law and order.' Maoists, who had plunged headlong into the Lalgarh movement, retaliated by kidnapping the erstwhile OC Sankrail PS and held him as a prisoner until the state government succumbed to their rational demand of freeing those innocent women. After Maoists forced the government to release these jailed women, the then CM Buddhadeb Bhattacharjee said that they would have been released anyway. When the women eventually came out of the jail gate, their main concern was how to get back to their village almost 100kms away. It was shameful that Bhattacharjee who swears by Marx and Lenin, showed extreme 'diligence' in putting those poor women in jails, but did not bother about how these hapless illiterate women would return home.

Women in Resistance

On 30 June, 2010, joint forces, once again backed by local CPI(M) henchmen, attacked and raped seven women in Sonamukhi village. What followed when a 70-year old woman tried to protest was a ghastly instance of the atrocities which the Junglemahal *Adivasis* had endured over the past years. Our 'brave' jawans danced on her feeble body and then just left her to die from the injuries they had inflicted on her. The other raped and ravaged women were turned away by medical facilities nearby on the plea that that they didn't treat Mahatos and *Adivasis*. Victims and their families went to the SDO for justice. But it was denied. Next day, thousands of women thronged the SDO office in Jhargram and met with a police barricade. On July 18, when villagers, mostly women, from Gosaidanga village near Dahijuri blocked the road, the joint forces attacked them repeatedly. At least 25 protestors were injured. But the villagers did not give up and organised an even larger march with the wounded to the BDO office demanding proper medical assistance. Outside the BDO office, in order to disperse the crowd, police and joint forces used every form of force, beating and arresting 86 women and two men. They were huddled up and taken into custody. But the gathering turned so strong that the unarmed 'army' of women was able to free everyone. On 20 July, a rally of almost 10,000 women reached the BDO office. Their question was eerily simple: 'You have raped us, insulted us, and even killed one of us. Now, you tell us where do we get medical treatment, who will take care of us?'

The President of the youth wing of Congress, Usha Naidu, came on a routine visit to Junglemahal. On meeting the women and hearing their plight, she was so stricken with 'grief' that she couldn't control her tears. Without going into the details of her 'humanitarian' visit, I would like to point out that her promise to ensure Rahul Gandhi's intervention to the aide of these hapless women was never kept. But that was hardly surprising, as the decision to deploy joint forces in the area was not the sole decision of state administration; the Congress-led UPA government at the Centre, too, played a crucial role in the crackdown. This truth was not lost on the hapless women of Junglemahal. So, they decided to stand up on their own: 'We will save ourselves.' That was the motto of *Nari Ijjat Banchao Committee* (NIBC) — Committee to Save Women's Honour. On 3 August, 2010, NIBC sent an open letter to Kabir Suman radical singer & rebel TMC MP describing their plight. But they still have no idea what would be his moves in response. On 9 August, women with NIBC participated *en masse* in the rally held at Lalgarh by *Santrash Birodhi Mancha* — Forum against Terror — of which the present chief minister Mamata Banerjee was the central figure. Ironically, people occupying the centre stage — Swami Agnivesh, Medha Patkar, Debabrata Bandyopadhyay et al — were so busy with themselves and so enthralled with Mamata that they hardly had any time to even look at these women. The women from NIBC did not go there to beg for any compensation, nor did they want any sympathy. They went there only to narrate their plight and the violence which women of Junglemahal had been facing every day.

On 27 December, almost 3,000 women of NIBC came to Kolkata to take part in a march to Writers' Buildings organised by Lalgarh Mancha (LM). Jyostna Mahato, convenor NIBC, said: 'As citizens of an independent country we've got police stations,...but we still don't have enough to eat, enough health or education and most importantly, we don't have *ijjat.* The people of Junglemahal formed PCPA to fight for our *ijjat*, our honour and dignity. We don't much care about our physical honour, what we care for is our self- esteem. Is that what you call Maoism? Our leaders and activists were tagged as Maoists and put behind bars. Lalmohan Tudu was killed in the darkness of night. We're branded as Maoists only because we raised our voice against State violence. We tried to tell our stories in every way we could, but nobody bothered to listen to us. Is every *Adivasi* a Maoist? The only thing you're to do is to brand a person as a Maoist; and after that, even if the person is raped or even murdered, nobody will say a word. Are we not citizens of this country? Yet, in spite of everything, the fact is that the struggle of PCPA cannot be stopped with rape, murder and imprisonment. We're growing in numbers. We know that the situation will get worse. We'll be assaulted, killed, displaced but our struggle will continue. We will fight for our land; for our self-respect; and I'm sure a day will come when government will finally learn to respect us.'

WOMEN AFTER '*PARIBARTAN*'

And then. After so much of rumbling, the long-awaited '*paribartan*' came and West Bengal had Mamata Banerjee as its first woman chief minister. But situation in Junglemahal has remained unchanged; on the contrary, in many respects, it has deteriorated to an alarming extent. In the name of providing employment, people of the same community are being set against each other — extra-judicial methods, as was the case with *Salwa Judum*, are being adopted and legitimised in the garb of giving police jobs. Mamata, in her Opposition avatar, promised to withdraw the joint forces. But she changed her tune after she came to power, she carried on with and intensified their operation. She is even trying to set up a new COBRA camp on *Adivasi* land, in violation of the Panchayat Extention Scheduled Act (PESA) . During her meeting on August 9 in Lalgarh, she promised that the 'encounter killings' of Lalmohan Tudu, Sidho Soren, Umakanta Mahato and others would be properly investigated and the guilty punished. But since the formation of the new government, not a single official responsible for those inhuman acts was either interrogated or punished.

People of Junglemahal, desperate for a change, voted for Mamata and her TMC for a change. But hope died almost as soon as they were born when CPI(M)-controlled *harmads* were replaced by TMC-sponsored *bhairabs*. A tragic incident that reflected the cruel absence of 'change' merits telling : a young couple had named their newborn '*Paribartan*.' Their passion for 'change,' however, went up in flames as they watched helplessly their baby being hurled away and their home set on fire by the *bhairabs*. Anti-CPI(M) sentiments are still running wild in Junglemahal. Taking advantage of that, the new entrants to the corridors of power, with the help of joint forces, are making no stone unturned to wipe out every other political organisation and opinion. On 13 October, 2011, Shibani Singh of a Belpahari village was raped by jawans because they could not find her husband Sushen Singh, a CPI(M) activist. Mamata denied the allegation of rape, made by Shibani herself, adding that 'such complaints are fabricated every time police move to nab criminals'. Her words were most shocking as they came from the mouth of Bengal's first woman chief minister. All these also make the entire concept of '*paribartan*' a huge farce. A different sense of fear and uncertainty has now gripped the entire region. Women are edgy about going out for even the most basic needs like gathering food and fuel, going to school and even bathing in the river as prying eyes of policemen and *jawans* are constantly there to relish the female 'flesh'. Custodial deaths have become almost as common as before. We may recall that during LF rule, Swapan Dasgupta, editor and publisher of a duly registered monthly magazine *Bangla People's March*, was put in jail under UAPA. He died in custody due to total negligence in providing medical treatment for his critical illness. Similarly, imprisoned under UAPA during the previous regime, Ranjit Murmu, a PCPA activist, died in Medinipur jail due to severe torture when the new government was already a few months old. He was declared mentally unstable and kept for several days in a lunatic ward stripped of all his dignity. 'Democracy in lieu of party-cracy' — this was the central electoral slogan of TMC against the CP(M), but the language of power is always the same. Let me cite an example: Rustam and Aimuddin of Chanditala, Garbeta are active members of Majdoor Kranti Parishad (MKP). Only because of this, Rustam was brutally beaten up by the TMC members. When they couldn't find Aimuddin in his house, they threatened the other family members. While thrashing Rustam, the TMC goons said: 'Either you join TMC or keep mum. Otherwise, whatever you do, we shall tell the police that you are a Maoist.'

In her last mass meeting in Junglemahal, Mamata almost threatened the local people. She was breathing fire on stage and her body language was extremely aggressive. By the way, who did she abuse as '*jangal-mafia*' or '*supari killers*!' They happened to be the political party with whom her government was supposedly trying to work out the peace process. Does it not mark the complexity of the political equations? This complexity was elucidated a few days later. On the pretext peace initiative, Kishenji, the top Maoist leader, was lured into a meeting and killed in cold blood. Who once, as the Opposition supremo in the state, demanded a neutral investigation of the 'encounter death' of Azad, has now as the head of state government, refused to comment on the entire incident and made a vain attempt to write an entirely different script. Here is a lesson in hypocrisy. Today, they are talking peace in Junglemahal. But, simply put, it's a reign of terror there with only the colour of the perpetrators changed. It is not hard to imagine the kind of brutality required to suppress the indomitable spirit of the people in Junglemahal. Even half-burnt bodies go unrecognised; no one wants to know the identity of a certain beheaded body.

(Translated from Bangla by Pritha Chatterjee)

Three Women from Junglemahal: Will Mamata Listen to Them?

Jury is still out on what went wrong in Junglemhal in the name of revolution and democracy, people's power and *paribartan* and who stood for dignity and development in the killing fields of Junglemahal. But a sustainable peace is possible in the much-gored land only if the new government tries to heal the wounds of all sides who suffered across the political divide. Will chief minister Mamata Banerjee listen to these three women who echo the plight of many of their sisters in Junglemahal?

Jyotsna Mahato

The frail frame of conceals her age. At 25 plus, she looks like a girl in her teens. But once one speaks to her, her passionate plea for justice for her people and her courage of conviction reveals a robust mind.

She does not offer any jargon-laden defence of her side in the context of contesting narratives in today's Junglemahal, where gun-barrels are still hot even amid an eerie calm. Jyotsna speaks of her experiences, her background, her dreams and disappointments. For police, she is a suspected Maoist and was one of moving spirit behind the *Nari Ijjat Bacho Committee*, officially dubbed as one of the Maoist frontal outfits. But the girlish woman from Barapal village under Jhargram sub division of West Medinipur insists that she does not understand politics and ideologies as we do. She became part of Junglemahal movement as late as in 2010.

Her marginal farmer family, with their four *bighas* of land, eked out a living out of sustenance farming. However, the additional income came from small-scale trading in Sal leaves, one of the crucial products of the fast depleting forest in Junglemahal. The village poor, belonging to the landless Sabars, Santhals and poor households of Mahatos, generally better off than the tribes and castes which are situated at the lower rung of socio-economic hierarchy, collect the Sal and Kendu leaves from forests to supplement their meagre income. After her father's death, Jyotsna and her two brothers collect the leaves from them and sell it at little profit to middlemen and wholesalers from neighbouring Odisha.

The only politics that her family got involved was over the land disputes with Jyotsna's uncle who allegedly got the better share of the ancestral land, courtesy his allegiance to the CPI(M). 'I had no time for politics and political rallies as I was busy in finding a livelihood. But the mass rapes by the joint forces and CPI(M) *harmads* last year (2010) in neighbouring Sonamukhi village changed my life,' Jyotsna recalled. 'I could not stomach the outrage and joined the women's rally to Jhargram to demand punishment of the culprits. This was first time I had ever walked in a procession. I was arrested for the first time in my life for being vociferous when police stopped us. I became angry after this arrest,' she said.

Buddhadeb Bhattacharjee government had dismissed the mass rape complaints as Maoist propaganda. The new government did not investigate into the complaint.

Her metamorphosis from a would-be home-maker into a women's organiser may be typical of many others of her sisters in Junglemahal. But her repeated reference to social customs in *'Mahato Samaj'* and women's plight amid the contest between government forces and their ruling party collaborators in one hand and armed Maoists and their supporters on the other provides a crucial social clue to women's involvement in the anti-police and anti-CPI(M) agitation that began in the fag end of 2008.

'Tumi jano na, Mahato samajer rit-rewaj keman. Police-er hate hok ba anna karo, dagi meye hale tar biye howa muskil. (You don't know the customs of Mahato community. It's difficult to get a girl married if she is arrested or outraged by police or others),' says Jyotsna. 'Their parents and brothers have to cough up more dowries, both in kind and cash. Many alliances were broken as they failed to do so. Hundreds of such

branded girls in Junglemahal had to suffer the shame and humiliation of being rejected,' she continued.

However, she parried the question whether her arrest led to similar social ostracism and disappointments in her life. But clearly, her voice betrayed her emotions. She said her committee's movement is not only aimed at protesting against the sexual assaults on women by the joint forces and their henchmen but also against the demands of heavy dowry demands in case of '*dagi*' girls. The rally against the Sonamukhi gang-rapes, she says, changed the 'police-fearing girl' into a different self. 'I am not scared of police-CRP any more. What has happened to many girls and married women may happen to me. But I don't care anymore,' she said evidently in desperation.

'Mamata is saying we are all Maoists. Believe me, I have never come across Akash-Bikash-Kishenji (Maoist leaders known by their nom de guerre) as you mentioned. But if fighting for the honour of Junglemhal women is Maoism, then they can call me a Maoist,' she said with a glimmer in her eyes.

Nevertheless, Jyotsna had other reasons to be angry. She had exposures to the wider world beyond her village prior to her clash with the joint forces. She had been to Cuttak where she learnt the skills of a private nurse while working at a nursing home.

But Jyotsna says she went there to train herself in a job what could be a passport to upcoming urban centres for a madhyamik-passed village girl. She came back home after four years looking for suitable jobs in sub-divisional or district towns. 'But it was difficult for us to admit patients from our area in Jhargram hospital after Sonamukhi incident. Police harassed patients and their families on their way to hospital, particularly after the dusk. Mohanpur health centre was far off. So, local clubs decided to open a community-managed health centre at Kurhashol. Local doctors including quacks joined in our efforts,' she remembered.

'The health centre gave me the opportunity to practise whatever I had learnt as a nurse. I used to spend hours in the health centre, making inventory of medicines collected from different sources as well as assisting the doctors. I gave injections to the patients and taught them about the medications and doses. It was the mostly the local poor who used to turn up at the centre,' the young woman said with an obvious pride and self-satisfaction. 'But police closed down the health centre after some time claiming that it was run by the Maoists. Tell me, is running a health centre a crime,' she asked. She said she did not support murders by the warring sides. 'It's wrong whoever kills. But a war is going on between the Maoists and government. We don't know which side is right. We were caught in the cross-fire. What are the crimes of women and other people of Junglemahal,' she questioned.

Asked what she would like to say to Mamata Banerjee if she gets the chance to meet her, Jyotsna said: 'She being a woman herself, I would ask her to realise the women's plight as one of us. She has given job to Lalmahon Mahato's wife (the Trinamul leader killed by the Maoists). But what about the widows of others who had been killed by the joint forces and *harmads*? Did her supporters alone vote her to power? We too want peace and development. But at what cost?'

Niyati Mahato

The housewife in her late thirties is not a political greenhorn like Jyotsna. But she is not a political activist either in the urban sense. Yet, Niyati, the better half of Chhatradhar Mahato, the leader of People's Committee against Police Atrocities has been compelled to take up many roles since her husband was put behind bars by erstwhile government.

She now supervises labourers in family farming, manages household chores as well as takes care of old in-laws and her two sons who are in hostels away from their home in West Medinipur's Amelia village.

Besides, she attends courts in different corners of the district on the days of hearing of multiple criminal cases including one under the UAPA against her husband and his friends. She visits Mahato at Medinipur central jail regularly, meets lawyers in Medinipur town and Kolkata in between attending rallies demanding the release of her husband and other PCPA leaders and their supporters.

'Amake doure berate hocche. Ar pere utchi na (I am running from pillar to post. I can't take it any more' smiles a visibly tired Niyati wiping sweat from her face with the *anchal* of her *sari*. With her traditional Bengali look complete with *sindur* and *sankha-loha* (religio-cultural signs of married status for Bengali Hindu women) bangles; she hardly makes a prototype of an activist, least of Maoist women.

Instead, she betrayed the emotions of a harassed and besieged house-maker of a peasant family. 'My old father-in-law has broken down completely. No more he looks after family cultivation. Some part of our 8-10 *bighas* of cultivable land has been left fallow due to lack of manpower in the family. Already he has lost his younger son Sasadhar (a Maoist guerrilla commander, killed in a suspected encounter),' Niyati said.

'My father-in-law was hoping that Mamata Banerjee would release my husband. Hope belied, he has cocooned himself. So many responsibilities and uncertainties, I can't take it anymore.' Tears welled up in her eyes as she spoke. But if we are to believe Mamata Banerjee's minions today, Niyati is the one of the major trouble-makers for the new regime, a rabble-rouser against the government's peace-enforcing efforts, kingpin in the PCPA's residual extortionist moves.

'Mamata is more peeved with her than Chhatradhar. She had been warned through well-meaning messengers but she did not listen to them,' confided a Trinamul leader in the know of the things.

Yes, she is not submissive. She makes aggressive speeches demanding release of her husband and other political prisoners. But clearly not comfortable with the craft, she reads out the written speech.

'Mamata has reneged on her pre-poll promises of withdrawal of joint forces and release of my husband and other prisoners. The government has changed but not the policies. The denial of our right to launch movement to press for our legitimate demands continues,' she said. 'We too want peace and development. But our dignity and identity come first. Government must release our prisoners and discuss with them,' she added.

Well, she may be echoing the Maoist position that the new

government has dismissed after the peace process between the Maoists and Mamata failed. She does not conceal her sympathies with the Maoists but denies her husband's link with the rebels. 'Maoists have taken up guns against injustice. My husband too fought against atrocities on poor people. He, however, believed in democracy. That's why he contested the assembly polls from jail,' she said.

Nevertheless, she has fond memories of younger brother-in-law, Sasadhar. According to her, younger Mahato was initially an introvert student who used to stay away from home. 'He became a disciple of Anukul Thakur (a Bengali Hindu religious guru with wide following) and stayed at *thakurbari* in Medinipur town to attend university. He became upset when CPI(M) sided with a section of my husband's greater family in a land dispute,' she recalled.

'We don't know how he grew links with the Maoists. My husband did not oppose him. Why should he? Each was following their own beliefs. He went to jungle carrying guns. My husband was a family man and led a mainstream life. They never crossed each other during the PCPA movement,' Niyati said. 'We are proud of Sasadhar. People of our village and neighbouring area respect and mourn him. He was killed in cold blood,' the sister-in-law of the slain guerrilla said.

However, the Mahato family was traditionally Congress-turned-Trinamul supporters, she revealed. 'My father-in-law was a Congress man. My husband was always anti-CPI(M) and once contested village panchayat poll as Congress candidate. He joined Trinamul after it was formed in late nineties,' Niyati said.

She too belonged to a Congress supporter's family and contested panchayat poll as the party's nominee. 'But I was essentially a housewife. I joined the first protest rally in my life after Chitamoni Murmu lost her eye following police rampage in their village.' Her as well as Chatradhar's bitterness about Mamata began before latter became chief minister. It was the assembly polls that lead to the clash between the two former allies against the CPI(M).

According to Niyati, Chhatradhar decided to contest the polls as independent candidate from jail to register his belief in democracy as well as to curve an independent niche for him as well as the PCPA which he had led. 'He wanted to counter the campaign that he was a Maoist just because Sasadhar was his brother. Also, he was not ready to wipe out the separate identity of such a widespread mass movement and popular organisation which he led. But Trinamul was not ready to leave any seat for him. Perhaps they were expecting that he would join or campaign for them directly. But he declined.'

According to Trinamul camp as well as pro-government civil society members who had tried to make peace between Mamata and Mahato at that time, the latter was asked to contest from any other seat except the strategic and prestigious Jhargram. But he refused to obey and finished poor third after Trinamul and CPI(M). 'Trinamul bagged the seat but Mamata did not forgive Mahato's intransigence. Chhatradhar lost his bargaining capacity due to his failure," said an insider of the negotiation in that period.

Niyati confirmed that Maoists did not approve Mahato's decision on the ground that it would divide anti-CPI(M) votes. 'Our supporters wanted him to contest. But Maoists did not campaign for him. We did not have money or manpower for his poll campaign. Despite being jailed for two years, he got 20,000 votes. Whatever Mamata says today, people will decide what their leaders should do. He listened to his people,' she says defending her husband.

According to her, Chhatradhar responded positively to Mamata's post-poll peace move. But he wanted the government to release him and his comrades first. 'He also said he would need a month's time to discuss with our people before joining discussion with the government. But government refused to listen to him,' she said. 'I am ready to meet Mamata. But will she listen to me? Will she remember that we too supported her to gain power?' Her wry but anguished tone was unmistakable.

Sabita Mahato

Unlike the other two, she was visibly docile, hapless and scared. Sabita Mahato has reasons to be so. The young widow of Umakanta Mahato, the key accused in the Gyaneswari Express derailment case that claimed more than 15O lives now herself lives under the shadow of police reprisals and death even after the killing of her husband in an 'encounter' by police. For intelligence officials, Umakanta was the kingpin of the heinous crime and a dreaded Maoist who had paid the price with his life. His mobile call to Maoist leadership about the accomplishment of sabotage mission was intercepted by police and that provided the clinching evidence for his role, they claimed.

For Sabita, it's hard to believe the police version as she remembers her husband in a different light. 'I never saw him fighting another person. He was at home on the night when Gyaneswari happened. It was I who informed him about the incident after listening to the radio news next morning,' she said.

'I don't know whom he called or what he told him over phone. But he told me he was not involved. I don't know whether he told the truth or not. He went underground after police came looking for him," she added.

Maoists denied the blame for Gyaneswari carnage while Mamata who had castigated CPI(M) before the polls for the crime now changed her position by putting the onus on the ultras, her friend-turned foes. We can only hope that truth about the crime and its perpetrators will come out of the mess of politically motivated allegations and denials.

According to Sabita, Umakanta, son of a relatively well-off peasant family in Bakshol village under Jhargram sub division, co-owned part of 8 *bigha* farmland and 10 *bighas* of cashew-nut field. He also ran sundry business and had a motorcycle, a symbol of relative prosperity in rural Bengal. Madhyamik-passed Sabita too belonged to a local trader's family. He was associated with social work in the area while being politically close to Aditya Kisku faction of Jharkhand Party since his teens. 'My husband was anti-CPI(M) from the beginning and opposed high-handedness of its local leaders. We had to suffer because of his political affiliation. CPI(M) supporters ransacked our home and he was out of home for two years in the 1990s,' she recalled.

Her husband joined Trinamul after it was formed. 'He brought TMC in our village. In 2009, he joined the agitation against the highly polluting sponge-iron factory in Jitushol and led a road blockade against it. I never heard him talking of Maoists and taking up guns,' Sabita said. 'But he was arrested and jailed as an accused in the case related to the killing of poll personnel in Kushbani forest during parliamentary polls. He became angry with police for falsely implicating him. After spending eight months in jail, he joined the PCPA in 2010,' the widow continued. He became its president after Lalmohon Tudu was gunned down by joint forces a few yards away from his home.

Fugitive Umakanta met his death in the similar fashion on his way home in August last year. 'Police claimed it was a gun-battle. But nobody believed," she said. Nevertheless, she is eager to bury her traumatic past but find herself enmeshed into her slain husband's political life. Police charged her in two criminal cases including one regarding blasting of a road culvert in Belpahari. She got anticipatory bails in both the cases. But she is worried about the future her four children if she is arrested eventually.

'Police still visit my home and threaten to pick me up. Believe me, I had no political life earlier and joined the PCPA rallies when my husband was active. I don't want bloodshed anymore. I don't want any other woman to lose what I have lost,' she said with moist eyes. Insisting that she and her late husband had always voted for Trinamul, Sabita said she had voted for Mamata's party in the assembly polls this year. 'But none of the Trinamul leaders visited us after Umakanta's death. I would request chief minister to withdraw the cases against me and allow me live a normal life. Politics would not feed my children. She is helping widows of other slain leaders. Do not my children deserve the same?'

* *All the interviews were conducted after Maoist politburo member Kishenji was gunned down in an 'encounter'* — Biswajit Roy

Medinipur Jail Diary

Nisha Biswas

[Hundreds of women (and men) from Junglemahal are in various jails, most of them lodged in Medinipur Central Correctional Home. The writer of this piece spent 43 days in its female ward in June-July 2010. Her experience, narrated below, provides an account of not only life in incarceration but also that of the oppressed, deprived and marginalised in general. We bring it here for our readers with the hope that it will provide a broader perspective to the issues involved so essential for building peace in Junglemahal — Editor]

It happened like this

Many evenings in April-May 2010 were spent in pondering over the conditions in Junglemahal under paramilitary forces, which had been sent there a year back on the pretext of suppressing the Maoist insurgency. The then home secretary declared that the security operation there was a 'laboratory experiment' for containing and exterminating Maoists. There were conflicting reports coming from Junglemahal: government was regularly issuing statements and planting propaganda stories regarding how normalcy was being restored by security forces; and, there were occasional reports from PCPA, in the form of letters to civil rights groups, providing details of the terrible state of affairs — how students were not attending schools because those had been converted into paramilitary camps; how women, children and old people were frequently beaten up and their dwellings ransacked; how they were unable to grow, tend and harvest crops; how *harmads*, in collaboration with paramilitary forces, were perpetrating unbearable atrocities. It was, however, heartening to learn that people, under the banner of PCPA, were continuing with the resistance. The exemplary courage of the poor, deprived, oppressed, so-called illiterate people of this country became the topic of our discussions. Junglemahal's was a fight for the right to live with dignity. People were not asking for any material thing, be it education for their children or health or drinking water or sanitation or food, which they had been systematically deprived of by all governments since 1947. The only thing they were demanding was that atrocities committed on them by police be stopped and they given justice. On the pretext of searching for Maoists, police had been ransacking their dwellings, beating up villagers, making indiscriminate arrests, and if those they came for were not found, detaining and torturing their wives, sisters and mothers, often booking them on charges of sedition.

By 2008, it was difficult to find a single household of which at least one person in a family had not been arrested or tortured. On the pretext of identifying young lads acting as couriers for Maoists, genitals of school-going kids were regularly inspected. In 2002, newly-wed Sulochana Kalindi was asked to strip during a police raid to give proof of her womanhood. It was such atrocities that people wanted stopped once and for all. The incident on 4-5 November 2008 of police assault on the women of Chhoto Pelia, in which Chhitamoni Murmu's eyes were damaged and eight other women injured, acted as trigger for the Lalgarh upsurge and the formation of PCPA. Roads were blocked and police barred from entering the area, people's demand being a public apology by the police officer responsible for the criminal assault. The State saw in it a challenge to its authority from the poor, illiterate, semi-starved, deprived and oppressed. The State was the ruler whose command was law; and, people were to be ruled, not heard.

For eight months, the movement spread to far corners of Junglemahal and gained great momentum. More and more people were participating in protest meetings and rallies, and almost every village was forming its own PCPA. They were also renovating wells, repairing hand-pumps, organising health camps and even fighting the local sponge-iron factories for the horrible pollution they were causing — concerns consistently ignored by whichever party ran the government. The State, of course, had its own compulsions and its own weird way of handling mass resistances. Response to the Lalgarh movement was no exception; and, therefore, in mid-June 2009, forces, both state and Central, were dispatched. A virtual curfew was imposed in the area while those who dared to go there were threatened with arrests. On one occasion, a group of almost a hundred activists were detained at Kharagpur and threatened with serious charges. So what option was left other than sneaking into the area? For me, it was not just a struggle for their dignity but mine as well. I had been to Lalgarh and other parts of Junglemahal several times before and shared the joys and sorrows of the people living there. The Kantapahari health camp, set up and run by PCPA with help from Kolkata activists and doctors, had become my weekend sojourn. The last trip was in the first week of June 2009, just a few days before the paramilitary moved in. Not being able to go there was like leaving dear ones in the lurch. How can one not stand by those who are carrying out such exemplary struggle?

Sneaking in

So, exactly a year later, on June 12, 2010, fellow activists, Manik Mondal and Kanishka Choudhury, and myself along with three journalist friends, set out for Junglemahal. We reached Pairachalli where our contacts, established from the phone numbers provided in the PCPA letters, were waiting for us. For the next three days, we visited Patri, Kalsibhanga and Rameswarpur, talking to villagers and Committee workers. Sometimes, we went with the women to collect leaves in the forest.

It's a hard life for the women: they go to the forest at sunrise, gather leaves and other forest produce, bundle them and return late afternoon; then, begin household chores — cooking, feeding children, washing, cleaning, so on; then, after a poor meal, they sit down to stitch leaf plates. The plates are then dried and two of such plates sewed together to make them marketable; such plates are then tied into bundles, hundred pieces each. The whole process takes three to four sunny days and quick mathematics told me that each woman with such bone-breaking labour can never earn more than ten rupees a day. Now, .with forces patrolling all around, leaf-collection had virtually come to a stop, as going to the forest ran the risk of being picked up as a Maoist. Things were really bad in Junglemahal but we also witnessed all round collective enterprise to work out a life of dignity. People were renovating wells and ponds as well as digging canals so that the faraway fields could be irrigated; quack doctors were providing free health service and organising health camps. What an amazing community activity! The positive energy exuding from all that was so inspiring that even for once I didn't feel tired. The emotions, though, were mixed: the hardship endured by the villagers was terribly painful; but then preparing for a better future was extremely encouraging.

JAILWARD HO!

15 June, we were sleeping on the roof of a local school in Rameswarpur. Suddenly someone shouted, 'Joint forces have cordoned the area.' I came down hurriedly and found forces all around. They were conducting a combing operation and bringing in suspects from nearby villages. Teenage boys were made to sit on one side and the rest here and there. They were checking their knees and ankles for, God knew what. A boy with red ink stains on his fingers was slapped for the imaginary crime of writing Maoist posters. A young couple taking their baby to the doctor on a bicycle was not allowed to proceed. A sympathetic officer who let them go had to face the wrath of his seniors. Amid all these, I didn't notice when they beat up Kshitij Mahato and broke his wrists. After rounding up everyone, young boys were allowed to leave with a warning. Around a hundred people, including us, were, however, asked to follow them. We were then made to walk miles in the scorching sun over dry, uneven harvested fields. After a point, I was unable to walk any more. So, I sat down and declared that I could not take a step further; and, if they so wished, they could shoot me down. After that, the forces started taking care, carrying my bag, getting me water and letting me walk at my own pace.

After two hours, we reached an asphalt road from where an anti-mine vehicle took us to the Pirakata police camp. The villagers walking with us were being allowed to go in batches and finally around thirty three of them ended up in the camp. Later, I learnt that one of them, face covered with a *gamchha*, identified 10 suspects who were then interrogated, beaten and arrested. Asit Manna was hung up-side-down and was beaten, the forces' boots squashing his legs. Asit is fine now but Kshitij's wrists are permanently damaged. He's unable to work in the field or earn any kind of livelihood.

In the evening, we were taken to Salboni PS and interrogated. Later, the journalists were released and we arrested. Next day, 13 of us, including the ten villagers, were produced in Medinipur court which sent us to jail for 14 days. The custody was subsequently extended twice; and that made for the 43 days of my stay in the women's ward of Medinipur Central Correctional Home.

In Good Company

Sprawled over a hundred acres, the two-hundred-years-old Medinipur jail is one of the oldest in the country. Before 1947, revolutionaries and political activists were incarcerated here and many of them hanged. The main part of the prison building is called 'Thirty-two cells.' On the first floor were lodged Chhatradhar Mahato, Prasun Chatterji, Raja Sarkhel (Tinku), Sukhshanti Baske and others; on the ground floor were all the accused in Gyaneshwari derailment case. Hiralal Mahato, Khagen Mahato and Bapi Mahato. Manik and Kanishka were sent to the first floor cells. Four wards were for under-trials and the rest for convicts.

Crossing Thirty-two cells, the jail library and a ward on the right, I was taken to the women's ward. The ward is surrounded typically by high red walls on which bold black letters in a semicircle declare it to be 'Medinipur Correctional Home (Female).' An officer unlocked the front lock and then passed the keys inside through a small opening to the warden, who then opened the door and took me in. The metal bell, tied to a rope with its end hanging outside, is the only means of communication between the ward and the jail. For supplying food or any information from the jail office — call for visitor or court date — is passed on only after pulling the rope and generating a big noise. The same bell tells the inmates that a new recruit is joining them. Entry of a new person is always a source of excitement in jail life. So, when the bell rang, most of the inmates gathered in front of the warden's office. I still don't know how they figured out I was a so-called Maoist. Anyone accused under Section 120 to 124A of the IPC are usually termed 'Maoist' and the case Maoist case.

A thin, short woman named Sandhya came forward to search my bag and body. The way she measured my body reminded me of that story by Taslima Nasreen in which she describes how male tailors take measurements of women's bodies. Then, she took my bag and dropped my belongings onto the floor. My clothes were a source of great amusement. After my arrest, I was able to send a message to Sampad (my husband) that I needed clothes and whatever he collected I managed to get them in through the high security. In the bag were some undergarments which made the women giggle. I had never felt such humiliation and, so, with tearful eyes I went through the processes of ripping off my dignity. Sandhya then brought me into the ward and after spreading a small sheet over a tattered mattress told me this was my 'file.' In jail, everything is a 'file' — the space allotted for sitting and sleeping is a file, inmate-counting queue is a file, the set of five half-cooked *rotis* is a file, even the rice-measuring ladle is a file. She also gave me an aluminium plate, a glass and a big, multipurpose bowl. One can have *dal* in it as well as use it as a mug for bathing or washing. Sandhya then gave me dinner — a file of *rotis*, some *dal* and vegetables. I ate very little.

Fate of Honesty

Once, in court lockup, Chhatradhar informed me that Satyarupa of Khejuri was also in the same jail. On my request, Sandhya introduced me to her. Satyarupa talked a lot but due to her local accent, unknown vocabulary and mental condition I hardly understood what she was trying to say. A simple woman, she had no idea why she was arrested and what UAPA was.

Talking to her, I learnt that she came from village Pankhai where she lived with her husband, two daughters-in-law — her three sons worked in Delhi, Odisha and Haldia — and five-year-old grandson. Her family owned a small piece of land and had a two-storied pucca house with no electricity. In all her married life, Satyarupa had taken up all kinds of jobs to run the household. She had vended vegetables, fish, incense sticks, and sold saris in the weekly bazaars.

For the past six or seven years, she had also been running self-help groups under various government schemes. Recently, she had taken training and her incense sticks were in great demand. She had started growing vegetables on her land which was sold in the market. The same land had, however, embroiled her family in a legal dispute with her husband's elder brother. With her meagre earnings, she had provided for the education of her sons and also their wives. One of her daughters-in-law was a part-time teacher and the other studying in a local college. She was proud that she had always been honest and truthful, not for once falling for dishonest means.

Her problem started with the renovation of a school pond under NREGS, Apparently, there were some irregularities with the project funds, but she had nothing to do with it. She never felt the need to give commission to any political group or person, which was why she was arrested. She believed that truth would eventually prevail and she had nothing to be afraid of. She was the first woman arrested under the draconian UAPA, which made her the biggest 'Maoist' in the jail. However, in my 43 days of stay with her, I found her least interested in politics; she never read newspapers and kept asking me who Maoists were and who I was; her only worry was when she would be back with her family and the losses she was incurring because of her incarceration. In jail both of us were 'Maoists,' but I enjoyed special status and privileges whereas Satyarupa did not.

Prisoners All

I was very tired — two and a half days in Junglemahal followed by two days' arrest process had numbed my nerves and I slept tightly. Next morning, my eyes opened with shrill shouts and I found the inmates queuing up and someone called Phul-*di* was counting in a loud voice and making vigorous gesticulations. This, I understood was *gunti* — head-counting.

Thereafter, the heavy door of the ward was opened. Each of us came out, some started sweeping, some washing dishes, and a few moving around aimlessly or plainly gossiping. It took no time to guess that I was the morning's topic. I looked for tea. Then Husanara, a sweet jovial woman, came to sit by my side and started talking. When she called me *baji* — elder sister, I began to cry, tears rolling down relentlessly. I know not what she understood, but I felt good. I had known that the State would never tolerate me, that I might be arrested; but I had never known that I would be so depressed when I was actually taken in. In the mental condition that I was in, someone introducing me to jail life, sharing puffed rice and biscuits, was a great relief. That first day with Husanara has stayed on in my memory.

Jails have been renamed 'Correctional Homes,' but are still run by old rules. In our ward, the gate used to open after *gunti* at six in the morning. Phul-*di* always did the counting — she was the 'writer.' Work was distributed among convicts according to their abilities. Like, Phul was the 'writer' and Sandhya 'mate.' Writer does office work and mate various chores in the ward. Phul's daily routine was counting and then informing those inmates who were to be produced in court on that day. Every alternate day, a doctor used to visit the ward and there, too, Phul made a list of those to be checked and gave out medicines as prescribed. One of her major job was to control the TV, whose remote was always in her custody. Everyone followed her dictates.

Her doctor husband was also lodged in the male ward. They had been convicted for the murder of a doctor friend. Her daughter was working in Kolkata with some reputed company. We all knew she belonged to an affluent family. Writer Phul and Mate Sandhya formed a caucus and both of them sought obedience from the rest of us. Medinipur is a transit jail for under-trials, not meant for convicts. Since under-trials are not supposed to do any labour, some convicts are always retained to manage the show. Our morning activity consisted of having tea, washing, bathing and playing ludo. Phul had told Satyarupa to teach sewing and take reading and writing classes in the evening, which just stopped with my entry.

Recounting used to be done at noon before we were locked up again — have lunch and stay locked. For three hours in the afternoon we were allowed out of the ward but from six in the evening we were locked again. From the female ward one had to cross six locked gates to reach the main gate of the jail. The ward was locked, the warden's office was locked from both inside and outside and the keys were kept in the office at jail gate. At daytime, a male convict was posted and the night warden was provided with a walkie-talkie for any eventuality. Inmates were locked and so were the wardens, both imprisoned.

Spiritual Succour

Jail-lexicon comes from some other world. I never knew that one could communicate in such a slang-filled lingo. I felt the inmates dreamt in that language. It probably enabled them to live such perfunctory life. The warden's tongue was hardly different. Both were imprisoned, the difference being that while one drew a salary for being confined, the other was compelled to live in the cage. Jail always encourages *pujas*. It's another exercise to make one lose confidence — don't take responsibility, leave everything to God; leave whatever happens to this life but work for betterment in the next; don't worry, almighty God is there to solve all your problems.

Every *Shanibar*, Saturday — there was quite a racket. Except five Muslim inmates, most of the women, including Satyarupa, fasted on account of *Shani-puja*. The puja was held in the evening in the open, near a small *Shiva-linga*. Inside the ward, there were a couple of tiny puja enclosures decorated with pictures of a variety of known and unknown Gods. Most inmates prayed there after bathing in the morning. The evenings were reserved for *kirtan*. Usually, *kirtan* was performed at one place but if there was discord, inmates split into two groups and competed with each other.

One day, a rather obese *Maharaj* from Ramakrishna Math came to visit, as he does once a month, to fulfil our spiritual needs. He, his entourage and jail officers sat on chairs while all the women went to touch his feet and receive his blessings. Never bothering to ask how they were, he gave a short speech, citing Hiroshima and Nagasaki (why not Bhopal?), on the futility of life. He left in 10 minutes after handing two pieces of *sandesh* to each inmate.

Sunday Night Fever

Sunday was a day of friendship. All the inmates gathered at one place and sang together. Apart from mate Sandhya, there were two more women of the same name. One of them worked as Phul's personal attendant and was frequently mistreated. The third Sandhya, who used to work with the forest department, was convicted for murdering her daughter-in-law. She, her husband and their son were awarded life-imprisonments. On my first Sunday in jail, while I was sitting quietly in my file, Husanara called me to see the fun. Much singing and clapping were going on there, and then I noticed something strange: the third Sandhya was hysterically banging her head and hands on the floor and asking them to sing louder and louder. Higher the pitch raised, more was the banging, with her hair flowing in all the directions. I remembered, once, when I was very young, I went to Chintpurni in Himachal to attend an aunt's son's (after six daughters) hair-giving ceremony. There, too, I saw women doing like this in front of the temple. Goddess Chintpurni's miraculous powers were said to have been transferred to those women in that manner; and with Her blessings, they were granted any wish they would make.

At some point, Bhabani, a trafficking accused, came and sat near her feet and asked her to vanquish her sins. Then, Mate Sandhya, too, came for atonement. The hysteric Sandhya held Bhabani by her arm and banged her head and free hand. At another end, *Ma Manasa* — the snake Goddess — landed on Kavita making her wriggle with cupped hands above the head like a hood. At this point, Husanara asked me to move away because Sandhya would now get up and stride around. It was enough for me; so, with a firm voice, I asked them to stop all that or else I would call the jailor. They stopped, but since then everyone went against me for my anti-god sensibility. They had seen many Maoists, they had seen women who had been so badly beaten that they couldn't go to the toilet, but they had never seen someone like me. It was fine if I didn't believe or participate in but I couldn't stop them from their obligations towards the Almighty. There was no separate cell here, but the ones in the discarded ward could be cleaned in a day, I might as well shift there without delay.

Next morning, the jail inspector came to the ward. After listening to the inmates, I was called. He tried to convince me that it was their belief and I should let them continue as long as they didn't disturb me. I tried to tell him that two women were sick and I couldn't see them suffering. He argued that the inmates were backward and we, the enlightened city folk, must respect their sentiments. I agreed but reminded him of our responsibility towards society. I asked him what the jail policy was; the jail being a government institution, does it encourage superstitions? Finally, he buckled and a doctor was sent for the treatment of Sandhya and Kavita. Both of them were given medicines and had no further attacks.

Outlawed In-laws

More than half the inmates of Medinipur jail were accused of dowry-murder. Among them was 80-years-old Champa-*mashi* — it was unthinkable that she could do something as dreadful as murder. She used to ask me lots of questions and look at me with amazement. But everyone was not Champa-*mashi*. That bride-murder is so rampant in Bengali society was a revelation to me. I used to think that it was predominantly an urban phenomenon; that in rural society, because women are directly involved in economic activities, even the poor had more freedom than urban middle-class women. I was so wrong! In cities, money helps avert arrest or manage bail, but in villages, the poor have no means to do that and they usually land in jail. Whenever I asked inmates accused of dowry-murder why they did what they did, the reply inevitably was that they had no role in the death. So, the discussion veered round to what drove a young, bubbling girl to take her own life. Her own family was responsible for her death — that was the usual answer.

A girl, if there's trouble in her in-laws' home, will normally share her pain with her parents, siblings, cousins or friends. But those confidantes, instead of helping her break free, force her to go back and face the misfortune. As long as we think daughters are liabilities and do not allow them to grow as an independent individual, many more will die. The absurd part of the story is that when a daughter dies, her own relations then show profound love for her and accuse the in-laws.

Money Can Buy Life

Take the case of Shibani Pal. She, her husband and son were accused of murdering the daughter-in-law. She got bail in six weeks after an out-of-court settlement for two lakh rupees. Kavita's case was opposite but no different. Her son and a neighbourhood girl used to take tuitions from a private tutor in her home. A relationship developed between the tutor and the girl and she became pregnant. The girl committed suicide because the tutor went back on her promise to marry. The girl's family accused Kavita as an accomplice in the crime. Meanwhile, the tutor got a job in a government school. The girl's father withdrew the case after receiving a lakh of rupees plus the expenses incurred so far. This bothered me a lot. Is the value of a girl's life just a lakh of rupees? How do you evaluate the price of life?

Around this time, came Sanchita alias Fantush. She was in jail because she had chopped her rapist's penis. The man, she said, was quite old and used to sneak into her room in the form of a cat. All day long she used to walk amongst us and groan. When her groaning became unbearable, mate Sandhya made her Sonu's daughter. Sonu, a sweet young mother of three, suffered from mental problem. Her husband, instead of providing her medical care, dumped her with her mother and remarried. One day in a fit of rage, she sacrificed her mother to Goddess Kali. She was much better after medication and care by other inmates. Sonu made a place in our hearts. She literally became Fantush's mother. But, her joy was short-lived as her *'beti'* left after four days.

Life is like that! Sonu was the adopted daughter of a Nepali army man who lived in Sejua with his wife. Later, he remarried and started living somewhere in Nepal. According to Sonu, he was a nice man and looked after them well. He passed away three years ago and now Sonu had no one. Every week she sent letters to her husband, kids, friends, cousins and others but no one ever bothered to respond. She pleaded to see her children, and so, her husband was summoned by the court. Instead of appearing, he sent a letter saying that, for all practical purposes, for him Sonu was dead.

Pastime Problems

Passing time is the biggest problem in jail. Medinipur jail is quite green and has lots of mango, jackfruit and blackberry trees. When I arrived, I saw big raw mangoes hanging from the mango trees, the jackfruit trees had fruits and there were tiny blackberries on the only blackberry tree in the female ward. To get fruits, a male convict was usually asked to climb the tree. Twice mangoes were plucked in my presence; we all got one each and the rest went to the office. It was such a happy occasion! Ripening of jackfruit was another story: after plucking, the raw fruits were covered with blankets and every day someone checked them; on ripening, everyone got one or two pods each. I had never eaten so much jackfruit in my life. It's not that everything went smoothly with distribution, but it was a great diversion. On Sundays, inmates were allowed to meet other family members, if husbands or sons also were in the male ward. It was a hectic day: those who had dates took bath and dressed in their best. They also saved puffed or pressed rice, and salted blackberries to give. I never found any men bringing such gifts for their women. For others, too, it was a matter of excitement as they were curious to know who said what at the meeting or if someone laughed or cried. It was to be the topic of discussion for the next few days. Jail too has its date with the consumer economy. Whether it was a family meeting with husband or son or an interview with family or friends from outside or an appearance in court, the female inmates women used to do makeup or dress to kill. They rubbed face-cream, daubed powder, wore lipstick, nail polish, kohl and what not. Those who were to be produced in Jhargram or Kanthi courts started putting makeup before dawn. The rampant use of Fair and Lovely was a shocking finding.

From the very first day in jail I got to read newspapers. Then, after a great deal of difficulty, I started getting books from the library. Inmates in the male ward read newspapers the same day, whereas the female ward got the papers of the day before. In the case of books, they sent the catalogue first and I had to select from it. Later, of course, I could see the library but nothing was easy. Most books in the library were religious. There were shelves after shelves of Ramakrishna, Vivekananda and other spiritual gurus. There were, of course, many good old books on history as well as novels and government reports. I managed to read quite a few novels and reports by British administrators. Just before my arrest, I was reading Varavara Rao's *Captive Imagination*, a collection of his writings from jail. His imagination and thoughtfulness is amazing. Every week Sampad brought magazines like *Tehelka*, *Outlook*, *EPW*, *Economist* and *Asian News*. *Outlook* once carried a story on Medinipur jail with the title 'Working class for Maoists.' It described in detail how jail workers were helping Maoists by training them in various occupations; it was accompanied by a half-page picture of Satyarupa working a sewing machine. I was shocked because Satyarupa was not really interested in sewing; even if she was, her specs were left behind at home due to which she couldn't thread the needle.

Arbitrariness, Corruption and Frugality

Sampad had left some writing paper for me to write a rejoinder, which the jail office did not pass it on to me. In protest I went on hunger strike. To assuage my feelings, the jail authorities sent junior inspector Nitai Chandra Das. Das had been friendly with everyone. Every morning he used to visit Chhatradhar, Tinku and Prasun in their cells and share a smoke with them. When he came to know that I also smoked, he gave me two cigarettes. I felt so happy that I smoked both at once. So he gave me two more for later. He tried his best to pacify me but I wasn't giving up easily. Instead, I asked for the jail manual and the petition form. The welfare officer admitted that he received the papers but didn't know what to do with them. Finally, after hours of discussions and arguments, I got all that I was asking for. Though I couldn't do anything about the *Outlook* story, the *pleasure* of troubling the jail authority gave me immense satisfaction.

Jail is a haven for corruption. If one has money, one can get anything: two rupees for a boiled egg or a piece of fish; two bananas or a lime or an apple for a rupee. One can get things from outside, too. It's also easy to smuggle in money. Champa-*mashi* had 50 rupees deposited in the office for her needs. Her family lived far away and couldn't visit her, so they made this arrangement. She asked the office to get her soap and a packet of puffed rice. For things that didn't cost more than 20 rupees, she had to sign on a bill for 50 rupees. Even mortgaging was carried out unchecked in the jail. Sonali mortgaged her gold nose-ring to buy a new dress. All the work of the sweeper was done by inmates for small favours like a few onions, a handful of green chilies, piece of soap, so on. Sujan and Amina used to do such work and, after they were transferred to Purulia jail, Manju and Sonali took over.

Again, it was in jail that I saw how dried *rotis* could be used as fuel for making tea, how 8-by-8-by-10-foot pit got half-filled in just four days with wasted food.

Gender Segregation

The jail took special care in guarding its female inmates from the male inmates. Male inmates had to come to the female ward for electrical or civil maintenance jobs, plucking fruits from trees, so on. Female inmates were always shooed away with the intimation of any such visit. I could never figure out what great misfortune would befall on us if we came within the range of male sight. During Ratha Yatra, male inmates took out the Ratha while females had to view it through a slit. There's no denying jail looks down upon women.

It's almost two years since I'm out of jail, but the memories have remained fresh. I can still feel the backache I developed due to sleeping on the hard floor. Even today, I miss the previous night's roti with dark, not so sweet morning tea.

Annexure I

Supreme Court Order, Planning Commission Report and Interviews with Indian Maoists

'Peace Talks Not a Child's Play': Kishenji

In the backdrop of the controversy over the peace talks between CPI(Maoist) and Mamata Banerjee government this is Kishenji's last interview to three Kolkata-based journalists — Pranab Mondol, Biswajit Bhattacharya and Chitradeep Chakraborty. He was no more by the time his replies reached them.

—Editor

ARE YOU INTERESTED IN THE PEACE TALKS AT ALL?

It's not easy to sit for peace talks. Conducive atmosphere is to be created. The present government could not build that atmosphere. We are saying from the beginning that no dialogue is possible if only one side is willing for it— either the government or our party. It is the same with the Central or state government. We made four demands [to be fulfilled] before any talks. First, all the villagers who have been arrested in the course of the Junglemahal movement have to be released. Second, joint forces have to be withdrawn from Junglemahal. Third, other political parties [apart from the ruling party] would have to be allowed to organise processions and meetings. Fourth, all the arms stacked in [CPI(M)] *harmad* camps in Junglemagal would have to be seized. We did not put up resistance against the joint forces' atrocities in villages since the last few months. Similarly, we did not retaliate against the [TMC-sponsored] *Bhairav Bhahini.* This means we want peace sincerely. But the state government does not want it. Its objective is clear to us : continue the security crackdown on the one hand and propagate on the other that Maoists do not want dialogue.

DO YOU HAVE FAITH IN THE MEDIATORS' TEAM?

We have discussed with thre members of the mediators' team several times. We informed them about our party's stand. After meeting us on

30 September, Sujatobabu [Bhadra] said that they would let us know about the next steps after meeting the chief minister on the 3rd [October]. But later we heard that the chief minister did not meet them. What kind of behaviour is this? She has no faith in the mediators' team that she herself had constituted.

Actually she wants to deploy the [Trinamul] leaders close to her. She is sending them repeatedly to Junglemahal in order to strengthen TMC and *Bhairav Bahini.* She wants to set up a rival interlocutors' team. They dropped several names as possible new mediators...

We think she should apologise to Sujato Bhadra, Chhoton Das, Prasun [Bhowmik], Asokendubabu [Sengupta], Kalyanbabu [Rudra] and Debasisbabu [Bhattacharya]. She did not give [proper] recognition to their committee. We won't accept any other team.

THE CHIEF MINISTER HAS URGED THE MAOISTS TO GIVE UP ARMS AND COME BACK TO MAINSTREAM. WHAT IS YOUR REACTION?

Our party's politburo and central committee reacted to these kinds of calls earlier. We are reiterating that Maoists have always been in the mainstream. They are not in any other stream. Our party is waging struggles together with the people and that's the mainstream. Now I come to the question of giving up armed struggle. Surrender of arms is not our principle. We arm people in order to carry on the People's War. What could have been done in the present context was ceasefire. We had already declared ceasefire for one month[in October 2011]. We did not go for any offensive during that period.

But what was the benefit? The state government unleashed the joint forces on us. That's why surrender of weapons is out of the question. But ceasefire is possible if both sides are committed to it. It can't happen that one side is holding fire while the other is continuing the attacks. We have already told this to the mediators. On behalf of the CPI(Maoist), we have told them that we are ready to go for the ceasefire if the government forces stop their operations. We are even ready for signing a bipartite agreement to this effect if such a thing materialises. But it has not happened. This is not child's play.

DID YOUR PARTY TAKE ANY INITIATIVE FOR THE PEACE TALKS IN THE STATE? OR, WAS IT A PLAN TO GAIN TIME ONLY?

The people of Junglemahal voted for Trinamul in view of the promises made in the party's poll manifesto. Besides, the people of Junglemahal did not want to vote for the CPI(M) after its diswal record pertaining to [quality of] their lives and livelihood in its 34-year long rule. Mamata, after coming to power, made announcements about the release of [political] prisoners and set up a review committee. She offered talks [with us]. But the problem began with the review committee. We wanted her to begin the release of prisoners. Mamata told [the committee] to submit a report in three months.

She said release would depend on case-to-case review. But not a single [Maoist] prisoner has been released after five months. On the contrary, the new government has begun arresting more people. We had done many developmental works in Junglemahal in the last five months. But the *Bhairav Bahini* has stopped those works everywhere. Actually, Mamata is not ready to allow any other political force to hold rallies and processions except TMC. She has reneged on her pre-election promises on Junglemahal. On the other hand, we desisted from resistance for a month. The people of Junglemahal have no faith in this infant government.

The government's agenda is not to hold dialogue but to mount attack on us. TMC promised many things here to garner votes. But nothing materialised. This shows the government's tactics. That's why we don't think there is congenial situation for talks. Let her first establish peace and bring development to Junglemahal. But instead of making such moves, she has undertaken a divide and rule policy by announcing to recruit police personnel from this area. To fight whom? Is Junglemahal is out of this state? Why Mamata is not telling mediators about these moves? Is she trying to build a *Bahadur Bahini* [to fight Maoists]? We committed only four per cent of the post-poll killings of [political] leaders; the rest was done by the TMC.

WHY DID YOU KILL TMC WORKERS?

We would not have killed them had they been supporting or working for TMC only. But they were working as police moles. We experienced this with the CPI(M)'s *harmad bahini* earlier. Villagers knew about them. We punished many such *harmads*. But the *Bhairav Bahini* came up within five months [after the polls] and began torturing villagers. They started informing the police. We came to know about them from villagers. They even formed a *Nari Samman Bachao Committee*. Police put up the committee's [anti-Maoist] posters and TMC leaders distributed leaflets issued by it. We are still saying that we won't object to those who work for CPI(M) and TMC. But we would resist if they work for police. We did the same with Babu Bose. He organised the *Gana Pratirodh Mancha* with the CPI(M) and became a leader of the *Bhairav Bahini* after TMC came to power. We have no objection to political struggle. If this government believes in democracy, let it discuss with the Opposition. Why are they stopping strikes (called by Maoists)? It's a democratic right.

ARE YOU STILL ACCEPTABLE TO THE PEOPLE OF JUNGLEMAHAL?

The residents of Junglemahal want food and development. Instead of sending her party leaders here, Mamata should send more food — rice, pulses and edible oil for the people. Now roads have been repaired and we are not obstructing anymore. Villagers have become tired after waging war for the last three years. Besides, a fair amount of rainfall has ensured good crops and people are busy in farming activities. We are also not going for attacks. But the new government is not taking care of Junglemahal properly. The local TMC leaders had either maintained a low profile or joined the PCPA during the Lalgarh movement.Now they have become active; this has created confusion among the villagers. At the same time, the government activities are politically motivated. For instance, Sushanta Ghosh [former CPI(M) minister accused of killings] was arrested alone while the rest of the *harmads* were spared. They are enjoying hospitality in camps. People did not want it. We have been maintaining ceasefire for long honouring the people's wishes. Still today 60-65 per cent of the people in Junglemahal are with us.

Are you not spending much time in Junglemahal these days?

It's a completely baseless propaganda. This has been going on since the days joint forces began operation. Journalists were fed the story about the route we had taken to 'escape'. It's ridiculous. Our party's leadership is still here and will continue to be so. The canard about my death was spread March 2010 onward. It continued for long. Then they spread the story of my injuries. These are aimed at breaking the morale of our workers. I am assuring you that our leaders and cadres are still in Junglemahal. We have not left.

Is there any problem in your party regarding the talks?

There is no problem among us. We decide our course after collective discussions. We were informed [by the party leadership about the moves to be taken] in respect of governments in Andhra and this state [West Bengal] in June [after the Assembly elections]. It was told what to do about the course of our moves regarding peace talks. We knew how much time the government would take for the talks. That's why I spoke to Sujato Bhadra, a member of the mediators' team. We signed an agreement [with the team members]. But later we found that the government was not paying heed to the mediators' team and avoiding them. But we on behalf of the CPI(Maoist) had moved ahead enough to hold the discussion with the government. But the situation changed in such a manner that we felt confused about whom should we talk to. Then we sent a letter on behalf of the party that the government should inform us about its position in writing. Because, Mamata, mediators and TMC were speaking in different voices. But we were communicating our position in a single voice.

(The Bengali version of the interview was published in a book titled 'Breaking News — Junglemahal' edited by Chitradeep Chakraborty We are carrying its translation in this collection, courtesy the authors. The words within brackets are added in this translation to make the context clear.)

CPI(Maoist) State Secretary's First Letter to Mediators in the Bengal Peace Process

Dear comrade,

Revolutionary greetings……I heard several programmes have been taken up on the release of political prisoners. The Junglemahal situation is still not normal. *Harmads* have not been arrested and their arms have not keen seized in core areas [of Junglemahal]. *Harmads* and joint forces carried major terror campaign since last two years. Even today both have relations and the joint attacks have not stopped. *Harmads* have been eyes and ears of the joint forces. Whatever Mamata says, she won't be able to stop the nexus between the two forces. The police officers who have been posted here earlier are still working here. The kingpins of [CPI(M) sponsored] *Gana Pratirodh Committee* have not been arrested, they won't be. Villagers are still living under fear. There are differences in police operation between now and then. The forces are not attacking the people as they did earlier. But they are threatening the villagers clearly. 'You people are forgetting what happened earlier and now joining the [Maoist-Orgauiseq] rallies and processions again,' they said. Whenever the joint forces get the information about our party's top leaders' movements, they are encircling us. This happened to com. Bikash, Suchitra Mahato and me. We survived because we were alert. Still now police network is active and new moles are being recruited during the patrolling. The counter-insurgency force led by Ajoy Nanda [Seuior IPS ofhicer] is increasing its strength and preparing for attack anytime.

New problem has cropped up now. TMC workers did not act as police informers before the [Assembly] polls in May 2011. Now a section of them are working as moles. They are spreading canards against us and threatening people. The lower-rung *harmads* and other reactionary forces are joining the TMC. Till now we have not included any *harmad* and CPI(M) worker in our party or mass organizations. Main leaders of the *harmads* have not returned to villages.... The. TMC is pursuing the politics of area domination and making hue and cry against us where they have not succeeded. We have not threatened or cautioned any TMC worker so far. Our own supporters who had joined TMC in March-April (in the run-up for the polls) now left the TMC. It is important to draw your attention to one thing. We have not stopped any developmental activities of the earlier government or this new one. They are carrying false propaganda against us. We had undertaken various developmental projects but joint forces stopped them. Despite that we succeeded in implementing them with the active participation of the people.

The mass meetings, held from 9 August 2010 Lalgarh rally [in which Mamata Banerjee had participated as Opposition supremo] to TMC programmes till April 2011, had witnessed good popular participation as we had taken the initiative. You are more educated and experieced. You may not agree with me. But TMC has backtracked on its pre-poll promises. We need to present the ground reality before you....newspapers reported that a team has been set up to discuss with the Maoists. But they did not elaborate on what transpired between the chief minister and the team.We want to know what exactly are the issues which Mamata and you have discussed and what responsibilities she has entrusted to the team. Also, we want to know that how much time she has given you (to accomplish your task) and what is the formal agreement and informal understanding between the both sides. I am inviting you to come and inform us all these matters......

Akash 8.7.2011

Akash's Last Letter to Mediators

Dada,

You have to make it clear what were the agenda of proposed discussion (with the mediators) because we have already made our stand clear in details earlier..But the situation deteriorated in last one month. Not only the joint forces but also TMC-led attacks have increased along with spreading of false propaganda and threats. We did not retaliate or take revenge keeping faith in you. Not only that, we did not obstruct joint forces. The propaganda about recent laying of mines by us is false as these mines were laid in 2009-2010. The story of ours mines being laid on the road that Subhendu [Adhikary, TMC MP from Haldia] travelled to reach Jhitka was a police fabrication.

.....But history showed that discussion was never possible when only one side came forward. .. Mamata's *Salwa Judum* model has become evident. We kept our promises [not to attack] for a month. But what was the benefit? You people individually recognized the Maoist commitment [to the ceasefire] but the government did not. The government did not even do the one per cent of what it was supposed to do. … you told us that you would meet the chief minister. But she did not meet you till 10/10//11. She did not even give importance to our discussion[between mediators and Maoists]… after that Mamata sent Mukul [Roy, TMC Union minister] who facilitated visit of …. to Midnapore jail. The move was aimed at prop up another mediator team with the tactics to mount pressure on you and confuse the public opinion. This drama has to be exposed….. I want to tell you again in this context that the fight is against the unscrupulous State and not any one else. Don't take it otherwise. Our party is professedly committed to peace, development, democracy, freedom of speech as well liberation from exploitation... If we can't join hand to oppose her *Salwa Judum* model in right time, it will not only In Crease attack on us but also liquidate people like you.

Akash.... . 31/10/11

**Translated from Bengali and abridged. Words in brackets are added to clear the context — editor*

Killing of Kishenji: Coordination of Democratic Rights Organisations' Fact-finding Report

Twenty two member team of four constituents of Coordination of Democratic Rights Organisation, namely, Association for Protection of Democratic Rights, Andhra Pradesh Civil Liberties Committee, Bandi Mukti Committee and Peoples Union for Democratic Rights (Delhi) undertook a fact finding into the alleged encounter killing of Mallojula Koteswara a Rao (aka Kishenji) on 1st December, 2011. The team visited Sorakatta hamlet of Burisole and Gosaibandh village of Paschim Medinipur. The team spoke to the residents of the two villages, the Sub Inspector and ASI of Jamboni Police Station, and visited the spot where the alleged encounter took place on 24th November.

Spot: The place where Kishenji's body was found is about 300 metres from the hamlet Sorakatta of Burisole village. It is barely 50 metres from the village football ground and surrounded by thin cover of Sal trees. Right next to where his body lay on the ground is a termite hill. All around is a thin spread of Sal trees giving the impression that there was little cover. The termite hill remains undamaged by all the alleged exchange of fire. Where the body lay on the ground there is a pool of blood where his head and torso lay but no blood spot marks where his legs lay. The trees which ostensibly carry the bullet marks show no burn marks caused by bullets. Indeed the contrast between the badly damaged body of the deceased with the undisturbed spot where his body lay gives rise to much doubt. If there was heavy exchange of fire there would be telltale signs around. What is most intriguing is that the termite hill, barely few inches away from the body, shows no corresponding damage if there was an exchange of fire and bullets flying all around him. Dried leaves show no sign of burn caused by sparks from bullet fire. Team members walked around to see for themselves signs of bullet-marks on the trees or termite hills and other signs of a gun-battle. But whereas some tress had cutmarks, not a single termite hill was damaged and no visible sign of burn or fire due to heavy rifle and mortar firing!

'VILLAGERS' ACCOUNT: At Sorakatta hamlet we were told that two days before the incident security forces movement became evident and it picked up by 24th November when in the morning, between 10-11 am, police personnel asked the villagers to stay inside their house and not to step out. According to the villagers during these three days of heavy security force movement no announcements were heard of any kind let alone of police asking Kisahnji to surrender. Between 4-5 pm of 24th they heard loud noise followed by sounds of bullet-fire for about 15-30 minutes. Significantly two villagers — a local quack, Budhev Mahato and a 20 years, old student Tarachand Tudu were picked up and implicated in the same case no. 46/11 dated 25/11/2011 and charged under S ection 307 and other sections I.P.C.

At Gosaibandh, which is about 5 kms from Burisole, one Dharmendra, third year student of geography at a local college, was picked up for allegedly sheltering Kishenji and the police claimed to have seized a laptop. The family said that the bag belonged to Dharmendra and there was no laptop in it instead Rs. 20,000 was stolen and family's ration card, certificates and OBC card were seized too.

POLICE STATION JAMBONI: The team members spoke to SI Sabyasachi Bodhak and asked him when did they receive information about the encounter, who informed them as well as who wrote the FIR since it fell in their jurisdiction. According to them they received the information from Additonal SP of Junglemahal Aloknath Rajori at night at around 10.30 pm. And it is the Addl. SP who wrote the FIR. It is important to note that the investigation has been entrusted to the DSP CB-CID whereas the complainant is a superior officer. This violates the basic principle of natural justice that a superior officer than the complainant officer investigate the crime.

We wish to recall the nature of injuries on the body of Kishenji. There were bullet, sharp cuts and burn injuries. Surprisingly there was no injury marks on his shirt and pant corresponding to his body parts.

1. Injuries on head and face:
   Right eye was hanging from the socket.
   Lower Jaw was missing instead there were burn marks.
   On the back side of the head part of skull and brain missing.
   At four places on the face there was bayonet like stab marks.
   One third of the throat was had been slash wound.
2. Right fore arm bone was broken without the skin showing any external injury.
3. The right arm has three Bullet Injury Marks.
2. Both legs ankles are broken and the left feet was half dangling.
3. The left sole skin was missing and burnt.
4. One third of the left hand index finger was removed.
5. There were more than 30 Bayonet like cut injuries on the body.

We were unable to get the Inquest Report prepared by the Executive Magistrate nor could we get the Postmortem report although team members have read and taken notes from it. Surprisingly none of the above injuries were recorded except the bullet entry and exit injuries.

Our observations: Considering the extent of the damage caused to the body against the rather undisturbed surrounding of the spot where the body lay raises our suspicion about the official version. The reported official version themselves suffer from inconsistencies. E.g. Whereas chief minister Mamta Bannerjee claimed that for three days a Kishenji and his companions were encircled and they were asked to surrender, but the villagers deny having heard any public announcerment over loudspeaker of any kind much less asking him to surrender. Mr Vijay Kumar, DG of CRPF went on record on 25th November that Kishenji along with three others were killed in an encounter whereas only a single body was found! The reported number of bullets fired said to be several hundred in the course of 15-

30 minute long encounter do not correspond to the spot where his body lay.

The killing of Kishenji took place against the background of fledgling efforts to initiate talks between the state government of West Bengal and the CPI(Maoist). With his death these efforts have been dealt a fatal blow. We cannot but wonder if this is a repeat of what transpired last year in July when Cherukuri Rajkumar , alias Azad was killed in a fake encounter.

We wish to point out that in the context of a crime committed in the area affected by armed conflict, investigation by one branch of the administration into the conduct of another branch)in this case CB-CID investigating the role of joint forces) can not be considered impartial and unbiased. We, believe that only an independent investigation by an SIT can help unravel the truth.

This tends to confirm our suspicion that this appears to be a case of custodial killing. Therefore, we demand :

1. An independent judicial inquiry headed by a sitting or retired Supreme Court or High Court judge into circumstances surrounding Kishenji's death.2. Register a criminal case under section 302 I.P.C

Debaprasad Roychoudhury (general secretary, APDR)
C H Chandrashekhar (general secretary, APCLC)
Bhanu Sarkar (secretariat member, BMS)
Gautam Navlakha (member, PUDR)
****

Press Statement from Co-ordination of Democratic Rights Organisations (CDRO) on behalf of 27 Democratic Rights Organisations:

We strongly condemn the killing of Mallojula Koteswara Rao alias Kishenji, politbureau member of the CPI(Maoist) at Burisole forest near Jhargram in West Bengal on 24th November, 2011. It is being claimed by the West Bengal police and the CRPF authorities that Kishenji has been killed in a '30 minute gunbattle' near Khushboni village in Burisole forests of West Medinipur district, while some other members of the Maoist squad escaped. However, this version of the police is riddled with contradictions, and also accounts from villagers in nearby villages strongly suggest that Kishenji has been killed in a fake encounter. According to local reports, Kishenji was captured during an operation by the joint forces in the area on 23rd November, and killed in cold blood on 24th November during a staged gunbattle. It is very surprising that a senior member of the CPI(Maoist) like Kishenji, who would normally have been surrounded by multiple layers of security manned by members of the Maoist squads, was the only victim of this alleged encounter. Also, not a single police personnel has been injured in this reportedly fierce gunbattle. Kishenji's body has reportedly been found with an AK-47 rifle lying by his side. All these is reminiscent of the killing of the spokesperson of the CPI(Maoist), Cherukuri Rajkumar alias Azad in an allegedly fake encounter on 2nd July, 2010. It is also highly condemnable that one of the seniormost members of the CPI(Maoist) has been killed in this manner while the party has been in the process of holding talks with the West Bengal government through government-appointed interlocutors, and the chief minister of West Bengal, Mamata Banerjee has been publicly maintaining that no operations are being conducted by the joint forces. The killing of Kishenji appears to be in keeping with the official policy of liquidating senior members of the CPI(Maoist) through extra judicial killings.

In its directive of 1996, NHRC had clearly stated that all cases of encounters are cognizable offence until the police version is verified by an independent investigating agency and that 'whenever information is received of encounter and death is ascertained as a result of firing by the police during the encounter, prima facie the ingredients of culpable homicide under appropriate sections of the IPC are satisfied and a magisterial inquiry shall be instituted against the encounter'. An Andhra Pradesh High Court's ruling on encounter killings states that 'the state is responsible to register an FIR against the encounter killing and the plea of self defence be proven before the court of law by the involved security personnel'.

In the light of all of this, we demand the registration of an FIR and initiation of an independent magisterial inquiry as per the NHRC

guidelines into the incident of killing of Kishenji immediately. We also demand that an independent, national level fact-finding team be allowed to go into the area and ascertain the facts behind the death. We also demand that the post-mortem on the body of Kishenji be conducted in presence of independent observers and the report be made public.
25. 11. 2011
****

PRESS STATEMENT FROM FRIENDS OF DEMOCRACY
We are deeply shocked in the death of M. Koteswara Rao aka Kishenji — a top leader of CPI(Maoist) party, in the hands of joints forces in West Medinipur. This death is totally unwarranted for and such operation during negotiation violates all established norms and protocols of peace initiative. We reiterate that the peace talk and war cry cannot go hand in hand. We demand a rapid judicial probe in this case as per existing rule of the land, because like Azad, his killing is also shrouded in mystery.

For the sake of lasting peace for the people of Jungle, we request all concerned parties to take initiative. Otherwise there will be more blood shed. The state government should act in a way to establish that it is not vindictive and not bent upon to take revenge.

We once again urge for the unconditional release of the political prisoners at the earliest, as well as withdrawal of joint forces from Junglemahal to establish a congenial atmosphere. We hope that good sense will prevail at last.

Subhas Sen, Biplab Chakraborty (Jt Convenors)RSVP - Sujato Bhadro
****

PRESS STATEMENT FROM ACTIVISTS NOVEMBER 25, 2011
We strongly condemn the cold-blooded murder and planned assassination of Kishenji alias Mallojula Koteswara Rao, Politburo Member of CPI(Maoist) in Burishol forest area, Paschim Medinipur District, Junglemahal, West Bengal on 24 November 2011. At the time

of this murder Kishenji was dealing with the process of peace talks through the interlocutors appointed by the chief minister of West Bengal, Mamata Banerjee. Such a heinous crime should be condemned by all justice-loving people.

According to the CPI(Maoist) statement issued to the media on today, Kishenji was arrested and tortured and then brutally killed. This murder looks much similar to that of Azad's in July 2010, when Azad was brutally tortured and killed while he was dealing with the Union Government's offer of peace talks through Union home ministry appointed interlocutor.

In these circumstances, the Joint Forces' story of a fierce gun battle in Burishol forest of Paschim Medinipur district comes out to be a concocted one. It is significant that the mother of Kishenji, Ms. Madhuramma while maintaining it is a fake encounter has also demanded a judicial enquiry. Under the circumstances, we demand :

1. The fake encounter killing of Kishenji should be investigated by a Judicial Enquiry Committee of a sitting or retired judge of Supreme Court.
2. Immediately register a case of Murder against the police, and paramilitary personnel who have claimed to have killed Koteswara Rao alias Kishenji, Politburo member, CPI(Maoist) in Burishol Forest area, Paschim Medinipur District, Junglemahal, West Bengal taken place on 24-11-2011.
3. All those who are the suspects and involved in this coldblooded murder should temporarily be removed from the office till the Judicial Enquiry is completed.
4. Kishenji's body should be airlifted to Hyderabad and handed over to his mother after proper post-mortem being conducted by the designated team of doctors and forensic experts not below the rank of civil surgeons.
5. Meanwhile, Kishenji's body should be preserved with appropriate embalming.

B D Sharma (Former National Commissioner for Scheduled Castes and Tribes) G N Saibaba (Deputy Secretary, Revolutionary Democratic Front)

Press Statement from MASUM

We, the friends of MASUM, severely condemn the killing of Kishenji, alias Koteswara a Rao, member of politburo of CPI(Maoist). It is alleged that Kishenji was killed in the custody of CRPF. We are alarmed at the killing of Kishenji, at this juncture of time, when the Government declared that it would proceed for a bi-lateral talk to resolve the problem due to Maoists' action and subsequently head towards peace. It is really unfortunate that the present government too, just like their predecessors, considers the problem of Maoists as a law and order problem, instead of looking it as a socio-political problem. Hence, we severely criticize the attitude taken by the governments ....

Even the police and joint force declaring with cheers, the news of death of Kishenji, alias Koteswara Rao; unfortunately no officer of the state government or from the central government felt that the bullet ridden body should be taken before any medical practitioner to confirm death. It seems that our police and joint force with sophisticated rifles / carbines in hands can declare officially the body is 'dead' by their own!! Without any certification from any doctor how the police , the civil administration and even the 'media' can claim the person is dead, is a matter of surprise. The police and administration left the injured body in open air for exhibition for hours together to claim their credit. The largest democratic system never felt to treat an injured person first with human approach. This is a shame…

25 November 2011

Source: sanhati.com

Excerpts from Interview of CPI(Maoist) Gen. Secy Ganapathy After Killing of Politburo Member Azad

In the interview you gave to Jan Myrdal and Gautam Navlakha you said that your party was ready for talks with the government. In the letter written by your spokesperson Azad to Agnivesh, he said your party was ready for simultaneous ceasefire from both sides. Now that the government had killed Azad in a conspiratorial manner, do you think it is possible to hold talks? Are you still reiterating the stand taken before the death of Azad?

In fact, you should put this question to Chidambaram and Manmohan Singh. For the past one and half year, comrades Azad, Kishenji and I have been stating our party's stand regarding talks a number of times. The government has been hiding the endless brutal violence it had been perpetuating on the people and has been announcing each time that talks would be held only if Maoists abjure violence. Chidambaram has been repeatedly shouting these words from the roof top. Keeping in view the war declared on the people and the difficulties they are facing due to it, Azad had continued declaring till the end that our party would be ready for simultaneous cease fire if the government is ready for it. His intention was to lessen the travails of the people to any possible extent. He mentioned the same demand in the letter written to Swami Agnivesh. Chidambaram and Manmohan Singh had not only killed him in a conspiratorial manner but are shamelessly performing the same charade once again. The fact is that the government doesn't feel any actual need for holding talks. If the peace wished by intellectuals, democrats and the people is to be established, then the most meaningless thing would be to demand that the counter-violence by people should be stopped while the government continues with its killing spree.

When Chidambaram announced that Maoists should stop violence for 72 hours and Kishenji responded by giving a time of 72 days. Chidambaram's answer was to target Kishenji and to intensify the attacks in order to kill him. Azad who had written the letter to Agnivesh was targeted and killed. As part of Operation Green Hunt nearly one lakh paramilitary forces and three lakh state forces have been deployed. Of these the major forces are Special Forces. Every day, every hour and every minute these forces are perpetuating countless atrocities on the people. They are targeting the people and democrats who are opposing this and putting them in jails under UAPA and other draconian laws of the states. Except for the reactionaries and their stooges in the media, nobody else is supporting this war on people in our country. Even if there are a few individuals who support it, it is not because they know the facts but because they innocently believe the false propaganda of the government. We feel that there is absolutely no conducive situation for holding talks now.

People like Agnivesh are asking us not to retreat from the dialogue process and to come forward for talks even after the cold-blooded murder of comrade Azad. We want to ask them if they would be able to stop such conspiracies and plots the government is hatching to kill our party leaders. Doubtless, comrade Azad was killed by the government in a conspiracy. The post-mortem and forensic reports too prove this beyond doubt. So we request all democrats, peace-loving intellectuals and human rights' organizations to come forward with the firm demand that judicial enquiry should be conducted on Azad's murder.

It is crystal clear that there is no conducive atmosphere for talks. In spite of this we request the people and democrats to demand the government to prove its commitment towards the process of talks by coming forward to implement the following steps.

1)Stop Operation Green Hunt. Withdraw the paramilitary forces. If the government stops its offensive on the people, then the counter-offensive of the people would also stop. As many intellectuals are saying, if the offensive of the government doesn't take place then there would be no need for the people to resist.

2)Ours is a political party like many other parties in this country and the world. Our party has an ideological and military line and aim and correct, clear-cut policies on matters relating to culture, caste, gender, nationality, ecology etc. Even according to the laws formulated by these ruling classes, democratic rights would apply to our party. So the ban on our party should be lifted. Ban on our mass organizations should be lifted. Absolute democratic opportunities should be created for mass mobilization. Only in conditions where we could work democratically, we can come forward for talks.

3)In Andhra Pradesh, comrade Riyaz who had participated in talks with the government in 2004 was caught and murdered after torturing him brutally. Others who participated in talks were targeted and attempts were made to assassinate them. Now comrade Azad who was working to facilitate the process of talks was murdered. So, it is not possible to believe the government and send underground comrades for talks. Therefore if the government releases our leadership comrades from jails, then they would directly represent our party in the talks.

So, you people should think about these three demands and place them before the government. We want to make it clear once again that any questions regarding talks should be put to the government first and not to us. GK Pillai, Prakash Singh, Chidambaram and such likes are saying that we would come into line only if pressure is built up on us through intensification of fascist military offensive on our party and massacring the people. They are living in a fools' paradise. Building pressure, creating illusions in the name of talks, deceiving and destroying the party - this is the strategy of the government. In fact, our party is fighting for peace too. They believe only in suppression and they are incompetent in facing us politically and ideologically. People are fighting under the leadership of our party with the lofty aim of establishing permanent peace by ending the exploitation, oppression, brutal suppression and violence in our country and in the whole human society. We see the issue of 'talks' and 'peace' as part of class struggle too. When class struggle intensifies, it would be in an armed form. In other circumstances it would be conducted in peaceful methods too. So it is completely false that our party would come for talks if pressure is built up.

And then, a false propaganda is being conducted through the media that there are differences in our party regarding talks and that they are mainly on the lines of erstwhile MCCI and erstwhile People's War. This is hundred percent false. This is nothing but false propaganda by the enemy to create doubts in peoples' minds about our party to carry on their aims. Our Unity Congress has taken a clear stand on the matter of talks. The struggle between correct ideas and wrong ideas is a continuous process in the party. We would solve our differences of opinion by abiding the principle of democratic centralism and in the light of Marxism-Leninism-Maoism. This would only lead to the development of the party. We achieved great unity with the merger of the two parties. Now any discussions or conflict of ideas which takes place in the party would be in the form of ideological and political discussions in a united party and not in the form of differences between erstwhile MCCI and erstwhile CPI (ML) (People's War). We categorically state that the differences would never ever take the form of conflicts before the merger.

CHIDAMBARAM AND MANMOHAN SINGH ARE REPEATEDLY ASKING YOU TO 'ABJURE VIOLENCE'. BUT THE ATTACKS OF YOUR PEOPLE'S LIBERATION GUERILLA ARMY ARE CONTINUING. DON'T YOU THINK THIS IS MAKING IT DIFFICULT TO ARRIVE AT A SOLUTION? IN THE BACKGROUND OF YOUR RECENT ATTACKS AT TADIMETLA (DANTEWADA), KONGERA (NARAYANPUR), SILDA (WEST BENGAL) AND LAKHISARAI (JHARKHAND), SOME PEOPLE ARE EXPRESSING THEIR ANXIETY THAT YOU ARE RESPONDING WITH MILITARY MEANS. THEY ARE SAYING THAT THIS WOULD FACILITATE THE DEPLOYMENT OF ARMY AND THAT IT WOULD LEAD TO MORE VIOLENCE AND GREATER LOSS OF LIVES OF ORDINARY CITIZENS AND *ADIVASIS*. WHAT DO YOU SAY?

It is nothing but a big deception and charade by the government to ask the people to abjure violence while the state continues its violence. It is violating its own laws and is massacring the people. So it is very necessary that every democrat and any politically conscious person questions the government on this and demands that it stop the violence and war on the people. They should demand that it is the government which should abjure violence. When the government says that we are practicing violence, it is just like a thief shouting 'thief, thief'. It is trying to divert attention from the real issue by doing so.....

All the members of our people's guerilla army are none other than masses who have armed themselves voluntarily. These masses who had been exploited and oppressed like slaves since generations have understood the laws of historical development of society and are fighting by arming themselves. Our party is repeatedly making this clear - there is only one way for the people to achieve their liberation and that is the armed way. It means arming themselves, forming themselves into an army and waging an armed struggle…..

The attacks carried on recently by our people's army under the leadership of the party and with the active support of the people at Tadimetla (Mukaram), Silda, Lakhisarai, Kongera etc., are all military attacks. Who is anxious about these attacks? Is it the ruling classes and its mercenaries or the people? People are celebrating each occasion of a successful raid like a festival. Each such attack is giving a political message in a practical manner and showing them the path of liberation. The people understand this exactly in this manner. On the contrary seeing all these, the ruling classes are trembling with fear.

However, people who do not understand our movement and those who are not clear about it are anguished about the losses on both sides. We can understand their anguish. But the people cannot stop their war and resistance just because they are anguished. What they should understand is why is such an intense war going on? Why are hundreds of people participating in each attack? Where are we getting the active support of the people? Why are we getting it? If they try to understand this it would become clear. Then they would realize the need for such big attacks, more such big attacks and the need for more such attacks to take place more frequently.....

As to the question if our attacks are facilitating the deployment of army — if people do not fight back, if they silently bow their heads and suffer exploitation and oppression which are going on since centuries, then there is no need even for police and paramilitary, leave alone the army. Then there would be no need for the ruling classes to carry on attacks too. .....In fact, the army had planned for counter-revolutionary *Salwa Judum* military campaign during Vajpayee's rule when Advani was the home minister. The home ministry approved it. The Congress which came to power after Vajpayee's government was toppled at the centre and the BJP which came to power in place of Congress in Chhattisgarh implemented this decision.

From then onwards, the army has been very actively using all its commands (Northern, Central, Southern, Western and Eastern), has formed special structures in all of them and has been giving all kinds of advices to the state police departments through them. It formulated the strategy for the war on people and is providing all kinds of training, intelligence, technology and deployment plans to the central home ministry.....

It is true that the deployment of the army would lead to more violence on the poor and the *Adivasis* and would lead to greater loss of lives. When people are fighting in self-defence it is the exploiters and their stooges who constitute just five percent of the population that are suffering casualties. But in the violence perpetuated by the state, it is vast masses of oppressed people who are facing losses. People who are in the form of PLGA, the Maoist party, mass organizations and *Janathana Sarkars* are losing their lives. So one should understand this. When ordinary citizens and *Adivasis* are suffering losses on such a large scale, one should firstly question as to why this is happening? It doesn't serve any purpose to make confused arguments, either innocently or deceivingly, that innocent people are dying. In this background of loss of lives, the oppressed people and the vast masses are putting a straight question to everybody — are you on our side or on the side of the rulers? It means there is no neutral ground left in between. So we request all those who express anguish about loss of lives to rethink in the background of this question……

The ruling classes of our country are saying that Maoists are not sincere about people's issues and they are not bothered about people's welfare and that their only aim is to 'overthrow the democratically elected government using armed force and establish communist rule.' What is your explanation for this?

The ruling classes are not at all morally qualified to hurl accusations against Maoists, who are sacrificing their lives for the people or to comment on their concern and commitment regarding people's interests, people's welfare and people's development. Our aim is to overthrow this 'democracy' and 'parliamentary rule' which are nothing but means for the dictatorship of the feudals and comprador bureaucratic bourgeoisie and which stand in complete opposition to 95% of the population's interests, using armed force and to establish new people's power. We feel it is wonder of the wonders to say that these elections and parliament are sacred and that the present rule is the highest form of democratic rule!....

This dictatorial and bourgeois parliament and state machinery which they had established by colluding with the imperialists would serve none else than those classes. They may be sacred for those classes but they are a big menace for the people. So it is their birth right to pull them down. It is their democratic right. They should establish a genuine democratic political system which constitutes new legislative bodies and a new constitution.

And, we are not the ones who are obstructing development. It is the ruling classes who are doing so. People are performing agricultural tasks while fighting back the horrible violence and destruction perpetuated by fascist gangs like the *Salwa Judum*, police and paramilitary in Dandakaranya. The militia is doing sentry in defence near the fields and reaping the harvests. The People's Liberation Guerilla Army is safeguarding the harvest of the people. The mercenary forces of the government are attacking such units and killing them. The government forces are wreaking havoc in the *Adivasi* areas by destroying their property, burning homes and whole villages, seizing hens, pigs, cattle and what not from the hapless poor people, destroying the fields and burning the harvest. This enormous destruction is the development policy of the rulers. Here, it is crystal clear that who are the bitter enemies of the people's welfare.

.....The development we are talking of is definitely not the one dictated by the IMF and the World Bank and also not the development policy proposed by Ahluwalias, Rangarajans, Manmohan Sings, Chidambarams and Pillais. The development policy we are proposing would change the relations of production qualitatively and thus would lead to the qualitative development of the productive forces. It is a real development policy which says that one should oppose placing the sovereignty of our country at the feet of foreign firms, that it should also be an independent and a self-reliant one, that the resources in our country should be used not for the imperialists but for the people. Many intellectuals and researchers who have visited our areas had already written that an alternative political power is being established in our areas…

MAMATA BANERJEE HAD DEMANDED JUDICIAL PROBE INTO AZAD'S MURDER. THE CPI(M) PARTY HAS BEEN REPEATEDLY HURLING ACCUSATIONS ABOUT THE CLOSE RELATIONS BETWEEN TRINAMUL CONGRESS AND THE MAOISTS? ARE YOU HAVING SOME UNDERCOVER RELATIONS WITH TRINAMUL EVEN WHILE DESCRIBING IT AS A BOURGEOIS PARTY? HOW DO YOU JUSTIFY THIS?

We are not at all surprised that Mamata Banerjee had demanded judicial probe into Azad's murder. Anybody who is familiar with the political situation of Bengal would not be the tiger they are facing on the front side. Now for them the tiger in the front is more dangerous than the bear which is at their back. But after they chase away the tiger they cannot escape the bear's hug. Our party would continue to caution the people about this danger too. We would ask them to chase away the bear too in the future. They would have to certainly fight against the bear too. Unless people get rid of these two menaces, any one of them would continue riding on the back of the people.

Tomorrow, even if Mamata Banerjee comes to power, she would not seize the lands of land lords and distribute them to the poor peasantry nor would she seize the industries of the imperialists and big bourgeoisie. People would not have a chance to participate freely in the elections too. This means that even if she comes to power there won't be any fundamental change. However, if Trinamul comes to power after a long rule of social fascists, it would definitely try hard to gain a tight grip over the administration. During this period keeping in view the election promises she had made, she may temporarily stop attacks on the people. But this would be only temporary. Later, people would have to fight against her government too.

And our party doesn't have any open or undercover relations with Trinamul. But on some occasions even ruling classes may talk in the interest of the people. They would take up some pro-people demands on some occasions for mobilizing the support of the people and for votes. They would even conduct some struggles. Such struggles also exist though their scope is very limited. When such people talk in the interests of the people, we would examine them concretely. As the contradictions among the enemies are indirect reserves for the proletariat, depending on the concrete situation our party would clearly state its stand. Our party would never support or oppose such things blindly. But people should seriously try to understand their class nature and their political and economic policies and should not entertain any illusions about them. If such illusions exist, it would be a task of our party to bring them out of it.When our stand is so clear, it is not at all proper to say as if we have relations with her party and as if we are justifying it.

Source: Maoist News Bulletin available at various websites.

Excerpts from Interview of Ganapathy by Jan Myrdal and Gautam Navlakha in January 2010

THE SITUATION IN THE EARLY DAYS OF THE LALGARH MOVEMENT WAS SUCH THAT INTELLECTUALS IN LARGE NUMBERS CAME OUT IN SUPPORT OF THE LALGARH MOVEMENT. BUT OF LATE, THE INTELLECTUALS HAVE HAD DIFFERENCES IN TERMS OF THE LATER STAGES OF THE MOVEMENT, AND THE FOCUS HAS BEEN SHIFTED TO SUCH ISSUES AS OPPOSITION TO LAWS LIKE UNLAWFUL ACTIVITIES PREVENTION ACT (UAPA). HOW DO YOU PERCEIVE THE SITUATION?

If I had the latest state committee report, it would have been easier for me to answer this question. But still I would like to say that initially there was lot of support among urban intelligentsia. Now depending upon the enemy's onslaught and the nature of struggle, it will also lead to changes in reaction to the support base. Some people may also go over to the opposition side of the Lalgarh movement. In Bengal, our influence in the Civil liberty groups and in urban areas is not much strong. We need to do more to develop this. We need to strengthen our work in urban areas. A lot would depend on our work there and the development of Lalgarh movement to a higher stage. There is a lot of difference between working among the basic masses and working among intellectuals. As the latter involves several complex factors. In this context, if the intellectuals are united around any issue, even being UAPA, considering that it is not in contradiction to the larger struggle, it would be positive for us. Those who cannot come to directly support the violent phases of the movement can come together in other issues like that. So, demands may change but these must be slogans of the people. And both, Lalgarh and new slogans need to be balanced. I would say that the Party will definitely take positive criticisms from any quarter of people even those who may not agree with our basic line but stood up for people. We welcome criticism from people to rectify our mistakes and strengthen our Party. The movement against UAPA is bound to be used in immediate and long term interest of the people. And in general terms, as such any mobilization in this field in the longer run is not contradictory to the interests of the Party.

WHERE DO YOU PLACE DEMOCRACY IN THE WORKING OF THE PARTY ? MEANING THE RIGHT TO STRIKE, THE RIGHT TO DISSENT, AND THE RIGHT TO FREEDOM OF EXPRESSION.

This is a very important question; however there is no confusion in our Party. We need a new democratic state in which other than CBB(Comprador Bureaucratic Bourgeoisie), the landlords and imperialists all others will have real or genuine freedom. Other than enemies of the people, for everybody there would be real or genuine democracy. In addition, I may say that while preparing Policy Program of Revolutionary people's Committees (RPCs)/*Jantana Sarkars*, we have studied the experience of *Graam Raajyaas* of historic Telangana armed agrarian revolution, Policy Program of Chinese Soviets, People's Barrio committees of Philippine, Revolutionary People's Committees of Peru, United Revolutionary People's Councils of Nepal and also studied the Great Proletarian Cultural Revolution. In accordance with above we have all the fundamental rights including that every voter has the right to recall any elected person. Even has the right to bring any one in position of authority, who works against interest of the people, to court in order to prosecute them. In terms of the four great freedoms declared by Chairman Mao during the Cultural Revolution, other than the character posters on the wall, all the rest freedoms have been ensured by the policy Program of the RPC/*Janathan Sarkar.* As the level of development in the *Janatana Sarkar* advances we would also follow the freedom for character posters. According to the constitution no physical punishment for political opposition will be allowed, anybody had right to politically differ and even unionize. The Indian state is trying to control dissent and therefore people want revolution. We would not repeat the same mistake. Besides, for any mistakes in prosecution, the person has the right to appeal to the village Revolutionary People's Committee, to higher levels and even to the Party. For instance, in one of the extension areas, there was an incident where in collusion with the Inspector General of Police, 33 members belonging to two villages became agents of the enemy. In this context our comrades went and handled the issue. While villagers wanted to give capital punishment to the main agent of the police, party interceded to give a chance to that person to realize his mistake.

What is your party's stance on Talks?

In general people and Maoist revolutionaries do not want violence or armed confrontation with anybody. In unavoidable condition only they take-up arms and resist their enemies and they are waging liberation war by learning from the history. So, we see this as a war of self-defense. In this context of all-out war, we must recognize that the state of Andhra Pradesh has 130 thousand forces, there are 45 thousand forces in Chattisgarh (to soon increase this by more than 20 thousand forces), 160 thousand forces in Maharashtra. Thus each state has a police force which is more than the national level forces of many European countries. The most cruel and dangerous special forces have been trained by the state along with various anti-people draconian laws. Bengal, Bihar, Odisha, Jharkhand, Chattisgarh, Maharashtra, Andhra Pradesh along with Uttar Pradesh and Madhya Pradesh have between them more than 700 to 800 thousand of police forces. Out of this, 250 to 300 thousand police forces are directly engaged against the people. And alongside 100 thousand central paramilitary forces have been deployed in these areas. Here people are combating against a stronger force than the movements in North East and Jammu-Kashmir. This is a brutal and violent repression campaign aimed at the suppression of the political movement of the people, and for exploitation of the minerals.

In this context, if possible we can hope for some respite. Longer the respite better for people. Democratic work needs this context. But while government is holding automatic gun on one hand, one cannot talk about this. People will keep fighting. While pumping bullets people never drop weapons and people never surrender. All democratic, progressive, patriotic forces need to unite and fight against the all-out war on the people by the central and state governments. To put concisely the main demands that the party has placed in front of the government for any kind of talks are: 1. All-out war has to be withdrawn; 2) For any kind of democratic work, the ban on the Party and Mass Organisations have to be lifted; 3) Illegal detention and torture of comrades had to be stopped and immediately released. If these demands are met, then the same leaders who are released from jails would lead and represent the Party in the talks.

Courtesy: sanhati.com/full text carried on the site on 12 February, 2010

Interview with K.G. Kannabiran on Andhra Talks

K.G Kannabiran, president of the People's Union of Civil Liberties (PUCL), has devoted his life to fighting for people's rights. He is one of the leading lawyers in Andhra Pradesh, and has taken up the legal cudgels against the state's attempts to suppress the people's movements and curtail the people's right to protest. He has been involved with the Andhra Pradesh Civil Liberties Committee since its inception 38 years ago and has fought every major legal case involving revolutionary poets, balladeers, fighters and sympathisers. He was the moving spirit behind the setting up of the Concerned Citizens' Committee that facilitated peace talks in 2004 between the government and People's War Naxalites, as the Maoists were known then.

What do you make of the Nallamalla encounter?

For the last 35-40 years, the government has been gunning down people and terming them encounters. This episode is nothing new. It was started by (former chief minister) Vengal Rao — the Naxalite problem was handed over to the police department. Today, the police department is not neutral. It has a vision which is anti-Naxalite. This is no different from Hitler's strategy of converting the police department into a political organ that hounded Jews. This policy is despicable and dangerous to democracy and human rights. How have the AP police silenced people's protests? The political character that the police department has assumed has reached the point that vigilante groups have been engaged to kill Naxalite supporters. They use indigenous weapons like the axe and sword and leave the weapon on the body (apparently as a warning to others). It's a deliberate act to terrorise people and silence them. After the murder of (rights activist) Kanakachary in Mahbubnagar (two years ago) the superintendent of police told the APCLC's vice -president Hargopal to close down the *Karuvu Vyatireka Samiti*. It's very unfortunate that an anti-hunger, anti-drought group was closed down. Everybody has lost the courage to protest.

DO YOU THINK THE PEACE TALKS OF 2004 BETWEEN THE NAXALS AND CONGRESS GOVERNMENT WORKED TO THE DISADVANTAGE OF MAOISTS?

The Congress cleverly used the promise of talks with Naxalites by incorporating it in its manifestos to come to power. The people wanted peace — this issue was one of the factors for the TDP's defeat. After the elections, the Congress, which is experienced in skulduggery, used the period of peace talks to go over Nallamalla forests (their hideout) with a toothcomb. The government behaved in a dastardly manner. Right from the beginning, they wanted to take advantage of the 'peace time'.

ON HINDSIGHT, DO YOU NOW THINK IT WAS NOT THE RIGHT THING TO DO TO PURSUE PEACE TALKS?

No, not really, but we unwittingly played a treacherous role in believing the bonafides of the government. While the Naxalites were here (in Hyderabad) for the talks, the (anti-Naxal police force) Greyhounds went to Nallamalla, spotted the hideouts and gained a strategic advantage. What is objectionable is that this happened after the Naxals were involved in the peace talks.

WAS NOTHING ACHIEVED BY THE TALKS?

I won't say we achieved nothing. It was the people's pressure that brought the government and Maoists to the table to talk peace. That was a victory for democracy.

DID THE MAOISTS REALLY BELIEVE THEY WOULD ACHIEVE ANYTHING THROUGH TALKS?

The Maoists honestly thought something would come out of the talks. They hoped to achieve at least land distribution. It they had achieved this then they would have achieved one of their main objectives without firing even one shot.

WILL THE ELIMINATION OF MAOIST LEADERS HIT THE MOVEMENT?
No, the movement won't be affected. This has gone on for 38 years. There will always be people driven by a desire for a better life, better society and a better country through alternative methods because mainstream politics is all rubbish. Nobody can call this government, either at the State or the Centre, a democracy. It is an anarchic situation.

WERE YOU HOPEFUL AFTER THE PEACE TALKS?
Somewhere along the way, I felt once we initiated a democratic process
it might have a multiplier effect. And the eight months of peace talks were the most peaceful period in the state. The peace talks gave me hope that we would be able to have genuine democracy, improve conditions of the people and fight against globalisation.

DO YOU THINK OF LATE THE VARIOUS PEOPLE'S MOVEMENTS HAVE BEEN WEAKENED IN SOME WAY?
After economic reforms and globalisation, the human rights movement has split… some think globalisation is good, some think it isn't. The movement has not only stagnated but also become fragmented like child rights, dalit rights, women rights and so on. Human rights is not perceived as an indivisible whole. All these issues are not linked holistically with the human rights structure.

THEN SHOULD ALL THE ISSUES BE BROUGHT UNDER ONE UMBRELLA?
Each issue has become something like property. The competitive ethics permeate the civil society movements. Each is confined to its own area and to its own fights. They should remember that a fragment cannot inspire democratic culture. Besides, the government has incorporated NGOs under various guises which is part of a strategy to silence people's voices and concerns.
Courtesy:Deccan Herald, 10 August,2006

Excerpts from
Supreme Court order on *Salwa Judum*

In The Supreme Court of India Civil Original Jurisdiction Writ petition no. 250/2007

Nandini Sundar and Ors. …Petitioners
Versus
State of Chattisgarh …Respondent

ORDER

1. We, the people as a nation, constituted ourselves as a sovereign democratic republic to conduct our affairs within the four corners of the Constitution, its goals and values. We expect the benefits of democratic participation to flow to us — all of us — so that we can take our rightful place, in the league of nations, befitting our heritage and collective genius. Consequently, we must also bear the discipline, and the rigour of constitutionalism, the essence of which is accountability of power, whereby the power of the people vested in any organ of the State, and its agents, can only be used for promotion of constitutional values and vision. This case represents a yawning gap between the promise of principled exercise of power in a constitutional democracy, and the reality of the situation in Chattisgarh, where the Respondent, the State of Chattisgarh, claims that it has a constitutional sanction to perpetrate, indefinitely, a regime of gross violation of human rights in a manner, and by adopting the same modes, as done by Maoist/Naxalite extremists. The State of Chattisgarh also claims that it has the powers to arm, with guns, thousands of mostly illiterate or barely literate young men of the tribal tracts, who are appointed as temporary police officers, with little or no

training, and even lesser clarity about the chain of command to control the activities of such a force, to fight the battles against alleged Maoist extremists.

2. As we heard the instant matters before us, we could not but help be reminded of the novella, '*Heart of Darkness*' by Joseph Conrad, who perceived darkness at three levels: (1) the darkness of the forest, representing a struggle for life and the sublime; (ii) the darkness of colonial expansion for resources; and finally (iii) the darkness, represented by inhumanity and evil, to which individual human beings are capable of descending, when supreme and unaccounted force is vested, rationalized by a warped world view that parades itself as pragmatic and inevitable, in each individual level of command. Set against the backdrop of resource rich darkness of the African tropical forests, the brutal ivory trade sought to be expanded by the imperialist-capitalist expansionary policy of European powers, Joseph Conrad describes the grisly, and the macabre states of mind and justifications advanced by men, who secure and wield force without reason, sans humanity, and any sense of balance. The main perpetrator in the novella, Kurtz, breathes his last with the words: 'The horror! The horror!'[1] Conrad characterized the actual circumstances in Congo between 1890 and 1910, based on his personal experiences there, as 'the vilest scramble for loot that ever disfigured the history of human conscience.'[2]

3. As we heard more and more about the situation in Chattisgarh, and the justifications being sought to be pressed upon us by the respondents, it began to become clear to us that the respondents were envisioning modes of state action that would seriously undermine constitutional values. This may cause grievous harm to national interests, particularly its goals of assuring human dignity, with fraternity amongst groups, and the nations unity and integrity. Given humanity's collective experience with unchecked power, which becomes its own principle, and its practice its own raison d'etre, resulting in the eventual dehumanization of all the people, the scouring of the earth by the unquenchable thirst for natural resources by imperialist powers, and the horrors of two World Wars, modern

constitutionalism posits that no wielder of power should be allowed to claim the right to perpetrate state's violence against any one, much less its own citizens, unchecked by law, and notions of innate human dignity of every individual. Through the course of these proceedings, as a hazy picture of events and circumstances in some districts of Chattisgarh emerged, we could not but arrive at the conclusion that the respondents were seeking to put us on a course of constitutional actions whereby we would also have to exclaim, at the end of it all: 'the horror, the horror.'

4. People do not take up arms, in an organized fashion, against the might of the State, or against fellow human beings without rhyme or reason. Guided by an instinct for survival, and according to Thomas Hobbes, a fear of lawlessness that is encoded in our collective conscience, we seek an order. However, when that order comes with the price of dehumanization, of manifest injustices of all forms perpetrated against the weak, the poor and the deprived, people revolt. That large tracts of the State of Chattisgarh have been affected by Maoist activities is widely known. It has also been widely reported that the people living in those regions of Chattisgarh have suffered grievously, on account of both the Maoist insurgency activities, and the counter insurgency unleashed by the State. The situation in Chattisgarh is undoubtedly deeply distressing to any reasonable person. What was doubly dismaying to us was the repeated insistence, by the respondents, that the only option for the State was to rule with an iron fist, establish a social order in which every person is to be treated as suspect, and any one speaking for human rights of citizens to be deemed as suspect, and a Maoist. In this bleak, and miasmic world view propounded by the respondents in the instant case, historian Ramchandra Guha, noted academic Nandini Sunder, civil society leader Swami Agnivesh, and a former and well reputed bureaucrat, E.A.S. Sarma, were all to be treated as Maoists, or supporters of Maoists. We must state that we were aghast at the blindness to constitutional limitations of the State of Chattisgarh, and some of its advocates, in claiming that any one who questions the conditions of inhumanity that are rampant in many parts of that state

ought to necessarily be treated as Maoists, or their sympathizers, and yet in the same breath also claim that it needs the constitutional sanction, under our Constitution, to perpetrate its policies of ruthless violence against the people of Chattisgarh to establish a Constitutional order.

5. The problem, it is apparent to us, and would be so to most reasonable people, cannot be the people of Chattisgarh,whose human rights are widely acknowledged to being systemically, and on a vast scale, being violated by the Maoists/Naxalites on one side, and the State, and some of its agents, on the other. Nor is the problem with those well meaning, thoughtful and reasonable people who question those conditions. The problem rests in the amoral political economy that the State endorses, and the resultant revolutionary politics that it necessarily spawns. In a recent book titled '*The Dark Side of Globalization*' it has been observed that: '[T]he persistence of 'Naxalism', the Maoist revolutionary politics, in India after over six decades of parliamentary politics is a visible paradox in a democratic 'socialist' India.... India has come into the twenty-first century with a decade of departure from the Nehruvian socialism to a freemarket, rapidly globalizing economy, which has created new dynamics (and pockets) of deprivation along with economic growth. Thus the same set of issues, particularly those related to land, continue to fuel protest politics, violent agitator politics, as well as armed rebellion.... Are governments and political parties in India able to grasp the socio-economic dynamics encouraging these politics or are they stuck with a security-oriented approach that further fuels them?'[3]

6. That violent agitator politics, and armed rebellion in many pockets of India hav intimate linkages to socio economic circumstances, endemic inequalities, and a corrupt social and state order that preys on such inequalities has been well recognized. In fact the Union of India has been repeatedly warned of the linkages. In a recent report titled '*Development Challenges in Extremist Affected Areas*'[4], an expert group constituted by the Planning Commission of India makes the following concluding observations: 'The development paradigm pursued since independence has aggravated the prevailing discontent among the

marginalized sections of the society.... The development paradigm as conceived by policy makers has always imposed on these communities.... causing irreparable damage to these sections. The benefits of this paradigm have been disproportionately cornered by the dominant sections at the expense of the poor, who have borne most of the costs. Development which is insensitive to the needs of these communities has inevitably caused displacement and reduced them to a sub-human existence. In the case of tribes in particular it has ended up in destroying their social organization, cultural identity and resource base.... which cumulatively makes them increasingly vulnerable to exploitation.... The pattern of development and its implementation has increased corrupt practices of a rent seeking bureaucracy and rapacious exploitation by the contractors, middlemen, traders and the greedy sections of the larger society intent on grabbing their resources and violating their dignity.' (paras 1.18.1 and 1.18.2, emphasis supplied)

7. It is also a well known fact that Government reports understate, in staid prose, the actuality of circumstances. That an expert body constituted by the Planning Commission of India, Government of India, uses the word 'rapacious', connoting predation for satisfaction of inordinate greed, and subsistence by capture of living prey, is revelatory of the degree of human suffering that is being visited on vast sections of our fellow citizens. It can only be concluded that the expert body, in characterizing the state of existence of large numbers of our fellow citizens, in large tracts of India, as 'sub-human', is clearly indicating that such an existence is not merely on account of pre-existing conditions of significant material deprivation, but also that significant facets that are essential to human dignity have been systematically denied by the forces and mechanisms of the developmental paradigm unleashed by the State. Equally poignantly, and indeed tragically because the State in India seems to repeatedly insist on paying scant attention to such advice, the Expert Group further continues and advises: 'This concludes our brief review of various disturbing aspects of the socio-economic context that prevails in large parts of India today, and that may (and can) contribute to

politics such as that of the Naxalite movement or erupt as other forms of violence. It should be recognized that there are different kinds of movements, and that calling and treating them generally as unrest, a disruption of law and order, is little more than a rationale for suppressing them by force. It is necessary to contextualize the tensions in terms of social, economic and political background and bring back on the agenda the issues of the people — the right to livelihood, the right to life and a dignified and honourable existence.

The State itself should feel committed to the democratic and human rights and humane objectives that are inscribed in the Preamble, the Fundamental Rights and Directive Principles of the Constitution. The State has to adhere strictly to the Rule of Law. Indeed, the State has no other authority to rule.... It is critical for the Government to recognize that dissent or expression of dissatisfaction is a positive feature of democracy, that unrest is often the only thing that actually puts pressure on the government to make things work and for the government to live up to its own promises. However, the right to protest, even peacefully, is often not recognized by the authorities, and even non-violent agitations are met with severe repression ... What is surprising is not the fact of unrest, but the failure of the State to draw right conclusions from it. While the official policy documents recognize that there is a direct correlation between what is termed as extremism and poverty ... or point to the deep relationship between tribals and forests, or that the tribals suffer unduly from displacement, the governments have in practice treated unrest merely as a law and order problem. It is necessary to change this mindset and bring about congruence between policy and implementation. There will be peace, harmony and social progress only if there is equity, justice and dignity for everyone.' (paras 1.18.3 and 1.18.4, emphasis supplied)

8. Rather than heeding such advice, which echoes the wisdom of our Constitution, what we have witnessed in the instant proceedings have been repeated assertions of inevitability of muscular and violent statecraft. Such an approach, informing the decisions of the Government of Chattisgarh with respect to the situations in

Dantewada, and its neighbouring districts, seemingly also blinds them to thefact that lawless violence, in response to violence by the Maoist/Naxalite insurgency, has not, and will not, solve the problems, and that instead it will only perpetuate the cycles of more violent, both intensive and extensive, insurgency and counter-insurgency. The death toll revealed by the Government of Chattisgarh is itself indicative of this. The fact that the cycles of violence and counterviolence have now lasted nearly a decade ought to lead a reasonable person to conclude that the prognosis given by the expert committee of the Planning Commission to be correct.

9. The root cause of the problem, and hence its solution, lies elsewhere. The culture of unrestrained selfishness and greed spawned by modern neo-liberal economic ideology, and the false promises of ever increasing spirals of consumption leading to economic growth that will lift everyone, under-gird this socially, politically and economically unsustainable set of circumstances in vast tracts of India in general, and Chattisgarh in particular. It has been reported that: 'Among the rapidly growing urban middle class, the corporate world is in a hurry to expand its manufacturing capacity. That means more land for manufacturing and trading. The peasants and tribals are the natural victims of acquisitions and displacements. The expanded mining activities encroach upon the forest domain.... Infrastructure development needs more steel, cement and energy.... Lacking public sector capacities, the income-poor but resource-rich states of eastern India are awarding mining and land rights to Indian and multinational companies.... Most of these deposits lie in territory inhabited by poor tribals and that is where Naxals operate. Chattisgarh, a state of eastern India, has 23 per cent of India's iron ore deposits and abundant coal. It has signed memoranda of understanding and other agreements worth billions with Tata Steel and ArcelorMittal, De Beers Consolidated Mines, BHP Billion and Rio Tinto. Other states inviting big business and FDI have made similar deals.... The appearance of mining crews, construction workers and truckers in the forest has seriously alarmed the tribals who have lived in these regions from time immemorial.'[5]

10. The justification often advanced, by advocates of the neoliberal development paradigm, as historically followed, or newly emerging, in a more rapacious form, in India, is that unless development occurs, via rapid and vast exploitation of natural resources, the country would not be able to either compete on the global scale, nor accumulate the wealth necessary to tackle endemic and seemingly intractable problems of poverty, illiteracy, hunger and squalor. Whether such exploitation is occurring in a manner that is sustainable, by the environment and the existing social structures, is an oft debated topic, and yet hurriedly buried. Neither the policy makers nor the elite in India, who turn a blind eye to the gross and inhuman suffering of the displaced and the dispossessed, provide any credible answers. Worse still, they ignore historical evidence which indicates that a development paradigmdepending largely on the plunder and loot of the natural resources more often than not leads to failure of the State; and that on its way to such a fate, countless millions would have been condemned to lives of great misery and hopelessness.

11. The more responsible thinkers have written at length about 'resource curse', a curious phenomenon wherein countries and regions well endowed with resources are often the worst performers when it comes to various human development indicia. In comparison with countries dependant on agricultural exports, or whose development paradigm is founded upon broad based development of human resources of all segments of the population, such countries and regions suffer from 'unusually high poverty, poor health care, widespread malnutrition, high rates of child mortality, low life expectancy and poor educational performance'.[6]

12. Predatory forms of capitalism, supported and promoted by the State in direct contravention of constitutional norms and values, often take deep roots around the extractive industries. In India too, we find a great frequency of occurrence of more volatile incidents of social unrest, historically, and in the present, in resource rich regions, which paradoxically also suffer from low levels of human development. The argument that such a development paradigm is necessary, and its consequences inevitable, is untenable. The Constitution itself, in no

uncertain terms, demands that the State shall strive, incessantly and consistently, to promote fraternity amongst all citizens such that dignity of every citizen is protected, nourished and promoted. The Directive Principles, though not justiciable, nevertheless 'fundamental in the governance of the country', direct the State to utilize the material resources of the community for the common good of all, and not just of the rich and the powerful without any consideration of the human suffering that extraction of such resources impose on those who are sought to be dispossessed and disempowered. Complete justice — social, economic and political — is what our Constitution promises to each and every citizen. Such a promise, even in its weakest form and content, cannot condone policies that turn a blind eye to deliberate infliction of misery on large segments of our population.

13. Policies of rapid exploitation of resources by the private sector, without credible commitments to equitable distribution of benefits and costs, and environmental sustainability, are necessarily violative of principles that are 'fundamental to governance', and when such a violation occurs on a large scale, they necessarily also eviscerate the promise of equality before law, and equal protection of the laws, promised by Article 14, and the dignity of life assured by Article 21. Additionally, the collusion of the extractive industry, and in some places it is also called the mining mafia, and some agents of the State, necessarily leads to evisceration of the moral authority of the State, which further undermines both Article 14 and Article 21. As recognized by the Expert Committee of the Planning Commission, any steps taken by the State, within the paradigm of treating such volatile circumstances as simple law and order problems, to perpetrate large scale violence against the local populace, would only breed more insurgency, and ever more violent protests. Some scholars have noted that complexities of varieties of political violence in India are rooted: 'as much in the economic relations of the country as in its stratified social structure.... [E]ntrenched feudal structures, emerging commercial interests, new alliances and the nexus between entrenched order, new interests, political elites and the bureaucracy, and deficient

public infrastructure andfacilities perpetuate exploitation. The resulting miseries have made these sections of the population vulnerable to calls for revolutionary politics....India's development dichotomy has also had a destabilizing impact on people's settled lives. For decades, the Indian state has failed to provide alternative livelihoods to those displaced by developmental projects. According to an estimate, between 1951 and 1990, 8.5 million members of ST's were displaced by developmental projects. Representing over 40 per cent of all the displaced people, only 25 per cent of them were rehabilitated.... Although there are no definitive data, Dalits and Adivasis have been reported to form a large proportion of the Maoists' foot soldiers.... A study of atrocities against these two sections of society revealscorrespondence between the prevalence and spread of Naxalism and the geographic location of atrocities.... The susceptibility of the vulnerable continues under the new emerging context of the liberalization, marketization and globalization of the Indian economy, which have added new dominance structures to the existing ones.'[7]

14. What is ominous, and forebodes grave danger to the security and unity of this nation, the welfare of all of our people, and the sanctity of our constitutional vision and goals, is that the State is drawing the wrong conclusions, as pointed out by the Expert Group of the Planning Commission cited earlier. Instead of locating the problem in the socioeconomic matrix, and the sense of disempowerment wrought by the false developmental paradigm without a human face, the powers that be in India are instead propagating the view that this obsession with economic growth is our only path, and that the costs borne by the poor and the deprived, disproportionately, are necessary costs. Amit Bhaduri, a noted economist, has observed: 'If we are to look a little beyond our middle class noses, beyond the world painted by mainstream media, the picture is less comforting, less assuring.... Once you step outside the charmed circle of a privileged minority expounding on the virtues of globalization, liberalization and privatization, things appear less certain.... According to the estimate of the Ministry of Home Affairs, some 120 to 160 out of a total of

607 districts are 'Naxal infested'. Supported by a disgruntled and dispossessed peasantry, the movement has spread to nearly one-fourth of Indian territory. And yet, all that this government does is not to face the causes of the rage and despair that nurture such movements; instead it considers it a menace, a law and order problem.... that is to be rooted out by the violence of the state, and congratulates itself when it uses violence effectively to crush the resistance of the angry poor.... For the sake of higher growth, the poor in growing numbers will be left out in the cold, undernourished, unskilled and illiterate, totally defenceless against the ruthless logic of a global market.... [T]his is not merely an iniquitous process. High growth brought about in this manner does not simply ignore the question of income distribution, its reality is far worse. It threatens the poor with a kind of brutal violence in the name of development, a sort of 'developmental terrorism', violence perpetrated on the poor in the name of development by the state primarily in the interest of corporate aristocracy, approved by the IMF and the World Bank, and a self-serving political class....Academics and media persons have joined the political chorus of presenting the developmental terrorism as a sign of progress, an inevitable cost of development. The conventional wisdom of our time is that, There Is No Alternative.... And yet this so widely agreed upon model of development is fatally flawed. It has already been rejected and will be rejected again by the growing strength of our democratic polity, and by direct resistance of the poor threatened with 'developmental terrorism'.

15. As if the above were not bad enough, another dangerous strand of governmental action seems to have been evolved out of the darkness that has begun to envelope our policy makers, with increasing blindness to constitutional wisdom and values. On the one hand the State subsidises the private sector, giving it tax break after tax break, while simultaneously citing lack of revenues as the primary reason for not fulfilling its obligations to provide adequate cover to the poor through social welfare measures. On the other hand, the State seeks to arm the youngsters amongst the poor with guns to combat the anger, and unrest, amongst the poor.

16. Tax breaks for the rich, and guns for the youngsters amongst poor, so that they keep fighting amongst [15] themselves, seems to be the new mantra from the mandarins of security and high economic policy of the State. This, apparently, is to be the grand vision for the development of a nation that has constituted itself as a sovereign, secular, socialist and democratic republic. Consequently, questions necessarily arise as to whether the policy makers, and the powers that be, are in any measure being guided by constitutional vision, values, and limitations that charge the State with the positive obligation of ensuring the dignity of all citizens.

17. What the mandarins of high policies forget is that a society is not a forest where one could combat an accidental forest fire by starting a counter forest fire that is allegedly controlled. Human beings are not individual blades of dry grass. As conscious beings, they exercise a free will. Armed, the very same groups can turn, and often have turned, against other citizens, and the State itself. Recent history is littered with examples of the dangers of armed vigilante groups that operate under the veneer of State patronage or support.

18. Such misguided policies, albeit vehemently and muscularly asserted by some policy makers, are necessarily contrary to the vision and imperatives of our constitution which demands that the power vested in the State, by the people, be only used for the welfare of the people — all the people, both rich and the poor — thereby assuring conditions of human dignity within the ambit of fraternity amongst groups of them. Neither Article 14, nor Article 21, can even remotely be conceived as being so bereft of substance as to be immune from such policies. They are necessarily tarnished, and violated in a primordial sense by such policies. The creation of such a miasmic [16] environment of dehumanization of youngsters of the deprived segments of our population, in which guns are given to them rather than books, to stand as guards for the rapine, plunder and loot in our forests, would be to lay the road to national destruction. It is necessary to note here that this Court had to intercede and order the Government of Chattisgarh to get the security forces to vacate the schools and hostels that they had occupied; and even after such

orders, many schools and hostels still remain in the possession and occupancy of the security forces. Such is the degree of degeneration of life, and society. Facts speak for themselves.

19. Analyzing the causes for failure of many nation-states, in recent decades, Robert I. Rotberg, a professor of the Kennedy School, Harvard University, posits the view that '(N)ation-states exist to provide a decentralized method of delivering political (public) goods to persons living within designated parameters (borders).... They organize and channel the interests of their people, often but not exclusively in furtherance of national goals and values.' Amongst the purposes that nation-states serve, that are normatively expected by citizenries, are included the task of buffering or manipulation of 'external forces and influences', and mediation between 'constraints and challenges' of the external and international forces and the dynamics of 'internal economic, political, and social realities'. In particular he notes: 'States succeed or fail across all or some of these dimensions. But it is according to their performance — according to the levels of their effective delivery of the most crucial political goods — that strong states may be distinguished from weak ones, and weak states from failed or collapsed states.... There is a hierarchy of political goods. None is as crucial as the supply of security, especially human security. Individuals alone, almost exclusively in special or particular circumstances, can attempt to secure themselves. Or groups of individuals can band together to organize and purchase goods or services that maximize their sense of security. Traditionally, and usually, however, individuals and groups cannot easily or effectively substitute private security for the full spectrum of public security. The state's prime function is to provide that political good of security — to prevent cross-border invasions and infiltrations, to eliminate domestic threats to or attacks upon the national order and social structure... and to stabilize citizens to resolve their disputes with the state and with their fellow human inhabitants without recourse to arms or other forms of physical coercion.'[8]

20. The primary task of the State is the provision of security to all its citizens, without violating human dignity. This would necessarily imply

the undertaking of tasks that would prevent the emergence of great dissatisfaction, and disaffection, on account of the manner and mode of extraction, and distribution, of natural resources and organization of social action, its benefits and costs. Our Directive Principles of State Policy explicitly recognize this. Our Constitution posits that unless we secure for our citizens conditions of social, economic and political justice for all who live in India, we would not have achieved human dignity for our citizens, nor would we be in a position to promote fraternity amongst groups of them. Policies that run counter to that essential truth are necessarily destructive of national unity and integrity. To pursue socio-economic policies that cause vast disaffection amongst the poor, creating conditions of violent politics is a proscribed feature of our Constitution. To arrive at such a situation, in actuality on account of such policies, and then claim that there are not enough resources to tackle the resulting socio-political unrest, and violence, within the framework of constitutional values amounts to an abdication of constitutional responsibilities. To claim that resource crunch prevents the State from developing appropriate capacity in ensuring security for its citizens through well trained formal police and security forces that are capable of working within the constitutional framework would be an abandonment of a primordial function of the State. To pursue policies whereby guns are distributed amongst barely literate youth amongst the poor to control the disaffection in such segments of the population would be tantamount to sowing of suicide pills that could divide and destroy society. Our youngsters are our most precious resource, to be nurtured for a better tomorrow. Given the endemic inequalities in our country, and the fact that we are increasingly, in a demographic sense, a young population, such a policy can necessarily be expected to lead to national disaster.

21. Our constitution is most certainly not a 'pact for national suicide.'[1] In the least, its vision does enable us, as constitutional adjudicators to recognize, and prevent, the emergence, and the institutionalization, of a policing paradigm, the end point of which can only mean that the entire nation, in short order, might have to gasp: 'The horror! The

horror!'

22. It is in light of the above that we necessarily have to examine the issues discussed below, and pass appropriate orders. We have heard at length the learned senior counsel, Shri. Ashok H. Desai, appearing on behalf of the petitioners, and learned senior counsel, Shri. Harish N. Salve and Shri. M.N. Krishnamani appearing for the State of Chattisgarh. We have also heard learned Solicitor General of India, Shri Gopal Subrahmanyam, appearing for the Union of India.

——————————J.
(B.SUDERSHAN REDDY)
——————————J.
(SURINDER SINGH NIJJAR)
New Delhi,
July 5, 2011

1. Joseph Conrad - *Heart of Darkness and Selected Short Fiction* (Barnes and Noble Classics, 2003).
2 Joseph Conrad - *Geography and Some Explorers*, National Geography magazine, Vol 45, 1924.
3. Ajay K. Mehra, *Maoism in a globalizing India* in *The Dark Side of Globalization,* eds. jorge Heine & Ramesh Thakur (United Nations University Press, 2011)
4. Report of an Expert Group to Planning Commission, Government of India (New Delhi, April, 2008)
5. Ajay K. Mehra, supra note
6. Joseph E. Stiglitz, *Making Natural Resources into a Blessing Rather than a Curse,* in 'Covering Oil", eds., Svetlana Tsalik and Arya Schiffrin, Open Society Institute (2005).
7. Ajay K. Mehra, supra note
8. *The Failure and Collapse of Nation-States — Breakdown, Prevention and Failure in When States Fail: Causes and Consequences,* Robert I. Rotberg, Ed, Princeton University Press (2004).18
9. (2005) 5 SCC 51758

Supreme Court Order: 'As Much a Lesson for the Maoists as for the Government'

Appeal to both the Maoists and the government to initiate peace talks on the basis of justice and constitutional principles, since ultimately that is the only way forward'— Nandini Sundar, Ramachandra Guha, Sriram Srinivasan, E.A.S. Sarma (Petitioners in WP 250/2007)

The petioners' statement on Supreme Court order dated 5.7.11 on *Salwa Judum*/SPOs by justice Sudershan Reddy and Justice SS Nijjar.

We warmly welcome the order by Justice Reddy and Justice Nijjar directing the State of Chhattisgarh to stop using Special Police Officers (SPOs) in counterinsurgency operations, disarm them and stop supporting vigilante movements by any name. We also welcome the order to the Centre directing it to cease from financially supporting SPOs to engage in counterinsurgency. Judging from the personal reactions we have had ' from a very wide variety of people many of whom we do not even know ' the order has been widely hailed as a landmark restatement of constitutional values. If the state is to be recognised as legitimate it must act lawfully and cannot sacrifice the law and Constitution for immediate expediency. As the judges have so succinctly observed the power of the people vested in any organ of the State, and its agents, can only be used for promotion of constitutional values and vision. However, judging by the reaction of the Home Ministry and the Chhattisgarh government, this basic constitutional principle is being willfully ignored. This simply reinforces the point that the judgement makes about the way in which the respondents are undermining the Constitution and thereby the basic human values enshrined in it. Instead of accepting the Court order for the sake of good governance and the national interest, they are talking about a review petition. Right from 2007 when the case was first heard before the Chief Justice of the Supreme Court, the highest court in the land has consistently maintained that the state cannot arm civilians. This, it is clear from the record, has been the considered opinion of not simply Justices Reddy and Nijjar, who issued the present order, but of the judges at previous hearings, such as Justice Balakrishnan, Justice Kapadia, and Justice Aftab Alam.

That the SPOs and *Salwa Judum* have been engaged in horrific crimes is a matter of record. The judgment therefore directs the State of Chhattisgarh investigate all previously inappropriately or incompletely investigated instances of alleged criminal activities of *Salwa Judum*, or those popularly known as Koya Commandos, filing of appropriate FIRs and diligent prosecution. At the same time, the judgment is as much a lesson for the Maoists as for the government. It makes it clear that the Maoists too cannot take the law into their own lands. For when the Constitution does swing into action, it has the power of people's aspirations behind it, and is a far more powerful and credible weapon in their hands than the gun.As the judges say, the fight against Maoist/Naxalite violence cannot be conducted purely as a mere law and order problem to be confronted by whatever means the State can muster. The primordial problem lies deep within the socio-economic policies pursued by the State on a society that was already endemically, and horrifically, suffering from gross inequalities. Consequently, the fight against Maoists/Naxalites is no less a fight for moral, constitutional and legal authority over the minds and hearts of our people. Our constitution provides the gridlines within which the State is to act, both to assert such authority, and also initiate, nurture and sustain such authority. We therefore appeal to the Maoists to join all right thinking citizens in hailing this historic judgment and to desist from harming SPOs, or any other group of citizens in any way. They should be allowed to peacefully reintegrate into their villages. We also appeal to both the Maoists and the government to initiate peace talks on the basis of justice and constitutional principles, since ultimately that is the only way forward.

Jul 10, 2011

source: Outlook magazine

Appeal for Talks with Broader Section of People's Struggles in the Forest and Mineral Belt

Aditya Nigam, Dilip Simeon, Jairus Banaji, Nivedita Menon,
Rohini Hensman, Satya Sivaraman, Sumit Sarkar and Tanika Sarkar

In the light of the recent demands raised by sections of the intelligentsia urging the government to heed the CPI(Maoist) 'offer of talks', we insist that 'civil society' should rather, put pressure on the government to initiate talks with representatives of all struggling popular and *Adivasi* organisations. The CPI(Maoist) cannot be treated as the sole spokesperson of all the people in the forest and mineral belt, convenient though this may be for the state and for that party. Does the government believe that violent insurgents are the only deserving interlocutors?

There is a common pattern to the emergence of Maoist violence in many areas. First a non-violent mass organisation like the PCPA in West Bengal or *Chasi Muliya Adivasi Sangh* (CMAS) in Odisha arises in response to marginalisation, displacement or violence against tribals by the police and paramilitaries. Then the Maoists step in, attempting to take over the movement and giving it a violent turn. The state responds with even more violence, which is directed not only against the Maoists but also against unaffiliated *Adivasis*. At this point, some *Adivasis* join the Maoists in self-defence, their leaders like Chhatradhar Mahato, Lalmohan Tudu, Singanna are either arrested or gunned down in fake encounters and large numbers of unaffiliated *Adivasis* are branded Maoists or Maoist sympathisers and arrested, killed or terrorised by the state. Clearly, Maoist violence in these cases obtains legitimacy because of the unbridled use of force by security forces and violations of the Fundamental Rights of the local people. On the other hand, the unilateral and doctrinal use of the language of warfare by one armed group obscures the political agency of the ordinary people who have had no say in this declaration. It also tramples on the human rights of the often desperately poor people who are obliged to seek a livelihood in organisations of the state. Furthermore, it is not clear that the CPI(Maoist) actually shares the rejection of this kind of 'development' by the people of the area, or whether it only wants to wrest control of this process from the Indian state.

The counter-insurgency operations mounted by the Central government in these areas has led to unprecedented bloodshed, massacres of civilian populations and rampant violations of constitutional rights in the area. The Central government insists on treating the affected areas as a 'war zone', and has shown little inclination towards tackling the huge backlog of tribal oppression that has created fertile ground for such violence. It is also true that whenever the government has conceded space, the conditions for this have been created by mass movements, not by the military actions of the CPI(Maoist). For example, the decision by the Ministry of Environment and Forests to put on hold the agreements with *Vedanta* and POSCO in Odisha because of non-compliance with legal requirements for obtaining the consent of local *Adivasis*, comes in the wake of sustained joint struggles by a range of political groupings.

We therefore urge all democratic sections to put pressure on the government to ensure that : (1) Regardless of whether talks with the Maoists materialise, talks should immediately be initiated with those *Adivasis* who are losing their land; and with representatives of the various mass-based organisations/mass movements, if necessary by securing their release from prison. (2) round-the-clock security from attacks by both Maoists and state-sponsored groups and security personnel, is provided to these representatives and their families, as well as to witnesses in cases like the Gompad massacre and their families; (3) the grievances voiced by these representatives be treated with the utmost seriousness and addressed as soon as possible.

Maoist violence flourishes in the foetid atmosphere provided by the destruction of the rule of law and rampant human rights abuses by the state. It is the task of the government to ensure that the rule of law is respected by all sides in the mineral and forest belt. If the rights of the *Adivasis* to freedom of association and of expression, including the right to oppose current 'development' policies, are respected, and crucially, if this dissent is taken into account by the government, Maoists will lose credibility. The party's violent methods, often designed to cause collateral damage, will lose the support it currently obtains among sections of the disaffected population in these areas.

Source : Kafila.org/posted March 2, 2010

Excerpts from Development Challenges in Extremist Affected Areas — Report of an Expert Group to Planning Commission, 2008

Investigating the People's Discontent and Support For Extremists

3.1.1 The analysis of roots of discontent, unrest and extremism rely upon extensive discussions based on official reports in the past, publications from the extremist groups, reports of human rights groups, books by observers of such developments, and media coverage in the background of field insight and interaction of members of the Expert Group. This has revealed that the causes are varied depending on characteristics of an area; social, economic and cultural background; a history of not working out solutions to lingering structural problems; and ineffective application of ameliorative steps undertaken since Independence and more so since the mid-sixties of the last century. Dissent movements, including the extremist Naxalite movement, are not confined to difficult hilly and forested areas but cover large contiguous tracts in the plains. They are not limited to dryland areas of recurring crop failures but extend to irrigated commands of major irrigation systems, as in the state of Bihar. The causes are, therefore, complex. The intensity of unrest resulting in extremist methods and effort to resolve issues through violent means as a challenge to State authority is in response to the gathering of unresolved social and economic issues for long durations. It creates the impression that policy making and administration responds to extreme means. The more recent development is in the emergence of CPI(Maoist) after the merger and consolidation two powerful Naxalite streams in September, 2004. This new formation, since its inception, is defining the official understanding of the extremist phenomenon of the level of the state as well as the Union government. This has appeared in the public perception as a simplisticlaw-and-order face-off between the official coercive machinery and this more radical extremist political formation. The social consequence results, then, in undermining instruments of social and economic amelioration as well as processes of democratic exchange to resolve persisting issues. This is the crux of the problem.

3.1.2 Perhaps due to the Union government's attention to the CPI(Maoist) (formed by the merger of CPIM-L (Peoples War) with Maoist Communist, Centre (MCC) in September 2004) and its association to the Naxalite phenomenon, that party and its method of functioning have started defining the official understanding of the Naxalite movement. That is neither factually accurate nor adequate for discussing the proper governmental response to it. There is no need to go into the history and genealogy of the Naxalite movement, but it is necessary to state that there are a very large number of Naxalite groups/parties, and their method of functioning differs in regard to the extent of mobilisation of the people, participation of people in their actions, role of armed underground cadre, etc., though all of them owe allegiance to the idea that the Indian State must be overthrown by force as a precondition of revolutionary change in our society. Some of them even have representatives in elected bodies from the panchayats to the legislatures. The unrest this report is concerned about is also not reducible to dramatic incidents such as blowing up or blasting of police stations but encompasses also mass unrest. Mass participation in militant protest has always been a characteristic of Naxalite mobilisation, not only in Bihar, but also elsewhere. The ban placed by many state governments, and at the national level by the Unlawful Activities (Prevention) Act, on the Maoist party and its mass organisations, and the formal and informal prohibition imposed by the police on such activity in the case of other Naxalite groups, has often rendered such mass activity virtually impossible. But that is no reason for ignoring the fact that the unrest this report is concerned with has often had mass character.

3.1.3 In what follows various issues concerning the life and livelihood of the people are discussed wherein the failure, inadequacy or injustice of State mechanisms and institutions created space for Naxalite activities. Such a description may help people to appreciate why Naxalites derive support. It is the purpose of this report to see how the government may eliminate the causes of unrest by constitutional and legal means and restore faith of the affected population in the system of governance established by the constitution and law.

3.1.4 However, the fact that the Naxalites employ methods of violence in tackling these issues has other consequences, which include injury, fear and disruption of normal life. It is also a fact that Naxalite activity is not confined to solving people's grievances. They are engaged in a violent fight against the State for overpowering and overthrowing it. This fight has its adverse consequences in terms of the injury and disruption it causes. The link between what the report deals with, and what it does not, lies in the fact that it is in the course of providing answers to the people's problems and needs that the Naxalite movement seeks to obtain their support from the masses.

Land Related Factors

3.2.1 The origin of the popular slogan 'land to the tiller' is in absentee landlordism, where the landlord would merely take the lion's share of the produce without contributing anything to the production of the crop. It was in this context that the freedom fighters demanded that the one who tills the land must own it, and the post independence government was committed to it. Absentee landlords do exist even today, but today's land relations are much more complex. So though the aspiration of 'land to the tiller' continues to be given, the focus of the Naxalite movement is on trying to provide land, whether the land of landlords or government land, to the landless. In occupying landlords' land, the Naxalites have not taken law as their reference point. It is not the ceiling-surplus land of the landlords that they have sought to put in the possession of the landless. Rather, they have targeted landholders whose holding is sizeable as they see it, or who are otherwise oppressive or cruel in their conduct, or hostile towards the Naxalite movement, even if they are not big landlords. Such landholders have in many cases been driven away from the villages and their land sought to be put in the possession of the landless poor. On some occasions, led by armed Naxalite cadre, the poor have sought to march on to the land and plant red flags in it, in symbolic occupation of the land. However, in many cases, the police have intervened, filed criminal cases against such landless poor, including cases under TADA/POTA when those Acts were in force, and ensured that the poor do not enjoy the land on the ground that they are encroachers. Where the landholder feels too threatened to come back and take possession of the land, the land remains fallow. This is the situation in parts of Andhra Pradesh. There is no estimate of the total extent of such land lying fallow in the State, but there is little doubt that it runs into tens of thousands of acres, especially in Warangal, Karimnagar and Adilabad districts.

The erstwhile landlord himself is in many cases willing to let the government of Andhra Pradesh assign the land to the poor identified by the Maoists provided some of it is left to him, but the government has resisted this resolution of the problem on the ground that it would sanctify lawlessness. Thousands of acres of land thus remain fallow. Where the landholder is prepared to re-occupy the land, as in much of Bihar, the entire efforts of the Naxalites to redistribute the land fails. But all said and done, considering the central place the slogan of land to the tiller has in Naxalite politics, their attempt at redistribution of private land has been meagre. And even that little has been defeated by the State's determined opposition to letting lawless means succeed, even for the beneficial purpose of giving land to the landless. If the government can get over these unnecessary qualms, it should be possible to devise legal means appropriate to each instance to ensure that the landless get the land. Some of the land can probably be taken over under land reform laws and distributed to the poor. Some may have to be purchased or acquired from the landholder. But where the landholder has been targeted by the Naxalites for political reasons and not because he has unconscionable extent of land, it may be the right thing to hand back the land to the landholder. Equity and law require that all lands of the owners having less than ceiling should be handed back to the owners subject to prevailing laws. Excesses of the Naxalites in this regard are not only unjustified but deserve utmost censure.

3.2.2 The Naxalites seem to have had greater success with government lands. Though no precise estimates are available, it is a fact that in some cases the Naxalite movement has succeeded in helping the landless to occupy a substantial extent of government land whether for homesteads or for cultivation. In Bihar all the Naxalite parties have attempted to assist, in their respective areas of influence, the landless Musahars, the lowest among the dalits, to take possession of a sizable extent of such land. But the poor remain without title to the land because the administration again feels that giving them title or even a conditional assignment (in which the assignee can use the land and pass it on to the heirs but cannot sell the land) would sanctify law-breaking and strengthen the Naxalites. Such qualms appear reasonable only if they are divorced from the reality that the government has the power to distribute such land to the poor, but has failed to do so. To defuse social tension government may regularise these occupations if the occupiers are otherwise eligible. [*Committee of Concerned Citizens (2002)*].

3.2.3 In the case of forest land, occupation by the *Adivasis* with the encouragement and assistance of the Naxalites, has taken place on an extensive scale in Andhra Pradesh, Chhattisgarh, the Vidarbha region of Maharashtra, Odisha and Jharkhand. In fact much of it is not fresh occupation but re- assertion of traditional usufructory rights declared by the law to be illegal. Properly conducted forest settlement proceedings should have protected at least the pre-existing rights, but much of forest settlement proceedings has taken place behind the back and over the head of the *Adivasi* forest dwellers.

3.2.4 The government's statistics show that 39% of what is called forest encroachment in the whole country has taken place in the above region. Much of it, as said above, is not encroachment but occupation that far pre-dates forest reservation and forest laws. Prior to 1980 the various state governments would off and on acknowledge this fact by regularising the occupation, thereby giving back what has been unilaterally taken away. But the Forest Conservation Act, 1980 put an end to such regularisation, and put the forest dwellers perpetually on the brink of eviction from their own habitat. This enabled the Naxalites to step into the vacuum to espouse the popular cause and secure popular support. The fear of Naxalite armed resistance deterred the repressive and depredatory moves of the authorities.

3.2.5 However, this occupation has remained a major bone of contention between the *Adivasis* and the State. While the forest department is inhibited by the threat of the Naxalites or the Naxalite-supported militancy of the *Adivasis*, the police see in the affected areas a 'Naxalite' in many a tribal and subject them to considerable harassment. A feeble attempt at providing a right of regularisation of at least pre-1980 occupation was made by the Union government in 1990 following the recommendations of the 29th report of the Commissioner for SCs and STs, but that remedy remained on paper — because the proof of occupation the claimant had to produce was onerous, and in any case no effort was made to educate the likely beneficiaries about the policy. But now with the enactment of Scheduled Tribes and Other Traditional Forest Dwellers (Recognition of Forest Rights) Act 2007 (Act 2 of 2007), it should be possible to resolve the issue by giving formal recognition to such rights. One can envisage some difficulties such as proof of occupation as on 13 Dec 2005, and if they are no dealt with imaginatively, the imaginatively drafted law may not deliver all that it promises. But it still holds a promise of a better deal for such forest dwellers.

3.2.6 In the matter of tenancy rights, in Bihar, the form of tenancy has over the years shifted to sharecropping in the areas of Naxalite influence. Perhaps a cmprehensive registration of sharecroppers on the lines of the registration of bargadars in West Bengal would consolidate this gain.

3.2.7. The High Level Committee constituted by the Planning Commission to review the National Mineral Policy (2007) has made several far reaching recommendations on simplification and streamlining of the procedures for granting mineral leases with a view to provide an impetus to mineral development. The [Central] government has considered these recommendations and, by and large, adopted them. Considering that mineral resources are largely located inthe predominantly tribal tracts in the country, it is important that mineral exploration and development activity is carried out in such a way that (i) it is consistent with and non-intrusive of the rights and privileges conferred on the tribals under the Fifth Schedule and (ii) it causes least disturbance to the ecology that surrounds the tribal habitats. In this regard, it is necessary to keep in view the guidelines laid down by the Hon'ble Supreme Court in the Samata case (referred earlier). The local tribal communities, through their Gram Sabhas, should be fully involved in any decision taken on mining in the first instance. Even if mining were to be taken up in exceptional cases, as already referred to, the Constitutional rights of the tribals in regard to ownership of the land and its resources should be fully protected.

Displacement

3.3.1 Internal displacement caused by irrigation/mining/industrial projects, resulting in landlessness and hunger, is a major cause of distress among the poor, especially the *Adivasis*. It is well known that 40% of all the people displaced by dams in the last sixty years are forest-dwelling *Adivasis*. Other forms of distress have added to this unconscionable figure. The law and administration provides no succour to displaced people, and in fact often treats them with hostility since such internally displaced forest-dwellers tend to settle down again in some forest region, which is prohibited by the law. The Naxalite movement has come to the aid of such victims of enforced migration in the teeth of the law.

3.3.2 Adivasis displaced by irrigation projects in Orissa (now Odisha) now have migrated to the forests of Visakhapatnam district of Andhra Pradesh in large numbers. They would have been evicted from there by the forest department of Andhra Pradesh but for the presence of the Naxalite movement. However, the perceived support of the Naxalites for these immigrants has led to harassment caused to them by the police. They have been repeatedly arrested and jailed for sheltering the Naxalites. Over the years, the administration too has come to accept the presence of these internally displaced *Adivasis*. And the recently enacted Forest Dwellers Act of 2007 may now put an end to the state's confrontation with them. However, a legal problem remains. The Presidential order issued under Art 342 of the Constitution declares the list of Scheduled tribes State-wise. A tribe that migrates from one state to another where it is not habitually resident would not be a Scheduled tribe in that State and would get none of the protection the law offers. The immigrants from Odisha were initially identified as the Samantha tribe, which finds no mention in the list of Scheduled tribes in A.P. The recognition that they are Kondhs has resolved the problem for these people, but such a situation could repeat itself. Unless the law declares that at least in so far as Central legislation or administrative orders are concerned, a Scheduled tribe recognised as such in any state is eligible for the benefits all over the country, internally displaced *Adivasis* who have crossed state borders will remain without any protection in law. Since non-inclusion of a tribe in a state's list only means that the tribe is not found there, and not that it lacks tribal characteristics in that state, such a prescription would do no harm to the purpose of identification of Scheduled tribes under the Constitution. Indeed there is no reason why the same rule cannot be adopted for state egislation too. A group of *Adivasis* recognised ST in any state should be recognised all over the country in respect of their legal and other developmental entitlements.

3.3.3 But displacement caused by major projects is not the only cause of migration. Landlessness, extremes of poverty and social oppression can also be causes of displacement. Landless *Adivasis* mainly of the Muria or Gothi Koya tribe of Chhattisgarh have long been crossing over into the forests of Khammam district of Andhra Pradesh in search of land, with the support of the Naxalites. Again, both the forest and police departments came down heavily on them and set their hamlets on fire in incident after incident from 1989 till about 2002. But due to the interventions of civil society bodies the immigrants have stood their ground and today their presence is informally accepted by the administration. The same Act of 2007 can come to their rescue but Muria is not a recognised Scheduled tribe in A.P., and the issue whether its other name, Gothi Koya, is the same as the Kottu Koya found in the A.P list of Scheduled tribes is as yet unresolved.

3.3.4. In many places local inhabitants formed resistance groups when the Naxalites severely interfered with their traditional life style. However these resistance groups were converted into vigilante groups sponsored by the authorities over a period of time. In Chhattisgarh, the group is called *Salwa Judum*. Some members of this group are appointed as Special Police Officers (SPOs). Some of them are given arms training and are provided with fire arms. Often these vigilante groups fight with armed Naxalite groups making the tribals fight the tribal. As a principle of good governance such a situation is not desirable.

3.3.5. These vigilante groups, inhabitants of tribal villages, who had moved out are put in camps along with some arterial roads. Such migrants have left behind their agricultural land, some of their livestock and other means of production and livelihood. Most of them do not like their camp life which has discipline and constraints.

3.3.6. Moreover, through this process of forced migration, many tribals have left their villages and even State and migrated into neighbouring States. This involuntary displacement and migration has caused further distress among the tribals and created administrative problems for the host State. In the State of Bihar, through social oppression, many dalits had to move from their traditional habitat and moved elsewhere. They were victims of upper caste atrocities. New habitats of such migrant dalits have become a source of further social tension. It is, therefore, time to think about a comprehensive policy frame in which such internal displacement of different groups of population, whether tribal or dalit, does not take place and in case it happens there should be a government policy to take care of such a situation. Through this process of forced migration large mineral areas got vacated where the mining corporate lessees are starting operation. Often the displaced persons look on hopelessly and sometimes they seek support of the Naxalite groups. Such situations create space for Naxalite interventions.

3.3.7 In Bihar, there have been many instances where dalits suffering social oppression, and in recent times victims of the massacres perpetrated by the caste senas such as *Ranbir Sena*, have had to flee their hamlets and settle elsewhere. Indeed, prevention of the depredations of the caste Senas is the state's duty in the first instance. It has failed not only in that but also in providing protection to the victims so that they are not forced to migrate, or at least shelter and livelihood at the places where they have migrated to. The victims have received that help from the Naxalites. The trauma of displacement for which the state does not provide succour creates space for violent movement.

3.3.8 Considering the widespread phenomenon of internal displacement in the country, it is time the [sentral government devised a policy to provide minimal security to such displaced populations. Their immediate problems are shelter and livelihood. In the absence of any policy in this regard, they are prey to all manner of exploitation. The Muria (Gothi Koya) immigrants from Chhattisgarh have, in their desperation, been a source of extremely cheap labour in building construction and civil works of all kinds in the parts of A.P that they have migrated to.

3.4 Livelihood

3.4.1 The Minimum Wages Act remains an act on paper in much of rural India. Agricultural labour is governed by the Act but the minimum wage rates under the Act are not implemented, except where the prosperity of the farmers and the demand for labour makes it unavoidable. In the areas of their activity, it is reported that Naxalites have ensured payment of decent wage rates, though they have not usually gone by the statutory minimum wage rates. The rates they have ensured are sometimes higher and sometimes lower than the statutory rate. Their orientation to rights is in general not governed by statutory entitlement but what they regard as just and fair, taking all factors that they believe to be relevant into consideration.

3.4.2 There are also large areas of labour not governed by the Minimum Wages Act. This includes categories where there is no discernible employer, which is for this reason included in the category of self-employment. Since the Naxalites are in any case not bothered whether or not there is a law governing the right they are espousing, they have intervened and determined fair wage rates in their perception in all labour processes in their areas of influence. This includes wages for washing clothes, making pots, tending cattle, repairing implements, etc. Naxalites have secured increases in the rate of payment for the picking of tendu leaf which is used for rolling beedies, in the forest areas of Andhra Pradesh, Chhattisgarh, Odisha, Maharashtra, and Jharkhand. This was a very major source of exploitation of *Adivasi* labour, and while the government knowingly ignored it, the Naxalites put an effective end to it. The exploitation was so severe that the rates have over the years increased up to fifty times what the tendu patta contractors used to pay before the Naxalites stepped in. It is therefore necessary for the State to provide for Minimum Support Price (MSP) for all types of minor minerals and forest produce and institutionally efficient procurement systems.

3.4.3 For quite some time the Central government has been toying with the idea of an umbrella legislation for unorganised labour, and in general for all forms of labour left out of labour welfare legislation. The Second National Labour Commission's recommendations are with the Government. Perhaps soon we will see a law made, but quite apart from the adequacy of the recommendations made by the said Commission and indeed the suitability of the very notion of a single umbrella legislation to provide a cushion in times of need rather than detailed entitlements, any such law will be of little use unless effective measures are taken to see that it is implemented. Otherwise, such law will meet the same fate as the Minimum Wages Act. The Report of the National Commission For Enterprise in the Unorganised Sector, August, 2007 recommends a legislation for the workers of this sector and also provides a draft of the proposed bill.

3.4.4 Enjoyment of common property resources as a traditional right by cattle-herds, fishing communities, toddy toppers, stone workers, has become vulnerable due to the appropriation of these resources by the dominant sections of society or by the others with their support. The Naxalites have tried to ensure the protection of this right wherever they are active. This is an area where there is in general no legislative protection at all of traditional rights, though some States have some policies which tend in that direction. Legislative protection of an umbrella nature should be considered by the Central Government.

3.4.5 The Equal Remuneration Act which mandates payment of equal wages for men and women for work requiring the same skill and effort is another law that is observed exclusively in the breach. The Naxalites too have not paid much attention to ensuring payment of equal wage for the sexes but it is without doubt a source of discontent.

3.5 Social Oppression

3.5.1 The fight against the social oppression that the dalits and the lower among the OBCs have been regularly subjected to is perhaps the most significant among the issues used by the Naxalite movement. Besides taking up and resolving individual issues, the movement has given confidence to the oppressed to assert their equality and demand respect and dignity from the dominant castes and classes. Impolite forms of address that the dalits were subjected to, and the prohibition in the matter of wearing clean clothes and footwear in the presence of upper castes, or while passing through their localities, and the compulsion to address them as dora or malik and other such oppressive practices, have by and large been brought to an end in their areas of work. The everyday humiliation and sexual exploitation of labouring women of dalit communities by upper caste men is another form of oppression that has been successfully fought. Forced labour (*begari* and *vetti chakri*) by which the toiling castes had to provide their caste obligations free to the upper castes was also put an end to in many parts of the country, especially the Telangana districts of Andhra Pradesh.

3.5.2 This is an area where the duty of the State is laid down unambiguously by the Constitution. The task of putting an end to social discrimination should not have required the threat of Naxalite-inspired militancy. Discrimination on grounds of caste, sex, religion, etc is barred by the Constitution in Articles 14 to 17. Positive enactments for penalising discrimination have been legislated in the case of the Scheduled castes and Scheduled tribes. The SC & ST (Prevention of Atrocities) Act, 1989 is not merely a penal law. It envisages the setting up of an elaborate system for prevention of such atrocities. The law has, however, been seen as merely a penal law which the victims have to set in motion. Its full potential has not been actualised by the administration. Instead much time is spent discussing its misuse.

3.5.3 *'Begar'*, or forced labour in all its forms is also prohibited by the Constitution in Article 23. The Bonded Labour System (Abolition) Act was enacted in the year 1976 to give concrete form to this prohibition. The Act is, however, concerned only with debt bondage and not all forms of forced labour. There is no law penalising forced labour in other forms. Therefore it flourished in the most medieval forms in the Telangana district in Karimnagar, and it took a major upsurge led by the Naxalites in the late seventies and early eighties of the last century to put an end to it.

3.5.4 Apart from the concrete issues undertaken by the Naxalites against social oppression, the fact that the cadre and also most of local leaders of the Naxalite organisations consist of poor villagers of castes looked upon as lowly has endowed the oppressed with much strength. A sense of powerlessness is a characteristic of the psychological make up of oppressed classes. The typical Naxalite cadre, however, is a confident (most probably gun-wielding) teenager from those very classes. To see young boys and girls of their own villages and their own class/caste active in the Naxalite movement, and wielding power over the 'big' men of the village and the high and mighty tahsildar has given a sense of empowerment to the oppressed that has inestimable value. This indeed was one of the benefits that the Panchayat Raj system was expected to give the oppressed communities, but with the empowerment of the local bodies as envisaged by the 73rd amendment to the Constitution remaining a mere promise in most States, and with the cooptation of the leaders generated by the Panchayat institutions in the corrupt political system, the hope has been largely belied. A very genuine empowerment of the local bodies and of the representatives of the oppressed communities within the system alone can fill this need.

3.6 ISSUES ARISING OUT OF NON- OR MAL-GOVERNANCE

3.6.1 Dissatisfaction with improper and often mal-governance created anger among the suffering population. The Naxalites exploit the situation for their own political gain by giving the affected persons some semblance of relief or response. Thereby they tend to legitimise in the eyes of the masses their own legal or even illegal activities.

3.6.2 In the initial stages, the Naxalite movement took advantage of the presence of forest department personnel in the *Adivasi* areas, and gave some relief to the *Adivasis.* The uncertain existence of *Adivasis* in the forests has resulted in tremendous power of harassment in the hands of forest department personnel. It is permissible to pick edible forest produce but not to undertake cultivation of the same produce in the forests. It is permissible to gather dry twigs and logs of uprooted trees but not to cut standing timber. It is permissible to graze cattle in the forests, but it should be ensured that the cattle do not nibble at the nurseries of the forest department. In some states timber can be gathered for house construction but not for any other purpose. Quite apart from the injustice of the restrictions, the dividing line between what can be done and what cannot is often so slight that there is considerable ground for arbitrary action by the enforcer of the restrictions. Wherever there is a basis for discretion on the part of government officials, forest personnel have had to be appeased in different ways to avoid harassment. It was only after the Naxalites entered the picture that the *Adivasis* got protection from this harassment, which was well known to the administration but was normally ignored.

3.6.3 But after the initial impact on extortionate practices of the forest department officials, the Naxalite movement's impact on official corruption has been slight. The level of corruption in the Naxalite affected areas is not noticeably less than elsewhere. It may be due to the understanding that corruption is an internal affair of the administration. Or that it cannot be rooted out within the present political-economic system. Whatever the reason it leaves the corruption intact and, therefore, the dissatisfaction among the people intact, unlike in a situation where, for instance, the minimum wages not ensured by the administration are ensured by the pressure exerted by the civil society. Cooption of some elements of Naxal movement into the corrupt system was a fact.

3.6.4 On some occasions the Naxalites have been able to put pressure upon lower level administrators to perform their job effectively. The pressure exerted by the Naxalite movement has had some effect in ensuring proper attendance of teachers, doctors etc., in Andhra Pradesh, Maharashtra and Chhattisgarh, but it is also true that such employees have made the presence of the Naxalites an excuse for not attending to their duties properly in the interior areas. In the matter of physical infrastructure like roads, school buildings, etc., the Naxalite movement has on certain occasions exerted pressure for its improvement, but in many places they have themselves obstructed the laying of roads for the reason that it would increase police and paramilitary raids. In Chhattisgarh they have demolished pucca buildings such as schools so that the police and paramilitary may have no shelter in the forests. All said and done, it cannot be said that there has been any general improvement in the administration in the areas of Naxalite influence.

3.6.5 The fact is that the Naxalites do not see it as their job to reform the administration, but to supplant it where possible and debunk it otherwise. Similarly, their hostile attitude towards the electoral process has meant that they have not had much effect on the political system and the functioning of the local bodies. Instead they have concentrated on establishing their organisations as alternatives. But since these organisations of parallel administration set up by them cannot replicate all the functions of the government, the gap remains and so does the dissatisfaction.

3.6.6 In the matter of resolution of disputes among the people and finding redressal, the contribution of the Naxalite movement has been significant. There is in general no administrative or judicial mechanism in our country for resolution of day-to-day conflicts and disputes. The people have been traditionally taking these disputes to local dispute-resolution mechanisms. In the best case the entire community sits and hears the dispute. This is usually the case in tribal villages. Outside the tribal areas, a dispute within a caste is usually — at any rate among tightly knit communities — decided by the caste panchayat. The caste panchayat itself may function democratically or under the dictates of a group of elders. Disputes between persons of different castes are decided by the two sides getting their respective caste elders (or persons they trust) to sit together. In some places disputes are commonly taken to the dominant person or persons in the village, whether or not justice is done. Sometimes there is a compulsion that all disputes must be brought to the village landlord, where the dispensation of justice is usually in favour of the strong. All told, the need of a quick, fair and effective dispute resolution mechanism remains.

3.6.7 The Naxalite movement has provided a mechanism (usually described as a 'Peoples Court') whereby these disputes are resolved in a rough and ready manner, and generally in the interests of the weaker party. It has the two elements of speed and effectiveness. Justice and fairness are however often disputed. In particular, use of force disproportionate to the issue involved is fairly common. Those who are not loyal to the Naxalites often do not attend the Peoples Court at all. It is attended only by loyalists who agree with the conclusion indicated and the resolution proposed by the Naxalites. Many times the consultation with the people is a mere formality. It is the Naxalite armed squad that decides the matter. While some sort of justice is attempted to be done in disputes arising from economic inequalities/ exploitation, decisions in other matters (particularly the matrimonial disputes for instance), have often been characterised by a degree of crudeness, highhandedness and even brutality.

3.6.8 Nevertheless these People's Courts, however imperfectly, have met some unmet demands of the community. Society must evolve a tradition of resolution of disputes by the local community in full knowledge of all the tangible and intangible, the express and the implicit aspects of the problem, and in a manner that inspires faith in its impartiality. Elected *Nyaya Panchayats* may be an alternative which should be explored with diligence and sincerity.

3.7 Policing

3.7.1 Efficient and impartial policing is an important requirement of good administration. But the fact is that the weaker sections of the people do not have much faith in the police. They have no faith that justice will be done to them against the powerful. Nor do they trust that the police will take interest in doing their duty where the poor alone are involved, because the poor do not have the wherewithal to make it worthwhile. Often it is as frustrating an experience to go to the police station as a complainant as it is fraught with danger to go as a suspect. Women who go to a police station to complain of sexual abuse or domestic harassment are made painfully aware of this fact. Here lies one of the attractions of the Naxalite movement. The movement does provide protection to the weak against the powerful, and takes the security of, and justice for, the weak and the socially marginal seriously. Even-handedness may still be a problem since instances where one party to an offence has influenced the Naxalite cadre are not unknown, but at least they have the satisfaction of being taken seriously. The other problem when the Naxalites interfere in providing security for one against another in society is that the level of violence they use tends to be on the high side. They tend to resort to severe corporal punishment, including capital punishment.

3.7.2 However, the Naxalite movement itself brings further police repression on the poor as a matter of State policy. Any agitation supported or encouraged by the Naxalites is brutally suppressed without regard to the justice of its demands. In such matters, it becomes more vital in the eyes of the administration to prevent the strengthening or growth of Naxalite influence than to answer the just aspiration. Often any individual who speaks out against the powerful is dubbed a Naxalite and jailed or otherwise silenced. The search for Naxalite cadre leads to severe harassment and torture of its supporters and sympathisers, and the kith and kin of the cadre. What is to be pointed out here is that the method chosen by the Government to deal with the Naxalite phenomenon has increased the people's distrust of the police and consequent unrest. Protest against police harassment is itself a major instance of unrest, frequently leading to further violence by the police, in the areas under Naxalite influence. The response of the Naxalites, at least the Maoists, has been to target the police and subject them to violence, which in effect triggers the second round of the spiral. Rural policing under the Panchayat system in the pattern of the old Bengal Rural Police Act 1913 might be tried in these areas.

3.7.3 The rights and entitlements of the people underlying these issues find expression in the Constitution, the laws enacted by the various Governments and the policy declarations. The administration should not have waited for the Naxalite movement to remind it of its obligations towards the people in these matters. But at least now that the reminder has been given, it should begin rectifying its own deficiencies. It should be recognised that such a responsibility would lie upon the Indian State even if the Naxalites were not there, and even in regions where the Naxalite movement does not exist.

Recommendations (Excerpts)

State Response

5.7.1 The public policy perspective on the Naxalite movement is overwhelmingly preoccupied with the incidents of violence that take place in these areas and its ideological underpinnings. Though it does concede that the area suffers from deficient development and people have unaddressed grievances, it views the movement as the greatest internal security threat to the country. Accordingly, the attention of the government is concentrated on curbing violence and maintaining public order to achieve normalcy. While area development is also being speeded up, security-centric view of the movement accords primacy to security operations. The contextualization of this violence is missing from this perspective. The scale, intensity and approach of security operations cause considerable collateral damage leading to greater alienation of common people. The strategy of security forces to curb violence has also encouraged formation of tribal squads to fight Naxalites, with a view to reducing the security force's own task and risk. This has promoted a fratricidal war in which tribals face the brunt of mortality and injury. Those tribal who are unattached to either the Naxalites or those opposing them, become victims of violence by all agencies — Naxalites, squads formed to fight them and the security forces. This approach to the movement is devastating the local tribals and causing hopelessness and despair. A change in policy perspective and strategy to deal with the movement is essential to create a positive image of the government in the local people, remove their sense of alienation and wean them away from its influence.

5.7.2 Encouragement of vigilante groups such as *Salwa Judum* and herding of hapless tribals in make-shift camps with dismal living conditions, removed from their habitat and deprived of livelihood as a strategy to counter the influence of the radical left is not desirable. It delegitimises politics, dehumanizes people, degenerates those engaged in their 'security', and above all represents abdication of the State itself. It should be undone immediately and be replaced by a strategy which positions an empowered task force of specially picked up responsive officials to execute all protection and development programmes for their benefit and redress people's grievances. This is the best strategy to eliminate the influence of radical left groups.

5.7.3 Authorities should encourage civil society groups, having knowledge of, and sympathy with, local tribals in assisting this task force for wider participation of people in implementation of the strategy outlined above.

5.7.4 There are reports of civil society groups on the numerous human rights violations by authorities. The government should take cognizance of these reports and enquiries into these episodes should be constituted so as to inspire confidence in victims and faith of the public in the rule of law.

5.7.5 It is not desirable to insulate the area and people from civil society groups, media, and political organizations and penalize those who seek to establish contact with affected people to gather information about the action of Naxalites and state agencies, and speak or write about their observations. Besides being undemocratic, it is counter-productive as well. Reverse this trend. Rather, seek cooperation of civil society organizations with good track record in providing credible information on the impact of the movement and of state action on the affected people, which may help in critical appraisal of the policy pursued by the state.

5.7.6 Mobilising the support of the people is also absolutely essential to weaken the support base of the Naxals. The political parties are not playing their role in this regard. The representatives of major political parties have virtually abdicated their responsibility.

5.7.7 A strategy of constructive management of conflict requires two key measures. At its present stage, priority should be accorded to search out creative policies that bridge gaps between state interests and those of tribal communities. Tribes are not opposed development. All that they want is to control its pace and influence, its pattern and direction so that they are enabled to prevent its damaging effects and enjoy some of its benefits. The autonomy and control over natural resources which tribal communities seek is consistent with national development. It requires dedicated interlocutors to work out its parameters in consultation with communities. PESA (1995) has made a beginning in this direction and provided a broad frame work.

5.7.8 Ensuring a life of respect and dignity for the *dalits*, *Adivasis*, women, and the poor in general, is not a task that can be left to the working out of a few laws. A concerted effort through the education system and the cultural media needs to be taken up. The education system should not shy away from speaking to the undemocratic practices that abound in our society. And purposive cultural interventions are very much needed. But the first pre-requisite at the level of the administration is that the administrators should be sensitised to these realities and their unacceptability. Government personnel exhibiting an attitude of indifference towards this issue must be deemed to have committed misconduct and proceeded against accordingly.

5.7.9 Mere provision of reservations for the SCs, STs, OBCs and women in the local bodies does notamo untto empowerment. Consequential steps need to be taken to ensure that they are actually able to exercise the responsibilities placed upon them, and that their powers are not appropriated by the dominant sections. In situations where the elected representatives from these communities are threatened or subjected to violence they should be ensured full and adequate protection by the administration. It should be the responsibility of the Panchayat Officer at the District level to ensure that the police do provide such protection. Cooperation of the administrative personnel in the exercise of the authority of such elected representatives should also be mandatorily ensured.

5.7.10 While condemning occasional bursts of wanton violence by the extremist groups, a government constituted by law and mandated to maintain rule of law can not commit any illegal act in countering rural extremism. government should strictly prohibit extra judicial killings by its security forces. Such acts of illegality by the authorities tend to legitimise extremist violence in the eyes of millions of non-committed on-lookers.

5.7.11 Security forces should undergo rigorous training not only on humane tactics of controlling rural violence but also on the constitutional obligations of the state to protect the Fundamental Rights, including human rights, of Indian citizens and implications and implementation of progressive laws in favour of the poor. Excepting casualties suffered by both sides in actual fire fights, there should be no killings, either by the security forces or any vigilante groups, covertly or overtly sponsored and supported by the government. Every such killing should be followed by a judicial enquiry to reinforce the faith of the ordinary masses in the rule of law.

Cowrfesy: planniug cmnmission if India

Annexure II

Peace Initiatives Between Left-wing Radicals and Governments in Asia and Latin America

NEPAL

We are publishing the excerpts from a study on the peace talks in the Himalayan kingdom-turned republic to add a larger South Asian perspective to the ongoing debates on war and peace in India. CPI(Maoist) has refused to give up armed struggle and join parliamentary democracy following the example of their Nepalese brethren. Tthe subsequent political stalemate that the latter are facing in pursuing their goals of 21st century socialism in the multi-party parliamentary system, has dampened the initial hopes expressed by different Circles regarding a path breaking ground in radical politics.

CIVIL SOCIETY AND INVOLVEMENT OF UNITED NATIONS IN ARMS MANAGEMENT IN NEPAL (Excerpts)

Bishnu Raj Upreti, PhD

1. INTRODUCTION

Civil society (CS) is a fuzzy term with no precise definition. Defining civil society, Bhattachan (2003 :34) writes, 'Civil society comprises different types of groups such as economic, social, cultural, religious, educational, informational, interests and lobby groups; civil organisations, non-governmental organisations, and public trusts. In Nepal minorities themselves are part of the civil society…'. Civil society for the purpose of this paper covers wide range of actors (other than military and security forces, government, political parties and international communities) such as professional organisations, business community, media, human rights activists, scholars and researchers, teachers, writers, lawyers, engineers, doctors, professional experts, NGO staff and religious groups who are engaged in activities

related to conflict transformation and peace building in Nepal. War and peace history has shown that civil society has tremendous potentiality and firm ability, far more than any one else, to enhance peace process .... Unquestionable reality is that creating and maintaining peace require an active engagement of all actors of society, from ordinary citizens, security actors to politicians. However, civic engagement in peace process in Nepal is not getting enough attention. It is very hard to realise genuine efforts from the state to promote public participation in peace process. Pragmatically, peace making and keeping is more than ending armed rebellion. It goes beyond to address root causes of conflict and it promotes peace transformation. Therefore, it is a political and social transformation process as it has to focus on structural change in governance, security and development, human rights policies and practice and regaining eroded trust (Barnes, 2002). In this respect, contribution of civil society for democratising peace process is vital in Nepal (Upreti, 2006). Civil society is the one who was advocating from the beginning to involve UN in Nepal's peace process and negotiation to end the ongoing armed rebellion. Involvement of UN in Nepal is widely discussed in this country and appreciated its contribution in establishing peace in different parts of the world.
****

3. Civil society in Nepalese peace process

Civil society has greatly contributed in conflict transformation and peace building in Nepal through public dialogue, rising their concerns, articulating governance reform, pressuring for peace talks and negotiation, organising mass meeting and rallies, (Dahal, 2005; Upreti, 2006). Civil society played crucial role in the April revolution and consequent regime change. When the king's regime was suppressing democratic political process and political parties were weak and unable to effectively oppose the royal takeover, civil society vehemently opposed the royal takeover and continuously and effectively came to street and protested the king's rule. The contribution of civil society in political development and regime change was highly appreciated by the Seven Party Alliance as well as the Maoists. Civil society has engaged in the following peace related areas of activities:

- Awareness raising on peace and peace empowerment
- Minimising effects of small arms and landmines
- Protecting / and or defending human rights
- Rebuilding the lost trust and reconciliation
- Working as coalition for peace
- Engage in humanitarian assistance
- Engaged in citizen diplomacy for dialogue
- Media monitoring
- Overseeing and fact-finding
- Opposing autocratic regimes
- Others

Professional alliances, business communities, artists, poets, women, youth, disabled people, organisations of indigenous communities, non governmental organisations, teachers, students, researchers, lawyers and in fact people of all walks of life have played important role in Nepal's peace process. However, there are several confusions on understanding civil society and serious criticisms in its functioning.....

4. UN in Nepal's peace process

In the past, the UN Secretary General Kofi Anan repeatedly expressed his deep concern on the deteriorating political and security situation in Nepal. He also appointed especial political officer (Mr Samual Tamrat from Political Division) to work on Nepal issues, who has been frequently visiting Nepal. In the past, several times, he had offered any

help from UN if the warring parties want, which CPN (Maoists) immediately welcomed. However, the governments in the past repeatedly rejected these offers on the ground of possible objection from big neighbours India and China if Nepal invites UN to help negotiated settlement...... When the issue of involvement of external mediators came in the debate, the resistance from India was always unbearable to weak politicians of Nepal. Once, the then Foreign

Minister Bhekh Bahadur Thapa clearly said in 2004 that 'our big neighbours India and China would not agree to accept UN as mediator'. However, now the situation has changed and the earlier strong resistance of India has been somehow softened and agreed minor role of UN in monitoring and managing arms. Civil society leaders, scholars and independent analysts demanded involvement of UN in settling Nepal's armed conflict since few years. Following were some of their arguments for engaging UN in Nepal's conflict transformation and peace building:

1. UN is an independent and neutral body with vast experience of mediating conflict around the world. 2. Nepal is a member of UN and it has legitimate concern if crisis occurs in its member state. 3. UN's experiences of holding/monitoring elections, disarming and demobilisation, arms and weapons management at the time of constituent Assembly elections can be used. 4. It is easier to generate the huge amount of financial resources required for post conflict reconstruction and rehabilitations once UN is involved. 5. Getting constructive support of India, USA and other countries may be easy when UN is engaged. Once UN involves in arms management and monitoring, it does not work in ad-hoc basis and follows rigorous procedures and specific provisions. For example, UN may ask both parties to furnish:

l Total numbers of armies, their compositions, responsibilities, capabilities, etc.

l Command and control structures of armies.

l Geographical locations of army bases and related information

l Detail of the possession of arms by both sides, such as i. Total numbers, ii. Names and other technical specifications (model, manufacturers, identification numbers, etc.) iii. Status of the arms and weapons.

l Other relevant information.

There could be different options in managing arms and weapons. Some of the possible approaches for our case could be:

l One of the most common methods used in managing arms in other conflict ridden countries is 'collection and keeping arms and weapons in armours/stores with multi-lock system'. Collected and properly labelled arms and weapons are contained in alarm-enabled armours with multiple locks and holding keys by agreed parties (i.e., UN, rebel groups and government) and strict surveillance and monitoring by UN monitors (may be civilian, military or combination of both types of monitors. But in Nepal, it may be unarmed civilian monitors instead of army). Nepal does not need UN armed monitors, which complicates situation)

l Another option could be declaring 'captive zone' or 'containment zone', where arms and weapons and armies are kept in defined specific geographical territory (for example, existing military barracks for government army and creating temporary barracks for rebel army, etc.) with joint management of concerned party and UN (for example Maoists and UN in case of Maoist army and government and UN in case of government army) monitoring and surveillance by UN.

l Another option could be to vacate some of the barracks of Nepal Army and bring in Maoist armies and arms, keep them in these barracks and monitor them. This could be more pragmatic in the sense that the same rules, procedures and monitoring mechanism can be used for both armies (government army and Maoist army). In arms and weapons management process, first step is to jointly recording and documenting all arms and weapons followed by collection and storage in armours and their monitoring and finally settling the arms issues (such as collectively destroying, handing over to rebels or government according to the previously reached agreement between the three parties (i.e., UN, government and rebels).

5. Possible Reasons of Maoist interests to involve UN

The Maoists repeatedly said that they want involvement of neutral third party and the UN was obvious choice. This has been reflected in the letter of Maoist Supremo Prachanda to Kofi Annan One of the paragraphs of the letter states: 'We hope the international community would appreciate the complexities of life and death struggle between feudal monarchical forces and progressive democratic forces currently going on in Nepal. In this context we would once again reiterate our commitment to find a forward-looking political solution through dialogue and peaceful means at an appropriate moment, but would feel duty-bound to resist armed onslaughts of the monarchical regime against the people fighting for their genuine democratic rights. Finally, we would appeal to the international community in general, and the UNO in particular, to do everything in their might to stop all foreign armed and otherwise interventions in Nepal and let the Nepalese people decide their own future themselves.' The possible reasons for international involvement are:

1. They did not trust the then government and Nepal Army. They became very suspicious of army after the objection of 5 KM agreement in the last negotiation in 2003 (see annex 1) and the Doramba killing. Hence, they want guarantee from a legitimate and neutral international power,

2. International involvement, particularly UN involvement gives legitimacy and recognition to their rebellion,

3. Perhaps another important reason might be to impress international community that Maoists are committed to negotiated settlement of the armed conflict,

4. They expect to rule the country and therefore want to demonstrate their openness and to establish international relations for future political and diplomatic course of actions and financial support. A letter of the Maoists leader Prachanda to Kofi Annan immediately after the breakdown of August 2003 Ceasefire had highlighted the justifications of 'people's war' (See annex 4). Since then CPN (Maoist) issued several press statements and its leaders gave several interviews to national and international media reiterating the need of third party facilitation. They asked international community to help in reaching a fair political negotiation. However, the subsequent governments until 2006 April were categorically refusing to involve third party in the negotiation process. Three days before reaching the 8 point agreement between the government and the Maoists, the Resident Representative of UN Mathew Kahane, while speaking in the Everest Press Club on 13 June 06 said that if both parties, the government and Maoists request UN for help in peace process and the arms management, UN

is ready. However, first of all they have to agree on what type of support they are seeking from UN.

6. Government Invitation to UN for Managing Arms

The fundamental basis to invite the UN was the 12-point understanding reached between the Seven Party Alliance (SPA) and the Maoists in November 2005. The 3rd point of the understanding states: 'Today, the country has demanded the establishment of permanent peace along with a positive solution to the armed conflict. Therefore, we are committed to ending autocratic monarchy and the existing armed conflict, and establishing permanent peace in the country through constituent assembly elections and forward-looking political outlet. The CPN (Maoist) expresses its commitment to move along the new peaceful political stream through this process. In this very context, an understanding has been reached to keep, during the holding of constituent assembly elections after ending autocratic monarchy, the armed Maoist force and the royal army under the supervision of the United Nations or any other reliable international supervision, to conclude the elections in a free and fair manner and accept the result of the elections. We expect reliable international mediation even during the dialogue process.' This 12-point understanding was also a foundation stone for the popular *Jananadolan II*, which I often call 'April Revolution'. After the successful April Revolution, the SPA came to power and peace talk between the SPA government and the Maoists started. Consequently, a summit level meeting between senior leaders of SPA and the Maoists was accomplished on 16 June 2006.

The summit level secret talk between the Prime Minister Girija Prasad Koirala and the Maoist supremo Prachanda first for few hours and then including other SPA leaders reached to an agreement to involve UN for arms management. The third point of the agreement states, 'requesting the United Nations to help manage the armies and weapons of both sides and to monitor it in order to ensure free and fair election for constituent assembly.' UN immediately welcomed the decision. In the Cabinet meeting of 3rd July 2006 the government decided to write a letter inviting the UN for supporting peace process. Subsequently a letter signed by Prime Minister Girija Prasad Koirala was handed over by his International Affairs Advisor Dr. Suresh Chalise to the UN Acting Resident Coordinator Junko Sazaki. The United Nations Office in Kathmandu sent the letter to the UN Secretary-General Kofi Annan. However, it is not known so far about the content of the letter. The process of preparing the letter was quite opaque that even cabinet ministers expressed their lack of knowledge about the content of the letter. Maoist leaders expressed their dissatisfaction for not being consulted before sending the letter. If UN involvement is their evergreen interest and provisioned in both the 12 point understanding between the SPA and Maoists in November 2005 and the 8 point agreement between the government and the Maoists in 16 June 2006, why they objected the letter from government of Nepal to invite UN for managing arms and armies? In a television interview, member of the Maoist Negotiation Team Dev Gurung said, 'it is unacceptable to our party because it was sent without consulting us'. The main reason of their objection might be in the procedure of the government while writing letter. As they are not in government and therefore they want to engage in drafting letter to be send to UN to make sure that their concerns are addressed or possible controversies are avoided. This issue became even confusing when Maoist leader Prachanda once said that they can mange arms internally and there may not be need of external support. This opinion came immediately after the meeting of Dr Babu Ram Bhattarai and Krishna Bahadur Mahara, influential duo in CPN (Maoist) with Indian Ambassador in first week of July 2006.

7. Role of Civil Society in Facilitating UN Engagement in Arms Management

Civil society plays important role in conflict transformation where management of arms and demobilisation is one of the important elements. Peace scholar Guenther Baechler argues that strong civil society within the framework of multi-track diplomacy is pivotal for conflict transformation and peace building. He writes, 'A strong civil society can serve as a guarantee for a sound societal fabric, one that can support civil conflict resolution (Baechler, 2005:4). Civil society was successful in bringing OHCHR in Nepal with its constant efforts (lobby, advocacy, producing evidences and justifying the need). The presence of OHCHR became instrumental in protecting human rights. It has demonstrated competency, commitment and credibility in Nepal. Similarly, civil society movement had also greatly contributed to make the *Jananadolan II* successful. UN System has bigger potential in facilitating not only peace process and managing small arms but also post conflict transformation. Therefore, even if government and the Maoists limit its role in managing armies and weapons, civil society could see UN role for post conflict transformation support and strengthening democratic institutions in Nepal, as it has resources and credibility. The following are some of the main tasks civil society could do in helping UN in managing arms and weapons.

7.1 *Creating conducive environment:* One of the important roles civil society played in the past was to create conducive environment. When political parties were not able to vitalise the Janandolan, it came to forefront ..... / Once there was a deep mistrust between democratic political parties it was active in developing trust between them. Similarly, if there are any possible problems or potential differences in settling critical issues between the government and the Maoist negotiation teams, civil society could facilitate a process to create conducive environment.

7.2 *Watchdog function:* Sometimes awkward conditions posed by the negotiating parties may create difficulties for UN where civil society could help by lobbying and advocating for a better option. UN is quite bureaucratic and formal organisation and many complications may arise when it engages in managing arms and armies. In both situations, constant vigilance may be needed if the bureaucratic and technocratic procedures and practices delay or hinder transformation process.

7.3 *Collaboration and support:* Civil society can and should collaborate with different actors active in conflict transformation. Once UN is involved in managing arms and armies, it needs collaboration and support from all actors to smoothly accomplish the responsibility, where civil society could constructively contribute. By nature, UN is a formal and rigid structure and it may not want to bring some of the contentious but serious issues or differences to be debated in public where civil society could facilitate such debate. There are several international bilateral and multilateral actors who want to positively contribute Nepal's peace process and support UN for arms management with whom civil society could collaborate.

7.4 *Exploring options:* During the course of negotiation and managing arms, several potential differences may arise and the arms management and negotiation process may disturb. At that time different possible options are needed where civil society could greatly contribute. Preparing ground work, mobilising people (in other word facilitating track three approach), and building public opinion are some of the potential activities of civil society that facilitate UN in managing arms.

8. *External concerns on UN involvement:* India was constantly resisting to involve any third party in negotiating Nepal's armed conflict. In this regard, Dev Raj Dahal (2005 :16) writes, 'the then Indian Ambassador to Nepal, Shyam Sharan, made it clear that his country was not in favour of any third party mediating in the Nepalese peace process. He was responding to the UN, Swiss and Norwegian willingness to mediate the conflict in Nepal'. However, after the royal takeover in general and successful April revolution in particular position of India in involving UN became somehow flexible but with some conditions. Sitaram Yechuri played instrumental role not only in bringing Seven Party Alliance and Maoists together but also softening Indian attitude towards UN involvement.

9. *Conclusion:* Arms management alone is not enough in facilitating peace process and negotiation. It is only a small part. Further, UN can not manage arms if SPA, government, Maoists and civil society do not cooperate. In this respect, success or failure of UN entirely depends upon the commitment, willingness and cooperation of the government and Maoists. Some worrying scenarios are emerging in Nepalese politics, particularly from the activities of the Parliament.

The recent activities of the Parliament (for example, obstructing initiatives of government negotiation team, disobeying the 8 point agreement reached between the SPA leaders and the Maoists, diverting from peace talks, etc.) are undermining peace process, negotiation and establishing lasting peace and transforming feudal state into an inclusive modern nation. Parliament and the government are also distancing from the concerns of people and perceiving civil society as their opponent. The activities of the parliament are creating suspicion and confusions that ultimately leads to mistrust and obstruction to peace process.

Twelve-point understanding between Seven Party Alliance and Maoists (Unofficial translation)

The long struggle between absolute monarchy and democracy in Nepal has now reached a very grave and new turn. Establishing peace by resolving the 10-year old armed conflict through a forward-looking political outlet has become the need of today. Therefore, implementing the concept of absolute democracy through a forward-looking restructuring of the state has become an inevitable need to solve the problems related to class, caste, gender, region etc of all sectors including political, economic, social and cultural, bringing autocratic monarchy to an end and establishing absolute democracy. We make public that, against this existing backdrop and reference in the country, the following understanding has been reached between the seven parliamentary parties and the CPN (Maoist) through different methods of talks. This was made public in Kathmandu on 22 November 2005.

Points of Understanding

1. Today, democracy, peace, prosperity, social advancement and a free and sovereign Nepal is the chief wish of all Nepalese. We completely agree that autocratic monarchy is the main hurdle in (realising) this. It is our clear view that without establishing absolute democracy by ending autocratic monarchy, there is nopossibility of peace, progress and prosperity in the country. Therefore, an understanding has been reached to establish absolute democracy by ending autocratic

monarchy, with all forces against the autocratic monarchy centralizing their assault against autocratic monarchy from their respective positions, thereby creating a nationwide storm of democratic protests.

2. The seven agitating parties are fully committed to the fact that only by establishing absolute democracy through the restoration of the Parliament with the force of agitation, forming an all-party government with complete authority, holding elections to a constituent assembly through dialogue and understanding with the Maoists, can the existing conflict in the country be resolved and sovereignty and state power completely transferred to the people. It is the view and commitment of the CPN (Maoist) that the above mentioned goal can be achieved by holding a national political conference of the agitating democratic forces, and through its decision, forming an interim government to hold constituent assembly elections. An understanding has been reached between the agitating seven parties and the CPN (Maoist) to continue dialogue on this procedural work-list and find a common understanding. It has been agreed that the force of people's movement is the only alternative to achieve this.

3. Today, the country has demanded the establishment of permanent peace along with a positive solution to the armed conflict. Therefore, we are committed to ending autocratic monarchy and the existing armed conflict, and establishing permanent peace in the country through constituent assembly elections and forward-looking political outlet. The CPN (Maoist) expresses its commitment to move along the new peaceful political stream through this process. In this very context, an understanding has been reached to keep, during the holding of constituent assembly elections after ending autocratic monarchy, the armed Maoist force and the royal army under the supervision of the United Nations or any other reliable international supervision, to conclude the elections in a free and fair manner and accept the result of the elections. We expect reliable international mediation even during the dialogue process.

4. Expressing clearly and making public institutional commitment to the democratic norms and values like the competitive multiparty

system of governance, civil liberties, human rights, the concept of the rule of law, fundamental rights etc, the CPN (Maoist) has expressed commitment to move forward its activities accordingly.

5. The CPN (Maoist) has expressed its commitment to create an environment allowing the political activists of other democratic parties displaced during the course of the armed conflict to return to their former localities and live there with dignity, return their home, land and property seized in an unjust manner and carry out their activities without let or hindrance.

6. Undertaking self criticism and self evaluation of past mistakes, the CPN (Maoist) has expressed commitment not to repeat such mistakes in future.

7. The seven political parties, undertaking self evaluation, have expressed commitment not to repeat the mistakes of the past which were committed while in parliament and in government.

8. In the context of moving the peace process forward, commitment has been expressed to fully respect the norms and values of human rights and press freedom and move ahead accordingly.

9. As the announcement of municipal polls pushed forward with the ill-motive of deluding the people and the international community and giving continuity to the autocratic and illegitimate rule of the King, and the talk of elections to Parliament are a crafty ploy, we announce to actively boycott them and call upon the general public to make such elections a failure.

10. The people and their representative political parties are the real guardians of nationality. Therefore, we are firmly committed to protecting the independence, sovereignty, geographical integrity of the country and national unity. Based on the principle of peaceful co-existence, it is our common obligation to maintain friendly relations with all countries of the world and good-neighbour relationship with neighbouring countries, especially India and China. But we request the patriotic masses to be cautious against the false attempt by the King and (his) loyalists to prolong his autocratic and illegitimate rule and delude the patriotic people by projecting the illusory 'Mandale' nationalism and questioning the patriotism of the political parties, and

appeal to the international powers and the people to support, in every possible way, the democratic movement against autocratic monarchy in Nepal.

11. We call upon the civil society, professional organizations, various wings of parties, people of all communities and regions, press and intellectuals to actively participate in the peaceful movement launched on the basis of these understandings centered on democracy, peace, prosperity, forward-looking social change and the country's independence, sovereignty, and pride.

12. Regarding the inappropriate conducts that took place between the parties in the past, a common commitment has been expressed to investigate any objection raised by any party over such incidents, take action if found guilty, and to make the action public. An understanding has been reached to settle any problem emerging between the parties through peaceful dialogue at the concerned level or at the leadership level.

****

Annex 4: Maoists' letter to the UN Secretary General Kofi Annan: 14 September 1, 2003

H.E. Kofi Annan
Secretary General,
UNO.

Your Excellency,

We highly appreciate the deep concern expressed by you on behalf of the august international body, the UNO, about the break down of peace talks between the old monarchical regime and the revolutionary democratic forces led by our Party in Nepal. We have also noted with high sense of responsibility your call for the solution of all outstanding problems through dialogue and peaceful means in future. As the entire international community knows, the fratricidal and regicidal 'King' Gyanendra has systematically usurped all democratic and civic rights of the Nepalese people, including the fragile parliamentary institutions since October 4 last, and imposed a royal military dictatorship through his traditional hold over the mercenary Royal Nepal Army (RNA). Our Party, along with other parliamentary and non-parliamentary democratic forces, has been leading a powerful resistance movement in the country against this royal dictatorship, and the autocratic monarchy totally isolated from the people has been surviving merely on brutal military force increasingly backed by some foreign powers.

However, taking into consideration the state of strategic equilibrium between the two armed forces and the sensitive geo-strategic positioning of the country, our Party opted for a ceasefire on January 29 last and entered into a negotiation process with the monarchical regime to find a forward-looking political solution to the problem. In the very first round of the peace talks on April 27 we proposed a three-point compromise formula of a round-table conference, an interim government and election to a Constituent Assembly to end the half century old contention between monarchy and democracy in a peaceful manner. But after much dilly-dallying the monarchical regime rejected the said proposal enjoying overwhelming support of every section of the people in the country and instead produced a very regressive political agenda to consolidate and continue with the hated monarchy and its RNA dictatorship in the third round of talks on August 17-19.

A cursory glance at the so-called 'Concept Paper' produced by the monarchical regime during the talks would suffice to expose its arch reactionary and anti-democratic essence to perpetuate the autocratic monarchy, which has been rightly rejected even by the parliamentary political parties agitating for minor reforms within the present set-up. This obstinate stand of monarchy and its principal support base, the RNA, against a forward-looking political solution through democratic means in the form of an elected Constituent Assembly objectively sealed the fate of peace talks, which were formally broken on August 27. Apart from this, whereas our Party and the People's Liberation Army (PLA) strictly observed the ceasefire throughout, the RNA provocatively flouted it all along killing dozens, the most blatant case being the brutal gunning down of 19 unarmed adres and general masses on the eve of third round of talks on August 17 in Dorambha (Ramechhap), eastern Nepal. To camouflage its essential anti-democratic and militarist character and objective termination of peace talks through denial of progressive political solutions, the monarchical regime has now unabashedly launched Goebbels-style disinformation campaign against the revolutionary democratic forces, which deserves to be exposed by one and all. We hope the international community would appreciate the complexities of life and death struggle between feudal monarchical forces and progressive democratic forces currently going on in Nepal. In this context we would once again reiterate our commitment to find a forward-looking political solution through dialogue and peaceful means at an appropriate moment, but would feel duty-bound to resist armed onslaughts of the monarchical regime against the people fighting for their genuine democratic rights.

Finally, we would appeal to the international community in general, and the UNO in particular, to do everything in their might to stop all foreign armed and otherwise interventions in Nepal and let the Nepalese people decide their own future themselves.

Looking forward to cordial and mutually beneficial relations,

(Prachanda)

Chairman,

Communist Party of Nepal (Maoist)

Courtesy: The author and Centre for Economic and Technical Studies (CETS). The original paper was placed at a seminar on 'Role of Civil Society in Conflict Mediation and Peace Building in Nepal' organized by the Ceutre in cooperation with Friedrich-Ebert-Stiftung (FES) on July 15 & 16, 2006

THE PHILLIPPINES

PHILIPPINE TALKS WITH MAOIST REBELS HIT AN IMPASSE/NOVEMBER

2011 (AP) Manila, Philippines — Negotiations to end one of Asia's longest-running Marxist insurgencies have stalled in the Philippines after Maoist rebels insisted jailed comrades be released and escalated attacks on government troops and mining companies, the government said Wednesday. The guerrillas wanted several more comrades freed after the government released five in recent months, one of whom is believed to have returned to fight with the rebels, government negotiator Alexander Padilla said. He said the government would not release more rebels.

Padilla called on the guerrillas to return to the negotiating table and said both sides may miss the mid-2012 deadline to complete the talks. 'We're no longer advancing because we keep going in circles,' Padilla said in a news conference. Norway, which has been brokering the talks, has tried to bridge differences between the Manila government and the guerrillas but has not brought them back to the negotiating table. Rebel negotiators refused to meet government counterparts in June and last month, demanding the release of 13 more jailed guerrillas. They said the 13 are consultants in the peace talks and are covered by a 1995 agreement that provided them temporary immunity from prosecution and arrest. Padilla said the rebels failed to produce proof the detainees are covered by the agreement. A list of 75 rebel consultants supposedly with pictures was deposited in a Dutch vault in 1996 by both sides and church witnesses so it could serve as a future basis for identifying guerrilla consultants who could be immune from arrests. Both sides, however, discovered in July that two diskettes containing the list have been damaged and its details could no longer be retrieved, Padilla said. 'We're not willing to accept any new list, that would be foolish,' Padilla said. Chief rebel negotiator Luis Jalandoni has said that the release of detained guerrillas is not merely a goodwill gesture but a 'commitment and an obligation' agreed by the two sides when talks resumed in February after being suspended for seven years. A recent wave of rebel attacks, including an assault by more than 200 New People's Army guerrillas that devastated three nickel mining complexes in southern Surigao del Norte province in October, has also damaged efforts to build trust, Padilla said. 'These attacks are not helping to create a conducive atmosphere for the negotiations,' he said.

Military officials have said the attacks were part of rebel extortion attempts. The guerrillas, however, accused the mining firms of causing massive environmental pollution and exploiting Filipino workers by paying them cheap wages in dangerous work conditions. The rebels have been fighting for a Marxist state since 1969, accusing successive Philippine administrations of subservience to U.S. interests and failing to improve the lives of the poor. Their numbers have dwindled to an estimated 4,000 fighters amid battle setbacks, surrenders and factionalism. They are listed as a terrorist organization by the U.S. and European Union.

PHILIPPINE GOVT, MAOISTS AGREE TO TALKS TIME-FRAME, 21 FEB 2011

Nesbru, Norway/Manila, Philippines, Feb 21 (Reuters) — The Philippine government and communist guerrillas whose conflict has taken 40,000 lives and stunted economic growth for five decades agreed on Monday to an 18-month timetable of formal peace talks. 'We have moved the peace negotiations forward, ending a six-year impasse,' said Luis G. Jalandoni, chief negotiator of the National Democratic Front (NDF), whose demands include land reform to benefit landless Filipinos. Among the forces Jalandoni represents is the Communist Party, New People's Army, whose more than 4,000 fighters are known for attacking political leaders and businesses such as mining operations, according to the International Crisis Group. Negotiations between the government and rebels have been held on-again-off-again for some 25 years, with Norway bringing the adversaries together several times over the past decade. Each side sent about 25 people to Norway but few analysts expected a breakthrough. Closed-door talks to revive contact between the adversaries and discuss social and political reforms ended late on Monday at a hotel outside the Norwegian capital.

'We have agreed on a timeframe of 18 months to produce substantive agreements on socio-economic reforms, on political and constitutional reforms and on the end of hostilities and disposition of forces leading to a final political settlement,' Alexander Padilla, chairman of the Philippine government delegation, said. Norwegi

facilitator Ture Llundh said setting a timetable with milestones was progress in itself. 'We did not expect any better than this,' he said.
In the Philippines, the political content of the Norwegian meeting was eclipsed by the arrest of a top communist leader on Feb. 14 and accusations that both sides have violated a ceasefire put in place for the talks. The conflict is one of two long-running insurgencies that have hobbled development and investment in the Southeast Asian nation.

The government attempts to suppress the Moro Islamic Liberation Front, or MILF, in southern Mindanao tends to get more international attention than the simmering conflict with Maoists active in 69 of 80 Philippine provinces. The NDF says on its website that it is fighting against a 'semi-colonial and semi-feudal' Phillippine state dominated by the United States. Jorge Madlos, known as Ka (comrade) Oris, NDF spokesman on southern island Mindanao, said soldiers had violated the ceasefire by going on patrols and attacking rebel positions in the mining province of Compostela.

'These violations are indelible marks of the government's hypocritical and disingenuous attitude towards the peace process,' Madlos said in a media statement.

Army commander Lieutenant-General Arturo Ortiz said it was the rebels who violated the ceasefire, saying soldiers had stopped Maoist New People's Army guerrillas from laying landmines on the central island of Samar on Saturday.

Seven years later peace talks resume between the GRP and the communist CPP-NPA-NDF

The Communist Party of the Philippines (CPP) was founded in December 1968 with its armed wing, the New People Army (NPA) established only a few months later in March 1969, originally with less than 60 fighters. Condemning the 'semicolonial and semifeudal' character of Philippine society, the CPP aims to arrive at a 'socialist revolution' after waging a 'national democratic revolution'. In addition to the revolutionary armed struggle, the other components of the 'protracted people's war' are land reforms and masse-base building.

Local communities are therefore seen by the CPP as indispensable allies with whom the CPP needs to build strong links through land reform, health, education and other 'mass campaigns'.

The revolutionary armed Left expanded nationwide during the 1970s despite the declaration of Martial Law in 1972. The National Democratic Front of the Philippines (NDFP) was formally established on April 24, 1973. Armed struggle intensified in the 1980s. By the time of the bringing down of Marcos dictatorship in 1986, the NPA has some 6,100 high-powered rifles. At the end of the 1980s, the NPA prioritized large military operations in the countryside in the context of its 'strategic counter-offensive' framework at the expense of work at the grassroots level to build mass support. From 1989 to 1994, the government's counter-insurgency operations Oplan lambat Bitag I, II and III succeeded in significantly weakening the NPA. Following a strategic re-orientation under what it called the 'Second Great Rectification Movement', the CPP-NPA-NDFP managed to expand and re-establish itself during the 1990s. In 2006, the NPA reported 'operating in more than 120 guerrilla fronts, which cover 800 municipalities in 70 out of 79 Philippine provinces'. Over the period 2000-2005 it was estimated that the NPA had between 8,000 and 11,000 fighters (UNICEF, October 2006). As of 2011, the number of fighters is believed to be closer to 5,000 (ICG, 14 February 2011, p.1).

Identifying the NPA as the country's greatest security threat, the government returned the primary responsibility for counter-insurgency to the AFP. In 2002, the government launched a five-year national counter-insurgency plan 'Oplan Bantay Laya' (OBL), which was extended five years later as OBL II, to crush the NPA by the end of President Arroyo's term in 2010. Ongoing since 1976, peace negotiations stalled in 2004. Peace talks did however produce one agreement: the Comprehensive Agreement on Respect for Human Rights and International Humanitarian Laws (CARHRIHL); as well as a Joint Monitoring Committee (JMC) to oversee the implementation of the agreement. The JMC continues to register complaints about human rights violations, although it has not reported to the panel since 2004. In June 2006, President Arroyo declared all-out war against the NPA and two years later decided to increase military spending in the fight against the NPA (UPI Asia, 27 March 2008). OBL priority regions particularly affected by the counter-insurgency activities include Central Luzon, Southern Tagalog, Bicol, Eastern Visayas and Northern Mindanao (Karapatan, January 2008, p.1).

Peace talks resume (2010-2011)

In October 2010, the new government decided to revive the peace talks with the CPP-NPA-NDF which had remained stalled since 2004 (ICG, 14 February 2011). Both parties met in Oslo in February 2011 under the auspices of the Norwegian government. As a result of the first round of meetings, a timeframe of 18 months was proposed to complete the following agreements : thecomprehensive agreement on socio-economic reforms by September 2011, the comprehensive agreement on political and constitutional reforms by February 2012 and the comprehensive agreement on end of hostilities and disposition of forces between June and August 2012. Both parties hoped to reach a final peace agreement within the first three years of Aquino's administration (GRP, 22 February 2011).

In another positive development, in April 2011, the Special Representative of the UN Secretary-General for Children and Armed Conflict, Ms. Coomaraswarmy, announced that the National Democratic Front of the Philippines (NDFP) had agreed to develop an Action Plan to ensure that no children are among the ranks of the New People's Army (NPA) or involved in the conflict (OSRSG for Children and Armed Conflict, 8 April 2011).

Hopes for a peace deal were dimmed in June when the main negotiator of the NDF threatened to suspend the talks until the government released 17 of their jailed NDF consultants. As a result, the government has been pressured by some parties to end the talks (Xinhua, 2 June 2011).

Peru

Peru Govt Seeks to Block Shining Path Party from Politics/January 2012

Weeks after the Shining Path guerrilla organization called for peace talks with the government, the justice minister has declared that those promoting terrorist groups will not be allowed to enter politics.

This announcement comes as the Movement for Amnesty and Fundamental Rights (known by its Spanish acronym Movadef) files for political party status. The organization is linked to the Shining Path (Sendero Luminoso) guerrilla group.

Justice Minister Juan Jimenez urged that the panel not approve the group's application, reports *La Republica,* declaring, 'We will not permit political organizations which correspond to armed groups that ... have not shown remorse with respect to the wrongdoings and crimes they have committed, to enter politics and destroy it.' In December, one of the remaining factions of the Shining Path publicly offered to begin peace talks with the government. The government has not accepted the proposal, and the guerrilla leader said that the authorities had rejected two previous attempts to make contact. This move to prevent Movadef from becoming a legal political party indicates that the government is unlikely to offer political concessions to the Shining Path in order to demobilize the group.

In neighboring Colombia, in contrast, President Juan Manuel Santos has been trying to push through legislation to allow demobilized members of the Revolutionary Armed Forces of Colombia (FARC) to take part in politics. An attempt in the 1980s to bring the rebels into the political system by launching a FARC-linked political party, however, ended in the murder of thousand of members, and the dissolution of the party.

Shining Path Rebel Leader Calls for Truce with Peru's Govt

One faction of Peruvian guerrilla group the Shining Path has issued a call for dialogue with the government, but the odds of the authorities taking them up on the offer are slim. Investigative journalism website IDL-Reporteros conducted an interview with alias 'Comrade Artemio', the head of one of the two remaining factions of the country's Shining Path (Sendero Luminoso) guerrillas, in which the rebel leader called for a truce with government forces and discussed the potential for demobilization. In the interview, Comrade Artemio (who officials have identified as Florindo Eleuterio Flores Hala) openly admitted that the group's 31-year war with the Peruvian state has been a military failure. The accompanying video, which is embedded below, shows Artemio looking slightly weary as he explains that the Shining Path's objective of provoking a mass insurrection remains the same, but 'in practice this is no longer possible today'.

He also called for a truce with the security forces, saying that he and his branch of the Shining Path, which is based in the Upper Huallaga Valley in the northern department of San Martin, 'have no intention to wield weapons of war in armed struggle." While Artemio said he would be willing to eventually demobilize, he stressed that this could not happen without a 'process of frank and real negotiations' with the government of Peruvian President Ollanta Humala, and a general amnesty for Senderista fighters.

Artemio admitted that his guerrilla faction has allowed cocaine production and trafficking in the Huallaga region, but denied that the group has ever profited from drug trafficking organizations. According to him, the rebels turn a blind eye to drug trade because they simply do not have the resources to take on local trafficking groups and the state at the same time. When asked how the group gets its funds, Artemio replied that they received support from coca growers, but 'never directly from narco-traffickers'.

This directly contradicts statements made by Peruvian officials, who say that Artemio is an active participant in the trafficking of cocaine. In July 2010 the US State Department put a $5 million ransom on his head, claiming that Artemio 'repeatedly invests his own and/or (Shining Path) money in drug trafficking ventures with local drug traffickers'. In December, former army chief General Otto Guibovich even referred to the Huallaga Shining Path as a 'drug cartel' in its own right. Meanwhile President Humala has made combating the group a central pillar of his administration, and has repeatedly stressed their alleged involvement in the drug trade.

For this reason the prospects for Artemio's proposed truce look grim. The guerrilla leader told IDL-Reporteros that he had already sent President Humala two letters proposing negotiations, but both were rejected. This may have been due to the rebels' lack of credibility than a lack of political will, however. As the *Guardian* notes, Artemio has announced ceasefires in the past, but each has ended with renewed guerrilla attacks on the security forces. What's more, Peru is known to look to the conflict in neighboring Colombia for guidance on counterinsurgency, and the precedent it sets for peace is not promising. After agreeing to a ceasefire in 1999, the Revolutionary Armed Forces of Colombia (FARC) used the time to regroup, continuing kidnappings and bombings.

A ceasefire with the Shining Path may not even be a legal option for Humala. Peruvian legal scholar Anibal Quiroga told La Republica that the truce is 'legally and constitutionally inviable', because the Shining Path is not a recognized belligerent group. The military incentive for a truce is also lacking. Peru's armed forces have had considerable success in targeting the Huallaga-based Shining Path, having captured Artemio's girlfriend and dealt a significant blow to the faction's support base amongst coca growers in recent months. It could be that Artemio is well aware that his group is on the ropes, and this latest move is simply a way for him to try to avoid being captured or killed, as Peruvian Defense Minister Daniel Mora has suggested. Whatever comes of Artemio's proposal, it most certainly will not apply to the other major Shining Path wing, which is based in the southeast Apurimac-Ene river valley (VRAE). Led by a 'Comrade Jose', the VRAE Shining Path have a reputation for being less political than their cousins in Huallaga, and are less ideologically close to the imprisoned Shining Path founder, Abimael Guzman. In a 2009 interview with La Republica, Guzman denounced the VRAE-based faction of the guerrillas as mere 'mercenaries', claiming they are actively engaged in cocaine trafficking. The VRAE group, and their alleged involvement in drug trafficking, are the main reason that the government has extended a state of emergency in the region.

COLOMBIA

1965 - Leftist National Liberation Army (ELN) and Maoist People's Liberation Army (EPL) founded.

1966 - Revolutionary Armed Forces of Colombia (Farc, the current largest guerrilla grouping) set up.

1970 - National People's Alliance formed as a left-wing counterweight to the National Front.

1971 - Left-wing M-19 guerrilla group emerges.

1978 - President Julio Turbay (Liberal) begins intensive fight against drug traffickers.

1982 - President Belisario Betancur (Conservative) grants guerrillas amnesty and frees political prisoners.

War against drug cartels stepped up

1984 - Campaign against drug traffickers stepped up following assassination of justice minister.

1985 - Eleven judges and 90 other people killed after M-19 guerrillas force their way into the Palace of Justice; Patriotic Union Party (UP) founded.

Nevado del Ruiz volcano erupts. An estimated 23,000 people are killed in four Andean towns.

1986 - Virgilio Barco Vargas (Liberal) wins presidential elections by record margin. Right-wing paramilitary groups begin murder campaign against UP politicians, amid continuing violence by left-wing groups and death squads run by drugs cartels.

1989 - M-19 becomes legal party after reaching peace agreement with government.

Liberal and UP presidential candidates murdered during presidential election campaign, reputedly at the behest of drug cartels; Cesar Gaviria elected on anti-drug platform.

1991 - New constitution legalises divorce, prohibits extradition of Colombians wanted for trial in other countries and guarantees indigenous peoples' democratic rights, but without addressing their territorial claims.

1993 - Pablo Escobar, Medellin drug-cartel leader, shot dead while trying to evade arrest.

1995 - Ernesto Samper Pizano (Liberal) elected president and is subsequently charged and cleared of receiving drug-cartel money for his election campaign.

Peace talks

1998 - Andres Pastrana Arango — a Conservative — elected president, begins peace talks with guerrillas.

1998 November - Pastrana grants Farc a safe haven the size of Switzerland in the south-east to help move peace talks along. The zone is off-limits to the army.

1999 January - Peace talks formally launched but proceed in stop-start fashion. Pastrana and Farc leader Manuel 'Sureshot' Marulanda meet.

1999 January - Powerful earthquake kills some 1,000 people. Cities of Armenia and Pereira badly hit.

Plan Colombia

2000 July - Pastrana's 'Plan Colombia' wins almost US$1 billion in mainly military aid from the US to fight drug-trafficking and rebels who profit and protect the trade.

2000 September - Government freezes talks; alleges Farc harboured hijacker of plane forced to land in safe haven. Later, Farc refuses to resume talks, accuses Pastrana of not stopping paramilitary groups.

2001 February - The Farc return to peace talks after meeting between 'Sureshot' and Pastrana. Pastrana extends demilitarized area for eight months.

2001 June - Farc rebels free 359 police and troops in exchange for 14 captured rebels. Farc accused of using safe haven to rearm, prepare attacks and conduct drug trade.

2001 October - Government, Farc sign San Francisco agreement, committing themselves to negotiate ceasefire. Pastrana extends life of safe haven until January 2002.

2002 January - Pastrana accepts Farc ceasefire timetable and extends safe haven until April.

TALKS FAIL

2002 20 February - Pastrana breaks off three years of tortuous peace talks with Farc rebels, says hijacking of aircraft hours earlier is final straw. He orders rebels out of demilitarised zone. Government declares war zone in south after rebels step up attacks.

2002 May - Independent candidate Alvaro Uribe wins a first-round presidential election victory, promises to crack down hard on rebel groups.

2002 August - Moments before Alvaro Uribe is sworn in as president, suspected Farc explosions rock Bogota. Twenty people are killed. Days later, Uribe declares state of emergency.

2003 October - 14 out of 15 of President Uribe's planned austerity measures and political reforms rejected by voters in referendum. Three ministers, national police chief resign.

2003 November - Fighters from right-wing United Self-Defence Forces of Colombia (AUC) begin to disarm.

2004 May - Farc's Ricardo Palmera, the most senior Colombian guerrilla ever captured, is jailed for 35 years.

2004 July - Right-wing AUC and government begin peace talks. AUC leaders address Congress. Colombia's 'drug barons' entered in peace talks. Demobilisation began. AUC fighters hand in weapons. AUC called ceasefire in 2002; peace talks began in 2004 Group listed as terrorist organisation in Europe and US. Most rank-and-file members will get full pardon and job training.

2005 January - Bitter 15-day dispute with Venezuela over the capture of a Farc leader on Venezuelan soil. The affair is resolved at talks in Caracas in February.

2005 June - New law offers reduced jail terms and protection from extradition for paramilitaries who turn in their arms. Rights groups say the legislation is too lenient.

2005 December - Exploratory peace talks with the second biggest left-wing rebel group, the National Liberation Army (ELN), begin in Cuba.

2006 February - Colombia and the US agree on a free trade deal. The agreement awaits ratification in both countries.

URIBE'S SECOND TERM

2006 March - Parties loyal to President Uribe win an overwhelming victory in parliamentary elections.

2006 May - President Uribe wins a second term in office.

2006 November - Court investigates possible ties between high-ranking politicians from Sucre department and right-wing paramilitaries.

2006 December - Detained paramilitary leaders say they are pulling out of a peace process. Government says demobilisation of right-wing groups will continue.

2007 January - Ecuador turns to the Organisation of American States (OAS) for help with its challenge to Colombia's coca crop-spraying programme along their common border.

2007 June - Government releases dozens of jailed Farc guerrillas, in hope that rebels will reciprocate by releasing hostages. Farc rejects move, saying it will only free hostages if government pulls back troops and sets up demilitarised zone.

2007 July - Hundreds of thousands protest in Bogota against kidnappings and conflict in the country.

HOSTAGE RELEASE TALKS

2007 September - In his role as mediator, Venezuelan President Hugo Chavez agrees to invite rebels for talks on hostage release deal.

2007 November - Colombia sets deadline of 31 December for President Chavez to reach deal with rebels on prisoner swap.

2007 November - Venezuelan President Hugo Chavez withdraws his country's ambassador to Bogota in a row over his role in negotiations between the Colombian government and rebel forces.

2008 January - The Farc releases two high-profile hostages, Clara Rojas and Consuelo Gonzalez, as a result of Mr Chavez's mediation. Mr Chavez calls on the US and European governments to stop treating Colombian left-wing rebel groups as terrorists, but Mr Uribe rejects the idea.

2008 March - A Colombian cross-border strike into Ecuador kills senior Farc rebel Raul Reyes and sparks a diplomatic crisis with both Ecuador and Venezuela.

2008 May - Colombia extradites 14 paramilitary warlords to the United States to stand trial on drug trafficking charges. US hails move as evidence Colombia deserves trade deal. Colombian opposition complains the extraditions mean that the militia leaders will not reveal their alleged links to political allies of Mr Uribe.

Farc announces death of its leader and founder, Manuel Marulanda.

2008 June - Colombia renews low-level diplomatic relations with Ecuador.

Betancourt freed

2008 July - Colombian army rescues the country's highest-profile hostage, Ingrid Betancourt, held in captivity for six years by Farc. She was among 15 hostages freed in an operation in the southern-central region of Guaviare.

2008 November - The sudden collapse of pyramid investment schemes - used by some of the poorest savers - triggers violent protests. Several towns are put under curfew.

2009 February - Farc rebels free six high-profile hostages, including a former provincial governor held since 2001.

2009 March - Farc releases a Swedish man thought to be the group's last foreign hostage, Erik Roland Larsson.

President Alvaro Uribe offers Farc rebels peace talks if they halt 'criminal activities' and declare a cease-fire.

2009 July-August - Relations with Venezuela deteriorate again after plans to allow US troops to use Colombian military bases as part of a drive to curb drug-trafficking are unveiled.

Venezuela withdraws its ambassador from Bogota and freezes relations after the Colombian government accuses Caracas of supplying arms to Farc rebels; Venezuelan President Hugo Chavez accuses Colombia of carrying out a military incursion into his country.

2009 October - Colombia and US sign deal giving the US military access to seven Colombian bases.

2009 November - Venezuelan President Hugo Chavez urges his

armed forces to be prepared for war with Colombia and orders 15,000 troops to the border, amid growing tensions.

Former army Gen Jaime Humberto Uscategui is given 40-year jail sentence for his role in killing of unarmed civilians by right-wing paramilitaries.

COMMON CAUSE

2009 December - The Marxist rebel groups — the Farc and the smaller National Liberation Army (ELN) — announce that they intend to stop fighting each other and concentrate on attacking the armed forces.

2010 July - Venezuela cuts diplomatic ties with Colombia after being accused of harbouring Farc rebels.

2010 August - Juan Manuel Santos takes over as president, having won easy victory in run-off election in June. He responds to a Farc offer of talks by insisting that the rebel group must first release all the hostages it still holds.

Colombia and Venezuela restore diplomatic ties.

2010 September - Farc steps up its campaign of violence. Colombian army kills senior Farc commander Mono Jojoy in air strike in Macarena region.

2011 February - Farc releases several hostages in what it describes as unilateral 'gesture of peace' to government.

2011 May - Senate approves law to compensate victims of civil conflict and return land to millions of displaced people. President Santos describes the new law as 'historic'.

2011 August - President Santos outlines new tactics against rebels, who have increasingly been resorting to hit-and-run raids.

2011 September - Former intelligence chief Jorge Noguera — a close ally of former president Alvaro Uribe — is sentenced to 25 years in prison for collaborating with paramilitary death squads.

2011 October - US Congress passes long-delayed free trade agreement with Colombia, despite concerns over country's poor record of labour relations.

Courtesy : BBC News Service. and other websites.

CONTRIBUTORS

Amit Bhaduri: Professor Emeritus at Jawaharlal Nehru University, Delhi, and visiting professor at various academic institutions abroad; internationally acclaimed economist known for his unconventional analysis of mass hunger and poverty in South Asia based on his fundamental critique of prevailing neo-liberal development model and globalisation; member of People's Union for Democratic Rights.

Aditya Nigam: Senior Fellow of the Centre for Studies in Developing Societies, Delhi; published extensively on Marxism, nationalism, identity and radical politics in both English and Hindi; a critic of CPI(M) and CPI(Maoist) both; writes for *kafila.org* regularly.

Amrita Paira: Political activist based in Jhargram town at the gateway of Junglemahal in West Medinipur district in Bengal; involved independent labour movement.

Amrita Paira: Political activist based in Jhargram town at the gateway of Junglemahal in West Medinipur district in Bengal; involved independent labour movement.

Amit Bhattacharya: Professor of history at Jadavpur University, Kolkata; authored books on Chinese and Japanese histories as well as modern India. Leading activists, written extensively on Singur, Nandigram and Lalgarh movements in EPW & Sanhati.com and other journals.

Asokendu Sengupta: Retired professor of Physics and member of the government-appointed team to mediate with Maoists in Bengal; active in pro-*Paribartan* civil society movement.

Anirban Roy: A close watcher of the Maoist and ethnic insurgencies in south-east Asia and the managing editor of *Seven Sisters Post*, an English daily in Guwahati.

Binayak Sen: A child and public health specialist by training and a human rights activist, known for his work among the poorest of the poor in Chattisgarh's tribal hinterland; vice-president of People's Union of Civil Liberties; his conviction and life sentence by the state high court on sedition charges triggered outrage in both in India and abroad; Supreme Court granted him bail in 2010; now with Planning Commission's committee on health.

Chhoton Das: Leading human rights activist involved in the campaign for the release of political prisoners and one of the mediators in the government-initiated peace process with Maoists in Bengal.

Debasis Bhattacharya: Veteran journalist, political and human rights activist and member of pro-*Paribartan* civil society in Kolkata.

Dipanjan Raichoudhuri: Retired professor of Physics, Presidency College, Kolkata; human rights activist and political commentator; contributes regularly for *Sanhati.com* and *Frontier*.

Dipankar Chakrabarti: Editor of a popular radical journal, *Aneek* and vice-president of Association for Protection of Democratic Rights; wriiten books on debates in International communist movement and people's resistance in India.

Dipankar Bhattacharya: General Secretary of the CPI(ML) Liberation; contributes to various journals including EPW.

Diptendra Raychaudhuri: Delhi-based veteran journalist with experiences both in print and electronic media; a closer observer of Maoist movement and author of an acclaimed novel, *A Naxal Story*.

G Hargopal: Teaches at the Centre for Human Rights, University of Hyderabad; professor/Senior Fellow at the Centre for Economic and Social Studies, Hyderabad; well-known human rights activist; one of the mediators in peace talks between Congress government and Maoists in Andhra in 2004-5; played key role in successful negotiations in Odisha in 2011 that led to the release of hostages taken by Maoists and activists illegally detained by the government.

Himanshu Kumar: Gandhian human rights activist; worked among tribals in Chhattisgarh's Dantewada amid the war between Maoists and security forces and Special Police Officers engaged in infamous *Salwa Judum*; his *Vanvasi Chetna Ashram*,. later razed by the BJP government, functioned as a bridge between tribals and a forgetful State; focused on teaching tribals about their entitlements and rights and encouraged community vigil.

K. Balagopal: Former Mathematics professor at Kakatiya University, Andhra; a lawyer and human rights activist; broke away from Andhra Pradesh Civil Liberties Committee on the issue of Maoist violence and founded Human Rights Forum; prolific writer with independent mind and keen insights, he wrote extensively on debates within the human rights movement on State and non-State terror; served as member of Expert Group on Development Challenges in Extremist Affected Areas, set up by Planning Commission of India in 2008.

Krishna Bandopadhyay: Veteran political activist and participant in people's movements in Bengal; former convener, *Lalgarh Mancha*; edits, *Khoj Ekhon*, a journal on women's issues; associated with the Calcutta Research Group.

Kunal Chattopadhyay: Teaches comparative literature at Jadavpur University, Kolkata, and edits a journal, *Radical*; a political activist and commentator, he has authored books and papers.

Mahasveta Devi: Acclaimed novelist and social activist; known for empathic portrayal of the struggle for survival of tribals and violations of their rights; works translated into many languages; regular media columnist; co-edits *Bartika*, a Bengali journal; backed Mamata-led regime-changing campaign in Bengal.

Manoranjan Mohanty: Retired professor of Political Science, Delhi University; currently with Council for Social Development, New Delhi; author of many books on social movements, human rights, development experiences and grassroots democracy in India and China; veteran activist of civil liberty movement and PUDR member.

Nandini Sundar: Head of the department of sociology, Delhi School of Economics; challenged with other activists the constitutional validity of the recruitment of Special Police Officers as the key instrument of State-run anti-Maoist *Salwa Judum* in Supreme Court which led to the court's historic verdict to disband the SPOs.

Gautam Navlakha: Noted political commentator, leading light of PUDR, Delhi; unsparing critic of the Indian State; raised voice against the violation of human rights across India, including Jammu and Kashmir; steadfast but not uncritical supporter of Maoist movement; visited rebel bases in Dandakaranya and conducted interviews with top CPI(Maoist) leaders.

Nilanjan Dutta: Senior journalist, independent researcher, documentary film-maker and human rights activist; conducted research on history of Civil Liberties Movement in India on a fellowship from School of Oriental and African Studies, University of London; several publications to his credit.

Nisha Biswas: Scientist at Central Glass & Ceramic Research Institute, Kolkata and an human rights activist in solidarity with the Lalgarh movement; rrested with two other intellectuals during a visit to Junglemahal and imprisoned for more than a month.

Nivedita Menon: Professor, Centre for Comparative Politics & Political Theory, Jawaharlal Nehru University, Delhi; works include edited volumes on gender and politics; commentator on contemporary issues in newspapers and weeklies like *Economic Political Weekly* and on *kafila.org*.

Premangsu Dasgupta: Rights activist and convenor, Little Magazine Samannay Mancha in Kolkata; took active part in the campaign in solidarity to Lalgarh movement.

Partha Sarathi: Independent researcher; authored books and papers on changing power-equations in rural Bengal during Left Front rule; offered insightful observations on Left parties, including Maoists focusing on question of democracy or lack of it in their party and mass organisations; contributor to EPW and other journals.

Partha Sarathi Roy: Scientist in a research university in Bengal; activist and alternative media practitioner; chronicled Lalgarh movement in films and the print media; writes regularly for *Sanhati.com* on people's movements across the country.

Rana Bose: Veteran freelance journalist and political commentator with international exposure.

Ranabir Samaddar: Head of Calcutta Research Group; leading political scientist; closely studied Junglemahal society and politics since colonial days in *Memory Identity Power, Politics in the Jungle Mahals 1890-1950*; a pioneer of peace studies; worked on issues of justice and rights in the context of conflicts, migration, refugee studies, and theory and practice of dialogue in South Asia.

Swami Agnivesh: Noted social activist; Arya Samaj leader and former Haryana minister; campaigner for abolition of bonded labour; recipient of the Rajiv Gandhi National Sadbhavana Award in 2004, Right to Livelihood Award from Sweden and M.A. Thomas National Rights Award 2006, Bangalore.

Samir Kumar Das: Professor of department of Political Science, Calcutta University, and member of the Calcutta Research Group; written extensively on peace studies in South Asia; edited books on peace processes and peace accords, particularly in the context of Northeast India.

Santosh Rana: Veteran of radical left politics in Junglemahal; elected MLA from Junglemahal in 1977; now leads of CPI(ML)-PCC and involved in people's movements demanding regional autonomy for Junglemahal, focusing on tribal and other under-privileged people's identities.

Saswati Ghosh: Teaches economics in City College, Kolkata; women's rights activist; participated in people's movements; took part in PCPA-administration negotiation before joint forces moved into Junglemahal; writes extensively on women's issues both in mainstream and alternative media.

Sujato Bhadra: Professor of history and leading figure in human rights movement in Bengal; written extensively on rights issues, both empirical and theoretical; headed team formed by Bengal government to mediate peace with Maoists; member of government-appointed review committee on political prisoners.

Sumanta Banerjee: Veteran journalist, political commentator and a leading social historian of 19th century Bengal; honorary fellow of Institute of Advanced Studies, Shimla; author of many books on society, politics and culture and regular contributor to *EPW, Frontier* and other journals; works include *In the Wake of Naxalbari*, *Naxalism — Views from the Other Side*; edited and introduced a collection of Naxalite poetry in English.

Sumit Chakravartty: Delhi-based veteran journalist and editor of *Mainstream* weekly; active in civil rights movement; written extensively on violations of peoples rights across India and corporate-government joint grab on farmland and other attacks on livelihood of land-dependent people from Singur-Nandigram to Kalinganagar.

Sumit Chowdhury: Independent activist, documentary film-maker and convener, *Lalgarh Andolan Sanhati Mancha*; active participant in popular resistance in Singur, Nandigram and Lalgarh; regular contributor to media on relevant issues.

Varavara Rao: Telugu revolutionary poet, public speaker, literary critic, teacher and civil rights activist; emissary of the Communist Party of India (Maoist) during the latter's talks with Andhra government, both in 2002 and 2004; founder member of Revolutionary Writers' Association; exposed systematic liquidation of Naxalites or Maoists by police in fake encounters; jailed intermittently by successive Andhra governments for his revolutionary beliefs.

Editor

Biswajit Roy: Senior journalist and independent researcher in media practices, politics and ideologies; co-authored books on role of media during Singur and Nandigram; edited special issues of Bengali journals on contests and engagements among ideologies — Orientalism, Marxism, Arab Nationalism, Islamic fundamentalism; published papers and articles on public health policies related to Indian Muslims; took part in international and national research works on impact of globalisation on informal labour economies.